Labour, Finance and Inequality

Following the 2008 "global" financial crisis, the viability of globalised financial capitalism was called into question. The resulting fear and uncertainty produced a momentary return to "Keynesian" policies. But as soon as emergency stimuli – and bank bail-outs – appeared to stabilise the situation, there was a sharp reversal; and successive British governments and the financial sector have since attempted to return to business as usual.

Historically, much smaller shocks have been able to produce dramatic change, with the 1978 "Winter of Discontent" providing a catalyst for the election of Margaret Thatcher, the ultimate abandonment of the post-war Keynesian consensus, and the ushering-in of neoliberalism. Nor is apparent success a guarantee *against* change, with Winston Churchill being swept from office by the first majority Labour government in 1945 – at a point which should have marked his greatest triumph.

In this book, these apparently inexplicable shifts in the conventional wisdom and the accompanying policy paradigm are explored through the lens of the interest groups that have jostled for position since the second industrial revolution. In this context, inequality, poverty, free market capitalism and the social welfare state have interacted in an uneasy, dynamic dance – the "insecurity cycle". The authors explore these interactions, their impact on the relationship between society and the economy, and the possible implications of Brexit and a re-energised political left.

Written in an engaging and accessible style, *Labour, Finance and Inequality* will be a key resource for academics and students of social and political economics as well as public policy. It will also offer considerable insight to policy makers and a more general non-specialist audience.

Suzanne J. Konzelmann is a Reader in Management at Birkbeck, University of London, UK. She is also Director of the London Centre for Corporate Governance and Ethics, Co-Executive Editor of the *Cambridge Journal of Economics* and a Research Associate in the Cambridge University Centre for Business Research.

Simon Deakin is a Professor of Law at the University of Cambridge, UK. He is also Director of the Cambridge University Centre for Business Research, Co-Chair of the University's Strategic Research Initiative in Public Policy, and a Fellow of Peterhouse. He is Editor in Chief of the *Industrial Law Journal* and a member of the editorial board of the *Cambridge Journal of Economics*.

Marc Fovargue-Davies is a Research Associate with the London Centre for Corporate Governance and Ethics, Birkbeck, University of London, UK. Formerly a strategic marketing consultant and brand development specialist, he is also a freelance journalist, specialising in socio-economic issues, politics and yachting.

Frank Wilkinson is Emeritus Reader in Economics at the University of Cambridge, UK. He is also Founding Editor of the *Cambridge Journal of Economics* and a Research Associate in the Cambridge University Centre for Business Research.

Routledge Critical Studies in Finance and Stability

Edited by Jan Toporowski

School of Oriental and African Studies, University of London, UK

The 2007–8 Banking Crash has induced a major and wide-ranging discussion on the subject of financial (in)stability and a need to revaluate theory and policy. The response of policy makers to the crisis has been to refocus fiscal and monetary policy on financial stabilisation and reconstruction. However, this has been done with only vague ideas of bank recapitalisation and 'Keynesian' reflation aroused by the exigencies of the crisis, rather than the application of any systematic theory or theories of financial instability.

Routledge Critical Studies in Finance and Stability covers a range of issues in the area of finance including instability, systemic failure, financial macroeconomics in the vein of Hyman P. Minsky, Ben Bernanke and Mark Gertler, central bank operations, financial regulation, developing countries and financial crises, new portfolio theory and New International Monetary and Financial Architecture.

For a full list of titles in this series, please visit www.routledge.com/series/RCSFS

Labour, Finance and Inequality

The Insecurity Cycle in British Public Policy

Suzanne J. Konzelmann,
Simon Deakin,
Marc Fovargue-Davies
and Frank Wilkinson

Routledge
Taylor & Francis Group

LONDON AND NEW YORK

First published 2018 by Routledge

2 Park Square, Milton Park, Abingdon, Oxfordshire OX14 4RN

52 Vanderbilt Avenue, New York, NY 10017

Routledge is an imprint of the Taylor & Francis Group, an informa business

First issued in paperback 2020

British Library Cataloguing-in-Publication Data
A catalogue record for this book is available from the British Library

Library of Congress Cataloging-in-Publication Data
A catalog record has been requested for this book

ISBN: 978-1-138-91972-3 (hbk)
ISBN: 978-0-367-59202-8 (pbk)

Typeset in Bembo
by Wearset Ltd, Boldon, Tyne and Wear

Contents

Preface

It is often said that change – along with death and taxes – is one of the few givens that life has to offer. However, by the time of writing, during the autumn of 2017, remarkably little change has so far resulted from the disruption caused by the 2007–8 "global" financial crisis and the socio-economic consequences of the decade of austerity that has followed it. Whilst the fear and uncertainty associated with the crisis produced a momentary return to "Keynesian" policies, as soon as the emergency stimuli and bank bail-outs appeared to have stabilised the situation, there was a sharp reversal as concerns about the resulting high levels of fiscal deficits and public debt trumped concerns about the nature of the system that had produced the crisis.

At present, the inter-related problems of mass unemployment, poverty and inequality remain unresolved; and the International Monetary Fund – arguably the strongest and most vociferous proponent of neoliberalism – is questioning its ability to deliver on its promises. But international finance appears to be back to "business as usual" and neoliberalism remains entrenched. By contrast, the decade of economic instability and industrial unrest during the turbulent 1970s – which ended with the "Winter of Discontent" – resulted in a complete reversal of the post-war "Keynesian" conventional wisdom in both economics and politics.

There are already a number of possible explanations for this, ranging from pure happenstance to the argument propounded by those who view economics as a "natural" science, with "free market" capitalism being the default setting for human interaction. But none of these provide a satisfactory explanation for the cyclical trends that Britain has experienced during its industrial and post-industrial phases of development as a consequence of shifting patterns of insecurity on the part of significant segments of society. Indeed, despite the economics profession lauding the "great moderation" – which preceded the most serious financial crisis of recent times – as a period during which the traditional problem of "boom and bust" had been solved, this cycle continues.

Nor have the poor – whose numbers shrank rapidly during the decades immediately following the Second World War – seen their lot improved. Far from it, in fact, with rapidly increasing inequality being a prominent feature of British society since the Thatcher government switched the focus of policy away from full employment to the control of inflation. Given that Clement Attlee's 1945 landslide election victory for Labour had been due in large part to the discontent experienced by the working and middle classes – and the collective sense of determination to create a post-war society and political economy that had been worth fighting for – poverty and inequality are certainly not new to Britain.

Labour, Finance and Inequality: The Insecurity Cycle in British Public Policy explores the dynamic inter-relationship between an ever-evolving economy, a rapidly developing society and the state – and the influence of this on the development of economic theory, public policy and subsequent events. The analysis is informed by the idea that not only poverty and inequality – but also the government policy framework that might (or might not) effectively address them – are cyclical. However, instead of moving in predictable, stable paths, they follow a dynamically non-equilibrium, evolutionary pattern of development. This raises two significant questions: What are the opposing interest groups driving the insecurity cycle? And what are the key factors that are likely to produce *either* relatively minor changes that can be accommodated within the existing policy paradigm, *or*, alternatively, a shift of the conventional wisdom and the policies informed by it?

To examine these questions, we explore the inter-related development of British society and economy since the industrial revolution, with reference to the dynamic processes driving the evolution of industrial techniques and organisation, democratic and political institutions, the legal framework and the values of the various interest groups, as they respond to the environment within which they interact. The notion of the insecurity cycle – and the key factors likely to produce change – emerges from this historical analysis of the dialectical processes involved.

Important in our study are the factors that lay behind what might be described as the "mood" of the different interest groups at any point in time. In 2010, for example, then Prime Minister David Cameron went so far as to try to measure the quality of life, tasking the Office of National Statistics with assessing the "sense of wellbeing" across various parts of Britain. However, the riots that swept the country's urban areas during early August the following year suggest that there might well have been greater variety in the way British people experienced life than Cameron had imagined. Indeed, the lack of coherent arguments offered by either side in the run-up to the 2016 referendum on membership of the European Union also suggests that the result may have been as much a consequence of the "mood" of parts of the nation as anything else.

However, moods can swiftly and unpredictably change. This is evident in the nation's response to the 2012 London Olympic Games: whilst the run-up to the event failed to energise "austerity Britain", the opening ceremony and the subsequent record-breaking performance of Team GB went a long way towards changing all that, with expectations of the British athletes being pushed ever higher since. Cameron's successor, Theresa May, also discovered just how quickly the electorate's mood can change: losing a 20-point lead in the opinion polls almost overnight, she also lost the Conservative majority in the snap 2017 general election, which she had hoped would deliver her an electoral mandate for Brexit. In no small part a result of the emergence of a revitalised Labour Party, led by Jeremy Corbyn, this shift of mood in politics has been sufficient for Corbyn to currently argue – with some conviction – that his party now represents the political mainstream. For sure, few can remember the last British political leader who, like Corbyn, has regularly been forced to seek ever larger venues for political rallies, or to climb on top of a fire engine to address an enthusiastic crowd.

Behind all this – as with the urban riots of 2011 – it is possible to discern the role played by the interest groups that drive the insecurity cycle, as well as the factors that lead to shifts, large or small. And contrary to conventional economic thinking, the insecurity cycle has so far followed a dynamic and non-equilibrium evolutionary path, with the interest groups with the most power dominating at any point in time.

Labour, Finance and Inequality: The Insecurity Cycle in British Public Policy also addresses the question of why, in the years since the arrival of the 2008 financial crisis, we have not (perhaps yet) seen a shift in the conventional wisdom of neoliberalism. We focus on the turns of two such cycles when there was a radical shift in economic thinking and policy. The first starts with the period leading-up to the "Liberal" social reforms preceding the First World War, followed by the attempt to restore the liberal economic order after the war's end. The second begins with the lead-in to the Attlee Labour government during the 1930s and 1940s and the "Keynesian" post-war consensus, followed by the return to pre-Keynesian "neoliberal" ideas and policies during the 1970s and 1980s.

The 2008 financial crisis marks the possible turn of a third cycle, when confidence in globalised financial capitalism and neoliberalism was severely shaken. But as yet, it is uncertain whether change will again take place, either *within* the conventional wisdom of neoliberalism or *of* conventional wisdom and associated public policies. We conclude with an examination of the current state of play among the factors that have historically driven shifts in the insecurity cycle, speculating on the most likely scenarios for future developments.

At the time of writing – a decade after the 2007–8 financial crisis – it is a rather sobering idea to imagine that policy may, for the foreseeable future at least, be doomed to swing between two old ideologies – economic liberalism and state interventionism – until a crisis of sufficient scale forces a fundamental rethink. However, currently emerging ideas about alternative approaches to economic theory and policy – potentially the most potent of the factors driving the insecurity cycle – represent reason for optimism regarding the prospects of building a more equitable British economy – with less insecurity all round.

In closing, we would like to acknowledge – with gratitude – the Cambridge Political Economy Society for its generous support of our research.

Sue Konzelmann
Simon Deakin
Marc Fovargue-Davies
Frank Wilkinson
31 October 2017

1 Introduction

Introduction

In the immediate aftermath of the 2008 financial crisis, the viability of globalised financial capitalism was called into question. The fear and uncertainty associated with the crisis shook confidence in the conventional wisdom of neoliberalism and there was a momentary return to "Keynesian" thinking and policies. But as soon as it appeared that these emergency stimuli – accompanied by the rescue of banks deemed "too big to fail" – had stabilised the situation, there was a sharp reversal in policy as concerns about the resulting high levels of fiscal deficits and public debt trumped concerns about the nature of the system that had produced the crisis; and austerity replaced stimulus, first in the Eurozone and then more broadly.

More than a decade later, despite widespread unemployment, growing social unrest, increasing poverty and an ever-expanding gap between the wealthy and the rest, remarkably little has changed. The litany of high-profile systematic misbehaviour on the part of financial actors and institutions – and the much criticised culture of the international financial sector – has failed to produce an effective response. Even the International Monetary Fund (IMF) – arguably the strongest proponent and promoter of neoliberalism – is questioning its ability to deliver on its promises.[1] All of this raises the question: Why has so little changed?

In his book, *The Affluent Society*, John Kenneth Galbraith emphasised the inherent conservatism of the ideas used to interpret economic and social life; and he identified the dominant set of such ideas as "conventional wisdom", the essence of which is acceptability. Thus, those who re-iterate the conventional wisdom are reassuring and afforded respect.[2] Galbraith (1999) went on to argue that the conventional wisdom gives way not so much to new ideas as to the "massive onslaught of circumstances with which it cannot contend" (p. 17). This makes space for alternative ideas to challenge the dominant orthodoxy. However, the alternative ideas that come to form the replacement conventional wisdom are not evolved in a vacuum; they are incubated by critics of the existing conventional wisdom, whose ideas gather increasing traction as the "massive onslaught of circumstances" builds up.

The purpose of this book is to address the question of why – in the years since the 2008 financial crisis – we have not (perhaps yet) seen a shift in the conventional wisdom.

The book's main focus is the United Kingdom (UK); but the UK is an integral part of the system of globalised financial capitalism, so the analysis will be located in this broader international context, in which Britain holds a unique position. It is one of the first countries to develop an industrial base and a centre for international finance; it is also one of the first to globalise, de-industrialise and re-financialise. Peculiarities of the British state also make it interesting. It is legally constrained in some ways through a flexible version of the rule of law; but relatively unfettered in others, as a result of having no codified constitution. These characteristics have remained relatively constant despite both globalisation and membership of the European Union (EU). The British state also has a long history of being intertwined with finance, from its early support for merchant trading companies and establishment of the Bank of England in 1694. It is also a fiscally stable and effective state that, contrary to popular opinion, has never been truly "laissez-faire", even during the nineteenth century. All of this suggests that the UK has the capacity to change and develop, despite the fact that the consequences of the 2008 financial crisis continue to plague the economy and financial reforms remain elusive. Exploring the reasons for this is a core component of our study.

This chapter lays out the conceptual and empirical puzzle regarding change in the dominant ideology of neoliberalism; and it develops the notion of the "insecurity cycle" as an analytical approach for explaining why, when and how change in the conventional wisdom – and the policies that accompany it – comes about. The evolution of this dynamic and non-equilibrium cycle is influenced by economic ideas; but vested interests and institutions are inextricably involved in the process, with the relative position of the key socio-economic actors – and the quality of their respective governing institutions, inter-relations and relationship with the state – having an important influence on both the evolution of the system and their location within it. The chapter concludes by drawing together the key analytical themes that will be explored in the sections and chapters to follow.

The "insecurity cycle"

During the century since the implementation of David Lloyd George and Winston Churchill's controversial "Liberal" social reforms, there has been an ongoing struggle between capital and the promotion of the "self-regulating" market, on the one hand, and, on the other, a functional welfare state which takes the view that the economy should serve society – rather than the other way round. This was very much Karl Polanyi's (1944) understanding of the relationship between economy and society, which forms the basis for beginning to discern what might be termed the "insecurity cycle". Other significant ideas informing its nature and dynamics can be found in Michal

Kalecki's (1943) assessment of "political aspects" of the cycle and the role of institutions and powerful interest groups in driving or inhibiting policy maintenance and change; in John Maynard Keynes's (1936) analysis in which cycles are driven by fundamental uncertainty – with the tendency of market capitalism to generate involuntary unemployment and excessive inequality – and an important role for the state in stabilising them; and in Hyman Minsky's (2008 [1986]) insight about the inherent instability of the free market economy – particularly with respect to finance – with financialisation being a long-term trend within capitalism.

The dynamic nature of such a cycle arises from two opposing tendencies within democratic capitalism – market liberalisation and social protectionism. Wolfgang Streeck (2016) describes democratic capitalism as

> a political economy ruled by two conflicting principles, or regimes, of resource allocation: one operating according to marginal productivity or what is revealed as merit by a "free play of market forces", and the other based on social entitlement, as certified by the collective choices of democratic politics.
>
> (p. 75)

He goes on to observe that whilst "governments are theoretically required to honour both principles simultaneously ... substantively the two almost never align" (ibid.). Moreover, because democratic politics is organised at – and confined to – the level of the nation state, there are limits on the ability of the democratic state to effectively intervene in the protection of society from the consequences of global market forces, particularly with respect to finance. Thus, central to our thesis is the idea that a capitalist economy must have an effective state or political realm, particularly in relation to finance; but that, at the same time, certain aspects of capitalism, including the nature of the international financial order, limit the capacity of nation states to protect society from the destabilising effects of the market.

In the British case, given that powerful vested interests and other institutions tend to mitigate in favour of free market capitalism – as does the narrowing of the political options available to the electorate – the cycle has historically been skewed towards market liberalisation. Movement away from this position has typically only ever been preceded by an extended period of high levels of uncertainty – and not a little fear – in some or all quarters, with free market capitalism giving ground only to preserve its assets and influence, ready to push back as soon as the appearance of stability returns.

To illustrate the cycle and the forces and factors within it, as well as to identify the tipping points likely to either drive or inhibit change, we will examine periods in British political and socio-economic development during the past century, when some of the most radical changes in the conventional wisdom – and the policies informed by it – took place. Building on the insights of Polanyi, Kalecki, Minsky and Keynes, discussed below, we will examine the circumstances that created the environment within which different ideas gained traction and ultimately reconstituted the dominant orthodoxy. As Keynes (1924a) observed, to make sense of contemporary economic developments, it is important to "contemplate the particular in terms of the general ... [and to] study the present in the light of the past for the purposes of the future" (p. 322). Thus, we will consider the question of paradigm change in the light of both history and current developments.

The study begins by tracing developments of the nineteenth century – during which a divergence in Britain's economy and society was first identified – in order to locate the twentieth-century shifts in insecurity cycle in context. We then turn to the Liberal social reform era that preceded the First World War – and the attempts to restore the pre-war liberal economic order that followed it. However, the experience of the Second World War – which seemed to justify not only "Keynesian" ideas about the role of the state in managing the economy but also its responsibility for social welfare provision – produced a post-war "consensus" that witnessed the retreat of laissez-faire and the advance of "Keynesianism". The "stagflationary" 1960s and 1970s reversed this process, with the questioning of Keynesianism and the promotion of pre-Keynesian "neoliberal" ideas. We are currently in what might – or might not – be a third Galbraithian episode, with neoliberalism being challenged by the money market frenzy that followed the 2007 credit crunch and the resulting crisis which paralysed the financial system, triggering the deepest recession since the 1930s. As yet, it is unclear what the new conventional wisdom might be as theorists and policy makers thrash around looking for alternatives – or, indeed, whether a replacement paradigm will emerge.

Conceptualising the insecurity cycle

Since the late nineteenth century, the British state has alternatively used its power to create and maintain the "self-regulating" market and to protect individuals and groups within society from its adverse effects. In this context, John Ruggie (1982) suggests that "states and markets are complementary institutions" (p. 383); but he warns that "markets that societies do not recognize as legitimate cannot last" (Abdelal and Ruggie 2009, 152). Streeck (2016) argues that the legitimacy of post-war democracy was based on the premise that states have the capacity to intervene in markets and correct their outcomes in the interest of citizens (p. 52).

The nineteenth-century liberal economic order was informed by the idea that an economy is a collection of (national and international) markets, with its own principles and logic, that is somehow separate from the social and political relations of the society in which it is situated. In this context, the free movement of goods, services and capital is assumed to deliver both economic efficiency and distributional justice. Polanyi (1944), however, contended that such "dis-embedded" markets – particularly in finance – are unsustainable as a consequence of their perpetual conflict with democratic forces in society.

Polanyi's historical research revealed that economic activity originally evolved to serve human needs – and that until the rise of nineteenth-century liberal capitalism, where they had existed at all, markets were subject to various social, religious and political controls to ensure that they did. However, during the nineteenth century – justified and reinforced by the conventional wisdom of the English Classical political economists, notably by the work of David Ricardo and Thomas Malthus – industrialisation and the rise of the laissez-faire market economy produced a radical shift, which Polanyi described as the "dis-embedding" of the economy from society.

From Polanyi's reading of history, this could be traced to a key event of 1834, the Poor Law Amendment Act, which sought to abolish (and in practice severely restricted) outdoor relief. This forced the unemployed poor, who were unable to access any other form of financial relief, either to enter the workhouses (which were becoming progressively more oppressive) or to obtain work at whatever wage was on offer. In Polanyi's analysis, this created a free market for labour. From this point onward, until the 1870s, after which various labour market protections, including rights for trade unions, were enacted, free market ideology enjoyed almost unchallenged ascendancy in Great Britain – and its influence rapidly expanded abroad. In mainstream economics and finance, it remained dominant until the 1930s.

Polanyi recognised that the market is embedded in a complex social, political and institutional context which ultimately defines and shapes it. Interested in the role of institutions in the organisation and functioning of the socio-economic system, he viewed the market as embedded in institutions – including legal institutions and the rule of law, civil society institutions, financial institutions and industrial relations institutions – all of which play an important role in its effective functioning by helping to support the trust, shared understanding and enforcement of contracts upon which market transactions depend. In Polanyi's view, the market forms part of the broader economic system, which itself is part of society; as such, instead of being an end in itself, the market economy serves as a means to more fundamental socio-economic objectives.

However, he identified a tension between what he considered to be the two organising principles of modern market society: "economic liberalism" and "social interventionism" (Polanyi 1944 [2001], p. 239), each with their own objectives and policies as well as support from the groups within society whose interests they are seen to serve. The aim of economic liberalism is to establish or restore the self-regulation of the system by eliminating interventionist policies that obstruct the freedom of markets for land, labour and capital. Through laissez-faire and free trade, social relationships are embedded within the economic system and subjected to unregulated market forces with support from the propertied classes, finance and industry. By contrast, the aim of social interventionism is to embed the economy within social relationships, thereby safeguarding human beings and nature through market regulation, with support from those adversely affected by the destabilising consequences of economic liberalisation and the self-regulating market – notably the working classes.

Polanyi argued that there is a conflict between the interest of capital in freeing itself from the constraints of society – and society's interest in protecting itself from the social dislocation of the market (particularly that of finance). This generates a "double-movement" of counter-reactions by both capital and society, mediated by politics and the legal process. Without compensating social intervention, Polanyi contended that the pressure on vulnerable individuals and groups within society, arising from attempts at market self-regulation, would generate resistance in the form of labour, civic, social and political movements. If these become widespread – and discontent with the damaging effects of the self-regulating market intensifies – social order becomes more difficult to maintain; and in an effort to safeguard the existing system, political leaders may attempt to deflect dissatisfaction by scapegoating. However, at some point, the state is likely to be put in the position of having to decide whether to intervene on behalf of those affected or to risk social breakdown. In turn, the impairment of market forces associated with protective regulatory measures could set into motion a counter-movement on the part of capital to attempt to protect its own interests by freeing itself from social and political constraints. In response, the state would have to decide the degree to which laissez-faire should be restored and social protections and market regulations relaxed.

Thus, for Polanyi, market forces are created and sustained through political decisions; and "re-embedding" the economy in society re-establishes social control over economic processes by means of democratic representative institutions. In his view, "socialism ... [is] the tendency inherent in an industrial civilization to transcend the self-regulating market by consciously subordinating it to a democratic society" (Polanyi 1944 [2001], p. 242).

Polanyi thus brings the role of government and politics to the centre of the analysis of market economies, as a consequence of the pivotal role played by the state and legislative processes in creating and maintaining socio-economic systems, by simultaneously promoting and regulating the market economy. In this context, because economies reflect the principles and values of the societies in which they are located – and the relative balance of power among the groups within – the question of whose interests they are designed and maintained to serve (special interests or the general interests of society as a whole) comes to the fore. Polanyi also highlights the contradictory nature of modern market economy and its potential for engendering "crises" when the pendulum swings too far in either direction or when a shock to the system occurs.

Kalecki (1943) drew attention to the "political aspects" of policy-making and their potential to serve as a driver of the economic cycle. Because such policy goals as maintenance of a high level of employment serve the interests of workers – despite also serving the general interest by delivering economic prosperity and having a positive effect on profits and the general price level – they are likely to draw opposition from powerful interests in industry as well as in banking and finance. He identified three main sources of opposition: "(i) dislike of government interference in the problem of employment as such; (ii) dislike of the direction of government spending...; (iii) dislike of the social and political changes resulting from the maintenance of full employment" (ibid., p. 324).

Kalecki identified investor "confidence" as an important determinant of economic performance, with confidence being dependent upon the extent to which the profit expectations of the owners of capital are reliably sanctioned by the distribution of political power and the policies to which it gives rise when business sees its interests threatened by political interference. From this perspective, commitment to a high level of employment can be expected to elicit responses in the form of the withdrawal of investment, fuelling a "political business cycle":

> In this situation a powerful alliance is likely to be formed between big business and rentier interests, and they would probably find more than one economist to declare that the situation was manifestly unsound. The pressure of all these forces, and in particular of big business ... would most probably induce the government to return to the orthodox policy of cutting down the budget deficit. A slump would follow in which government spending policy would again come into its own.
>
> (Ibid., pp. 325–6)

Kalecki concluded that to be sustainable, "'full employment capitalism' will ... have to develop new social and political institutions which will reflect the increased power of the working class" (ibid., p. 326), drawing attention to the critical role played by interests and institutions in the process of socioeconomic stability and change.

Building on Keynes's "investment theory of the cycle", Minsky's analysis also emphasises the central importance of institutions – including government, the legal system, the structure of regulation, businesses and financial institutions – the role of investor confidence and the dynamic, non-equilibrium processes that generate change. According to Minsky (2008 [1986]), the capitalist economy is only "conditionally coherent" (p. 117) and during "periods of tranquility" (p. 197), market forces tend to push the system towards instability because they encourage increased risk taking and innovation. In Minsky's view, the processes generating instability are "natural" and endogenous to the system. Thus, Minsky adds a third tendency of market capitalism – instability (ibid., pp. 112, 315) – to Keynes's original two, these being unemployment and inequality.

Minsky's analysis of cycles – building on Keynes – begins with the contention that decisions regarding investment are inherently unstable because they are made under conditions of fundamental uncertainty regarding prospective future income streams. As a result, they are based on subjective expectations and subject to wide swings between optimism and pessimism that determine the aggregate level of investment, which in turn (and with a multiplier effect), influences output and employment.

Agreeing with Keynes's contention that the maintenance of an approximately full employment level of effective demand requires policies aimed at promoting *both* investment *and* consumption, Minsky criticised the post-war policy focus on investment-driven growth on the grounds that the benefits never "trickle down" to the poor and that it tends to increase inequality and instability (Minsky 2008 [1986], pp. 323–6); and he famously wrote that "if there is a road to full employment by way [of market adjustments alone] … it may well go through hell" (ibid., p. 198). Minsky argued that "[t]he policy problem is to devise institutional structures and measures that attenuate the thrust to inflation, unemployment and slower improvements in the standard of living, without increasing the likelihood of deep depression" (ibid., p. 328). However, he recognised that policy success could only ever be temporary because the economic system is in constant flux, with continual adjustments in policy being required in response to ever-changing circumstances.

The insecurity cycle is illustrated in Figure 1.1. In this context, the definition of "insecurity" is taken from the *Oxford Dictionary* as "the state of being open to danger or threat; lack of protection", where lack of protection of the

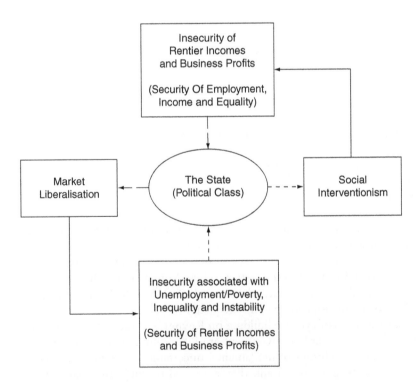

Figure 1.1 The insecurity cycle.

interests of various groups within society is a key source of their perceptions regarding insecurity.

During periods of market liberalisation, in response to the insecurity associated with the resulting increase in unemployment, poverty, inequality and instability, affected groups can be expected to put growing pressure on the state for social protection and market regulation to mitigate its damaging socio-economic effects. However, as these social and political constraints are seen to impinge upon investor rights and the property claims of capital – rentier incomes and business profits – affected groups can be expected to respond by pressuring the state to relax them and to scale back social protections through market liberalisation. This, in turn, can be expected to generate socio-economic insecurity and a further counter-movement on the part of society – in a continuing cycle of perceived insecurity and responses to it on the part of those affected. In this process, as discussed below, policy makers will search for ideas to support and justify their policy choices; and they can be expected to work within the existing policy paradigm – and in so doing to preserve and maintain it – to the extent possible.

Does free market capitalism increase insecurity?

One interpretation of the policy cycle we have just described is that insecurity is an inevitable feature of capitalism, which can at best be alleviated or attenuated on a temporary basis, but can never be entirely removed from the system. The basis for this view is the idea that capitalism does not just produce insecurity as one of its by-products; insecurity is vital for capitalism to function. If this is so, the role of the state must ultimately be to perpetuate the conditions for insecurity.

But capitalism is not synonymous with the market. Markets not only existed before the historical emergence of capitalism; they could be found in various forms in state socialist systems associated with the Soviet model; and they exist today in low-income countries which have few of the features of more developed capitalist economies. So markets are not unique to capitalism. Nor does "the market" describe the whole of capitalism. Historically, as Polanyi emphasised, capitalism is associated with a number of inter-linked institutions and practices, at the core of which are a particular type of production, based on *wage labour*, and a specific variant of finance, identified with *equity capital*.

According to Marx (1867), the form of the employment contract under capitalism is the source of capitalist dynamics, creating inequality and subordination, on the one hand, and the potential for innovation and technological change, on the other. The employment contract is a bargain of a special kind: what the worker sells to the capitalist is not finished labour, but their labour capacity or power to work. With wage labour or employment – as opposed to independent contracting or self-employment – the worker is placed at the disposal, or under the authority, of the employer. Exactly what the worker must do to earn the wage cannot be fully specified at the point when the bargain is struck. This creates a gap between what is contracted for in the market, and what the capitalist firm then extracts from the worker during the process of performance. In Marx's analysis, this gap is the basis for the "surplus value" generated by the capitalist mode of production, which is the property of the capitalist firm and, residually, of the firms' members, the shareholders, and so is the basis for the creation of equity capital in its strict sense.

Equity capital is a type of intangible property that takes the form of shares and similar corporate securities which can be traded in their own right. This tradability makes it possible for equity capital to be freed from its connection to tangible forms of property and put to different uses across society, hence the role of the "capital market" in allocating resources to different uses depending on their expected rate of return. Debt as a form of finance, or credit, probably originated at the same time as the first organised human societies (Graeber 2011); but in a capitalist economy, debt finance changes its function and mode of operation: it coexists with equity capital, is complementary to it in various ways, but ultimately serves it and follows its logic, which is the logic of capital accumulation.

Equity capital is a relatively recent phenomenon in historical terms. Its origins can be traced to the appearance of the institution of joint stock in the economies of western Europe, most prominently Britain and the Netherlands where the first trading companies, including the British and Dutch East India companies, were formed during the early seventeenth century (Harris 2000).

Wage labour, similarly, has only existed in its modern form since about the same time; and it has evolved gradually to reach its present position as the predominant mode of contracting for work in mature industrial economies (Deakin and Wilkinson 2005). The phenomenon of virtually the whole population of a country accessing the means for its subsistence, directly or indirectly, through the sale of labour power, is a feature of advanced economies with institutions of a particular type, which include those of the welfare state.

There has been much debate in the social sciences about the nature of "institutions" and of their relationship to firms and markets; and there are good grounds for thinking that it would not have been possible for labour and capital markets – in the sense just described – to exist without an effective state, consisting, in part, of a legal system capable of identifying and enforcing property rights as the basis for exchange relations (Deakin *et al.* 2017). However, the functions of the legal system are not confined to defining contract and property rights.

Capitalism has developed since the first emergence of wage labour; and the employment contract – which for Marx was a mechanism of exploitation and the source of social stratification – has over time had inserted into it a range of social rights. The most fundamental of these are those relating to workers' rights to self-organisation or freedom of association. Legally protected rights also underpin several of the institutions which are characteristic of the modern welfare or social state. These include social insurance, health and safety legislation, employment protection laws, and rights to equal treatment. The process of inserting these rights into the contract of employment gathered pace across the industrialised world, including Britain, in the final decades of the nineteenth century as the democratic franchise was extended to cover the working class.

Today the function of the welfare state is still to channel the risks which are inherent in the operation of a capitalist labour market. These risks include subjection to the power of another in the workplace and exposure to the risk of loss of income through unemployment, illness, age and social discrimination (Deakin and Wilkinson 2005). The welfare state qualifies capitalism; but it also, in a fundamental sense, both presupposes it and endorses it. There is nothing in social insurance or protective labour legislation to alter the fundamental "subordination" inherent in waged labour. Tellingly, "subordination" is the condition for "protection" in labour law discourse.

In essence, the welfare state captures part of the "surplus value" created by capitalist modes of production and applies it to the financing of various public or collective goods. As we have seen, this is part of the Polanyian "double movement". The system of public finance draws on the surplus from production − through income tax and corporation tax − to fund universal health care and public education systems, along with the rest of the apparatus of government. In doing so, it reinforces − and does not undermine − the logic of capitalist forms of production.

So the effect of the welfare state has been to make capitalism more sustainable, as well as, in the final analysis, less unjust. For many of the proponents of social reform in Britain, such as William Beveridge and the Webbs, this was its explicit purpose. Legal and institutional support for collective bargaining and access to social insurance helped to sustain effective demand for goods and services, while the reduction of social conflict associated with the recognition of workers' freedom of association rights helped to ensure that capitalist firms could operate with minimal interruption.

It would be wrong to describe the welfare state as a thing of the past. However, the welfare state has been seriously eroded over the course of the past four decades. This tendency has been attributed to many things, including changing work patterns, the narrowing of the tax base, the decline of the nation state, the freeing up of capital flows, the growth of international trade, and so on. Together with this erosion or decline has come an increase in social inequality and a perception that the nation state is losing its capacity to deliver social guarantees (Supiot 2015).

What has happened to the relationship between the welfare state and capitalism to put the functioning of social guarantees into question? Social rights are a charge on the capitalist firm, so even if firms collectively benefit from the provision of public goods, including orderly industrial relations, individual profit-seeking enterprises will take whatever opportunities they can to minimise or avoid social or fiscal commitments. Nation states themselves compete, as they increasingly see it, to attract capital. In this process, they have begun either to tolerate regulatory avoidance or – according to theories of efficient "regulatory competition" – openly encourage it.

At the same time, there has been a change in the institution of the corporation. The idea of "shareholder primacy", although contested, has taken hold in company law and corporate governance since the 1980s (Hansmann and Kraakman 2001). The rise of the shareholder value norm is associated with developments in corporate finance, including the rise of hostile takeovers and more recently the salience of shareholder activism. These are all ways of re-asserting the original claim of capital to the residual from production. The modern "shareholder" has many identities – including hedge funds, pension schemes and sovereign wealth funds – which use their collective power not only to put pressure on managers to prioritise shareholder interests but also to lobby governments for investor-friendly legal reforms.

The exclusion of worker well-being from anything more than an ancillary result, or by-product, of the operation of the capitalist firm – rather than one of its objectives – has been justified in various ways. These include being a technical precondition for the operation of the firm, without which even workers' interests would ultimately be harmed; being an inherent feature of shareholders' private property rights; and being an unavoidable consequence of the need to promote innovation-based technological change. But whatever the precise justification given, the effect of the logic of "shareholder value" is to dis-embed the corporation from its societal context, and to bring about a radical re-ordering of its goals. As the welfare state declines, the logic of finance as a mode of resource allocation and, ultimately, of social organisation, takes its place.

Thus in the capitalist systems of the global north – and increasingly at an international level – the capital market no longer operates simply (or even primarily) to finance business firms. Instead it is becoming a universal mode of governance for evaluating social and political projects. This idea finds its clearest expression in contemporary finance theory, which sees firms' retained earnings as, in principle, dead capital which should be freed up ("free cash flow") through takeover bids and restructuring, or through higher dividends and share re-purchases. The objective of this process is to permit an economy-wide re-allocation of resources of the kind credited, for example, with having created Silicon Valley and America's economic revival during the 1990s. The idea that the same mechanism of re-allocation should apply across society – and not just the economy – lies behind the contemporary marketisation of public health and education services and the introduction of various "private finance" initiatives into the public sector. It also implies a strict limit on how far the state can be allowed to interrupt the flow of profits from firms to capital markets – and back again – through taxation and regulation.

But focusing on the proximate causes for the decline of the welfare state in the global north – and its underdevelopment elsewhere – may get us only so far. The question prompted by a consideration of the nature of capitalism – and of its historical evolution – is whether the current decline of the welfare state is in some sense necessitated by capitalist dynamics. In this, there seem to be two alternative scenarios.

In the first scenario, the welfare state is seen to be incompatible with capitalism, and only survived for a brief interlude during the middle of the twentieth century as a consequence of a number of contingent circumstances. Because these no longer hold, the erosion and disappearance of the welfare state – and its replacement by unfettered capitalism – is considered inevitable.

The alternative scenario suggests that because the welfare state made capitalism sustainable, its failure would put capitalism itself at risk. From this perspective, there is nothing within capitalism which makes it infeasible to reconstruct the welfare state, perhaps in some new or evolved form.

In the chapters that follow, we will explore the degree to which these competing scenarios contain the most convincing prognosis for the UK. As we shall see, there have been periods in the past century when Britain's own distinctive variant of capitalism has been stabilised by the institutional and regulatory interventions led by the state; and the same is true of other so-called advanced market economies. The distinctiveness of the British situation, however, lies in the particular fragility and cyclicality of these interventions.

For a period from the early 1970s, Britain's membership of the EU enabled it to import institutions and mechanisms from other EU member states which proved successful in striking a balance between the competing pressures for marketisation and liberalisation. But this process of institutional learning was, at best, incomplete. This is because the influence of the EU over British social and economic policy was limited by constraints on the EU's competences, many of which were a direct consequence of British influence. How Britain is likely to fare in a post-Brexit world – in which it is no longer tied so closely to mainland European institutions and practices – is another question that will be explored in greater detail later in the book.

The drivers of change: the dynamics of the insecurity cycle

Since the arrival of the 2008 financial crisis, longstanding debates about the nature and extent of change in economic theory and policy paradigms – and the causal role that crises play in this context – have been reignited.[3] Peter Hall (1993) defines a "policy paradigm" as "an interpretive framework of ideas and standards that specifies not only the goals of policy and the kind of instruments that can be used to attain them, but also the very nature of the problems they are meant to be addressing" (p. 279). Such a framework may be destabilised by a "crisis", or an extended period of economic difficulty, that the conventional wisdom did not anticipate and cannot explain or ameliorate. This is particularly the case if it leads to widespread public and political dissatisfaction and a search for alternatives. But crises do not always produce shifts in the conventional wisdom; and paradigm change may come about without the dominant ideology having been destabilised by a crisis.

The academic literature on economic policy change is rooted in a range of institutional perspectives:[4] *historical institutionalism* focuses on macro-level dynamics, in which political actors and interest groups operate within a set of historically constructed institutional opportunities and constraints. In this context, power asymmetries, path dependence and unintended consequences are features of institutional development and change. Historical events are characterised by periods of relative continuity, interrupted by "critical junctures" during which significant institutional change takes place, through a process where ideas have an important influence on political contestation and outcomes. From this perspective, Galbraith's "massive onslaught of circumstances" can be considered a critical juncture that places "institutional arrangements on paths or trajectories which are very difficult to alter" (Pierson 2004, p. 135).

Rational choice institutionalism focuses on micro-level dynamics in which economic policy is affected by the behaviour and interactions of individuals and groups, who are assumed to be rational utility maximisers in pursuit of their own material self-interests. From this perspective, political outcomes are a result of strategic interactions within an institutional environment, the development of which is shaped by a process of competitive selection.

Economic constructivism focuses on a combination of micro- and macro-level dynamics in which individual and group behaviour and interests are seen to be governed by ideas (as opposed to institutions or self-interest) at a micro-level; and at a macro-level, ideas serve as a pre-condition for policy innovation and change because policy change requires the existence of a set of intellectually coherent and politically appealing ideas from which a new paradigm can be built.

To these three "new institutionalisms", Vivien Schmidt (2010, 2011) adds a fourth, which she identifies as *"discursive" institutionalism*, focusing on the substantive content of ideas about political action and the institutional context and processes by which these ideas are generated and communicated. She describes the exchange of ideas within the specialist policy sphere as "co-ordinative discourse" and the communication of these ideas to the general public as "communicative discourse" (Schmidt 2008, pp. 310–11). Between these two spheres of discourse, Alan Finlayson (2013) identifies a third, the "intermediate sphere", which he describes as "a sphere of political action and debate that joins formal expertise with political activists, party supporters and interested citizens, united by membership of the same ideological family" (p. 71).

What these analytical frameworks share – which is important for our purposes – is an appreciation of the key role played by institutions, interests and ideas within the policy-making and paradigm change process. Also important are insights from the now substantial literature on path dependency[5] in contributing to our understanding of policy stability and the literature on critical junctures in conjunction with the more recent, less developed, literature on "process sequencing",[6] which offers insight into policy evolution and change.

The academic literature suggests that the vitality of a policy paradigm will be influenced by features of the crisis or challenge to the conventional wisdom; ideational factors; the political and institutional means of support for the dominant orthodoxy (and the policy paradigm informed by it) – or for the development and implementation of a new one; and the ability of affected groups within society to recognise and mobilise support for their interests.

Benjamin Braun (2015) distinguishes between "explosive" crises – requiring an immediate response in order to avert perceived catastrophe – and "slow burning" crises that unfold over an extended period of time, allowing policy makers to search for and experiment with alternative approaches and theoretical justifications. However, if experimentation with new ideas and policy instruments within the existing paradigm fails or makes the situation worse, the authority and competence of government will be challenged, creating fear among policy makers of the consequences of *not* responding effectively. Thus, the relative severity and duration of a crisis or challenge to the conventional wisdom plays an important role in the stability of the existing policy paradigm.

When a challenge to the conventional wisdom occurs, how it is conceptualised has an important influence on the policies formulated and implemented to address it. Colin Hay (2013a) argues that "[c]rises are, in effect, what we make of them; and what we make of them determines how we respond" (p. 23). A decisive factor in this process is the correct diagnosis of the underlying cause of economic difficulties. However, this is a necessary but not sufficient condition for effectively resolving them. The cause of a crisis can be misidentified either wilfully, as a result of excessive confidence in a particular ideology, or accidentally (as, for example, were inflationary pressures during the 1970s). Mark Blyth (2013) makes the point that what the most powerful members of the group or society believe will determine how the crisis is conceived and in turn how it is approached. At present, the diagnosis of the current crisis as a "crisis of debt" (as opposed to a "crisis of growth") is serving to reinforce rather than challenge the neoliberal paradigm, providing a partial explanation for why we have yet to see any meaningful shift in economic thinking or policy (Hay 2013a, p. 23).

The narration of a crisis therefore plays an important role in the policy change process. But only if the crisis discourse is "paradigm-threatening" – as opposed to "paradigm-reinforcing" – is a shift in the conventional wisdom – and the policies informed by it – likely to occur (Hay 2013a). In this context, ideas that provide an interpretive framework for making sense of what is going on serve to reduce uncertainty and make possible collective action (Blyth 2002, p. 32). They not only tell us what to do, they also tell us how doing so will promote our interests as well as what those interests are in the first place.

James Silverwood (2013) identifies "policy consolidation" as being the implementation of policies that reinforce the conventional wisdom; and he differentiates this from "policy innovation" and change. Analysing the evolution of UK economic policy during the inter-war years, he concludes that rather than "the slow evolution of the ideas and policies of Keynes, ... [the orthodox paradigm proved remarkably resilient], maintained by the process of creative consolidation" (p. 13). This may provide an explanation for the current endurance of neoliberalism as well.

Colin Crouch (2008) argues that the transition from one policy paradigm to another requires not only the availability of a persuasive set of alternative ideas but also the existence of a class, the pursuit of whose interests is seen to serve the general interest (such as the mass consumer class that supported the neoliberal paradigm), and mechanisms for expressing and pursuing societal objectives. In this context, an important catalyst for change will be the existence of political resources that allow for the mobilisation of countervailing power (Streeck 2016) and the construction of a broad coalition in support of the new alternative (Baker 2015).

An effective legitimating discourse that not only tells a persuasive causal story but also resonates with shared experiences and ideas thus plays a key role in the policy change process (Stanley 2014). Vivien Schmidt (2010, 2011) suggests that agents' background ideational abilities enable them to create and sustain internal institutions that structure policy learning processes while their foreground discursive capabilities enable them to communicate critically about them, to maintain or to change them. But there is a tension in the literature about the relationship between economic events and the ideas used to interpret – and remedy – them. Ideas can serve as both weapons in the struggle for institutional change and "institutional blueprints"; they can also create the conditions for institutional stability (Blyth 2002). However, the process by which new ideas inform policy is a complex and opaque one, in which competing interests and institutions have a central role to play;[7] but new ideas do not always succeed in informing the direction of policy (Goldstein and Keohane 1993).

Drawing on Kuhn's (1962) theory of scientific revolutions, Hall's (1993) seminal analysis of paradigm change in macroeconomic policy-making in Britain between 1970 and 1989 develops a model based on a process of "social learning" involving three levels of policy change: (1) adjustment in the "settings" of existing policy instruments; (2) adoption of new instruments; and (3) adjustment of the hierarchy of policy objectives and the intellectual framework within which the policy-making process takes place. Hall identifies the first two as "normal policy-making" in which the overall terms of a given policy paradigm are not challenged and which do not necessarily lead to level three change and a paradigm shift. From this perspective, a once stable policy paradigm could be threatened by the appearance of "anomalies" – developments that cannot be fully understood or explained by the existing paradigm. As these accumulate and ad hoc attempts are made to resolve them, the intellectual coherence of the paradigm may be weakened. In this context, the failure to provide effective solutions to policy problems could undermine the government's authority, leading to a political contest which ends when the advocates of a new paradigm succeed in institutionalising it.

However, because paradigm failure does not necessarily lead to a comprehensive change in the existing policy framework, building on Hall's (1993) model of "paradigm revolution", Michael Oliver and Hugh Pemberton (2004) propose a model of "paradigm evolution". Analysing British political economic development starting with the "Keynesian Revolution" of the 1930s and 1940s – followed by the 1960s revision of the Keynesian paradigm, the unsuccessful "Monetarist Revolution" of the 1970s and the "Neoliberal Revolution" of the 1980s–1990s – they describe a process by which the failure to effectively institutionalise a new policy framework leads to a period of policy learning in which new ideas are incorporated into the existing paradigm and used in further experimentation with new settings and instruments. They suggest that this evolutionary process can be expected to continue until the battle to institutionalise a new policy framework is won – and the new paradigm gains acceptance as the replacement for its predecessor.

Distinguishing structural transformation, involving regime change, from conjunctional transformation, when change is sought within the existing policy framework, Hay (1999) contends that an extended period of seemingly unsuccessful experimentation within an existing regime may result in the emergence of a new paradigm if – as a consequence of the gradual accumulation of contradictions – it leads to narration of a structural crisis. However, because economic crises do not come complete with a new set of economic ideas to replace old ones, the absence of a coherent set of novel ideas might help to explain the absence of a paradigm shift since the 2008 financial crisis (Hay 2011).

Paradigm change may also be impeded by the tendency of political actors, during times of crisis or deep uncertainty, to resist change and fall back on familiar formulas, which if successful result in institutional reproduction (Thelen 2004). But institutions evolve in order to survive so change should never be ruled out, particularly if a crisis or period of uncertainty persists for an extended period of time.

Because crises on their own cannot generate processes producing alternative institutional arrangements – only human agency can – politics determines how a crisis will be played out; and there are political battles over how crises are defined, and hence, over proposals for resolving them. The political institutional setting – involving policies, political institutions and politics – therefore shapes the reform process and is key to understanding it (Schmidt 2009). Policy change also requires the political and institutional means of translating new economic ideas into policy. Because governments depend upon the belief by citizens that their decisions are worthy of being obeyed, they respond to threats to that legitimacy. As a result, regime change often follows "perceived" state failure (Hay 1999). In this context, political and ideational mediation of state and economic failure plays an important role in the process by which the transition occurs.

In this context, John Keeler (1993) identifies three mechanisms shaping the socio-political context through which policy reforms take place. The "crisis mandate" mechanism serves to discredit the ideas of incumbent government; the "urgency" mechanism permits reform to be imposed without caution regarding procedures; and the "fear" mechanism allows radical reforms to be imposed immediately without opposition, due to intimidation against resistance. Severe crises have the potential to empower governments with a mandate creating an extraordinary policy-making context where authorisation, party pressure, urgency and fear produce an outpouring of reform legislation. Thus, the window for reform is determined by both the severity of the crisis and the degree of partisan support.

Andrew Gamble (2014b) argues that lasting shifts in the conventional wisdom require a long-term strategic vision of what the future of the economy should look like, the change that is required to achieve it, identification of the short-term steps that are desirable in themselves, and the political will to seize opportunities as they arise. In this, direct backing by a major political advocate will be important (Béland 2005). Thus,

> the triumph of a new policy framework depends upon the preparedness of interest groups to adopt it, on the ability to promote the new ideas and to secure its endorsement by those in power and in the subsequent adoption by the institutions of economic policy.
>
> (Oliver and Pemberton 2004, p. 419)

The success of a new paradigm therefore relies upon a coherent set of ideas to justify and support it as well as the creation of a widespread network advocating the associated policies, forming a climate of opinion favourable to their adoption. In this, financial and political journalists and the media have a potentially pivotal role to play in simplifying new ideas, communicating them to the public and making them politically intelligible (Oliver and Pemberton 2004).

Some suggest that there is also an important role for some sort of exogenous shock in securing the triumph of the new policy paradigm in this institutional battle.[8] Oliver and Pemberton (2004) argue that

> [the full institutionalization of a new paradigm requires an exogenous shock capable of destroying confidence in the possibility of stabilizing the existing policy framework … the lack of sufficient shock to the system [may allow] vested interests successfully to resist radical change.
>
> (pp. 435–6)

In short, the relative resilience of a policy paradigm – and confidence in the government's economic management capabilities – will be influenced by the severity of a crisis – or challenge to the conventional wisdom – and length of time it persists; its conceptualisation and diagnosis (whether it is paradigm-reinforcing or -threatening); the availability, articulation and promotion of an intellectually coherent and politically appealing set of ideas in support of an existing paradigm (or from which a new paradigm can be built and justified); the persuasiveness of the legitimating discourse (for policy maintenance or change); the political and institutional means of supporting the dominant orthodoxy (or developing and implementing a new one); and the degree to which different groups within society are affected by the economic situation, are able to recognise and articulate their interests and mobilise support for them.

Exploring the insecurity cycle

Labour, Finance and Inequality: The Insecurity Cycle in British Public Policy is a study of the interaction between politics, economics, social dynamics and the legal framework – and the process of change in the conventional wisdom and the policies informed by it. These are examined against the backdrop of British history from the industrial revolution to the present to assess both why change comes about and why it doesn't always happen when it is expected to. Important in this context are the influence of shifts in the conventional wisdom; the relationship between the state and the market, the state and society and the market and society; and the relative power of key segments of society. We also take account of shifts in the relative power of the state and international business and finance, and how this has affected both the policy options available to national governments and their relative effectiveness.

Our contribution is to draw together ideas about socio-economic change and the nature of market capitalism into a theory that conceptualises change as being cyclical – and inevitable. Whereas the conventional wisdom of neo-liberalism views the economy as self-regulating if unimpeded – and tending towards stability – our analysis shows that socio-economic development is *actually* characterised by dynamic *non-equilibrium* processes, with stability (if ever) being fleeting. We also include insight from the literature on policy resilience and change – and the role of crises in this context – to identify combinations of factors with the potential to inhibit or catalyse change.

Chapter 2 examines how features of the British state – and its legal and institutional system – as they have evolved since the industrial revolution, have contributed to the inherently cyclical nature of Britain's socio-economic development, and to movement between the "self-regulating" market, on the one hand, and the social welfare state, on the other. Chapter 3 sets the turns in the insecurity cycle that can be discerned from the early twentieth century into their longer historical context. Chapter 4 explores the developments leading up to the Liberal social reforms preceding the First World War. Chapter 5 focuses on the inter-war years, which witnessed both the attempt to restore the pre-war liberal economic order and the social and economic reforms of the 1930s. The focus of Chapter 6 is the period leading up to the Attlee Labour government in 1945 and shift in ideology accompanying the post-war "Keynesian" consensus. Chapter 7 investigates the questioning of Keynesianism and the resurrection of pre-Keynesian "neoliberal" ideas during the "stagflationary" 1960s and 1970s. The rise of Margaret Thatcher, and the translation of these ideas into policy during the decades that ultimately produced the 2008 financial crisis, are the subject of Chapter 8. Chapter 9 considers the aftermath of the 2008 financial crisis, and the question of whether we might be in the throes of a further turn in the insecurity cycle. Chapter 10 considers what a post-Brexit regulatory model might look like. Chapter 11 concludes.

Notes

1 See, for example, Ostry *et al.* (2016).
2 Galbraith (1999, chapter 2).
3 See, for example, Baker (2015); Braun (2015); Cohen (2012); Crouch (2008, 2011); Gamble (2014a, 2014b); Hay (2011, 2013a); and Mirowski (2013).
4 See, for example, Hall and Taylor (1996); Schmidt (2011); and Silverwood (2013).
5 See, for example, Mahoney (2000); Mahoney and Thelen (2010); and Streeck and Thelen (2005).
6 See, for example, Haydu's (2010 and 1998, p. 353) discussion of "reiterated problem solving", Howlett and Rayner's (2006, pp. 13–14) analysis of "process sequencing" and Mahoney's (2000, p. 509) examination of "reactive sequencing".
7 See, for example, Blyth (1997); Berman (1998); Hall (1989, 1993); Hay (2001); and Walsh (2000).
8 See, for example, Greener (2001) and Oliver and Pemberton (2004).

2 The influence of the legal and institutional framework

Introduction

In recent years, the United Kingdom (UK) has shown itself to be more likely than many of its European neighbours to arrive at unexpected economic – and especially political – decisions. Whilst some of these have appeared to be inexplicable, and at times positively wilful, there are in fact reasons why Britain does not rigidly adhere to a given policy paradigm, supported by a well-rehearsed line of argumentation; and in the absence of significant change – perhaps through deeper integration of European Union member countries or the adoption of a system of proportional representation – this tendency is likely to continue for the foreseeable future.

So what makes Britain so prone to unanticipated change? What effect if any, has European Union or international law had on British legal systems, policy-making and social evolution – and what might be the effect of leaving the European bloc?

A number of factors underpinning the structure and evolution of the British state, along with its legal and institutional system, help to explain the tensions at the heart of the "insecurity cycle" as well as the mechanisms that contribute to its dynamism. This dynamism is evident in shifts between market liberalisation, on the one hand, and social interventionism, on the other. Thus, contrary to the idea of the "self-regulating" market, the "market" for liberty or social welfare does not appear to tend towards stability, but instead is in a constant state of flux, in response to changes in socio-economic circumstances and associated shifts in the prevailing ideology.

Absence of a written constitution

Whilst it is not true to say that the UK has no written constitution, there is no single document that sets it out. Thus the British constitution is accurately described as "uncodified". In this respect it is virtually unique. Almost every other country has developed formal, systematic rules for the organisation of government and separation of powers between the executive, legislature and judiciary (Elkins *et al.* 2009). By contrast, the British constitution comprises a body of documents drawn from statute law, common law (decisions of judges), Parliamentary and other conventions, and "works of authority", of which the most relevant is the set of written rules governing Parliamentary process. All four of these sources are continuously evolving, and as such, are subject to change; and pending withdrawal from the European Union, they together operate within the context of membership in the European bloc.

The absence of a single, codified constitution means that Britain has no embedded legal commitment to the protection of social rights. This does not mean that the concept of social protection is absent from UK law; but it does mean that it has been a contested policy rather than a constitutionally protected right as it is in most other countries, including virtually all other member states of the European Union.

In countries with a codified constitution, it is normal to find explicit legal guarantees for human rights, along with a clear demarcation of powers between the different branches of government (Comparative Constitutions Project 2017). Most national constitutions in Europe contain at least some reference to social rights, which vary from one country to another but generally include at least one of more of the rights to health, housing, social security and fair treatment at work. It is generally the task of the courts to define these rights and to defend them from legislative or executive interference.

In the UK, the power of judicial review is much more limited. The British courts can control the improper use of executive powers, but they have no capacity to overrule Parliament on the grounds that the legislation it enacts is incompatible with human rights. This is the effect of the doctrine of Parliamentary sovereignty, which, at least since the late seventeenth century, has been understood to mean that legislation passed in accordance with Parliament's procedures takes priority over all other sources of law, including the case law developed by the courts. It is also taken to mean that one Parliament can always undo or modify the work of its predecessors (Dicey 1885). The result is that human rights, even when contained in legislation, cannot be entrenched against later change.

In 1998, the Westminster Parliament adopted the Human Rights Act, which incorporated parts of the European Convention on Human Rights and Freedoms of 1951 into UK law. The Convention was, and is, a treaty, which binds the UK in international law. However, the UK – again in contrast to most other European countries – does not regard a treaty as part of its own national or domestic law, unless it is incorporated into the domestic legal order by statute. Even when incorporation of this kind takes place, its effects are limited. Because Parliament is sovereign, the Human Rights Act 1998 enjoys no special protection against repeal by a later Parliament; thus it is not entrenched against legislative action in the way that it is normal for constitutional protections in other countries, which generally require a supermajority or similar special procedure to change part of the constitution (Elkins *et al.* 2009).

As long as the Human Rights Act 1998 remains in place it enjoys a certain special status, in the sense that the courts will interpret later laws, as far as possible, in such a way as to ensure that they comply with the Convention rights it sets out. This is a limited concession to constitutionalism and the British courts have been hesitant to use it even so (Hickman 2011).

The Human Rights Act has had little or no effect in the area of social protection for another reason. Nearly all the provisions of the European Convention relate to civil and political rights, such as the right to free speech or the right to privacy (Dorssemont *et al.* 2013). These rights are important but they do not generate a comprehensive right to social protection. Rights to housing, health, social security and fairness at work are contained in a separate legal instrument, the European Social Charter of 1961 (Bruun *et al.* 2017), which, although also binding on the UK in international law, has not been incorporated into British domestic law.

The Convention right which has had the most significant bearing on social protection is Article 11, which sets out the right to freedom of association. Although this right has been interpreted by the European Court of Human Rights in a dynamic fashion to include a right to collective bargaining and a right to strike (Ewing and Hendy 2010), the British courts have developed their own jurisprudence on the meaning of Article 11, which is more limited in its scope than that of the Strasbourg court (Bogg and Dukes 2017). The result is that British workers, almost uniquely in a European context, enjoy no constitutional guarantee of collective participation in decisions affecting their pay and conditions of employment. Meanwhile, Britain has come to have one of the lowest rates of collective bargaining coverage of any developed country (Ewing *et al.* 2016).

The position is different with European Union (EU) law. As a signatory to the EU treaties, the UK is bound in international law to implement EU law at domestic level. The European Communities Act 1972 achieved this in a far-reaching way. Treaty provisions, directives (akin to legislation), regulations and rulings of the Court of Justice of the European Communities (CJEU), all flow into UK law without the need for specific implementing legislation (unless and to the extent that this is inherent in the form of the relevant EU legal instrument, as is the case with directives). The CJEU is the final arbiter on the meaning of EU law, and has developed legal doctrines ("supremacy" and "direct effect") to ensure that EU law takes priority over national law in the event of any conflict between them, and that EU law will be applied and enforced by national courts.[1] During the 1980s and 1990s, the UK courts came to accept the radical implications of these arrangements for labour and employment law, among other areas (Deakin and Morris 2012, chapter 2). On the one hand, UK law which was in conflict with EU law could be, to that extent, dis-applied. On the other, many aspects of EU law would be applied directly in UK national law, conferring legally enforceable employment rights on UK citizens. One of the first instances of this new departure in UK constitutional practice was a case in which a female employee seeking to establish equal pay with a male colleague was able to assert an EU-law right to equality in the face of a UK statute which would have barred her claim.

In contrast to the position under the European Convention on Human Rights, EU law recognises a wide range of social rights and, on the whole, grants them equivalent legal status to civil and political rights. Among the rights given a high level of protection by EU Treaties are the right to equal treatment (non-discrimination) in employment and the right to health and safety at work. Directives set out employee rights in a wider range of social policy contexts, including redundancies, business transfers, collective employee information and consultation, and the rights of part-time, fixed-term and temporary agency workers.[2]

However, not all areas of social policy are covered by EU law. There is no EU-wide minimum wage, nor a general EU-level legal instrument governing termination of employment. The EU has no competence to adopt directives relating to freedom of association or the right to strike. The EU Charter of Fundamental Rights sets out a number of social rights on matters which are outside the current scope of social policy directives; for example, it acknowledges the existence of a right or freedom to take collective industrial action. However, there is less to the Charter than meets the eye: although its provisions can be called in aid when interpreting provisions of the Treaties and directives, it does not create new rights in areas of law beyond the scope of these existing legal measures (Deakin and Morris 2012, chapter 2).

Thus, EU law is very far from providing a comprehensive code of social rights and protections. It is as limited as it is very largely as a result of the influence wielded by successive UK governments. Since the late 1970s, the UK has followed a twin-track strategy of opposing new social policy initiatives and, when opposition was no longer possible (as not all directives require unanimity on the part of member states), ensuring they were watered down and their implementation delayed. For a time, the UK was completely outside the scope of new rule-making powers embodied in the Social Chapter of the Maastricht Treaty, agreed in 1992. Partly through fear of losing its influence over the Union's evolving social policy, the UK opted back into the Social Chapter in 1997 and promptly resumed its strategy of opposition to new social initiatives (Kenner 2003; Barnard 2012).

Even so, it was now too late for British policy makers to reverse the effects of EU law-making in the field of social policy. EU law, in this area as in others where the Union has been active – such as financial regulation and competition policy – provides the nearest thing the UK has ever had to a set of constitutional norms protected against executive interference and political expediency. The impact on social protection, in areas as wide-ranging as equal pay, LGBT rights, age discrimination, working time and transfers of undertakings, has been profound (Barnard 2012).

Brexit will put these developments into reverse. Even if many of the social protections currently derived from EU law were to be re-adopted as part of

UK domestic law after Brexit, they would be vulnerable in future to legislative revisions. Indeed, if proposals being debated by the Westminster Parliament in the course of the session which began in 2017 are followed through, the process of removing social and other rights from UK law after Brexit will be streamlined, with statutory orders and other forms of secondary legislation, with minimal Parliamentary scrutiny, sufficing to achieve the necessary legal changes.[3]

Brexit has thrown other aspects of UK constitutional law and practice into sharp relief. It is now clear – if there had been any real doubt – that the UK's membership of the European Union did nothing to change the fundamental nature of the British constitution. The insertion of EU law into domestic law was essentially the result of one statute, the European Communities Act 1972 (and related legislative variants of that model). The supremacy of EU law over domestic law rested entirely on a domestic legal measure. That measure, in turn, enjoyed no special legal protection from revision or repeal by a later Parliament. Remove the European Communities Act, and the entire body of EU law, in so far as it is part of UK domestic law, simply falls away (at least in relation to its prospective effects, and subject to any savings clauses introduced by later legislation[4]).

All of this was made transparently clear in the *Miller* litigation which in 2017 clarified the need for Parliamentary authorisation of Brexit. Although the UK government lost that case, the decision of the Supreme Court was a strong reassertion of constitutional orthodoxy: Parliament remained supreme and the UK's forty-plus years of EU membership had changed nothing.

The issue at stake in *Miller* was not whether the referendum vote of June 2016 was in any way binding on Parliament (it wasn't), or whether the EU legal rights apparently guaranteed to UK citizens and those of other member states could be removed through legislation adopted by the Westminster Parliament in the normal way (they could). It was whether the executive act of triggering the UK's withdrawal from the EU under Article 50 of the Treaty on the European Union necessitated an Act of Parliament. The Supreme Court held that it did, on the narrow ground that, on this issue, the government's prerogative power to conduct foreign policy had been restricted as a result of the passage of the European Communities Act 1972. What Parliament had done, it had to undo. Parliament duly obliged and legislative authorisation for the triggering of Article 50 was provided in the form of the European Union (Notification of Withdrawal) Act 2017. In British constitutional terms, it was irrelevant that legislating to quit the EU in this way would have the effect, in due course, of eliminating legal protections in the areas of social policy and free movement which British and other EU citizens had come to regard, over several decades of legal and political practice, as fixed and irreversible.

The *Miller* case had wider ramifications for the British legal and constitutional system (Elliott 2017). One of the issues put before the Supreme Court concerned the relationship between the Westminster Parliament and the devolved legislatures of Scotland, Wales and Northern Ireland. It was argued that the consent of the devolved legislatures would be needed for Article 50 to be triggered. This was because of a constitutional principle known as the Sewel Convention, according to which the Westminster Parliament will not legislate on a matter affecting a devolved legislature without its consent.

In the case of the relationship between the UK Parliament and the Scottish Parliament, this convention was no longer just an understanding or assumption based on previous practice; it had been recognised in legislation of the Westminster Parliament itself. In *Miller*, the Supreme Court held, in essence, that this counted for nothing, and that the Sewel Convention was, like other constitutional conventions, a political understanding, not a legal guarantee of a division of powers between the different levels of government. Thus, the consent of the Scottish Parliament was not needed in order for the Westminster Parliament to authorise the triggering of Brexit. Nor was it relevant that majorities of those voting in the referendum in Scotland (and Northern Ireland) had opposed Brexit.

To sum up, Britain has a constitution and legal system which are, in a very real sense, pre-modern. The UK's institutions never underwent the kind of revolutionary transformation which the Americans and French experienced in the late eighteenth century and which then spread around the world in the decades which followed (Elkins *et al.* 2009). The checks and balances which characterise constitutional law and practice in virtually every other country in the world, and certainly all economically developed ones, are absent in Britain. In their place, informal understandings and the shared values and assumptions of the political class focused on Westminster, together with the higher judiciary and civil service, set the parameters within which public power is exercised. EU law introduced a period of partial and belated modernisation, which will be reversed if Brexit proceeds as expected. When that process is completed, Britain's constitutional *ancien régime* will be fully restored.

The rights of capital: corporate and financial law

The nature of the constitution is not the only influence that contributes to the adversarial nature of the British institutional structure; the separate evolution of corporate and financial law, on the one hand, and the rather more halting development of laws relating to the labour market, on the other, have also contributed to this tension.

From very early on, British financial and business law was under considerable pressure to evolve, particularly with the progression of the first – and especially the second – industrial revolution. The new technologies driving change required very large amounts of capital, especially for the construction of infrastructure, including canals and railways. So the legal framework evolved in order to provide it.

The Bank of England had been set up in 1694, as a private institution to provide the King with large amounts of capital. At the time, this was motivated by the need to fund a much more powerful navy with which to both defend and establish trade routes. The fleet also engaged in military activities and, subsequently, the expansion of the British Empire.

In this process, the "City" of London soon emerged as the international centre for finance; and as it was largely independent of the state, the City has rarely accepted intervention from that quarter (Kynaston 1994). Even so, finance had problems of its own. Whilst it had experience of raising large amounts of capital for wars and imperial expansion, financing the industrial revolution was far more problematic.

Being the first country to industrialise, Britain had little experience to draw upon – and no road map. Consequently, the industrial revolution was a step into an unknown future, where not only individual businesses, but even whole new technologies might fail to find a foothold. Raising sufficient capital therefore also meant finding ways of providing protection for investors and limiting their liability in the event that the enterprises in which they chose to invest were unsuccessful. As it was, Britain was comparatively late to adopt the corporate form, with the normal legal mode of operation for early manufacturing firms being a hybrid of the trust and the partnership (Harris 2000). Statutory recognition for the principle of shareholders' limited liability was delayed to the middle decades of the nineteenth century by concerns over its potential to leave unsecured creditors and workers without adequate protection in the event of business failure.

However, once the legal shift to a corporate economy had been made, the courts did not look back; and by the 1890s, they had conclusively ruled that limited liability protected shareholders from exposure to business losses. As a consequence of this gradual evolution, British industry became heavily reliant on the stock market as a source of finance for expansion beyond what could be raised and re-invested from operational returns.

UK company law continues to be influenced by the initial conditions of British industrialisation and by the emphasis given to shareholder protection at various stages of its development (Ahlering and Deakin 2007). It is myth to say that shareholders are the legal "owners" of companies, or that directors have a duty to "maximise" shareholder value. UK company law, in common with its equivalents in other countries, maintains a strict separation between the property of the corporate person or entity, on the one hand, and that of its members, the shareholders. Shareholders can, in general, freely trade their shares; and they can exercise income, voice and control rights to the exclusion of other "stake-holders" such as the company's employees and creditors. However, the management of the company's business is legally vested in the board of directors, which has the power to delegate responsibilities to officers and employees. At least since the last quarter of the nineteenth century, the British courts have recognised that ownership of a share of stock – understood as a transferable corporate security – does not equate to part ownership of the corporation's assets; nor does it confer a right on the shareholders, collectively or individually, to give instructions to management on how to run the business (Ireland 1999).

The modern business firm is, in essence, a complex exercise in delegation, and the role of company law is to facilitate its operations, including capital raising and the coordination of production, by reducing transaction costs (Armour *et al.* 2017). In this fundamental respect, British company law is no different to that found elsewhere. There, are, however, some differences, which place British company law at one end of the spectrum, internationally, when it comes to protecting the rights of shareholders (Deakin 2017a). Although shareholders do not have powers to manage the company in its day-to-day affairs, UK company statutes provide shareholders with more extensive rights to intervene in managerial decisions affecting corporate strategy and major assets than is normal among advanced industrial countries. UK company legislation also prevents boards entrenching themselves against removal by a simple majority of the voting shares. In law, at least – and often in practice – British business firms are shareholder democracies, even if democracy, in this case, is based on the principle of one share, one vote, rather than one person, one vote.

During the nineteenth century, the evolution of British company law was driven by the expansion of stock markets, creating a growing class of rentier investors, and by a series of corporate scandals which revealed the weakness of the legal regime when it came to protecting the new shareholder class against self-dealing and other forms of managerial opportunism. In this context, shareholders' rights to receive information from the board and to hold directors to account for their performance developed in stages, largely by reaction to the fallout from phases of financial expansion such as the railway mania of the 1840s and the banking crisis of the late 1860s.

The middle decades of the twentieth century, by contrast, were a period of corporate consolidation and merger; and as significant parts of industry came under state control, the rise of shareholder power was checked. This was a period during which managerial autonomy was at its height, and investor pressure muted at best. It was also a time when British industry was in a position to accommodate a greater role for employee voice in the organisation of workplace relations, and, through collective bargaining, an increasing share for labour in corporate profits.

But shareholder power was to revive during the final third of the twentieth century through the conjunction of several trends (Cheffins 2008). Pension funds – themselves the result of the tendency towards corporate consolidation and intended to provide workers in larger enterprises with long-term income security in return for their commitment to the firm – came to occupy a pivotal role as investors in listed companies; and the concentration of power and resources which they represented led to a revival of interest in the issue of shareholder rights. Governments at this time – keen to reform a private sector which they associated with restrictive practices and a reluctance to innovate – saw shareholder power as a lever for the modernisation of industry. After 1979, successive privatisations further reinforced the dominance of the pension funds and other institutional investors as the ultimate "owners" of British industry, while, from the 1990s, the growing influx of overseas capital and the appearance of new actors aimed at enhancing shareholders' financial returns, including hedge funds and sovereign wealth funds, directed policy makers' attention to the issue of company law reform.

The initial developments in the rise of "corporate governance" as an area of policy concern took place largely outside the legal system, instead taking the form of codes of practice drawn up by financial and legal interest groups in the City of London – and largely operated by them. The first of these, the Takeover Code, originated in the late 1950s, and was intended to ensure that minority shareholders were not shut out from the gains resulting from hostile takeovers. The Code was extended during the late 1960s and has continued to evolve ever since, largely in the direction of enhancing shareholders' information and income rights (Johnston 2011). The model of shareholder empowerment underlying the Code became the basis for an EU directive in 2004, and by those means came to influence mainland European practice; it has also had a substantial impact on the evolution of takeover regulation in other parts of the world, including Latin America and East Asia (Katelouzou and Siems 2015).

During the mid-1990s, the first corporate governance codes were adopted – again largely as a result of self-regulation by City interests – although with some prompting from government. The impetus for the Cadbury Code of 1992 was the need to address the accounting and governance failures which had been revealed by the collapse of several large listed companies. The Cadbury Report put in process the development of standards for board structure and an expansion of the role of non-executive directors.

The Cadbury model was ostensibly designed to ensure that managers of listed companies could more effectively be held to account through a combination of independent director monitoring and market influence. But it also entrenched the idea that the principal purpose of the company was to serve the interest of shareholders, as the role which other corporate constituencies might have played in ensuring managerial accountability was recognised only by its striking absence. The principle that companies should have the option of complying with the Code's recommendations or disclosing their reasons for non-compliance – "comply or explain" – reflected the contemporary preference for "light-touch" regulation and the use of market mechanisms in place of direct enforcement (Sanderson *et al.* 2017). As in the case of the Takeover Code, the UK's corporate governance codes have become a template for global practice, with countries around the world adopting Cadbury's recommendations for independent boards and light-touch enforcement through the principle of "comply or explain".

When company law reform eventually arrived in the shape of the Companies Act 2006 – which followed nearly a decade of Law Commission reports and government-sponsored reviews – it confirmed the shift to a legal regime focused on shareholder primacy. Attempts to instil a more pluralistic account of corporate purposes in company legislation were rebuffed during the long process of review which ran from the late 1990s to the mid-2000s, while the statutory re-definition of directors' duties contained in the 2006 Act aligned the concept of the corporate interest more closely with the realisation of shareholder value than before (Keay 2013). The Operating and Financial Review, a proposed expansion of corporate reporting requirements to include a wider range of social and environmental outcomes, which even reached the stage of being formally enacted, was watered down at the last minute as a result of institutional investor pressure.

The Companies Act 2006 came into force just as the "global" financial crisis of the late 2000s was beginning. In the UK, this took the form of the near-failure of those financial institutions which had most actively pursued the strategy of shareholder value maximisation (Deakin 2011). Northern Rock and HBOS had been building societies before their conversion to listed company status, a process encouraged during the 1980s by statutory reforms and an acquiescent judiciary. RBS was the result of mergers in the banking sector which had been driven by hostile takeovers aimed at generating a surplus for investors. These companies were all highly leveraged at the point when the credit crunch began in 2007, making them uniquely vulnerable to the subsequent collapse in liquidity; and they all had to be rescued by the government.

The corporate bail-outs were not interpreted – as they might easily have been – as a practical refutation of the policies which had dominated British corporate and financial law for the preceding three decades. Aside from some minor changes to corporate governance standards affecting banks, there were practically no policy or legal responses of any significance to Britain's experience of the global financial crisis.

British company law today is still highly shareholder-orientated. It is closely aligned with what has become a deeply financialised economy, in which takeover bids and share re-purchases designed to "return capital" to investors have a significantly higher incidence than in other countries, but which is also characterised by low levels of investment in research and development and a patchy record of innovation (Driver and Thompson 2018). Yet elements of this model are fairly recent; and it is not irreversible. The underlying legal structure is capable of supporting alternative forms of enterprise based on worker and customer participation and state involvement (Deakin 2012); and there is a growing debate about the "dark side" of shareholder value, which is manifest in growing pay inequality and the shifting of risks from business to the state (Talbot 2012). British company law remains contested terrain.

Social (in)security: from the poor law to the welfare state – and back again

The history of the laws regulating the labour market is the converse of those governing capital markets and the system of finance. Since the time of the poor laws, the treatment of workers, the unemployed and those in poverty has been characterised by waves of coercive state intervention and social engineering – far from "light-touch" regulation – aimed at maintaining labour discipline and ensuring a supply of low-cost labour to firms. These policies were not consistently successful and the costs they engendered led to periodic attempts to build alternative models based on mutual assistance and collective security against labour market risks (Deakin and Wilkinson 2005). Thus, here – as in other areas – policy has oscillated between two extremes, although the recent trend has been in the direction of greater coercion and control.

The British poor law was a remarkably enduring institution which had its origins in the post-feudal economy of the late middle ages and persisted up to foundation of the modern welfare state during the middle decades of the twentieth century. Indeed, many of the assumptions of the poor law continue to shape contemporary social security law and practice.

The poor laws played a pivotal role in Britain's early industrialisation by providing the growing industrial labour force with alternative means of subsistence at a point when waged employment was becoming the norm and access to the land was limited by the process of enclosure (Wrigley 1988). In this context, the poor laws were used to manage the migration of labour from the towns to the cities and to cushion some of its effects on communities and families. Poor relief was not designed to be generous. But replacement rates for the predecessors of unemployment benefit were, for some areas of the country, comparable to those payable today; and at the turn of the eighteenth century, expenditure on poor relief in Britain was substantially higher than in other western European countries (Solar 1995).

Although many intellectual currents informed the evolution of the poor laws– including the stigmatisation of the poor as responsible for their own fate – other ideas also played a part. Thus, according to an early eighteenth-century legal text written for the local justices responsible for administering the law, the poor were to be thought of not as "vagabond beggars and rogues" but "those who labour to live, and such as are old and decrepit unable to work, poor widows, and fatherless children, and tenants driven to poverty; not by riot, expense and carelessness, but by mischance" (Dalton 1746).

However, this comparatively enlightened view did not survive the social upheaval caused by the rapid growth of British industry during the century after 1750; and by the 1830s the "old" poor law was crumbling away, its decay most evident in the practice of wage subsidisation known as the "Speenhamland system". Unable to pay a living wage because of rising competition and falling prices, employers pressed for the extension of "outdoor relief" – cash payments – from the unemployed to those in work. This only led to further falls in wages and rising expenditure on poor relief to fill the gap (Deakin and Wilkinson 2005, pp. 126–34).

Parliament's response was the Poor Law Amendment Act of 1834, which aimed to make "indoor relief" – the provision of benefits in kind, conditional on forced labour under workhouse conditions – mandatory for the "able-bodied" poor. The workhouse model was premised on the theory of "less eligibility", according to which standards of poor relief should be no better than the worst conditions available to the "independent labourer" in waged employment (Deakin and Wilkinson 2005, pp. 134–42). It was assumed that once wage subsidies were removed and incentives for the supply of wage labour restored, wages would automatically rise to meet workers' subsistence needs; in other words, the market would deliver a living wage.

This idea, in its turn, was tested to destruction during the course of the nineteenth century (Williams 1981). Although the law prohibited the payment of outdoor relief in urban and manufacturing districts – a more flexible approach was applied to rural areas – it often continued as a matter of practice where wages failed to rise and no alternative forms of subsistence were available; and it was frequently supplemented by private charity. Increasingly, however, more workhouses were constructed and their living conditions made systematically more demeaning in an effort to bring about the expected adjustment in labour market conditions. As late as the first years of the twentieth century, "test workhouses" in the major cities were being designed to impose especially harsh regimes of forced labour and family separation on those deemed able to take up independent work (Deakin and Wilkinson 2005, pp. 142–8).

The modern welfare state was born out of the realisation that the workhouse system could not be made to work, no matter how much resource was devoted to it. As the Webbs discovered, rather than allowing wages to rise to subsistence level, the test workhouse, by degrading the delivery of poor relief, was undermining wages and employment conditions and entrenching poverty (Webb and Webb 1909). The pioneering social research of Booth and Rowntree revealed that in-work poverty was much more extensive than previously realised, and that a stable income was out of reach for between a fifth and a third of the urban population. Efforts were thus begun to put into place a legal floor under wages in low-paying trades and to extend the reach of collective bargaining; and during the first half of the twentieth century, access to both sickness and unemployment benefits and old age pensions was extended through legislation establishing social insurance schemes which were to be directly managed by the state. By 1946, the National Insurance Act had established a comprehensive system for the public financing of social security benefits, which Beveridge, its principal designer, described as a new "national minimum" (Deakin and Wilkinson 2005, pp. 160–8).

In Beveridge's scheme of national insurance, social security would be a legal entitlement, based on a wage-earner's contributions throughout a working lifetime, and no longer a matter of private charity or of public assistance based solely on need (Beveridge 1942). The involvement of the state would reduce transaction costs and avoid the "cherry picking" associated with private insurance schemes, which mainly protected those in stable and well paid employment and imposed risk-related premia on the lower paid and those in casual trades. Thus, national insurance was inherently redistributive and based on the premise that risk-pooling across the whole working population was both the fairest and most cost-effective mode of delivering economic security.

At the same time, Beveridge intended the benefits delivered by national insurance to be minimal. Individuals were to be encouraged to make additional provision over and above the basic protections provided by the state scheme. Alongside national insurance, therefore, the state subsidised private, employer-based ("occupational") pension schemes through the tax system. When a fully earnings-related state retirement pension was introduced during the mid-1970s, provision was made for employer-based occupational schemes to be contracted out of it. From the mid-1980s the state earnings-related scheme was gradually wound down, leaving most pensioners reliant on a combination of the basic state pension, means-tested pension credits and income from private schemes (Deakin and Wilkinson 2005, pp. 175–85).

The Beveridgian model also depended critically on the widespread availability of stable and well-remunerated employment (Beveridge 1944). Long-term unemployment would undercut the financing of the state scheme, as would any persistence of casual and low-paid work. Thus, active state management of the economy, designed to maintain effective demand, was an integral part of the model, as was the use of state power to promote collective bargaining and stable work in both the public and private sectors, and to de-casualise employment in low-paying trades.

From the 1980s, the removal of these beneficial external conditions made the Beveridgian approach to social security unsustainable. Governments responded to high levels of structural unemployment by lowering replacement rates for unemployment and sickness benefits, and making their receipt increasingly conditional on claimants accepting work at rates of pay below those set by collective bargaining, even as contributions were rising in an attempt to restore fiscal equilibrium to the national insurance fund (Deakin and Wilkinson 2005, pp. 185–9).

From the 1990s, policies of wage subsidisation were revived, in the form of tax credits paid to low-income households, and later in the unified tax-benefit system of universal credit, which was rolled out in stages from 2013. A national minimum wage, introduced with effect from 1999, was designed not as a means of reducing poverty, but in order to limit expenditure on tax credits, an aim it was barely able to realise in the face of rising numbers of the low paid; in 2016, around one-fifth of the workforce was receiving less than two-thirds of the median wage, and a quarter was paid below a needs-based living wage (Deakin 2017a).

Social security policy, it seems, has come full circle. It is estimated that between 1780 and 1800, expenditure on poor relief increased by over 300 per cent, largely as a result of the growth in wage subsidies during this period (Snell 1985). Between 1999 and 2010, the numbers in receipt of tax credits increased by over 500 per cent (Puttick 2018). While no-one is now suggesting the revival of the workhouse, "workfare" – working for an employer in return for receiving basic social assistance – has made a return for the long-term unemployed. Conditionality in the payment of unemployment benefits is being tightened, with the numbers of claimants sanctioned for reasons including not actively seeking work or not taking up or leaving a place on a workfare programme totalling nearly a million cases in one year alone (2014). The universal credit system extends conditionality to those in work if they are receiving tax credits as a supplement to wages; unless they maintain their hours of work at a threshold of thirty-five hours (which for this purpose is deemed to be the normal full time working week), their tax credits are docked. The aim of this policy – known as "in-work progression" – is explicitly disciplinary, as it sanctions those who lose pay without "good reason" (Puttick 2018). It is also likely to lead to a further growth in "mini jobs" and other casual and precarious forms of work (Adams and Deakin 2014a).

In the very long run of British social security policy, the twentieth-century experiment with the welfare state now appears as the exception. Universal credit signifies a return to that particular mix of state coercion, labour discipline and wage subsidisation which characterised the poor law in previous centuries. However, history suggests that the present model will not prove very durable, and that before long there will be a reconsideration of the case – on the combined grounds of fairness and efficiency – for social insurance.

Regulating employment relations: labour law and collective bargaining

Closely related to social security law, and integrating the operation of the labour market with the organisation of business firms, is labour law, the body of law governing the employment relationship, the determination of pay and conditions of employment, and the activities of trade unions, including collective bargaining. The evolution of British labour is closely tied to the trajectory of trade unionism, with the law at different points restricting and then supporting independent unions.

During the nineteenth century, not having democratic representation did not deter workers from pursuing alternative channels of expression; and the trade union movement provided a means of identifying and securing independent representation for the interests of workers in particular occupations and industrial sectors. The early trade unions were strongly resisted by both employers and the state, with union rights and legal status becoming a bone of contention almost from the start – and this remained a recurring feature throughout the nineteenth century and right up to Tony Blair's New Labour government a century later. In this process, both statutory and common law moved first in favour of one side before swinging back to the other.

From their beginnings, trade unions were not restricted to negotiating conditions of employment; and there was a concerted effort to reform democracy as well, notably via the Chartist movement. Although this was

– officially at least – finally rejected in 1858, almost all of its demands would eventually be met. During the twentieth century, the trade unions mostly supported the expansion of the welfare state, while expressing concerns that the absorption of worker-led forms of mutual assistance into the state social security scheme might eventually weaken their position. From the 1980s, as social security became once again more disciplinary and coercive in nature (Deakin and Wilkinson 2005, chapter 3), this fear turned out to be well founded.

For most of the twentieth century, British labour law supported trade unionism indirectly (Deakin and Morris 2012, chapter 1). Unions and their officials were provided with forms of immunity from liability in tort for organising industrial action; and the law encouraged employers to recognise trade unions for the purposes of collective bargaining, without making collective bargaining compulsory. Except in wartime, legal enforcement of basic rates of pay was confined to sectors without effective trade union organisation, where trade boards, and later wage councils, were established to set minimum wages and other terms and conditions of employment that established a floor of rights with legal effect. Outside the wages council sector, successive governments supported the establishment of voluntary machinery for pay determination at industry or sector level, and put into place legislative measures designed to ensure that sectoral agreements were extended to non-unionised firms, thereby ensuring that wages were taken out of competition. Shortly after the Second World War, over 80 per cent of British workers came within the coverage of one or the other of these forms of collective wage determination. This was also the high point of earnings equality in Britain (Deakin and Wilkinson 2005, p. 243).

The spread of collective bargaining did not imply the disappearance of the individual contract of employment. Wages and conditions of employment set by collective bargaining were incorporated into individual contracts and could be enforced by workers by individual action where necessary. Just as plant- or company-level bargaining could improve the minimum terms set by sector-level agreements, so individual agreements could be made to improve on terms set collectively. In practice, up to the 1960s, individual bargaining had ceased to play a meaningful role in the regulation of pay and conditions for the vast majority of British workers.

However, from this point onward, British labour law began to change, for a number of related reasons. Governments of both political parties saw a more prominent role for individual employment law as a means of "modernising" workplace relations. Unfair dismissal laws, introduced by a Conservative government in 1971, were designed to provide low-cost access to a new type of labour court – the industrial (later employment) tribunals – in the hope of reducing the incidence of unofficial ("wildcat") strikes over disciplinary and dismissal-related disputes. Employment protection legislation was later expanded and came to be seen as a mechanism for achieving workplace justice; but its corporatist origins have continued to shape its development and have limited its effectiveness as a mode of redressing employee grievances (Collins 1992).

Another development dating from the 1960s was the attempt by government to exercise greater control over the processes and outcomes of collective bargaining. For a time this was associated with the "modernising" agenda of the Labour government's proposals for trade union reform – *In Place of Strife* (1969) – and the Conservative government's Industrial Relations Act (1971–4), both of which the unions were successful in opposing (Deakin and Wilkinson 2005, pp. 261–4).

From the early 1980s, in the very different economic climate of rising unemployment and downsizing in industries such as steel, shipbuilding and coal, where the unions had been strongly represented, they were less effective in resisting a new round of legal reforms which sought more directly to undermine the sources of their power. Under Margaret Thatcher and John Major, successive Conservative governments not only rolled back the immunities which had protected strike action, they also imposed new balloting requirements and removed statutory support for sector-level collective bargaining. In this context, collective bargaining coverage began to fall, along with union membership, which had reached a post-war high in 1979, while earnings inequality rapidly increased (Deakin and Wilkinson 2005, pp. 264–71).

In complementary legal reforms, the powers of the wages councils were reduced after 1986; and between 1993 and 1999 there was no statutory minimum wage of any kind. As we have just seen, tax credits were expanded during this period in an attempt to fill the resulting gap in household incomes; and the reintroduction of a minimum wage from 1999 was intended to dovetail with the tax credit system, not to replace it. Setting a minimum rate which reflected employers' concerns regarding the affordability of higher pay was made a priority for the body tasked with advising ministers, the Low Pay Commission (Simpson 1999).

In addition to bringing back the minimum wage, the New Labour government, elected in 1997, strengthened certain aspects of employment protection legislation, adopted a number of new EU legal norms by virtue of its decision to end Britain's opt out of the Social Chapter, and passed a new measure to require employers to recognise trade unions for the purposes of collective bargaining where they could show a certain threshold of support (generally a majority) in a relevant bargaining unit. But New Labour did not reverse the most significant of the changes to strike law which had curtailed much of the labour market power of trade unions – in particular, the legal limits placed on solidarity or "secondary" strike action – nor did it take steps to restore sector-level collective bargaining.

The highly collectivised labour market of forty years ago has become one in which union presence is dispersed and collective bargaining fragmented. Trade union membership in 2018 – at just over 6 million people – is less than half what it was at the peak in 1979. Union density (membership as a proportion of the active labour force) has fallen to below 25 per cent, and the coverage of collective agreements to below 30 per cent. But 40 per cent of all workers report that a union has a presence of some kind in their workplace, a figure which rises to over 80 per cent in the public sector; and workers in around 40 per cent of larger workplaces (those employing more than fifty people) have their pay governed by a collective agreement (BEIS 2017).

Thus the British labour market is by no means de-unionised, and the trend towards declining union membership is one that is mirrored in the experience of other industrialised countries (Visser *et al.* 2015). Where the UK is different is in the limited coverage of collective bargaining. But this indicator is weakly correlated with other measures of union influence: France and Germany have lower levels of union membership than the UK but higher levels of collective bargaining coverage, thanks to laws which support sectoral agreements and their extension to workplaces where unions are not recognised. With a different legal framework, the sectoral coverage of collective agreements could once again be expanded in Britain (Ewing *et al.* 2016).

Declining union influence in sectors such as retail and services is reflected in the growth of precarious forms of work, including zero hours contracts and false self-employment. Given the weakness of collective bargaining in these and other sectors, unions have re-focused their attention on the use of litigation and other legally orientated strategies to try to counter the effects of growing insecurity at work. Over the course of the 1990s and 2000s, this led to a huge increase in the numbers of complaints being heard by employment tribunals. In 2013, these peaked at over 300,000 claims, an increase of over 200 per cent from the late 1990s. The Conservative-Liberal Democrat coalition government responded by introducing a system of tribunal fees, requiring claimants to pay up-front sums ranging from a few hundred pounds to over two thousand. During the years following the introduction of the new system in 2013, although the government had argued that any fall in the number of claims would be around 8 per cent, depending upon the type of claim, the number actually fell by between 66 and 70 per cent (Ford 2018).

In July 2017, the UK Supreme Court ruled that the order introducing the fees system was unlawful, due in part to its infringement of constitutional protections traceable to Magna Carta (1215), which guaranteed unfettered access to justice. The fees order was also contrary to EU law requiring effective remedies for breaches of social rights. Had the fees order been contained in primary legislation, and in the absence of the entrenchment of rights through EU law, it is likely that the case would have been decided in the government's favour, on the grounds that the British courts have very limited powers, if any, to overturn an Act of Parliament.

The fees litigation – which was initiated by the trade union Unison – illustrates the potential of employment law to counter the effects of a changing industrial economy and labour market structure on the ability of unions to organise at workplace level. In other recent cases, the unions have used litigation to remedy historic pay inequalities based on stereotyped assumptions about the need for male workers to receive a breadwinner wage (Deakin *et al.* 2015), and to challenge the use of false self-employment by so-called "gig economy" firms such as Uber (Prassl 2018). These decisions, in addition to helping the litigants concerned attain redress for breaches of employment rights – which in the case of the equal pay claims directly benefited tens of thousands of workers – raise the public profile of the unions and help to shift public opinion on what counts as acceptable employer behaviour. The fees litigation also highlights the potential threat posed by Brexit, which will put many employment rights – and the means of enforcing them – at risk.

The electoral and political systems

The evolution of Britain's electoral and political system has also played a role in the cyclical nature of policy. Initial reforms of representative democracy had been spurred by the 1789 French Revolution, which caused an explosion of interest in democratic government in Europe. It also produced not a little fear – which is another powerful influence in the insecurity cycle – amongst the ruling classes. In Britain, these unfolding events – and the turmoil and bloodshed that accompanied the birth of democracy in France – were watched with considerable alarm.

However, the process of democratic reform in Britain was remarkably slow. Since giving more ordinary people a vote would undermine the influence of those with property, the idea was met with strong resistance; and even by the end of the Napoleonic Wars with revolutionary France in 1815, only about one in seven men – and no women – were enfranchised. This is a situation which, despite several Representation of the People Acts during the nineteenth century, would not radically change until the end of the First World War, with universal suffrage only finally being achieved in 1928. One of the key effects of this was to shift politics decisively to the left, with the first Labour administrations coming to power during the inter-war years.

Britain's "first past the post electoral system" – as opposed to a form of proportional representation – also plays a role in the recurring shifts between governments of different political leanings. By polarising the outcome of general elections, allocating power and influence to a limited number of parties and making both minority governments and coalitions correspondingly rare, the party in government typically has the ability to pursue its own policy agenda. Whilst this has the potential to shift the insecurity cycle one way or another – or to maintain the status quo – following a change of administration, there is every possibility that the direction of travel will be reversed.

Shifts in the direction of policy are themselves subject to both the availability of sufficiently divergent political alternatives for the electorate to choose from and the representativeness of the population by voters. For extended periods of time in Britain's history, one or other of these conditions – if not both – have not been present; and this has typically produced pressure for change, followed by a shift in the insecurity cycle.

Following the initial appearance of the Whig and Tory factions, for example, for most of the nineteenth and early twentieth centuries – until the split within the Liberal Party over the introduction of social welfare reforms – the political choice was a relatively narrow one, between the Liberal Party and the Conservative and Unionist Parties. However, the development of early socialist thought and the beginnings of the trade union movement gave rise to the Labour Party, which – greatly assisted by the progressive extension of the electoral franchise – provided a far more polarised choice between right and left wing ideologies and policies.

But the forces continually at work within the insecurity cycle meant that this situation was no less subject to change than those before it. With the eclipse of trade union influence during the 1980s and the emergence of "New Labour" during the 1990s, electoral choice was narrowed once again as the "new" New Labour policies were closely modelled on those of the Conservatives – up to and including labour and trade union legislation.

This shift also coincided with the emergence of the "Westminster Bubble", a term first used in 1998 to describe an insular community of politicians, journalists and civil servants, seemingly detached from the life experience of much of the rest of the British public – particularly that section of it which is struggling. At the same time, as professional politicians and technocrats came to largely displace those with experience of employment prior to becoming a Member of Parliament, ministers tended to be more technically and ideologically driven – and further distanced from the life experiences of the majority in society.

In this context, the rise of parties such as the Scottish Nationalist Party (SNP) and United Kingdom Independence Party (UKIP) – as well as movements such as "People's Momentum", powered by growing popular support for Jeremy Corbyn and giving rise to the re-emergence of the political left as a force in British politics – should come as no real surprise.

The dynamics of the insecurity cycle

Taken as a whole, the factors described above help to explain the origins and tensions inherent in the British legal, institutional and political systems. The adversarial nature of these systems contributes to the opposing interests that power the insecurity cycle. Whilst these interests have been present in one form or another throughout the life of the cycle – from the beginnings of the industrial revolution to date – they are not in themselves the cause of the various shifts that have been discerned in either direction; instead, they provide the latent potential for them.

For a significant movement in the insecurity cycle to occur, a combination of four further "event"-based factors is required. The occurrence of one or two of these factors – whilst providing pressure for change – will usually be insufficient to trigger a significant movement in the cycle; the presence of all of them is more likely to support a shift.

The influence of crisis

The principal catalyst for change is some sort of crisis. Some crises take an "acute" form, being sudden, unexpected events that strike with little warning, whilst others take a "chronic" or long-running form. From the point of view of the insecurity cycle, a chronic crisis is likely to be far more influential. A chronic crisis might involve a recession, sometimes due to exogenous factors and sometimes self-inflicted, as a result of austerity policies, for example. A key characteristic of a chronic crisis is that it lasts over at least one general election cycle, often resulting in at least one administration being elected as a result of claiming to be able to rectify the problem. If this expectation is not realised, then pressure for change will continue.

This is the sort of process that followed the 2008 financial crisis. Whilst most of the financial sector quickly got back to "business as usual" – including headline-grabbing bonuses but largely ignoring the litany of governance failures – large parts of the British population saw erosion of their incomes and public services as a consequence of austerity policies. The resentment generated by this resulted in movements like "Occupy" – a classic example of a strong democratic upsurge, and a key part of the insecurity cycle. However, whilst this was a headline-grabbing movement, it failed to produce much actual change. The obsession with austerity policies has now passed through its third general election cycle, providing the time for both new ideas to emerge and new movements to coalesce. It has also witnessed the emergence of a new political leader and focus. Both new ideas and political leadership are also, as discussed below, key factors in triggering a shift in the insecurity cycle.

Whilst no two crises are exactly alike, there is a clear difference in impact of an acute (short-term) crisis and a chronic crisis. An acute crisis, if resolved quickly and effectively – as, for example, was the General Strike of 1926 – can serve to enhance both the reputation of the incumbent government and the economic values to which it adheres. But it is also possible for politicians to create an acute crisis, such as that following in the immediate aftermath of the European Union referendum. This crisis has yet to be resolved; and is already exhibiting signs of evolving into a chronic crisis – and perhaps sowing the seeds for a further shift in the insecurity cycle in the process.

Fear is another key aspect of crisis; and it has the ability to significantly influence the insecurity cycle in a number of important ways. David Cameron's fear of the rise of UKIP, along with its potential effect on his own party, was a driving force behind his commitment to holding a referendum on European Union membership, probably exacerbating already existing divisions in the process. Ironically, the vote in favour of leaving the European Union was a direct result of the failure of "Project Fear".

The two world wars, on the other hand, had a completely different effect. In this case fear – or radical uncertainty – was far more general; and the result was to unify purpose, rather than to divide it. In both cases, it also provided a test bed for the involvement of the state as a significant – or indeed the guiding – economic actor. By the end of the Second World War, fear of the reaction of de-mobbed soldiers to any attempt to return to "normal" could well have been a factor in the landslide Labour victory in 1945 and the subsequent evolution of the post-war consensus.

Democratic pressure – and political support

Strong "democratic" pressure is also a key determinant of a shift in the insecurity cycle; and this is true of a move in either direction. Whilst strong trade union pressure was a factor in both the evolution of the British welfare state and extension of the voting franchise, union activities also played their part in the downfall of James Callaghan and the election of Margaret Thatcher.

However, in the British context, democratic movements have rarely been sufficient in themselves to produce significant change. This is perhaps because democratic movements tend to be much clearer about what they *do not* want than being able to articulate ideas about policy alternatives. An illustration of this can be found in the differential influence of the "Occupy" movement, which failed to produce lasting change, and the more recent "People's Momentum", which appears to be having significant influence on the direction of politics.

Occupy grabbed headlines and made the policies it opposed very clear; but without the support and focus of a credible political leader, it was unable to articulate an alternative or a clear path forward for implementing it. Like the trade unions before it, Occupy was forced to communicate by means of direct and disruptive action, which produced a legally based response by the state – as well as the use of force. As evident in the case of Momentum, political support also allows a movement to operate within the accepted apparatus of the state and democratic process; and as a result, it may then exert an influence in proportion to its levels of support.

Alternative policy ideas

Given that a significant body of public opinion, along with the support of one or more significant politicians are key elements in a shift in the insecurity cycle, it is also important that they have ideas that differ significantly from the existing policy paradigm. Thus, alternative policy ideas are the fourth element contributing to a shift in the cycle. However, there are variations in the way by which alternative ideas influence movement in the cycle.

As discussed in Chapters 3 and 4, whilst the combined effect of trade union activity, pressure for democratic change through Chartism, the emergence of early socialist thought and the Liberal social reforms of the early twentieth century together produced a degree of change, the basic, overarching "laissez faire" paradigm remained in place. Effectively, changes took place within the existing policy paradigm.

A complete paradigm shift – such as the shift from "laissez faire" to "Keynesianism" or back again – requires not only an intellectually coherent overarching and politically appealing set of alternative ideas; it also requires a combination of crises and fear of a scale sufficient to match the degree of change being propounded. This degree of change – particularly a turn towards social interventionism – has typically only ever occurred when the resistance from vested interests has morphed from self-interest into self-preservation. It would seem that this is a relatively rare set of circumstances; and self-preservation often means that assets and influence remain intact, ready to lend their weight to another turn of the cycle as soon as the opportunity presents itself.

The penetration of new ideas – even more than resurrected old ones – into the policy discourse are, like democratic pressure, reliant on significant political support. Whilst David Cameron was able to largely ignore a major report by the British Red Cross on poverty in Britain, for example, Lloyd George paid attention to the report of his friend, Seebohm Rowntree, on the causes of extreme poverty in York – which was subsequently influential in shaping policy during the Liberal reform era.

Turns of the insecurity cycle so far

Since the industrial revolution, it is possible to discern two complete "revolutions" of the insecurity cycle, where there was a lasting shift in the policy paradigm – and in the ideas informing it. However, this is a relatively rare event; and existing policy paradigms have proven "sticky" to varying degrees, with their proponents resisting change and viewing crises that challenge the conventional wisdom through their own ideological prism. The result has often been "real politic" responses, producing a degree of movement, but not complete change.

It is also clear that movements towards market liberalisation have been much faster and more decisive than those towards social protectionism. This is probably due to two main influences. First, almost by definition, those needing social protection most often have not only little influence in politics or the private sector but also few assets to mobilise in support of their interests. The opposite is true of the proponents of market liberalisation. Second, most upward pressure comes via the electoral cycle, which means that whatever voice is available to the electorate is only available every few years via local and national elections. Meanwhile, capital is able to press for change in its favour at more or less any time of its choosing.

Whilst there have only been two discernible complete revolutions during the period under investigation, there have also been significant shifts in between, resulting in what might be regarded as "hybrid" policy approaches. Breaking the insecurity cycle into its component shifts – towards market liberalisation, social protectionism and back again – there have been five significant movements; and it may well be that a sixth is currently in progress. These include:

1   the emergence of "laissez faire" during the eighteenth and nineteenth centuries;
2   the Liberal social reforms preceding the First World War;
3   the attempt to return to pre-war "normality" during the inter-war years;
4   the shift to "Keynesianism" and the post-war "consensus" following the Second World War;
5   the re-enshrining of economic liberalism during the 1970s and 1980s, continuing into the twenty-first century;
6   the aftermath of the 2008 financial crisis.

Each of these shifts will be discussed in greater detail in the chapters that follow, with particular reference to the causal factors described above.

Conclusions

The nature of the British state – and its legal, electoral and institutional system as they have evolved since the industrial revolution – makes it especially prone to a cyclical tendency. The result has been a continuous movement between the two extremes of the "self-regulating" market, on the one hand, and the social welfare state, on the other.

Actual movements in the cycle have generally been the result of events, and in particular, the coincidence of four key drivers for change: crisis, democratic pressure, and alternative policy ideas and political support. However, this is not a model for predicting shifts in the cycle into the future. Like many shifts in fashion or the stock market, the cycle is ultimately the result of human feelings, which as Keynes himself noted, are subject to wild – and often irrational – swings.

Notes

1   See our further analysis in Chapter 10.
2   See our further analysis in Chapter 10.
3   At the time of writing (winter 2017-18) the Westminster Parliament is debating the European Union (Withdrawal) Bill. This first repeals the European Communities Act 1972 and then makes provision for most of EU law to be re-enacted as UK domestic law, at the same time conferring power on ministers to repeal certain of these provisions by statutory order.
4   See previous note.

3   The economy and society diverge

Setting up the insecurity cycle

Introduction

Prior to the start of the first industrial revolution during the mid-eighteenth century, day to day life for most of the British population had remained essentially unchanged for thousands of years. The economy was largely an agrarian and merchant economy, with many existing on a subsistence basis; and, especially by comparison with what was to come, it was relatively organised, stable and familiar.

The transition to an industrialised economy, which took only about a century and a half, was extraordinarily rapid; and it changed almost everything that those in power – and those with no power at the time – thought they knew about the way that the economy and society worked. Out of this transformational experience emerged both a new economy and a radically changed – and much larger – society. It was far more factionalised, with an increasing number of groups competing for influence and power; and it contained far greater numbers of poor people. But it also offered the possibility of great prosperity, on the one hand, and radical social change, on the other.

The nineteenth century, in particular, also witnessed the development of many and various theories attempting to explain not only what was going on in both the social and economic spheres, but also what could or should happen next – and how to deal with the rapidly increasing numbers in poverty. These ideas ranged widely, from that of the "self-regulating" market at one extreme, to early ideas about socialism at the other.

The changes wrought by the industrial revolution set it out as being as much a social revolution as an industrial one; and this created the tensions that have provided the basis for the insecurity cycle ever since. Whilst some degree of social upheaval had occasionally been contemplated in the past – notably by the Levellers, who amongst other things argued for the abolition of the monarchy and democratic reform following the English Civil War in 1651 (Hoyle 1992) – the dominance of large land owners in the affairs of state had rarely, if ever, been seriously challenged. The technical and social transformation accompanying the industrial revolution, however – along with a sharp increase in both the population generally, and the urban poor in particular – would result in the appearance of new interest groups, whose shifting fortunes, influence and ideas would soon provide a succession of challenges which ultimately neither the culture nor the waning influence of the existing aristocracy would be equipped to resist. After centuries of dominance, major land owners would eventually have to become accustomed to at least sharing power.

This was partly a consequence of the rapidly expanding urban population, with no close ties to the structured land-owning hierarchies. With industrialisation, separation of the population from the land and its concentration in urban areas would come a growing sense of social cohesion among participants in the new cash economy. In this context, a range of identifiable groups would eventually emerge – most significantly capital, labour, land owners and politicians. But their interests would only rarely appear to coincide, with a gain for one usually being seen as a loss for another – with the dynamic interaction of these interest groups giving rise to the insecurity cycle.

The discovery of mechanisms to press for countervailing influence would eventually lead to significant change in the structure of society during the nineteenth century and into the twentieth; but the power of existing interests would still be considerable, with many seeing no need to give ground. As a result, the nineteenth century would produce one of the longest running disputes of the age: who should have a say in how the country is governed – and whose interests should the economy and society serve?

The journey towards universal suffrage, a fanciful notion for many at the time, would be a long one, which would not be fully realised until almost a third of the way through the following century; and as Chapter 4 will show, sufficient progress would be made by the time of the Liberal social reforms preceding the First World War to suggest that a politician might be able to build a platform on the ideas and needs of the new electorate. But as this chapter will demonstrate, although there was certainly no shortage of democratic pressure, crises and new ideas, there would be little political support for change – often the final piece required for a lasting shift in the insecurity cycle – so none would be forthcoming.

This chapter considers how new interest groups emerged to challenge the established dominance of large land owners, along with their aims, grievances and interactions – and how these together achieved a sort of dynamic equilibrium. That balance would be disturbed by significant political intervention; but the slow progress of franchise reform, in spite of the best efforts of the Chartists and the Reform League, would make it a fruitless risk – at least until the early decades of the twentieth century.

The emergence of new interest groups

Prior to the industrial revolution, many lives revolved around the land. The population was dispersed; but it was also highly integrated socially and life was relatively stable. Whilst bad weather and harvests were always a threat, the societal routine was based around well understood tasks, at predictable times of the year. However, the industrial and agricultural revolutions, along with a programme of common and waste land, would change all that. Decoupling significant numbers of people from their existing social structure, moving them from a rural to an urban environment – and from a subsistence to a cash economy – would create new interest groups; and whilst they did not have a great deal of formal power, they did have numbers on their side.

The new working and middle classes were not, however, the only new groups to emerge. Manufacturing and new technology were now the socio-economy's main drivers, and the engineers and factory owners had a very different world view to their agrarian compatriots. But these new "entrepreneurs" would have been powerless to act without the capital to design and build the infrastructure that was beginning to displace human labour. The ability to concentrate large amounts of capital would also result in the rapid growth and development of finance – and those who managed it.

The differing ambitions, political and world views, influence – and, hence, insecurity – of these emergent groups as they began to interact both with each other and with established interest groups would lay the foundations of the insecurity cycle.

The growth of the new working and middle classes

The merchant class and landed aristocracy were the most influential groups within British society prior to the early decades of the nineteenth century. But as the industrial revolution progressed, the economic and political power of industrial and finance capital increased – and the balance of power in society began to shift. The industrial revolution radically improved transport and productivity; it also resulted in the transformation of the British population – with far reaching economic and social effects.

During the late eighteenth century, the increasing size of the population resulted in discussion about its effects on society; and in 1798, Thomas Malthus's *Essay on the Principle of Population* set out the argument that this growth in the number of mouths to feed had the potential to outstrip food production, leading to famine and starvation. John Rickman, a civil servant and statistician, along with politicians such as William Wilberforce and Charles Abbot, disagreed; and Rickman proposed introducing a census of the population (Nissel 1987). This resulted in the 1800 Population Act; and the first census was conducted the following year. Malthus's work thus served as a catalyst for the first United Kingdom census (Jeffries 2005, p. 3); and the first "modern" census – recording every member of a household instead of local summaries – was conducted in 1841 and served as the model for all future censuses.

Whilst the population in 1750 had probably not exceeded 7 million, by the time of the 1801 census it had risen 18 per cent, to 8.29 million, with further increases of nearly 80 per cent (to 14.85 million) by the census in

1941, and 43 per cent (to 21.29 million) in 1871. This trend would continue on an upward trajectory; and by the time of the 1951 census – towards the middle of the post-war consensus – the population would nearly double to reach 41.16 million.[1]

For some, the transformation of society and the economy that accompanied the industrial revolution was clearly beneficial. The increase in population had been fuelled by more and earlier marriages, better child survival rates, generally better health and improved agricultural techniques, which brought more reliable food sources.

Many skilled workers in regular employment were also covered by a social welfare net of their own making, through membership of friendly societies and trade unions (Boyer 1988). These associations provided various benefits, including education and support for sickness, old age and in some cases, unemployment, with benefits being reliant upon the willingness and ability of members to keep up the subscriptions, particularly when times were good.

Organisation of the labour force was initially the preserve of skilled workers, with roots in the guild system; but as the industrial revolution accelerated, it developed into a movement, eventually drawing in semi-skilled and unskilled workers. Anti-union legislation soon followed, with the Combination Acts of 1799 and 1800. These were, in theory, intended to prevent workers from holding the government to ransom by striking during the Napoleonic Wars of 1799–1815 with revolutionary France; but they were only briefly repealed in 1824 before being re-instated in 1825 as a consequence of the spike in strikes that had followed the Act's repeal. Thus, whilst unions were not banned as such, their ability to strike was severely restricted; and it was not until the Trade Union Act of 1871 and the Trade Disputes Act of 1906, respectively, that unions and strikes were effectively legalised.

An incident that took place less than a decade after the 1825 Combination Act illustrates the strongly held views on both sides. The six men who would become the "Tolpuddle Martyrs" had set up a "friendly society" – effectively a trade union – as a result of the serious erosion of agricultural wages. The fall in wages was particularly pernicious since it took place at a time when tariffs were being imposed on cheaper imported grain under the Corn Laws, to keep food prices high in an attempt to boost agricultural profits. The local land owner objected to the formation of the society, but since it had done nothing illegal under the Combination Act, in the 1834 case of "*R v Lovelass and Others*", the society's members were instead prosecuted under the 1797 Unlawful Oaths Act – originally passed to curb mutinies in the Royal Navy. The sentence was harsh: each of the six men was to be sent to Australia for penal servitude of seven years. However, the public response was equally assertive: a high-profile march and a petition with the best part of a million signatures followed rapidly; and with the support of the reformist, Lord Russell, all six were pardoned – but only on the promise of good behaviour.[2]

Major marches and even bigger petitions would follow – but they would soon prove themselves unreliable sources of major change.

The Chartist movement

Chartism, which centred on publication of the People's Charter in 1838, was a mass movement in search of electoral reform, which was promoted by mostly peaceful and constitutional means.[3] The People's Charter made six key demands, which are worth considering in some detail, since, with only one exception, they were all subsequently achieved. These demands include: (1) a vote for every man of twenty-one years of age, sound mind and not undergoing punishment for a crime; (2) a secret ballot to protect the voter; (3) no property qualification for Members of Parliament (MPs) in order to allow constituencies to return the man of their choice; (4) payment of MPs, to enable working men and others of modest means to leave or interrupt their livelihood to attend to the nation's interests; (5) equal constituencies, securing the same amount of representation for the same number of electors instead of allowing less populous constituencies to have greater weight than more populous ones; and (6) annual Parliamentary elections, presenting an effectual check to bribery and intimidation, since no purse could afford to buy a constituency in each twelve-month period.

When the movement was launched, there were mass gatherings throughout England, Scotland and Wales, culminating in a National Convention in London in 1839. A petition, with 1.3 million signatures was presented; but the MPs voted heavily against hearing the petitioners, resulting in heightened tensions and even plans for uprisings, with shots being fired and significant casualties at Newport in Wales. Although this didn't help the Chartist image or cause, three years later a second petition – this time with 3 million signatures – was submitted to Parliament; but it, too, was rejected.

The year 1842 also brought recession, and with it wage reductions, as factory owners and farmers alike attempted to maintain profits. As a consequence, demand for wage restoration was added to the People's Charter; and the "Plug Plot" – named after the tactic of removing the plugs from boilers, so that steam-powered machinery could not be used – probably represents the first time a large body of workers withdrew their labour, with collective political and financial aims in mind. The government responded by making several hundred arrests; but it failed in its attempt to prosecute most of the Chartist leaders (Smith 2002).

When Feargus O'Connor, a key Chartist organiser, was elected MP for Nottingham in 1847 – and with the 1848 "Year of Revolution" in Europe (Jones, P. 2013) – a third Chartist petition followed the now familiar format of a gathering and a march, with the intention of delivering the petition to Parliament. Estimates of the numbers that gathered vary widely; with the government's estimate of around 15,000 being the most conservative and O'Connor's own figure of 300,000 being the highest, most writers settle on a number somewhere in between. Whatever the truth, there was clearly a sufficient number of petitioners to make the authorities nervous enough to ban them from crossing the Thames from Kennington – and to bring in 100,000 special constables to reinforce the police. In the event, things went peacefully; and the third petition was duly handed over – this time with 6 million signatures. When it was rejected, the response was once again not entirely peaceful; and with the potential for further uprising, anti-conspiracy legislation was passed. The Chartist movement soon fragmented before going into a rapid decline (Saville 1987).

Chartism had been popular amongst the trade unions – in particular, London's tailors, shoemakers, carpenters and masons – due to their fear of the influx of unskilled labour; and in Manchester and Glasgow, engineers were active in the movement. Whilst none of their objectives had yet been achieved, the act of putting the movement together in the first place, and managing it over twenty years, had taught its members many of the techniques and political skills that would later inspire trade union leadership. Thus, although the Chartist movement appeared to have failed, its legacy would be longer-lived.

The trade union movement – and collective action

Aside from campaigns like the Chartist movement – and in no small part due to their restricted legal status – the early British trade unions tended to be local or regional in orientation. However, following the experience of the Chartists – and with the appearance of organisations like the National Political Union, a pressure group that had been set up in 1831 to push for Parliamentary reform – the trade unions started to set their sights on becoming a more national movement.

The impetus for change in the legal status of trade unions, perhaps surprisingly, came from a Conservative Prime Minister, the Earl of Derby, who set up the Royal Commission on Trade Unions in 1867 (McCready 1955). Although no trade unionists were appointed to the Commission, a trade union member did serve as an observer. The resulting Majority Report opposed the idea of de-criminalising trade unions, recommending instead that they be regulated in a similar way to corporations; it also recommended that unions be registered. Whilst this would, to a degree, shield them from criminal law, it would seriously curtail their activities because the Registrar of Friendly Societies would be obliged to strike down any union rules that permitted strike action, supported the idea of a closed shop or allowed action in support of union members elsewhere.

A significant Minority Report was also produced, written by Frederick Harrison (a pro-union member of the Commission), Thomas Hughes, MP for Lambeth (a notable lawyer and author as well as being a social reformer and supporter of the cooperative movement) and Thomas George Anson, Earl of Lichfield. The Minority Report took an opposing view to the Majority Report, with agreement on rule registration being the only area of common ground. However, even on this there was dispute, with the Minority Report being firmly opposed to the Registrar striking down union rules. It also argued in favour of unions having protection from both criminal and the law on restraint of trade, as well as the ability to secure their own funds. The Minority Report won the debate and formed the basis of the 1871 Trade Union Act, which, with some modification, would largely endure until 1974.

As well as the Royal Commission on Trade Unions, 1867 also witnessed publication of the first volume of Karl Marx's *Das Kapital*, an analysis and critique of the capitalist paradigm of his day. The following year, there was a first meeting of the Trades Union Congress (TUC) at the Mechanic's Institute in Manchester, followed by a second meeting in Birmingham. The TUC had been initiated by the northern Trades Councils, partly to counteract the increasing influence of the London Trade Council, which, perhaps as a consequence of its proximity to the seat of government, was felt to be becoming too dominant within the movement.

The combined effect of the de-criminalisation of trade unions, creation of the TUC, experience of running national campaigns – and perhaps even a little influence from Marx – supported the emergence and development of "new" unionism; and the British trade union movement became increasingly national in scope, as opposed to tending towards local or regional organisation, as previously. Underpinning the shift in character – and justifying the soubriquet "new" in the process – was the recruitment of both semi- and unskilled workers into the movement (Fraser 1999, pp. 88–92; Charlton 1999). Whilst union membership had hitherto been composed of skilled craftsmen, the recruitment of semi-skilled and unskilled workers into the movement not only strengthened membership in existing sectors, it also helped to organise entirely new sectors and groups. The results were rapid, and there were soon strikes, including the "Match Girls' strike" at the Bryant & May match factory in 1888 and the London Dock Strike the following year.

The industrial action at Bryant & May's "model" factory at Bow was one of the first notable – and successful – examples of strike action by women.[4] Although it was triggered by the dismissal of three employees for purportedly "telling lies" to Annie Besant, a socialist commentator and journalist, the strike was the result of a combination of factors, including long hours, poor pay, fines for all kinds of minor misdemeanours, such as "dirty feet" or talking.

Worse still were the diseases associated with working with white phosphorus without any suitable protection. The most notorious of these, "phossy jaw", was the result of being forced to take meals at the work bench, resulting in the ingestion of phosphorus. The first symptom was serious toothache, followed by gum disease and bone abscesses; eventually, the infected bones would even glow a greenish white in the dark. The prognosis promised further misery, in the form of brain damage; and if not treated by removal of the affected bones, death was the likely outcome.

The dispute escalated rapidly; and conditions at the factory became the subject of an article by Besant entitled "White Slavery in London", in her weekly magazine, *The Link*, in 1888. Whilst Besant didn't actually instigate the strike, with the factory's 1,400 women and girls refusing to work, she certainly helped to organise and support it. The factory owner, Frederick Bryant, was not slow to respond, claiming that relations with his employees had been "very friendly until they had been duped by socialist outsiders" (Charlton 1999, p. 17).

As well as being an able journalist, Besant also understood the importance of organisation and funding; like the Chartists and the Reform League, she helped organise mass gatherings in London parks, ran campaigns for donations from both middle and working classes alike and publicised each contribution in *The Link*. A major turning point was finally reached when the strike committee called upon the London Trades Council for help. The Council, which had hitherto reserved its efforts for skilled trades and workers, agreed to support the strikers; and perhaps in that decision, "new" unionism took its first step. The London Trades Council's secretary, George Shipton, negotiated the settlement with Frederick Bryant – which included setting up a union, one of the very first for semi-skilled and unskilled workers.

This high-profile action encouraged further union activity among the semi- and unskilled workforce. The National Union of Gas Workers and General Labourers was set up; and with the threat of strike action in 1889, it quickly achieved an eight-hour day at the Beckton Gas Works. The Match Girls' strike was probably also a catalyst for women to press for the right to vote. Whilst the famously militant suffragettes would be a product of the twentieth century, they were not the first movement to press for women's suffrage, as a decade after the Match Girls' Strike, the National Union of Women's Suffrage Societies appeared in 1897 (Smith 1998).

But union action against low wages and poor working conditions was not limited to single companies. The potential effectiveness of more general collective action is illustrated by the success of the 1889 London Dock Strike.[5] Organised by Ben Tillett and Tom Mann, among others, the strike involved the five London Dock companies well as a group of wharf businesses on the employer side, and mobilisation of semi- and unskilled workers – ably and enthusiastically supported by women – on the other.

Whilst skilled and highly organised workers such as the stevedores would play a key role in the success of the strike, unskilled workers had sheer numbers on their side. Giving evidence to a Parliamentary Committee, the general manager of the Millwall Dock Co, Colonel G.R. Birt, painted a bleak picture of the condition of these casual labourers:

> The poor fellows are miserably clad, scarcely a boot on their foot, in a most miserable state ... These are men who come to work in our docks who come on without having a bit of food in their stomachs, perhaps since the previous day; they have worked for an hour and have earned 5d; their hunger will not allow them to continue; they take the 5d in

order that they may get food, perhaps the first food they have had for 24 hours.

(Quoted in Black *et al.* 2015, pp. 1423–4)

At the time of the strike, London Docks were operated by five competing companies, employing a highly differentiated workforce, ranging from the essential skilled and better paid "stevedores", to casual unskilled workers – the "zero hours contract" employees of their time – who were chosen every day from an assembled crowd. According to Ben Tillett, a socialist, politician and union organiser, who had played a major role in founding the Dockers Union:

> Coats, flesh and even ears were torn off ... The strong literally threw themselves over the heads of their fellows and battled ... through the kicking, punching, cursing crowds the bars of the 'cage' which held them like rats – mad, human rats who saw food in the ticket.
>
> (Quoted in Torr 1956, p. 281)

The dock workers' situation had been deteriorating as a consequence of increasing competition among the dock companies, which, in an attempt to maintain profits, were finding ways of reducing workers' pay. The basic wage rate was supplemented by a bonus called the "plus" – a mysterious figure whose workings were never fully set out – theoretically related to both tonnage and speed of job completion. It was this "plus" that would finally trigger the strike.

The strike's leader, Tillett, had set up a new port union – the Tea Operatives and General Labourers' Union – two years previously; and when the "plus" on a ship called the "Lady Armstrong" resulted in a dispute, the situation escalated rapidly. Tillett not only managed to secure solidarity among the various trades within the docks, skilled or not, he also sought help from other organisers in raising funds and influencing public opinion; and Eleanor Marx (Karl Marx's youngest daughter) acted as volunteer secretary, whilst the women of the docks organised a rent strike.

The dock companies, despite Colonel Birt's apparently sympathetic comments, were firmly entrenched; but the ship owners were moved to settle quickly. Although not all of the unions' demands were met, the basic rate of pay was increased to 6d (the "Docker's Tanner"), the "plus" was abolished and contract-based employment was agreed. The dispute also produced a new union, the Dock, Wharf, Riverside and General Workers, which included 18,000 members and served as a model for other unions around the country. It had a more mixed membership, including various trades, both skilled and unskilled, as well as women; and it was committed to improving the lot of its members, with militancy, if necessary.

Britain's total union membership of about 1.5 million would soon be sharply reduced by a combination of recession, technological change and countervailing management activities. But the labour movement would continue to evolve – this time into both local and national politics.

Political activism

At a local level, socialists were beginning to make practical progress. The Progressive Party was formed in 1888 to contest local government elections in London. Allied with the Liberal Party, the labour movement and the Fabian Society, in 1889, the same year as the London Dock Strike, the Progressives won the first London County Council elections and held power until 1907. The result was a significant improvement in London's infrastructure and service network, including some of the first social housing in the country, better roads and sewage management – a major influence on public health – and a child welfare clinic. Events at Bradford City Council started to move in a similar direction three years later; and in 1898 West Ham Borough Council became the first to be controlled by Labour, with one of its first moves being expansion of the council's labour force and improvement in working conditions, including a minimum wage, eight-hour day and annual fortnight's holiday.

The performance of MPs sponsored by the trade unions, however, was less encouraging. The first of these – William Abraham and Joseph Arch – had been elected in 1885 through a loose alliance with the Liberals. The increasing influence of the urban electorate, resulting from their large numbers and the steady expansion of the franchise, had attracted the attention of the Liberals; and they sought to exploit this situation by not opposing union-sponsored candidates, provided that, if elected, they would support both the interests of working-class voters and Liberal policies. However, from the point of view of the unions and their electorate, the performance of union-sponsored MPs was disappointing in that their support for Liberal aims appeared stronger than for trade union and social objectives.

In this context, the Manningham Mills strike in 1890 served as a significant catalyst for formation of the Labour Party (Barker 2013). The cause of the strike is by now all too familiar. In response to the erosion of profits as a consequence of intensifying international competition, Samuel Lister, the silk mill's owner, announced pay cuts that would affect approximately 20 per cent of the factory's 5,000 employees; and a lock-out was threatened if these were not accepted. Although the mill's employees were not heavily unionised – and they had no fund for strike pay – they withdrew their labour anyway. It turned out to be a harsh winter; and the Poor Law Amendment Act of 1834 meant that there was little or no chance of receiving "outdoor" support from the local authority. So the strike was broken.

But the association with unashamedly pro-free market Liberals was also seriously damaged. It was now clear that the culture and policy of the Liberal Party was increasingly incompatible with the objectives of union-sponsored MPs. The founding conference of the Independent Labour Movement in 1893 would lead to development of the Labour Party. The chronic insecurity of the working classes was about to create pressure for a shift in the insecurity cycle.

The growth of poverty

The combination of shifting patterns of employment and exponential growth in the population produced a parallel increase in the number of poor people. Many of these were semi- or unskilled workers; but they also included a high proportion of women, children, elderly people and the sick.

Mechanisation had transformed agriculture and food production, resulting in more plentiful and reliable food sources for those who could afford them. It had also pushed many agricultural workers off the land and into the cities, where they were introduced into a cash, rather than a subsistence economy. So whilst food prices increased as a result of marketisation, for many of these new city dwellers – the semi- or unskilled workers in particular – wages usually moved in the opposite direction. This resulted in the numbers of the poor being regularly swollen by increasingly regular recessions and crises.

The effect was a disproportionate increase in the numbers of the poor, by comparison to the rest of the population. According to Jackson Spielvogel, "poverty was already a highly visible problem by the eighteenth century, both in cities and in the countryside ... an estimated ten percent of the people depended on charity or begging for their food" (Spielvogel 2018, p. 555). The following century, however, would see this figure rise dramatically. The first of Charles Booth's seventeen-volume *Life and Labour of the People in London*, published in 1889 – the year of the famous Dock Strike – put the number of those in east London who were "poor or in want" at 35.2 per cent of the population, a figure that dropped only slightly, to 30.7 per cent, if the whole of London was included.

Booth's work was followed up by Seebohm Rowntree's 1899 study in York, which, as well as offering an independent study of the living and working conditions of the poor, also allowed a comparison between the metropolitan city of London and the relatively small urban centre of York. Rowntree came up with a similar figure of 27.84 per cent of the city's residents being in either primary or secondary poverty. Rowntree's approach improved on the methodology employed by Booth in a number of ways, including systematically interviewing families and setting an absolute poverty line of 21 shillings and 8 pence per day for a man, woman and three children (Chinn 1995, p. 25). This figure provided no opportunity for indulgence, being seen as merely the figure to provide "physical efficiency".

Rowntree also set out what trying to live on this figure would be like:

> And let us clearly state what 'merely physical efficiency' means. A family living upon the scale allowed for in this estimate must never spend a penny on railway fare or omnibus. They must never go into the country unless they walk. They must never purchase a halfpenny newspaper or

spend a penny to buy a ticket for a popular concert. They must write no letters to absent children, for they cannot afford to pay the postage. They must never contribute anything to their church or chapel, or give any help to a neighbour which costs them money. They cannot save, nor can they join sick club or trade union, because they cannot pay the necessary subscriptions. The children must have no pocket money for dolls, marbles or sweets. The father must smoke no tobacco, and must drink no beer. The mother must never buy any pretty clothes for herself or for her children, the character of the family wardrobe as for the family diet, being governed by the regulation 'nothing must be bought but that which is absolutely necessary for the maintenance of physical health and what is bought must be of the plainest and most economical disposition'. Should a child fall ill, it must be attended by the parish doctor; should it die, it should be buried by the parish. Finally, the wage earner must never be absent from work for a single day.

(Rowntree 1901, pp. 133–4)

His findings on how people reached, or fell below, the poverty line – and the proportion of the population in each of these categories – made equally depressing reading:

1 "Death of chief wage earner" (15.63 per cent).
2 "Incapacity of chief wage earner through accident, illness or old age" (5.11 per cent).
3 "Chief wage earner out of work" (2.31 per cent).
4 "Chronic irregularity of work (sometimes due to incapacity or unwillingness to undertake regular employment" (2.83 per cent).
5 "Largeness of family. i.e. cases in which the family is in poverty because there are more than four children, though it would not have been in poverty had the number of children not exceeded four" (22.16 per cent).
6 "Lowness of wage, i.e. where the chief wage earner is in regular work, but at wages which are insufficient to maintain a moderate family (i.e. not more than four children in a state of Physical Efficiency)" (51.96 per cent)" (Rowntree 1901, pp. 119–20).

This situation had arisen partly because the Poor Laws – originally designed to address a completely different situation in 1601 – had failed to keep pace with socio-economic developments resulting from the second industrial revolution, in particular. The much larger and more concentrated numbers of poor meant that these outdated approaches were being overwhelmed and becoming increasingly expensive to operate.

The problem was exacerbated by the tendency of systems like "Allowance", "Roundsman" and "Speenhamland", where local parishes were responsible for topping up low wages. Not only did these systems incentivise employers to pay as little as possible; they forced workers to scramble for fragments of work in order to access in-work benefits, thereby putting enormous power into the hands of employers – particularly unscrupulous ones – who gained an unfair competitive advantage by transferring the benefit into profit. Attacked by David Ricardo, who set out his "Iron Law of Wages" arguing against the transfer of private wage bills to the public sector, these systems were essentially an early form of in-work benefits that would re-emerge during the 1970s, with similar effect (Wilkinson 2001, p. 94).

In response to the rising cost of poor relief in agricultural areas, in 1832, Parliament had set up a Royal Commission into the operation of the Poor Laws, which recommended the abolition of outdoor relief, with relief being made available only in the workhouse where conditions were to be worse than the worst conditions outside of it, thus serving as a deterrent to the able-bodied poor. To avoid the workhouse, the poor were thus forced to accept any available employment, whatever the wage and conditions. The resulting Poor Law Amendment Act of 1834 had been strongly influenced by Malthus's *Essay on the Principle of Population*. Malthus's view was that the population would always expand at a greater rate than the food supply, inevitably resulting in the appearance and persistence of poverty. He went on to argue that support for the poor would therefore be futile, as it would encourage them to have more children, thereby increasing the numbers of those needing support and setting up a vicious cycle.

At the time, without data from researchers like Booth and Rowntree to provide an accurate view of the extent and drivers of poverty, a piece in *Fraser's Magazine* in 1834 summed up the deeply held opinion of many at the time that the urban working poor were "characterised by their reckless improvidence, depravity and profligacy" (Froud *et al.* 1834, p. 72). Even twenty years later, William Lucas Sargent – a commentator generally friendly toward the working class – observed that nothing was more common to hear than the "denunciations of the wasteful spending of working people, of the imprudence of their early marriages, of their lack of frugality, and of their drunkenness" (quoted in Chinn 1995, p. 40). The largely unchallenged view, up until the close of the nineteenth century was thus that the poor were largely responsible for their own condition.

Booth's and Rowntree's evidence-based studies of the reality of poverty did not simply look at the wages and working conditions of the poor; they also scrutinised their living conditions. From these, it became clear that not only had the rapid growth of urban populations outgrown the Poor Laws, it had also outgrown the available accommodation and sanitation. Accommodation was a significant source of income for some; and the combination of high rents, low wages and even lower housing standards would become a major issue.

Of Britain's twelve largest cities, eight had seen the most significant rates of expansion during the first two decades of the nineteenth century. The effect on the quality of housing was dire, with landlords making minimal investment with the objective of maximum return. Dr Alfred Hill, Birmingham's first

Medical Officer of Health, observed that the poor were invited to rent homes that were likely to be "built on an impure foundation, with mortar consisting of dirt instead of sand, and only enough lime to swear by" (quoted in Chinn 1995, p. 78). His counterpart in Manchester expressed a similar view: "[whilst] the old houses are rotten from age and neglect, [the new ones] often commence where the old ones leave off, and are rotten from the first" (ibid.) Housing and health would also be on the list of problems assessed by the social reformers.

Finding political "voice"

At the beginning of the nineteenth century, suffrage was very limited, as only about one in seven men had a vote, whilst women, regardless of their position in society were entirely disenfranchised. As a result, neither of the two main factions in Westminster – the Whigs or the Tories – initially took any account of the needs or desires of the general public.

The electoral system was rooted in the pre-industrial political economy and therefore heavily skewed in favour of large land owners – especially as a result of property qualifications – since many controlled more than one borough and could therefore effectively dictate who the MP(s) representing it would be. Even by 1821, the Whig, Sydney Smith, wryly observed that "the country belongs to the Duke of Rutland, Lord Lonsdale, the Duke of Newcastle and about twenty other holders of boroughs. They are our masters!" (quoted in Moore and Strachan 2010, p. 26).

It was a highly questionable arrangement, with these "nomination" or "pocket" boroughs – some with the number of electors approaching single digit numbers – being numerous. William Pitt's speech in the House of Commons on 14 January 1766 revealed that there was already significant awareness of the lack of justice of this system:

> or will you tell him that he is represented by any representative of a borough – a borough that perhaps its own representatives never saw? This is what is called the rotten part of the constitution. It cannot continue a century; if it does not drop, it must be amputated.
>
> (Quoted in Copeland *et al.* 1999, p. 156)

His comments also proved prescient, as the Representation of the People Acts of the following century would not only do away with the "rotten" boroughs; they would also transfer their MPs' seats to the rapidly expanding cities. However, achieving this would be a slow process, fought against entrenched and vocal opposition, coming perhaps strongest from the House of Lords, but by no means absent from the Commons.

The first Reform Act

The passage of the Great Reform Act of 1832 illustrates the difficulty of achieving any sort of concessions from entrenched vested interests – even when there is a clear need for them.[6] The process of getting the bill passed also represents an almost complete dress rehearsal for the struggle over Lloyd George's "People's Budget" nearly eighty years later, when in spite of continuing shifts in economy and society, vested interests appeared to have hardly moved at all. In this context, it would take an unprecedented set of circumstances – such as a chronic or acute crisis – before sufficient support to attempt change might be garnered.

In 1829, an acute crisis was provided by the Catholic Relief Act enacted by a Tory government led by the Duke of Wellington.[7] Whilst designed to prevent unrest and violence in Ireland, the Act would trigger far larger changes. Effectively, it repealed a number of legal restrictions affecting Roman Catholics – including standing for Parliament. Whilst most attempts at electoral reform had hitherto come from the Whigs, there was a significant faction of Tories who were prepared to endure; and to counter this potential threat, they were also prepared to consider Parliamentary reform, notably the overdue enfranchisement of the expanding industrial cities – none of which favoured Catholicism.

It was not just politicians that felt the need for change; electoral reform was a key issue in the 1830 general election and a number of highly active political unions had advanced the cause. One of the most influential was the Birmingham Political Union, which represented a fast growing industrial city. Like many others, the Union comprised an alliance of both working- and middle-class members. Thus, added to the pressure of the acute crisis associated with Wellington's Catholic Relief Act, there was also growing democratic pressure.

The Tories won the ensuing election, but Wellesley's flat rejection of any need for Parliamentary reform proved to be his undoing; he lost a vote of no confidence and was forced to resign, being replaced by the pro-reform Whig, Earl Grey, who immediately put change on the agenda. The resulting Bill completely disenfranchised the sixty smallest boroughs and reduced the number of MPs by forty-seven. Some of these seats were simply abolished, whilst others were reassigned to the industrial cities, the counties, Scotland and Ireland. The Bill also systematised the borough franchise and increased the electorate by a modest number of around 500,000. The stage was now set.

However, the Bill did not survive the Commons. A packed house passed the second reading by only one vote, with various amendments to follow. Grey gave up and called an election, which resulted in a Whig victory in almost all of the seats not controlled by vested interests, whilst most of the "rotten" boroughs remained in Tory hands. The Bill subsequently made it through the Commons with relative ease; but it was met with hostility and voted down by the House of Lords. The result was an outbreak of public disorder in various parts of the country, which included setting fire to the home of the Duke of Newcastle – one of Sydney Smith's "Masters" – and taking over the city of Bristol for almost four days.

A more strategic response came from the hitherto local political unions, which now sought to unite to form a national movement. This possibility generated fear on the part of the government, which declared the National Political Union illegal. Although this had little effect on its leadership, the Birmingham Political Union remained local, venting some of the pressure. Soon after, following a motion of confidence in Grey, a lightly revised Reform Bill was again passed by the House of Commons and sent back to the Lords.

Fearing the consequences of rejecting the Bill a second time, the Lords instead sought to transform it through amendments; and it attempted to retain the "rotten" boroughs. This left only one alternative, which was to create a sufficient number of pro-reform peers to flood the Lords and pass the bill. But this could only be done by the King, and William IV refused. Grey therefore resigned; and William invited the unpopular Wellesley to form a government.

Wellington was known for his opposition to electoral reform. The response was predictable and immediate, with some even predicting revolution. At the time, the possibility of revolution was credible. The "Days of May" that followed included calls for tax boycotting and an orchestrated run on the Bank of England – reducing its stock of gold by almost a third in less than a week – and demonstrating that there was little enthusiasm for either Wellesley or the status quo. Meanwhile, the National Political Union petitioned the Commons to cease government funding, in an attempt to force the Lords to capitulate. There were even calls for the abolition of the aristocracy – and especially worrying for William IV, abolition of the monarchy as well.

Wellington's attempt to form a government was doomed to failure, and the King was forced to again turn to Earl Grey. This time, there could be no resisting the threat of creating a group of new Whig peers. But the Lords, realising the future implications of this, abruptly switched from self-interest to self-preservation and passed the Bill; and the new Whig peers never materialised.

This saga illustrates in miniature, the workings of the insecurity cycle, with the interaction of crises, democratic pressure, some new ideas and the political support. But in this case, the issue at stake was not a fundamental paradigm shift; nor was the status quo easy to defend. The episode does, however, show that the cycle is very firmly based on human feelings and perceived injustices on both sides.

But it was not the end of the matter, since those still without a vote were forced to look elsewhere for a means of expressing their views. The retention of the property qualification meant that the new Act had provided votes for much of the middle class, but not for labour – skilled – or otherwise. This separated labour's interests from those of the middle class and soon resulted in the Chartist movement. Others looked for a voice more locally, through the early trade union movement, whilst there were also those who would eventually create new organisations – especially following the decriminalising of trade unions, the obvious effectiveness of strike action and increasing militancy by women. The pressure for further electoral reform would not be relaxed for long.

Extension of the franchise

The next move wasn't long in coming; the People's Charter, with its six-point demands for reform of democratic process arose from the trade union movement and was published in the same year as the Poor Laws were amended. This is discussed in greater depth above, when looking at the evolution of the trade union movement. But whilst Chartism was in principle dismissed, most of its demands would eventually be conceded; it also showed the potential of large, well organised but peaceful gatherings; and it taught both unions and social reformers alike a great deal about publicity and coordination as well as managing both messages and large groups of people. Whilst Chartism had lost much of its popular support by 1858, it would not be long before a new movement emerged to continue the pressure for electoral reform.

The Reform League – set up in 1865 – emerged from the Universal League for the Material Elevation of the Industrious Classes which had been set up by the Marquis Townshend – one of the few reform-oriented lords. The League had aimed to promote the reduction of working hours, the extension of the franchise, the "international fraternity" of workers as well as educational and sporting opportunities for the working class. However, with Gladstone's apparent conversion to the reform agenda, the League shifted its focus to franchise reform, and a Universal League Reform Committee was set up. The Marquis sought a position of control, which proved incompatible with the views of committee members; and little more than a year after it had been set up, the Universal League was no more.

The Reform League, however, quickly gathered support, with branches appearing in London and around the country; and by early 1866, it had become a national movement and "Manhood Suffrage" was firmly on the agenda. But Gladstone's Reform Bill seemed to please no-one; and an amended Bill soon brought down the government. Robert Lowe, the first Viscount Sherbrooke and a Liberal MP, took the opportunity to suggest that whilst there was a national mood for reform, the views of some had to change; and he dismissed the working class as "impulsive, unreflecting, violent people" given to all kinds of "venality, ignorance, drunkenness and intimidation" (quoted in Maccoby 2002, p. 90).

It was rapidly becoming clear that the Parliamentary route would be difficult to navigate; so the League turned to some of the methods previously favoured by the Chartists. Within weeks, a mass gathering was held in Trafalgar Square; there were allegations that the League would not support any Reform Bill that did not conform to its demands; and for the first time, the red flag was flown.

The Hyde Park demonstration that followed was even larger. So alarmed was the government that the Home Secretary, Walpole, attempted to declare it illegal; the gates of the park were closed, chained and guarded by police. This resulted in three days of what were described as "skirmishes" and "riots" as the League attempted to enter the park. The problem was settled by the "Hyde Park Railings Affair" when it transpired that the park railings were considerably less sturdy than the gates – and around 200,000 people rushed into the park. With the meeting proceeding as planned from that point, and both the police and military keeping their distance, it was agreed to return to Trafalgar Square the following evening.

In spite of Walpole's concerns, this demonstration also proceeded peacefully. But news of these events did little to improve the Tory government's case; and support for the reform movement continued to grow, with its generally well behaved and peaceful nature contributing to its increasing favour among the middle classes as well. The pressure was maintained, despite news of another Reform Bill being in the pipeline; and there were further rallies in London and elsewhere, finally resulting in success with passage of the 1868 Representation of the People Act. This Act served to enfranchise much of the urban working class for the first time, and made further alterations to the electoral boroughs, with representation being redistributed to the rapidly growing cities.

In the process, the Reform League had fundamentally changed the game. A further Representation of the People Act followed under Gladstone in 1884, proposed by the Liberal government without significant outside pressure. This Act extended voting rights to those employed in urban areas and to rural constituencies; all men paying an annual rent of £10 or holding land of an equivalent value now also had the vote. But this was not greeted with enthusiasm by the Conservatives, who felt that it would undermine their influence and support in the counties; so there was significant resistance in both the House of Commons and the Lords. The Conservatives were somewhat appeased by the Redistribution Act the following year which transferred representation from the rural areas to the towns and established the one MP for each constituency standard.

Although not all men were yet enfranchised – and as yet, women had yet to make any sort of progress – it was a landmark political event. Women would eventually adopt similar strategies to the Chartists and the Reform League; and the National Union of Women's Suffrage Societies was set up in 1897. But they would end up abandoning peaceful protest in the fight for female suffrage.

By now, it was clear that politics could never be the same again. Dominance had been wrested from the large land owners, and the balance had shifted somewhat to the left. But the electorate still had only the choice between two traditional old parties, of which the Liberals – or at least some of them – had probably done the most to reach out to the new electorate. Whilst the Liberal Party would be split within less than a decade – and a spent political force in less than two – the Conservatives would endure. But they would face a brand new adversary – the Labour Party – born out of a combination of the trade union movement and the extension of the franchise.

Free market capitalism – and the new "entrepreneurs"

The industrial revolution would not have been possible without both the new breed of factory owners and engineers and the rapidly developing financial system that supported them. These two separate but vital developments were in no small part a consequence of the move away from absolute monarchy in Britain, although this would persist in much of the rest of Europe for a number of decades. Decentralising both finance and control proved to be a major factor in the rapid development of the private sector, especially relating to manufacturing and transport, but also having a significant impact on agriculture.

The Glorious Revolution and the origins of modern finance

The ousting of James II in favour of William and Mary in 1688 brought an end to "absolutism" in England and many financial developments, most of which were along the lines of the system already in place in the Netherlands. The first issue of English government bonds took place a year before the foundation of one of the first central banks, the Bank of England, in 1694. Shortly afterwards, with the evolution of the stock market – where investors could trade their shares, and companies could raise capital – large chartered joint stock companies began to grow rapidly.

With Parliament, rather than the Crown, now in charge of state finances – and with many bond holders also being MPs – the interests of investors were automatically represented at the highest level. This minimised the risk of default; and as a result, the cost of borrowing was notably lower than for other states – providing a significant competitive advantage for the City of London and strengthening the ability of the government to raise capital to fund public spending.

Mercantile capitalism, particularly as represented by the large chartered, joint stock companies, such as the Muscovy Company and the East India Company, did not operate on a laissez faire basis – particularly as the state was usually involved as a significant economic player. In the view of Francis Bacon, the idea of mercantilism was "the opening and well balancing of trade; the cherishing of manufacturers; the banishing of idleness; the repressing of waste and excess by sumptuary laws; the improvement and husbandry of the soil; the regulation of prices" (quoted in Clark 1961, p. 24). This attention to the sources of wealth was also noted by Karl Polanyi who argued that mercantilists "never attacked the safeguards which protected two basic elements of production – labour and land – from becoming the elements of commerce" (Polanyi 2001 [1944], p. 73); he therefore made the case for the state as a regulator as well as an economic actor and went on to contend that since there was not, in his view, a competitive labour market in England prior to 1834, this must mark the beginning of industrial capitalism.

One effect of mercantilism had been to provide England with considerable capital; whilst the end of absolutism – and the new, Dutch-inspired financial institutions and instruments – made it much easier to raise more. This, along with the eventual development of Britain's industrial economy, weakened the role of the state as both a regulator and an economic actor. New ideas such as those set out by Adam Smith in his *Wealth of Nations* (1999 [1776]) attacked the concepts that lay behind mercantilism. And the concept of laissez faire began to develop.

Whilst major land owners had typically inherited their wealth and influence, embedding both long-term economic and state structures in the process, the arrival of new technologies – and the opportunities they provided – would present a powerful challenge to the established order. Not only did the move away from the land produce a massive increase in the working urban population, it also created a new breed of entrepreneurs – engineers, investors and financiers.

Technologically and conceptually, the industrial revolution was both fast paced and unpredictable; and it required large volumes of capital to fund the new technologies incorporated into new factories, machinery, railways and underground systems. This heavy and sustained demand accelerated the concentration of capital in the hands of engineers, factory owners and their investors, whilst at the same time supporting technological development and strengthening the position of financial markets and actors.

Prior to the industrial revolution, financial crises had been relatively rare. With industrialisation, the construction of new factories and investment in new technologies and infrastructure put an emphasis on finance. Whereas the South Sea Bubble had been an early indicator of the potential for (especially international) financial speculation to cause crises on a previously unknown scale, this would become a familiar part of life, with somewhere between a third and a half of the nineteenth century witnessing recession or depression and financial crisis – or both at the same time.

The ability of free market capitalism to generate both chronic and acute crises created pressure for movements in the insecurity cycle, which started early. The post-Napoleonic War recession began in 1812 and lasted for almost a decade, with further recessions following in 1848, 1857 and 1867, and the "great depression" of 1873 – which was downgraded to the "long depression" when the depression of the 1930s arrived. These crises coincided with increased trade union activity and pressure for democratic reform from the disenfranchised. As discussed above, this process of change would also undermine the political influence of the landed aristocracy, which in time would not only have an impact on who governed Britain; it would also fundamentally influence the relationships and balance of power between the state, industry, labour and finance.

The concentration of capital and protection of investor interests required legal change, which advanced at a much faster rate than the development of the Poor Laws. The laissez faire approach to business was considered to be the best way forward; and theories were developed to explain and justify why this should be the case. Even Darwin's *On the Origin of Species* published in 1859 had an (unwitting) influence on the debate.

Industrial entrepreneurs

The initial laissez faire approach to business was largely free of legislation. The workplace was effectively unregulated, partly as a consequence of efforts to keep costs down and as a means of maximising profit; it was also a result of prevailing attitudes about the poor. Given that the objective of industry was to produce ever higher quantities at higher speed and lower cost, working conditions were typically very poor. By 1808, the poet William Blake was already able to refer to the "dark satanic mills" blackening the sky over Lancashire.

Effectively then, labour law was at a "pre-regulation" stage, with many factory owners doing their best to get the most out of their employees in a variety of ways. However, the effects of these conditions, combined with the development of early trade unions and friendly societies, and the ideas of more philanthropic mill owners such as Robert Owen, slowly created the conditions for building a legal framework around conditions of employment.

This process began during the early nineteenth century, with passage of the Health and Morals of Apprentices Act in 1802 – the precursor to a succession of Factory Acts. The Act concerned mainly the health, maintenance and education of apprentices, but failed to include an effective inspectorate – with the result that the new rules were widely flouted. The same problem afflicted the 1819 Cotton Mills and Factories Act. Although it was supposedly based on a proposal by Robert Owen, a reforming factory owner who ran the Mill at New Lanark, not only was the Act a pale imitation of the original; like its predecessor, compliance was effectively voluntary.

In 1825, the government tried again. John Hobhouse had discovered that in the twenty-six years since the previous Act, there had been only two prosecutions; and he proposed a Bill to enable magistrates not only to investigate themselves, but also to summon witnesses to attend proceedings. George Philips, MP for Wootton Bassett opposed the new Bill; but he conceded that the 1819 act had been more or less ignored, adding that

> the provisions of Sir Robert Peel's Act had been evaded in many respects; and it was now in the power of the workmen to ruin many individuals,

by enforcing the penalties for children working beyond the hours limited by that Act.

(Quoted in Hansard 1826, p. 646)

On that basis, he felt that the Act should be repealed. William Evans, MP for East Retford and also a mill owner, put the opposing view, agreeing that there was "much that requires remedy" (ibid., p. 650). He, too, doubted "whether shortening the hours of work would be injurious, even to the interests of the manufacturers; as children would be able, while they were employed, to pursue their occupation with greater vigour and activity" (ibid.).

The entrenched nature of the debate is clear from the number of Factory Acts – and abortive attempts at them – which took place: in 1832, two in 1833 (as well as a Factory Commission), 1836, 1838, 1839–41, 1843, 1844, 1847, 1850, 1856, 1867, 1870, 1871, 1874, 1878, 1891, 1895 and a further four in the twentieth century.

Whilst one of the early aims of the various Factory Acts had been to limit the working day for children, factory owners were also faced with pressure for shorter working days for all their employees. Robert Owen had started pushing for a ten-hour day, and had already introduced it in his New Lanark mill as early as 1810. Whilst this was followed by a revised aim of an eight-hour day for all employed labour, it was another thirty-seven years before women and children achieved the ten-hour working day. Meanwhile, the move for a shorter working day – and resistance to the idea – did little to discourage the growth of either the Chartist or trade union movements. Given the resistance to early attempts at regulation and the extension of labour law, it is not difficult to discern the beginnings of significant "insecurity" amongst the new entrepreneurs, which gave rise to the feeling that their profits were being needlessly limited, adding fuel to the other side of the insecurity cycle.

Long hours, low wages and poor working conditions were not the only possibilities open to factory owners, when it came to maximising profits. According to Sidney and Beatrice Webb they also included circumventing agreed pay rates. Payment in goods (at the employer's valuation) rather than in currency had been a persistent cause of discontent – and legislation – since the fifteenth century. But as well as this particular practice, the industrial revolution produced two further refinements. The first – as the Match Girls at Bryant & May's model factory in Bow had discovered – was the imposition of arbitrary and heavy fines for the apparent wastage of materials. The other, was either part or complete payment in tokens (often referred to as a "Tommy Ticket") which were only redeemable at the company's own store – usually at excessive and unjustifiable prices. The Truck Act of 1831, which repealed all previous legislation, was intended to address this problem; but like the Factory Acts, it would need to be revisited, although rather less often.

As well as resisting legislation from Parliament, many employers were equally keen to resist initiatives creating pressure from within their own factories. The emergence of the early trade unions, aided by considerable nervousness following the French Revolution, generated legislation that included the various Combination Acts, which received Royal Assent at the end of the "Terror" in 1799. Employers' response to the "new" unionism was equally chilly, even resulting in some owners and managers organising themselves in a direct response to militant union activity.

But not all employers were entirely focused on profits. Some, such as Robert Owen and William Morris would pioneer other ideas and approaches. Whilst Owen introduced a ten-hour day at his mill at New Lanark and then campaigned for a general eight-hour day, with the mantra "Eight hours work, eight hours leisure, eight hours rest", Morris, a committed social reformer and at the time a member of the Social Democratic Federation (SDF), envisioned a completely different approach to manufacturing.

In the third of a series of four articles, "Work in a Factory As It Might Be", published in *Justice*, the SDF's weekly newspaper in 1884, Morris sets out much of his ideal:

> I have tried to show in former articles that in a duly ordered society, in which people would work for a livelihood and not for the profit of another, a factory might not only be pleasant as to its surroundings, and beautiful in its own architecture, but that even the rough and necessary work done in it might be so arranged as to be neither burdensome in itself or of long duration for each worker; but furthermore the organization of such a factory, that is to say, a group of people working in harmonious cooperation towards a useful end, would of itself afford opportunities for increasing the pleasure of life.
>
> (Morris 1884, p. 2)

However, there was still more than enough collective resistance to any sort of regulation, let alone utopian world views, to build significant pressure in the insecurity cycle.

The land owners dig in – but power is shifting

Large land owners unwittingly helped to swell the large and growing labour force as a result of the various Enclosure Acts, which had also considerably extended their land holdings at very little expense to themselves. Not only did this make a gift of what had previously been common or waste land, it also allowed them to charge high rents to the people who had previously been peasants but were now effectively tenant farmers. This resulted in many relocating to the cities in search of better pay and conditions. At the same time, the Enclosure Acts – along with new agricultural techniques – also had helped to make the land more productive, and therefore able to feed the new urbanised groups more effectively.

Many large land owners had therefore done well out of the industrial revolution, with land sales and rents for accommodation in the cities and suburbs generating considerable profit – and increasing income from the marketisation of agricultural production having replaced subsistence farming. But the industrial entrepreneurs, who employed most of the new workforce, were the group that was rapidly becoming more influential than the landed aristocracy. They were also accumulating considerable wealth as their products were becoming of greater importance to the economy.

But the landed aristocracy would not concede further influence without resistance. With strong representation in Parliament, particularly in relation to the working classes, the land owners still had significant power; and they attempted to use it to slow – if not halt – the growth in influence of these other new segments of the economy and society as well as to bolster their own profits to the extent possible.

In line with the tenets of mercantilism, which favoured price regulation aimed at limiting imports and maximising exports, the government had already considered the imposition of tariffs on grain imports. Whilst this would protect the profits of land owners, its impact on the urban labour force was – initially at least – of less concern; and the first Corn Law was duly passed by the Tory government of Lord Liverpool in 1815.

It is impossible to argue that members of the Whig and Tory factions – particularly prior to the formation of modern political parties – had general and consistent views or represented a particular class of people. But the Tories, especially those in the House of Lords, exhibited a general tendency to support large land owners whilst the Whigs, who had been largely supportive of the Glorious Revolution, tended to have a bias towards the entrepreneurs of the industrial revolution. As the industrial revolution progressed, some factions within the Whig movement began to take note of the potential electoral support that was growing within the growing urban classes; the Tories, by contrast, tended to regard them with deep suspicion.

Nonetheless, the Whig governments that followed Lord Liverpool's Tory administration failed to repeal the Corn Law, which had not only been immediately unpopular; it had since sparked a growing nationwide movement for its repeal. Richard Cobden, one of the movement's leading advocates, articulated four key benefits of repealing the Corn Law:

> first, it would guarantee the prosperity of the manufacturer by affording him outlets for his products. Second, it would relieve "the Condition of England" question by cheapening the price of food and ensuring more regular employment. Third, it would make English agriculture more efficient by stimulating demand for its products in urban and industrial areas. Fourth, it would introduce through mutually advantageous international trade a new era of fellowship and peace. The only barrier to these four beneficent solutions was the ignorant self-interest of the landlords, "the bread-taxing oligarchy, unprincipled, unfeeling, rapacious and plundering".

> (Quoted in Briggs 2014 [1959], p. 271)

The landlords responded with accusations of their own, suggesting that Cobden – a factory owner himself – was merely wanting cheaper food, so that he could reduce wages and thereby increase profits. With the Anti Corn Law League on one side and the Duke of Richmond's Agricultural Protection Society on the other, little progress was being made – until successive poor harvests in England and famine in Ireland created fear of serious disorder, which served as the catalyst for the repeal of the Corn Law in 1846.

New ideas: early alternatives to free market capitalism

It was not long before the early laissez faire theories put forward by Adam Smith, John Stuart Mill and others were met with alternative ideas about how the economy and society might work. However, whilst free market theories were, on the whole, relatively similar and consistent in nature, the various alternative streams of thought provided considerable variety – and not a little debate amongst themselves.

For most of the nineteenth century, the Whig movement supported the tenets of liberal capitalism, with many of their MPs being factory and mill owners themselves. Alternative ideas, on the other hand, acquired political support slowly, only really gathering momentum as a consequence of the progressive extension of the franchise – which itself was an indirect result of the regular recessions and financial crises that appeared to be an inescapable feature of free market capitalism. Although the beneficiaries of alternative streams of thought had had very little representation at the start of the century, this changed significantly by the end of the Victorian era – as did attitudes with regard to ways of assessing capitalism and its relationship with society.

Challenges to the conventional wisdom of liberal capitalism came from a variety of sources, including mill and business owners, such as Robert Owen and William Morris; thinkers and writers, such as Karl Marx, Friedrich Engels and John Ruskin; union leaders such as Thomas Mann; and others, like the Fabians, who laid the foundations of several of the country's modern political institutions.

There were already a few MPs in support of change, and even in the House of Lords – dominated as it was by Conservative large land owners – there was at least one dissenting voice. Lord Byron was fully in support of improving the conditions of the working class; and in 1812, in an address to the House of Lords, he declared:

> I have been in some of the most oppressed provinces of Turkey; but never, under the most despotic of infidel governments, did I behold such squalid wretchedness as I have seen since my return, in the very heart of a Christian country.
>
> (Byron 1844, p. 156)

But without the efforts of those who sought to take advantage of the potential support of the newly enfranchised electorate, change would have taken far longer.

Robert Owen had already been considering how mills might be run in a more philanthropic manner early on in the nineteenth century, having introduced a ten-hour day at his New Lanark mill in 1810. Seven years later, he became a socialist and started pushing for a further reduction to an eight-hour day. Prior to the enactment of the Truck Acts – which made the practice of paying employees in tokens that could only be cashed in at the company store illegal – Owen had taken a very different approach. An early supporter of the cooperative movement, Owen used the power of bulk buying to supply his employees with better quality goods at cost plus a small margin.

One of the first major academic works examining the effects of the industrial revolution on its new urban work force was produced by Friedrich Engels in 1844 – *The Condition of the Working Class in England*. This was soon followed by a joint work with Karl Marx, espousing alternatives to the capitalist system itself, with the *Communist Manifesto*, published in 1848. Marx's (1859) *A Contribution to the Critique of the Political Economy* was a precursor to his more famous *Capital*, published in German in 1867. In this, Marx accepted the labour theory of value, as set out by David Ricardo. But unlike Ricardo, who had distinguished between use value and value in commodities – but failed to convincingly address the relationship between them – Marx had been able to do so. The book also includes a scientific theory of money and money circulation. The first print run sold out quickly, as did Marx's other major work prior to *Capital: Theories of Surplus Value*, written in 1863 – which is widely regarded as one of the first histories of economic thought.

The industrial revolution, and the factory system in particular, were not without their critics for other reasons as well. The view that the division of labour was not only dehumanising but also separated the craftsman from the end product, gave rise to the Arts and Crafts movement. In this, John Ruskin's early publications included a series of essays that were later compiled into a book, entitled *Unto This Last*. The essays first appeared in a new magazine, *Cornhill*, edited by the novelist William Makepeace Thackeray. But unlike Marx's early work, Ruskin's essays were met with such a negative public reaction that Thackeray limited him to only four.

Ruskin's first essay, "The Roots of Honour", focuses on the relationship between employers and workers, proposing that all work be paid at an equal rate for a given job, so that workers are not pitted into competition with each other such that the work of the less able or reliable can pull down the wage of the others. "The Veins of Wealth" makes the case that getting rich is always at the expense of someone else and that wealth – rather than being accumulated material goods – is power over men's labour. He goes on to argue that society benefits from the equitable sharing of the nation's wealth among the greatest number of citizens. In "Qui Judicatis Terram" ("Who Judge on Earth"), Ruskin maintains that when men are justly treated and paid, everyone has a chance to rise in economic status. The final essay, "Ad Valorem" ("According to Value") provides an alternative conceptualisation of value, wealth, price and production to those proposed by the political economists of his day. In Ruskin's view, value supports life; wealth is "the possession of useful articles *which we can use*" (Ruskin 1921 [1860], p. 95, emphasis in the original); price is "the quantity of labour given by the person desiring it in order to obtain possession of it" (ibid., p. 104); and production is tied to consumption, with "consumption [being] the end and the aim of production, so life is the end and aim of consumption" (ibid., p. 116).

William Morris was another leading member of the Arts and Crafts movement, as well as being the owner of an influential design and manufacturing company. However, this seems to have put him in a conflicted position with respect to the implications of production automation. Whilst he introduced a profit sharing scheme for some of his staff, production workers were paid on a piecework basis, which was standard practice for the time. Though very much a progressive, Morris justified this hybrid approach on the basis that it was impossible to operate a business along socialist lines in a competitive capitalist economy (MacCarthy 1994, pp. 454–8; Mackail 1899, p. 61; Thompson 1955, pp. 319–22).

Nonetheless, like many in the Arts and Crafts movement, Morris espoused socialism; and in 1883, he joined the essentially Marxist "Democratic Federation" and travelled to Lancashire the following year, where he delivered various lectures on socialism to the workers taking part in the great cotton strike. He also contributed to the Federation's manifesto "Socialism Made Plain".

The Federation's change of name – to the "Social Democratic Federation" (SDF) – in 1884, however, revealed a split in the views of its members. Although some SDF socialists espoused a conventional political route for change through Parliament, others felt that the existing system was so heavily weighted in favour of vested interests, that it should be bypassed. In an early example of what would become a not uncommon feature of the socialist movement, Morris and a number of others split from the SDF to form the more Marxist "Socialist League" in 1885.

However, not all of the members of the SDF took such a purely intellectual view of the way forward. Thomas Mann, who had read Marx and Engels's *Communist Manifesto*, had embraced its views in 1886. He rapidly became an activist, organising the SDF's activities in the north of England. He managed Keir Hardie's electoral campaign in Lanark, supported both the Match Girls' and the London Dock Strikes, and was a founding member of the Independent Labour Party. As such, Mann did a great deal to advance his cause by supporting both practical and institutional developments.

This more structured approach was adopted by others within the Arts and Crafts movement, contributing to an acceleration in the development of its institutional structure. Sidney and Beatrice Webb were early members of the Fabian Society, which promoted the concept of sustained resistance and gradual change, rather than Marxist revolution. Sidney Webb, who was a supporter of the eight-hour work day movement, was also a prolific writer, having published *Facts for Socialists: From the Political Economists and Statisticians* in 1887, "The Basis of Socialism" in *Fabian Essays in Socialism* in 1889 and many others. He would go on to co-found the *New Statesman* in 1913 and draft the famous "Clause IV" for the Labour Party manifesto. Meanwhile Beatrice Webb, whilst perhaps most noted for the Minority Report of the Poor Law Commission, which would eventually provide the basis for the Labour Party's radical 1945 manifesto, was also a rent collector for the East End Dwellings Co., which provided good quality accommodation for casual and unskilled workers in London at affordable prices.

As it turned out, Thomas Mann's faith in Keir Hardie was not misplaced. He had initially helped to organise Scottish mining unions in both Lanark and Ayrshire; and although these were ultimately unsuccessful, Hardie had demonstrated the energy and organising talent required to become the first secretary of the Scottish Labour Party in 1888; and he was elected to Parliament as MP for West Ham South in 1892 as a result of the Liberal-Labour pact, under which the Liberals, whilst neither supporting nor providing funding, did not put up a candidate of their own to oppose him. In 1893, Hardie went on to help found the Independent Labour Party; and seven years later, he organised a meeting of trade unions and socialists to form the Labour Representation Committee, with Hardie himself becoming one of its first MPs. The urban working classes now not only had more votes – they also had a clear choice within the political establishment and Parliament.

Whilst many early socialist ideas sprang from the middle classes, a gradual increase in the franchise, along with democratic pressure – particularly as a result of the social conditions produced by regular recessions – encouraged a more broadly based socialist movement. The initial organisation was largely provided by the trade unions, who also played a key role in the extension of the franchise. When the labour movement began to coalesce and build its own countervailing political institutions, a move in the insecurity cycle would soon become possible.

Conclusions

Having examined some of the key economic and social developments of the nineteenth century, the parallels with circumstances a century and a half later are striking. The rapid expansion of (especially urban) communities, with its attendant effects on both the availability of adequate quality affordable accommodation and employment at satisfactory rates of pay would be depressingly familiar to many in the 1880s; and the casual workers involved in the 1889 London Dock Strike bear a close resemblance to today's "zero hours contract" workers.

Along with echoes of the dubious practices at Bryant & May's match factory in the various corporate scandals of recent years, it is also possible to discern the reappearance of pressure for change coming from groups of individuals with few other alternatives available to them. Today the loss of many skilled trades – and with them, independent representation – has put those faced with low wages, poor housing and, as a result, poor health, in much the same position as the semi- and unskilled workers of the late nineteenth century.

Given the dynamic nature of the insecurity cycle, they have responded in a similar manner to those before them; but instead of forming a trade union, they are using social media to organise within the labour movement – providing pressure for representation and returning the Labour Party to the left. Then, as now, the laissez faire paradigm is being challenged; but although battered, it remains largely in place.

The industrial revolution not only gave rise to new interest groups, it also eventually produced not only ways for them to express their views, but also varying degrees of power and influence. The initial laissez faire approach adopted by many of the new entrepreneurs – and Liberal politicians – might well theoretically maximise profit. But, as has been demonstrated, there are limits to the degree to which exploitation will be tolerated, before some kind of push back results. In their turn, the various Reform Acts, Factory Acts and Truck Acts, were stoutly resisted by their own sets of vested interests.

In many ways, this is the problem that those exploring alternatives to free market capitalism were trying to solve; and Ruskin, Morris, Marx and Owen – amongst many others – were in essence, effectively looking for a solution to the insecurity cycle. Whilst there are certainly differences between the present and the latter part of the nineteenth century – most notably, the existence today of a National Health Service and other remnants of the welfare state – there is a strong feeling that these are under threat; and it is a *feeling* that lies behind the very human nature of the insecurity cycle. This sense of familiarity between events in the past and those of the present will be a perceptible thread that spans and connects the chapters of this book.

Notes

1 These figures are drawn from census data in GB Historical GIS (2017). The individual census documents can be found at: www.visionofbritain.org.uk/unit/10061325/cube/TOT_POP.
2 See, for example, Webb and Webb (1920, chapter 3).
3 For further information about the Chartist movement, see, for example, Chase (2007); Jones, P. (2013); Saunders (2008); Taylor, M. (1996).
4 See, for example, Beaver (1985); Charlton (1999, pp. 15–27); Emsley (2000); and Raw (2009).
5 See, for example, Lovell (1969).
6 See, for example, Ertman (2010); O'Gorman (1989); Philips and Wetherell (1995); and Warham (1995).
7 See, for example, Davis (1997, 1999); Kingon (2004); Linker (1976); and Machin (1979).

4   The state steps in – and then back out again

Introduction

Although the "laissez faire" view of industrial development – unlike that of the earlier mercantilists – ascribed no economic role for the British state, the government occasionally intervened with regard to prices; an example of this is the Corn Laws, enacted at the end of the Napoleonic Wars. However, the role of the state was about to change. Instead of import price controls, the British state would soon become involved in the initial phases of construction of the social welfare state; and during the First World War, it would flirt with the idea of both state control of industry and cooperation with the trade unions.

Behind all of this, the forces driving the insecurity cycle that had sprung from the industrial revolution would serve as the engine for change; recessions and low wages would give rise to both crises and democratic pressure for change. But this time, a combination of the expanded franchise, better understanding of the extent and causes of poverty, and – most important of all – the full and strong commitment of David Lloyd George – a more than credible politician, with little love for the landed gentry – would create the conditions conducive to activating processes of significant change.

The fundamental drivers of change would be amplified – to no small degree – by fear. The threat of social disorder would not disappear; and British naval supremacy – along with the empire itself – would come under threat from Germany's aggressive naval expansion. With the launch of the revolutionary new battleship, *HMS Dreadnought*, in 1906, all others became obsolete overnight – including the rest of the British battle fleet. It would now be a race between navies to build more of these new (and hugely expensive) ships. But with social reform to pay for as well, this would mean a fundamental – and permanent – reappraisal of the system of public finance. The question of who defines policy, as well as the intended beneficiaries, was now firmly on the table.

Attitudes about poverty and unemployment

At the dawn of the twentieth century, accumulating evidence about the extent and causes of urban poverty put increasing pressure on governments to address it. Better understanding of poverty and its causes had already begun with the work of the Victorian social reformers, researchers and journalists who drew attention to the lives and living conditions of the poor. Influential among them was Henry Mayhew, who in 1849, as metropolitan correspondent for the *Morning Chronicle*, wrote an extensive series of newspaper articles based on interviews with the poor in London which were later published in a three-volume series entitled *London Labour and the London Poor; Cyclaepedia of the Conditions and Earnings of Those that Will Work, Those that Cannot Work and Those that Will Not Work*. A fourth volume, co-written with Bracebridge Hemyng, John Binny and Andrew Halliday, focusing on London's prostitutes, thieves, swindlers and beggars, was published in 1861. In Mayhew's words:

> My earnest hope is that the book may serve to give the rich a more intimate knowledge of the sufferings, and the frequent heroism under those sufferings, of the poor – that it may teach those who are beyond temptation to look with charity on the frailties of their less fortunate brethren – and cause those who are in "high places", and those of whom much is expected, to bestir themselves to improve the condition of a class of people whose misery, ignorance, and vice, amidst all the immense wealth and great knowledge of 'the first city in the world', is, to say the very least, a national disgrace to us.
>
> (Mayhew 1851, p. iv)

Others also drew attention to the squalor and misery of the urban poor. George Sims, for example, wrote a series of articles in 1883 in *Pictorial World*, entitled "How the Poor Live", which were later published in a book, entitled *How the Poor Live and Terrible London* in 1889. Reverend Andrew Mearns wrote *The Bitter Cry of Outcast London: An Inquiry into the Condition of the Abject Poor*, and William Thomas Stead wrote a collection of articles in the *Pall Mall Gazette*, including "Outcast London: Where to Begin?" in 1883. These journalistic accounts, which attributed the problem to over-crowding in the slums, led to the 1885 Royal Commission on the Housing of the Working Class, which concluded that poverty was the result of over-crowding, high rents and low wages (Wohl 1977, pp. 210–31).

At the end of the nineteenth century, the recorded numbers in receipt of poor relief amounted to only around 3 per cent of the population (Ogus 1982, p. 167). It was against this background that the social surveys of Charles Booth and Seebohm Rowntree revealed evidence on the much greater extent of poverty and destitution which existed beyond the operation of the poor law system.[1]

In *Life and Labour of the People in London*, Booth introduced the concept of a "line of poverty" – a minimum level of income below which it is not possible to afford what is required to attain the nutritional standard for good physical health. His inquiry into the living conditions of Londoners, conducted between 1886 and 1903, revealed that 30 per cent of the population was living in poverty.

Rowntree's survey of the living conditions of the poor in York, *Poverty; A Survey of Town Life*, reached a similar conclusion. Rowntree's survey was an advance on Booth's London study because it involved a detailed study of a larger number of households. Moreover, it provided an answer to those critics of Booth who believed that he had uncovered a special "metropolitan problem" of a quite exceptional nature (Briggs 1961). In preparing his survey Rowntree based his definition of poverty on the nutritional requirements for maintaining individuals, or more precisely families, in a state of *physical efficiency*. This bare subsistence measure allowed him to draw a distinction between *primary poverty* – that of families whose incomes were insufficient to provide the base necessities of physical efficiency, no matter how wisely and carefully their incomes were spent – and *secondary poverty* – that of families who were obviously poverty-stricken although they received incomes large enough to live above the "poverty-line" if their income had been spent differently.

Rowntree used evidence related to workhouse diets and selected, as his standard efficiency diet, one less generous than that recommended for an able-bodied pauper. This was then re-valued at the prices the poor would have to pay for basic-level goods and services, and to this was added the cost for clothing, rent, light and heat, in turn parsimoniously estimated.

Rowntree's research found that 15 per cent of the working-class population – and 10 per cent of the total population – of York could not reach even this lowest possible subsistence level, which he classified as *primary poverty*. A further 18 per cent of York's population were found to be in *secondary poverty*. On this basis Rowntree concluded that the average level of income earned by workers in York was lower than the physical efficiency level if they were married with three children.

Rowntree's work directed attention to what was soon understood to be a social problem of enormous dimensions.[2] Public policy came round to the view that a combination of thrift and self-help for the "deserving" poor and discipline for the rest was an inadequate substitute for a programme based on full employment and social security. But the poor law was slow to fade, and for the first half of the twentieth century it overlapped with the emerging social security system put into place by the Liberal social welfare reforms, discussed below.

Like Keynes forty years later, Seebohm Rowntree had powerful political connections that would ultimately help gain support for his ideas. He was a close friend of Lloyd George, whom he had met in 1907 after Lloyd George became President of the Board of Trade. Along with Winston Churchill,

Lloyd George considered the concentration of wealth and influence as being as much a threat to liberty as government interference, if not more so. As a result, they sought reform in terms of remedying the balance between capital and labour. In this context, Rowntree's work convinced a significant Liberal faction that they needed to conquer poverty; and it was an important influence on the Liberal social reforms of 1906–14 – the first serious package of social reforms in Britain undertaken with the expressed intent of redistributing wealth.

The studies of Booth and Rowntree both revealed that much of the poverty they observed was caused by age-specific and cyclical factors – predominantly unemployment, under-employment, low wages and ill-health – that were beyond the control of the poor, rather than "idleness and moral weakness"; and they provided valuable statistical evidence in support of genuine concern for the poor. The environmental explanation for poverty also found support in academic research. The Cambridge economist Alfred Marshall's work on short-term fluctuations in the trade cycle, for example, demonstrated that a significant part of unemployment – and hence poverty – is structural.

The belief that chronic poverty was a consequence of environmental and systemic, rather than moral and individual factors, helped promote the idea of "social justice" and a growing role for the state in the regulation of social and economic life. Most Britons now accepted the notion of "socialism" that suggested a legitimate role for the state in combatting extreme poverty and promoting prosperity (Harling 2001, p. 114). But little progress was made in addressing the social problem of poverty, with many advocates of reform continuing to take a harsh view of the "undeserving poor"; and social legislation of the Victorian and Edwardian eras reflects a strong desire to provide decent treatment for the "respectable" and "deserving poor" whilst separating them from the "residuum" of casual workers, loafers and unemployables (Harris 1972, pp. 42–3, 141–2; Thane 1982, pp. 10–11; Himmelfarb 1991, pp. 123–5; Stedman Jones 1971, pp. 312–14). Politically, the Conservatives and Liberals were in power and the Fabians, who championed an interventionist agenda, backed-up by detailed and well-researched proposals for reform, remained at the margins of the political spectrum, despite playing an important role in London municipal politics.

Developments in the British economy – and concerns about "national efficiency"

Developments in the British economy had an important influence on attitudes towards social reform among political leaders and policy makers during the early twentieth century. In financial terms, Britain was still the dominant economic power. But having been the first country to industrialise and the largest imperial power, Britain was now falling behind Germany and the United States in industrial production. Whereas Britain had been the world's leading industrial economy in 1870 – accounting for 31.8 per cent of world manufacturing production, compared with the USA's 23 per cent and Germany's 13.2 per cent — by 1913, the pattern had been reversed, and Britain produced 14 per cent, behind the USA's 35.8 per cent and Germany's 15.7 per cent (League of Nations 1945). At the same time, economic growth was also slowing and Germany was aggressively expanding its navy.

In this context, revelations about the poor physical condition of many of the men who had sought to enlist in the army during the 1899–1902 Boer War in South Africa raised serious concerns about Britain's ability to defend itself and its empire (Harling 2001, p. 118; Hay 1983, p. 31; Gilbert 1966, chapter 2). This led to the establishment of the Interdepartmental Committee on Physical Deterioration, the findings of which eventually helped to pave the way for the introduction of free school meals for poor children, routine school medical examinations and physical education programmes; many of its recommendations were ultimately adopted, as discussed below. The Committee's 1904 Report went so far as to conclude that "it may be necessary ... for the State ... to take charge of the lives of those who, from whatever the causes, are incapable of independent existence up to the standard of decency it imposes" (p. 85).

Concern's such as these regarding "national efficiency" cut across party lines, raising social reform to the level of respectability as a political issue; and national efficiency entered the political parlance of the time. As threats to Britain's economic position increased, attention was drawn to the potential social and economic benefits to be derived from the provision of education, health and social welfare services; and many looked to Bismarck's Germany for a model of social legislation and the funding of social provision through a system of contributory social insurance (Gilbert 1976, pp. 1060–1).

Working-class attitudes and pressures

Even after the creation of the Independent Labour Party (ILP) in 1893, the Liberal Party was generally regarded as the party of the organised working class. But by the end of the nineteenth century, a series of anti-union laws had been passed which significantly weakened the position of the unions, with the 1896 case of *Lyons v Wilkins* outlawing most peaceful picketing. British trade unions therefore realised that they needed a stronger independent voice in Parliament if they were to represent and defend their interests politically.

In this context, the ILP formed an alliance with the Liberal Party that permitted cross-party support in elections and the consequent emergence of a small Labour contingent in Parliament; and in 1900, the unions agreed to use some of their funds to set up a new organisation, the Labour Representation Committee (LRC), as a Parliamentary pressure group, to coordinate efforts to support Members of Parliament sponsored by the trade unions, to represent the interests of the working population and to unite British trade unionists and other left-wing organisations in a single political movement. In so doing, the trade unions developed a close relationship with the political left.

This bond was strengthened by the 1901 Taff Vale Judgment which supported the right of the employer, the Taff Vale Railway, to sue the Amalgamated Society of Railway Servants for the loss of profits sustained during a strike, effectively making strikes prohibitively costly for unions to organise. The outrage cause by this decision encouraged many trade unions to join the LRC – and its membership rose from 350,000 in 1901, to 450,000 in 1902 and 850,000 in 1903.

With expansion of the labour movement – and adult male suffrage – many observers and politicians believed that the newly enfranchised workers would seek to promote their class interests by pressing for interventionist legislation, prompting politicians and policy makers to focus on social issues. The political motivation for social reform was also fuelled by a desire to legitimate the capitalist order in the eyes of the working classes – a desire that was strengthened by the 1905 Russian Revolution (Hall and Schwartz 1985; Saville 1957–8). The usefulness of social policy was expressed by the Conservative politician, Arthur Balfour, in a speech in Manchester in 1895: "Social legislation ... is not merely distinguished from Socialist legislation, but is its most direct opposite and its most effective antidote" (quoted in Scally 1975, p. 98); whilst Joseph Chamberlain's policy of "ransom" reflected "the belief that revolution must be headed off by timely social reform" (Adams 1953, p. 56).

But the emerging Labour Party was more interested in state neutrality than state intervention as a consequence of prior anti-union rulings, such as Taff Vale; and reversing such judgements became a major objective. Added to this was working-class suspicion of central government, resulting from the moral intrusiveness of much of the social legislation adopted in the name of "national efficiency" and the discipline of the urban "residuum" in the interests of the "respectable" (Harling 2001, pp. 120–1). Working people also valued independence, having been accustomed to looking to themselves for social provision. This encouraged the unions to look to Parliament for social justice and "fair play" rather than state-sponsored forms of social welfare (Pelling 1968, pp. 1–18; Thane 1984).

New ideas about poverty

Both the majority and minority reports of the Royal Commission on the Poor Laws of 1909 recommended the dismantling of the post-1834 Poor Law system. Beatrice Webb had been a member of the Commission; and the Minority Report was drafted by Beatrice and Sidney Webb. Part II of the Minority Report made a case for wide-ranging reform which came to underpin many subsequent legislative developments; and it is the pivotal text in the early twentieth-century reconstruction of labour market regulation.[3]

The essence of the Webbs' critique was that the new Poor Law of 1834 had failed on its own terms: it was unable to discipline the truly "work shy" or to offer adequate support to "the respectable able-bodied man or woman" (Webb and Webb 1909, p. 96). It was founded on a false premise, namely that destitution was always and everywhere the result of personal irresponsibility, and this was the result in turn of the attention placed in 1834 on "the demoralisation of character and waste of wealth produced ... by an hypertrophied Poor Law" (ibid., p. 4). For the Webbs, the issue was how to understand more effectively the multiple causes of poverty and destitution and to deal with them appropriately. Their proposal amounted to a conceptual revolution in which the language of "pauperism" gave way to the "modern terminology" of *unemployment*.[4]

"Unemployment" connoted a condition of worklessness brought about by the operation of industrial and commercial forces. But the Webbs did not believe that the "personal character" of those in poverty was completely irrelevant since it was "of vital importance to the method of treatment to be adopted with regard to the individuals in distress". Yet it was not "of significance with regard to the existence of or the amount of Unemployment" (Webb and Webb 1909, p. 4).

They proposed a four-fold classification of the unemployed, based not on individual characteristics of workers but on the nature of their employment prior to becoming jobless: "the men from Permanent Situations, the Men of Discontinuous Employment, the Under-Employed and the Unemployable" (Webb and Webb 1909, p. 165). The purpose of the distinction was to diagnose the conditions under which unemployment arose. The next step in the argument presented by the Minority Report was to link casualisation not just to employers' practices in particular industries (the docks were identified as the main culprits), but to the operation of the Poor Law itself. The final link concerned the combined impact of the Poor Law and casualisation on the family, and the further consequences for labour supply.

The solutions advanced by the Minority Report reflected its diagnosis of the problem. The first aim was to remove the "able-bodied" from the reach of the Poor Law. The key mechanisms for achieving this end were labour exchanges, the function of which was to provide a register of unemployed which could then be matched with the demands of employers seeking workers; it would thereby reduce the costs of search for the unemployed and under-employed. More than this, supporters of the labour exchange model saw it as breaking the power which employers had to maintain "pools of labour" in reserve, waiting for work (Webb and Webb 1909, p. 261). The Minority Report also addressed the issue of unemployment compensation as an alternative to Poor Law relief, arguing in favour of a hybrid public-private system, under which government would have the power to subsidise the private insurance schemes already run, at that point, by certain trade unions, and covering around 2.5 million workers (Ogus 1982, p. 186).

The second and related objective was to put in place a series of measures aimed at "absorbing the surplus" of employment which caused under-employment and unemployment. Some of these measures were based on the improvement and extension of labour standards, including proposals to set a maximum working week for railway and transport workers (for whom long hours had been identified as a particular problem), and a general minimum employment age of fifteen years. Others were more straightforwardly aimed at limiting labour supply.

The third main component of the Minority Report's proposals was, in effect, the institutionalisation of the breadwinner wage:

> we have chosen so to organise our industry that it is to the man that is paid the income necessary for the support of the family, on the assumption that the work of the woman is to care for the home and the children. The result is that mothers of young children, if they seek industrial employ-ment, do so under the double disadvantage that the woman's wage is fixed to maintain herself alone, and that even this can be earned only by giving up to work the time that is needed by the care of the children. When the bread-winner is withdrawn by death or desertion, or is, from illness or Unemployment, unable to earn the family maintenance, the bargain which the community made with the woman on her marriage – that the mainte-nance of the home should come through the man – is broken. It seems to us clear that, if only for the sake of the interest which the community has in the children, there should be adequate provision made from public funds for the maintenance of the home, conditional on the mother's abstaining from industrial work, and devoting herself to the care of the children.
>
> (Webb and Webb 1909, p. 211)

The removal of unemployment from the reach of the Poor Law therefore occurred under precisely defined conditions; traditional notions of family structure remained firmly in place and, indeed, were strengthened by the shift from the new Poor Law to social security. What did change, decisively, was the prevailing attitude towards regulation of the employment relationship. The nineteenth-century faith in the self-correcting properties of supply and demand could no longer be maintained in the face of evidence of their daily failure. The case advanced by the Minority Report was that even when the administration of the Poor Law was at its harshest, and outdoor relief most severely restricted, wages did not automatically rise to the point where they coincided with subsistence, and continuous employment remained the excep-tion, not the norm, for those in or near poverty. It was not simply that "dis-tress from want of employment, though periodically aggravated by depression of trade, is a constant feature of industry and commerce"; it was also the case that "this misery has no redeeming feature" (Webb and Webb 1909, pp. 241–2). Thus while the experience of degradation and humiliation under the unreformed Poor Law was a disaster for those who came into direct contact with it, all sections of the community, and not just the recipients of relief, were affected: "a hundred different threads of communication connect the slum and the square" (ibid.). In this way, the case for social security was constructed on an appeal, not only to the general good, but also, specifically, to the interests of the propertied classes.

The 1909 Royal Commission, divided as it was between Majority and Minority Reports which diverged on the role to be played by the state in the reconstruction of poor relief, did not produce an immediate blueprint for legislative reform; and the Webbs' proposals would have to wait another three decades before finding their way into policy, with the Beveridge Report of 1942. But the Webbs' analysis of the labour market was to have a major influence on the subsequent development of the social insurance model; and as unemployment compensation evolved, the separation of unemployment benefit from the Poor Law was gradually, if haltingly, achieved.

Whilst further new ideas – with evidence to back them up – were a major factor inspiring the Liberal reforms of 1904–14, the decisive factor was heavy-weight political backing.

The Liberal social reforms of 1906–8

By the 1906 general election, Britain faced the problem of how to fund simultaneously the enormous and growing costs of military preparedness as well as expanded social welfare provision. Both the Conservatives and the Liberals committed themselves to supporting both, although neither party made poverty an important election issue.

The Conservatives campaigned in favour of tariff reform and protectionism, aimed at revitalising Britain's ailing staple industries and strengthening its empire. The Liberals argued in favour of progressive (direct) taxation and free trade, maintaining that protectionism would generate inflation and depress real wages whilst damaging employment opportunities in the country's export sectors. They also argued that the burden of tariffs would fall disproportionately on the working classes, to the benefit of the rich.

Positioning themselves as the "party of the people", the Liberals won a landslide victory, with 377 Liberals, 132 Conservatives, 83 Irish Nationalists, 29 Labour Representation Committee supporters (soon to be re-constituted as the Labour Party), 25 Liberal Unionists and 24 Liberal-Labour men – marking one of the largest swings to the left in British democratic history. But the House of Lords had 355 Conservative peers, 124 Liberal Unionists and 88 Liberals.

The background of the Liberal victory, however, was a period of great national anxiety – about empire, following the Boer War in South Africa, which witnessed the death of thousands of women and children in British concentration camps; about national security, in the face of Germany's military expansion; about the economy, and fear that Germany and the United States were over-taking Britain's industrial lead; about poverty and unemployment; and about women's suffrage, standard of living and quality of life (Morgan 2017 [2011]).

Against these cumulative anxieties, the Liberal cause of free trade promised to promote affordable food for the working classes and lower raw materials prices for industry – as well as full employment, economic growth and prosperity. This "New Liberalism" was one of social reform; and the Liberal government – led by Henry Campbell-Bannerman, with Herbert Henry Asquith Chancellor of the Exchequer, David Lloyd George President of the Board of Trade and Winston Churchill Under-secretary for the Colonies – began introducing wide-ranging measures as soon as it took office. But the 1906 Liberal victory was not so much a public expression of enthusiasm for the Liberal Party as it was one of opposition to the Conservatives (Gilbert 1976).

Lloyd George was acutely aware of the strengthening Labour Party and sought to address the challenge to the Liberal Party with policies supported by labour and an active social policy. During the first session of Parliament in 1906, the government succeeded in passing the Trade Disputes Act, reversing the Taff Vale judgment and enhancing unions' rights to picket and strike; the Workmen's Compensation Act, granting new forms of compensation for injury at work; and the Merchant Shipping Act, improving conditions for sailors. It also passed the Provision of Meals Act, allowing (but not requiring) local authorities to provide free school meals for needy children. But the Lords vetoed the Plural Voting Bill.

During the second session in 1907, tax reform, differentiating earned and unearned income was passed, along with the Administrative Procedures Act, requiring medical inspection of children and permitting medical treatment. But the Lords vetoed the government's bills for Irish councils, Scottish small-holdings and land valuations; and the Education Bill was amended to such a degree that the Liberals refused to accept any of the amendments. Thus, by 1907, it was becoming clear that measures favoured by a majority of voters were likely to be stifled whilst those mild enough to pass the House of Lords would meet with voter opposition (Watson 1953).

The Liberals thus confronted two major problems: (1) how to satisfy the voters who had brought them to power with reform legislation when they also had to contend with the House of Lords' veto; and (2) how to maintain the Labour vote without destroying the conservative wing of the Liberal Party in the House of Lords (Watson 1953).

In a speech in Oxford, Lloyd George verbally attacked the Lords – to the great displeasure of the King (Lee 2008, pp. 10–11):

> I think that the time has come, if the House of Lords insists on maintaining its claim to reject legislation that comes from the representatives of the people, to consider another great question. If the dissolution comes sooner or later, it will be, in my judgement, a much larger measure than the Education Bill that will come up for consideration, if the House of Lords persists in its present policy. It will come on an issue of whether this country is to be governed by King and Peers or by the King and his People.
>
> (Quoted in Lee 2008, p. 10)

Nevertheless, in 1908 the government succeeded in passing the Children's Act, dealing with child neglect, setting up juvenile courts and remand homes, prohibiting imprisonment of children and banning children from pubs and buying cigarettes. It also passed the Coal Mines Regulation Act, introducing a maximum eight hour working day for coal miners.

In 1909, the government passed the first Old Age Pensions Act, providing government-funded weekly pensions to those over seventy. Although these pensions were very small and very few pensioners received them (since the life expectancy of the time was fifty-five years at birth), it was a landmark Act in its acknowledgement that the "respectable" elderly could be poor through no fault of their own and that state support was a right of citizenship (Collins 1965). The government also succeeded in passing the Labour Exchanges Act, setting up labour exchanges where employers with vacancies could advertise positions, thereby making it easier for the unemployed to find work. This was an important Act in the sense that it provided further evidence of an acceptance of the belief that able-bodied workers could find themselves out of work and at risk of poverty through no fault of their own, with the state accepting a role in helping them to find new jobs. The Trade Boards Act – setting a minimum wage in the occupations of tailoring, box making, lace making and chain making (which in 1913 was extended to cover six more sweated trades) – was also passed, marking a return to the state's involvement in wage setting, from which it had withdrawn with the repeal of the relevant part of the Elizabethan Statute of Artificers in 1814.

The "People's Budget"

From 1907 onwards, the government had faced a crisis of public finance as a consequence of the coincidence of falling tax receipts resulting from cyclical recession and of increased expenditures required to fund both an accelerated programme of battleship construction in response to Germany's military build-up and expanded social provision.

The 1909 budget was a product of the new Prime Minister Asquith (following Campbell-Bannerman's resignation due to ill health); and it was championed by Lloyd George (Chancellor of the Exchequer) and Churchill (President of the Board of Trade). In his 1909 budget speech, Lloyd George concluded by declaring:

> This is a war budget. It is for raising money to wage implacable warfare against poverty and squalidness. I cannot help hoping and believing that before this generation has passed away we shall have advanced a great step towards that good time when poverty, and the wretchedness and human degradation which always follow in its camp, will be as remote to the people of this country as the wolves which once infested its forests.
>
> (Quoted in Lee 2008, p. 36)

The People's Budget was to fight literal as well as metaphorical wars. Since German re-unification in 1871, the balance of power in Germany had shifted in favour of the Second Reich; and in 1908, Germany began a massive pro-gramme of naval re-armament, which appeared to be a direct challenge to Britain's naval dominance. Concerned about Germany's military build-up, the First Lord of the Admiralty Reginald McKenna asked for six of the new Dreadnought battleships. When Lloyd George and Churchill maintained that four would be enough, Asquith intervened, suggesting a compromise of four, with a further four if required. Stirred by the daily papers and news reels, public opinion was heightened by fear of war and supported Asquith – and eight new battleships were delivered, along with social welfare.

The 1909 budget was an unprecedented peacetime budget, with a total expenditure of £16 million, of which £3 million was required for new naval construction and £8.75 million for Old Age Pensions (Murray 2009). It thus included proposals to meet the burden of defence against war as well as poverty, by including a graduated income tax; a super-tax on incomes over £5,000; and land valuation making it possible to tax unearned increments on the value of land, taxes on undeveloped land, and a 10 per cent duty on the benefits accruing to lessors at the end of a lease. An increase in death duties was also proposed; and there were spirit duties and motor and petrol taxes for a Road Fund.

The budget had a stormy passage, remarkably similar to that of the first Reform Bill in 1832; it passed the House of Commons on 4 November 1909 before progressing to the House of Lords. The Lords, who were entitled by convention to reject but not amend a money bill, had not vetoed a budget in 200 years. Despite the King's private urgings that the budget be passed to avoid a crisis, on 30 November 1909, the House of Lords rejected it with a vote of 350 to 75; but they indicated that they would be prepared to accept it once an electoral mandate had been obtained. The Liberals countered by proposing to reduce the power of the Lords by flooding the House of Lords with new Liberal peers. In response, the King made it clear that he would require two general elections – one to coerce the Lords on the budget by obtaining an electoral mandate for it and a second to justify the use of the King's prerogative of creating Liberal peers to the Lords to pass the constitutional change.

Parliament was dissolved on 3 December 1909; and in January 1910, the general election delivered a hung Parliament, with a coalition government being formed, returning the Liberals to power with a reduced majority. The budget was re-introduced and on 28 April 1910, the Lords accepted it. King Edward died in May 1910 and in November, the new King George V secretly agreed to follow his father and require a further election before flood-ing the House of Lords with new Liberal peers (Watson 1953). In the second general election in December 1910, the Conservatives were again defeated by their combined opponents, the Liberals, Labour and Irish Nationalists.

In 1911, when faced with the threat that the new King would flood the House of Lords with new Liberal peers to give the Liberals a majority or near majority there, the Lords passed the Parliament Act of 1911. This Act removed the House of Lords' right to veto money bills (concerning taxation and government expenditure), replacing it with the right to reject public bills, with a maximum delay of two years, and reduced the maximum term of Parliament from seven to five years. In its preamble, the intention is clear: "it is intended to substitute for the House of Lords as it at present exists a second chamber constituted on a popular instead of hereditary basis" (quoted in Murray 2009, p. 13).

The long-term significance of the 1909/10 budget was the modernisation of the British system of public finance, being the first budget in British history with the expressed purpose of redistributing income from the wealthy to the rest. And – aside from the land value tax – as a revenue-generating mechanism, it was a success, delivering annual surpluses with no new taxes until the outbreak of the First World War in 1914. Land taxes, however, proved more costly to implement than they generated in revenue; and they were repealed by Lloyd George's coalition government in 1916, with the revenues that had been collected being returned to their contributors (Murray 2009).

The Liberal social reforms of 1910–13

Lloyd George's People's Budget was followed up in 1911 with the National Insurance Act, establishing a nation-wide system of support for unemployment, illness and maternity care. This Act went further than the recommendations in the Minority Report by instituting a fully state-administered system. But the form of unemployment compensation which initially emerged was similar to that discussed (but rejected as unfeasible) in the Minority Report, namely a system of compulsory insurance "applied only to particular sections of workers or to certain specified industries, under carefully considered conditions".[5] The passage of the National Insurance Act is widely considered to represent the birth of the British welfare state (Morgan 2017). Like the Old Age Pensions Act of 1909, the National Insurance Act – although limited in its redistributive effects due to its contributory nature – set an important precedent for state intervention by allocating tax revenues for the provision of basic medical care and assistance to able-bodied workers who had lost their jobs – and faced the prospect of poverty – as a consequence of factors that were beyond their control.

The government was also successful in passing the 1911 Payment of Members of Parliament Act, which provided for an annual salary of £400 per year to be paid to Members of Parliament, thereby permitting the working classes to afford to enter politics. The Shops Act was also passed, giving shop assistants a statutory half day off per week.

In 1912, after the Miners Federation of Great Britain sanctioned a national ballot for a general work stoppage to secure a minimum wage – and the vote in favour was four-to-one – the government rushed a (Coal Mines Minimum Wage) Act for the coal industry onto the statute books, setting up local boards to fix minimum wages in each district. But the miners rejected the government's offer and carried on with their action.

In the following year, the 1913 Trade Union Act was passed, reversing the Osborne judgment of 1909 that had prohibited trade unions from imposing a political levy on their members in support of the Labour Party. By allowing the trade unions to divide their subscriptions into political and social funds, the Act helped to secure a solid financial base for the Labour Party – which ultimately witnessed its ascent to replacing the Liberal Party as party in opposition to the Conservatives.

As a whole, the Liberal reform measures involved the state in a wide range of activities, including the provision of child and old-age welfare, health and unemployment insurance, assistance to the unemployed in finding work, as well as wage setting and industrial arbitration. But these were strictly limited; the poor law continued to serve as the basis for social security; and the general view was that the "proper" role for the state was to establish a framework within which the economy and society could regulate themselves (Bronstein and Harris 2012).

In short, with crises, insecurity and fear, democratic movement, new and alternative ideas – and significant political support – change began to take place. Although the Liberal social reforms appeared to represent a significant advance in the degree of state intervention on behalf of British society, a substantial pro- portion of the working-class people they were intended to help viewed them with resentment. Much of the new social legislation was considered intrusive; and skilled workers tended to dislike health and unemployment insurance as a consequence of its contributory nature. Nevertheless, and despite the very diffi- cult pre-war period – characterised by labour disputes, violence and the threat of a general strike; militancy by the suffragettes; and the possibility of civil war in Ireland – in many ways, this was the high point for the Liberals before the war.

"New unionism" and the "great unrest"

In Britain, as elsewhere, the pre-war period was one of massive industrial unrest. Outside of Britain, the wave of unrest included the 1903 railway workers strikes in Holland; the 1905 Russian Revolution and miners' strikes in the Ruhr; the 1907 New Orleans dock workers general strike; the 1909 general strikes in Barcelona, New York and Sweden; the 1912 general strike in Brisbane; the 1917 Bolshevik Revolution; the 1917 general strikes in Aus- tralia and Spain; and the 1918 general strike in Switzerland.

In Britain, between 1900 and 1906, the combined effect of anti–union legislation, strong employers' organisations and a very uncertain economic environment had put workers at a disadvantage and union strength declined (Cronin 1987, p. 163). In 1906, the reversal of anti-union legislation and an improvement in the demand for labour produced an increase in trade union membership and strength; but it fell off again in 1907–9.

In this context, the government's failure to deliver many of the labour market policies sought by trade unionists, such as the "right to work" and the eight-hour day – and the resentment, particularly among young workers, of both the Parliamentary Labour Party's support for the Liberals' social welfare programmes and the trade unions' active role in administering them – only served to intensify pressures that were fuelling unrest. In this context, expanding trade union membership; grievances over poor working conditions and discipline at work; rising prices and stagnant or falling real wages; intransigent managers and growing labour militancy together served as a powerful stimulus; and following the depression of 1908–9, there was an explosion of industrial action that continued even into the initial stages of the First World War. This period – known as "The Great Unrest" – is an era about which little has been formally recorded and which "chroniclers, with their eyes on the battlefields, have been inclined to under-estimate" (Adams 1953, p. 55).[6]

Table 4.1 details the pattern of annual work stoppages and the associated numbers of days lost during the years preceding the First World War. Whereas the 1902–6 period had witnessed between 300 and 400 strikes per year, during which the days lost to strikes averaged 3.6 million per year, between 1910 and the outbreak of war in 1914, the annual number of strikes ranged from over 500 to nearly 1,500, with an average of 16.1 million days lost per year, with a peak of 40.8 million in 1912 (Pugh 2012, p. 147; Fraser 1999, p. 121).

As the Great Unrest progressed, the pattern of participation in industrial action shifted – towards workers in transport and industry and away from skilled crafts, prominent among which were the railway men, dock workers, miners and textile workers. Since most of these strikes were successful – 44 per cent resulted in outright victory, 42 per cent in compromise and only 14 per cent in defeat (Cronin 1987, p. 164) – they catalysed a further increase in trade union membership, which reached 4.1 million, or 27 per cent of the industrial workforce, by 1914 (Pugh 2012, p. 147).

The role and attitude of the government also shifted. The 1896 Conciliation Act, which had charged the Board of Trade with responsibility for looking into the cause of industrial disputes and offering mediation to those involved, meant that there was a branch of government involved in the continuous monitoring of industrial relations. The state was also involved in

Table 4.1 Work stoppages and days lost due to strikes

Year	Stoppages	Days lost (thousands)
1909	422	2,687
1910	521	9,867
1911	872	10,155
1912	834	40,840
1913	1,459	9,804
1914	972	9,878

Source: Fraser (1999, p. 121).

voluntary triangular relationships with both sides of industry in an effort to keep industrial peace. But whilst the Liberals acknowledged the right to strike, they did not hesitate to use force against strikers who were considered to be a threat to public order; and troops were sent to the coalfields in Wales in 1910. Police and warships were dispatched to Liverpool in 1911; and in 1912, troops were deployed against the threat of generalised unrest, with entire regions of the country being put under martial law.

The labour unrest of 1910–13 was led by the rank and file, in the face of fierce and sustained employer opposition and often in rebellion against union leadership, who were perceived as having close ties with the right wing of the Labour Party. Their reluctance to sanction industrial action forced workers to take unofficial action. The militants leading the industrial action of this period were generally socialists; but they were also influenced by the ideas of syndicalism and industrial unionism.

By the end of this period, the trade union leadership had begun to regain control. The formation of the so-called "Triple Alliance" between the miners, railway men and transport workers, for example, was in reality a measure designed to impede spontaneous and unofficial collective action and to prevent future outbreaks of irrepressible militancy on the part of the rank and file. But the discontent continued.

Despite the use of force when the consequences of labour unrest gave the appearance of being uncontrollable any other way, the government preferred to mediate and conciliate, favouring the stable organisation of workers and employers and their relations with each other. This was accentuated with the coming of war in 1914, during which the government sponsored greater organisation of both sides of industry and the overall balance of advantage swung towards the workers (Cronin 1987; Garside and Gospel 1982; Wrigley 1982).

"War socialism"

With the outbreak of war in 1914, the voluntary enlistment of a large proportion of the male workforce into military service put the remaining labour force – organised and unorganised – in a relatively strong position. Female employment increased significantly; and women moved away from domestic services and other traditionally female occupations and into transport, engineering, banking and insurance, and local and national government. But as a consequence of the unrestricted recruitment of male workers from the munitions trades – including 22 per cent of miners, 24 per cent of chemical and explosives workers, 24 per cent of electrical engineers and 20 per cent of engineers (Dewey 1984; Winter 1986, pp. 26–9) – the nation's capacity for producing the necessary materials for war was seriously impeded.

In response, Churchill, then First Lord of the Admiralty, proposed the issuance of "admiralty service badges" to prevent the further migration of skilled munitions workers into military service. Cabinet authority was granted on 26 December 1914 and the first such badges were issued to the employees of Admiralty contractors and to workers in the Royal Docklands. In March 1915, the scheme was adopted by the War Office – and it was estimated that by the end of 1915, more than 1.5 million men of military age were engaged in the munitions trades (Woodward 1967, pp. 468–9).

The extent of the munitions shortage was soon ruthlessly exposed in one of the early battles of 1915, the Battle of Neuve Chapelle, resulting in the "Shell Crisis of 1915". In response, the Munitions of War Committee was set up to direct resources to the production and supply of light and heavy arms, ammunitions and explosives. But on 15 May 1915, *The Times* headlined an article, "Need for Shells: British Attacks Checked: Limited Supply the Cause: A Lesson from France"; and on 21 May, "The Shell Scandal: Lord Kitchener's Tragic Blunder" appeared in the *Daily Mail*. So damaging was the scandal that the Liberal government collapsed and a coalition government was formed. Asquith remained Prime Minister; and in July, the Munitions of War Committee was superseded by the Ministry of Munitions, with Lloyd George being assigned the role of Minister of Munitions.

The 1915 Munitions of War Act gave the newly established Ministry of Munitions the power to declare munitions factories "controlled establishments", to oblige manufacturers to take on government work and to transfer machinery and skilled munitions workers from private to state-managed factories. To stop skilled workers from using shortages to push up their earnings and to prevent firms from poaching skilled workers from one another, the freedom of workers to leave employment was restricted by a system of certificates and tribunals. Work stoppages were prohibited, with compulsory arbitration taking their place. Restrictive work practices were suspended; and a system of statutory wage regulation was instituted. The unions agreed to make the sacrifices required in exchange for guarantees that the terms of the Munitions of War Act would extend only for the duration of the war and that the pay and position of union workers would not suffer as a result.

Strict controls were also placed on businesses and shareholders: profits were strictly limited by the Inland Revenue to an amount not exceeding 20 per cent more than the average profits of the two fiscal years prior to the outbreak of war; limits were also placed on the income of shareholders in these controlled establishments. A Controlled Establishments Department was set up to oversee and ensure both the efficient operation of firms which were brought under Ministry Authority and that managers and employees obeyed the ministry's regulatory codes, with special courts being set up to hear cases involving infractions.

The Munitions of War Act thus vastly expanded the state's role in industry; and the objective of winning the war brought an unprecedented degree of cooperation between government, industry and labour. The top levels of the Ministry of Munitions were staffed by businessmen, loaned by their companies for the duration of the war, to coordinate the needs of big business with those of the state. Because the support of trade unions was also required, they were called into consultation with the government as never before. The Trade Union Congress (TUC) was consulted on a wide range of issues at the highest levels of government (Martin 1980, chapter 5; Clinton 1977); and union officials and shop stewards were given a consultative role in the organisation of work as well as being included on tribunals that supervised workplace conditions. Whilst this ultimately created a "paradox" – of collective bargaining being pushed upward to national level and bargaining over work organisation and conditions being pushed downward to the shop floor – that created tensions between the rank and file and trade union leadership, it also strengthened trade union power and influence. This served as a catalyst for employers' organisations to come together; and the Federation of British Industries was formed in 1916.

To coordinate the manpower requirements of war, a National Registration Act was passed in August 1915, requiring all working men and women between the ages of fifteen and sixty-five to report the nature of their occupations and skills. This information was compiled into a statistical view of the British labour force for use by the Ministry of Reserved Occupations Committee.

Instructional workshops were set up to increase the supply of workers with the requisite skills and to improve production efficiency; and skilled trade unionists were compelled to train and supervise the scores of unskilled workers that entered their shops so that they mastered the small and repetitive tasks assigned to them in a process of "dilution". Since this created insecurity among skilled workers due to fear that dilution would put downward pressure on wages and lead to de-skilling, the Amalgamated Society of Engineers (ASE) agreed to dilution only on the condition that women workers were paid the full craft rate. Although employers resisted on the grounds that the dilutees' work covered only part of the skilled craft job, the Munitions of War Act was duly amended to require that all dilutees be paid at craft rates. The resulting opportunities for reasonable pay for women raised many households of unskilled workers out of poverty. But the ASE signed a separate agreement with the government guaranteeing that all women "dilutees" would be forced out at the end of the war in order to protect the jobs and wages of the men (Fraser 1999, p. 135). Statutory guarantees that trade union rules would be restored with the return of peace were also provided.

Between 1900 and 1913, membership in British trade unions had doubled – and it nearly doubled again during the war. By 1918, trade union membership exceeded 6.5 million, or 36 per cent of the workforce, with growth continuing for another two years to reach a peak of 8 million in 1920 (Fraser 1999, p. 129). Trade unionism was boosted by higher wages and better working conditions as well as by the fact that the government required collective agreements in many industries and insisted that employers recognise the unions as a means of ensuring that war production was not disrupted.

But trade union involvement in carrying out dilution and other changes in shop floor working practices often led to conflict between union leadership and their members at local level. Thus, whilst the number of strikes declined during the war, dissatisfaction with union officials did not disappear; and as the war progressed, inflation, food shortages and overcrowding in munitions-producing regions contributed to growing discontent. This provided the impetus for a national shop stewards movement, which adopted a strategy of supporting union leaders when they represented the interests of their members and acting independently when they did not.

Although the British state had extensive powers over labour under the Defence of the Realm Act (DORA) and the Munitions of War Acts, the needs of war and the strong position of labour sometimes made it difficult – or unrealistic – to enforce these powers; and the government soon learned that little could be achieved through direct confrontation. In 1915, when 20,000 south Wales miners went on strike over changes to back-shift and night-shift pay, the government pressed the employers for concessions, which were duly agreed (Fraser 1999, p. 129).

J.A.R. Marriott (1948) summed up the government's policy:

> no private interest was to be permitted to obstruct the service, or imperil the safety of the state. Trade union regulations must be suspended; employers' profits must be limited, skilled men must fight, if not in the trenches, in the factories; manpower must be economized by the dilution of labour and the employment of women; private factories must pass under control of the state; and new national factories must be set up. Results justified the new policy: the output was prodigious; the goods were delivered.
>
> (p. 376)

"Whitleyism"

As early as 1916, the British government, industry and trade unions were looking forward to the return of peace. Partly in response to the industrial unrest of the early years of the war – and in the wake of the establishment of the shop stewards movement and the widespread protest action against dilution – the government felt that the period of post-war reconstruction offered an opportunity for improving industrial relations. But even before the war's end, there were signs of renewed trade union militancy, given fresh impetus by the 1917 Russian Revolution.

A subcommittee of the Ministry of Reconstruction – chaired by the Deputy Speaker of the House of Commons, J.H. Whitley and known as the Whitley Committee – was set up, involving representatives from the employers' associations, trade unions and academia. Tasked with responsibility for developing proposals to secure "a permanent improvement in relations between employers and workmen and to recommend ways of systematically reviewing industrial relations of the future" (quoted in Jackson *et al.* 1993, p. 7), the Committee published its first recommendations for industrial relations reform in March 1917.

The Whitley Committee's *Report on the Relations of Employers and Employees* – the Whitley Report – re-affirmed commitment to a voluntary system and rejected expansion of the state's role in industrial relations, emphasising that employers and unions should work together with minimal government involvement. Endorsing workplace cooperation as the key to curbing industrial unrest and improving efficiency, the Committee's first report proposed establishing a hierarchy of industry-wide, district and workplace joint employer-worker industrial councils – known as "Whitley Councils" – with equal representation for employers and employees, to discuss workshop methods and industrial policy. Its second report recommended extending the system of trade boards – that Churchill had introduced in 1909 – into sectors with little or no existing organisation and establishing a system of joint councils with some government assistance in poorly organised industries. The final proposal was for an Arbitration Council to which, as a last resort, disputes could be referred. More specific recommendations aimed at reforming employee representation and consolidating union control.

In general, Whitleyism was a recognition of the changes the war had brought about in the sense that it involved an acceptance by government that unionism and collective bargaining were fundamental to industrial relations. The Whitley recommendations won government approval and the Ministry of Labour – which the TUC had long pressed for and which had been set up by Lloyd George to gain Labour's support for his coalition government – worked to secure their adoption. There was a general hope that peace would bring more orderly and cooperative industrial relations; and the Federation of British Industry – which saw the potential for industrial development taking place on a tri-partite basis of cooperation between government, employers and unions – committed itself to joint discussion regarding wages and working conditions.

An important motivation of the Whitley recommendations had been to establish Whitley councils in the private sector, in particular in those industries most affected by the wave of industrial unrest to offset the demand for workers' control – a demand that was rapidly gaining ground after the Russian Revolution.

But the Whitley scheme proved disappointing to its champions. Established employers believed that Whitley councils impinged on managerial prerogative; and trade union officials opposed them on the basis of their potential to bypass their own traditional roles. The large trade unions mainly ignored the Whitley Report's recommendations; and they were rejected by the coal, engineering, shipbuilding, iron, steel and textile unions. Only the unions in less organised and newer industries – and the public sector – recognising the opportunities offered by the scheme, embraced it.

Conclusions

Britain's early experience with industrialisation had been accompanied by significant confrontation and mutual mistrust, especially following the development of "new" unionism during the 1870s; and this contributed in no small part to the adversarial nature of the British state.

However, by the turn of the twentieth century, Booth and Rowntree's research established poverty as a problem of the employing system rather than the shortcomings of the poor; and in their Minority Report, the Poor Law Commission identified the role of ineffective labour regulation and the working of the Poor Law in perpetuating a cycle of unemployment, under-employment and poverty. They argued that the labour yard, which provided the jobless occasional outdoor relief under strict conditions, facilitated and encouraged casualisation and under-employment. Furthermore, the work-house eligibility test and poor terms and conditions in the labour market were mutually enforcing and tended to drive each other down.

The refuting of supply side explanations for poverty progressively shifted public policy from being based on thrift and self-help for the "deserving" poor and discipline for the rest to one based on full employment and social security. And the decade or so before the First World War saw the introduction of employment initiatives as alternatives to the workhouse to combat cyclical employment; the nationwide establishment of labour exchanges at which the unemployed could register for work; old age pensions, and the beginnings of contribution-based unemployment compensation and health insurance. But the Poor Law remained in place for those outside the scope of the statutory social insurance and assistance schemes.

The doubling of trade union membership solidified the Labour Party's base of support whilst Labour's participation in the wartime coalition helped to legitimise it as a viable party of government.[7] That coalition presided over a series of important social insurance extensions. Increasingly generous war pensions were provided to the dependents of those killed or seriously wounded in battle; demobilised servicemen were given non-contributory "out of work" pensions; and the families of servicemen were granted separation allowances. The 1918 Representation of the People Act created universal male suffrage and extended the franchise to women over thirty, serving to treble the size of the electorate overnight (Harling 2001, p. 140).

Whilst collective fear provided a common enemy for the duration of the First World War – and progress had been made in relations between the unions, industrialists and the state – on the cessation of hostilities, it soon became apparent that this had not been strong enough to transform these relations permanently. In fact, since Lloyd George's objective as Minister of Munitions had been to limit these new working arrangements to the duration of the war, adversarial attitudes returned almost immediately – with predictable results on both sides.

The insecurity cycle had produced significant results over the previous two decades. Whilst some, such as the proto welfare state, would prove long-lasting, others, such as more cooperative industrial relationships and working arrangements, proved more fleeting. Nevertheless, although "laissez faire" proved resilient as the dominant conventional wisdom, the conspicuous success of state involvement in industry left a lasting legacy. But fundamental change would require greater intervention from the insecurity cycle.

Notes

1 See Williams (1981, chapter 3), on the effect which the disciplinary policy of the new Poor Law had in terms of reducing numbers in receipt of relief at the end of the nineteenth century. The 3 per cent figure did not take into account pauperism among the non-able-bodied poor, in particular the elderly; this increased the figure to nearer to 30 per cent in parts of London. Booth's work of classification of the elderly poor demonstrated the ineffectiveness of the policy of restricting, on disciplinary grounds, outdoor relief to the old, and thereby helped pave the way for the introduction of old age pension based on legal entitlement. Thus "Booth should be remembered not as the man who discovered poverty, but as the man who diminished pauperism" (Williams 1981, p. 344).

2 But for a much more sceptical account of Rowntree's work, suggesting that his "technicist" approach to the definition of poverty prefigured later difficulties in the operation of the welfare state, see Williams (1981, chapter 8).

3 For an extended discussion and analysis of the Minority Report and the associated reforms to the Poor Law and unemployment compensation, see Picchio del Mercado (1992, chapter 3). For the background to the Royal Commission on the Poor Laws and its reports, see Gilbert (1966, chapter 5); Harris (1972); Woodroofe (1977); McBriar (1987); Burnett (1994, chapter 5). On the development of the Webbs' strategy and philosophy of labour market regulation in the period prior to their involvement in the Minority Report, see Harrison (2000).

4 The term "unemployment", although certainly known in the early nineteenth century and relied on in Parliamentary reports, began to be generally used to describe the condition of joblessness in the 1880s (Burnett 1994, p. 149); it was legally defined in the 1900s and 1910s, above all in the context of national insurance legislation and the reform of the outdoor relief orders; and it was adopted for statistical purposes in the 1920s, replacing the term "in want of work" (Williams 1981, p. 180). The emergence of a political and institutional discourse centred on the notion of "unemployment" during this period is analysed by Mansfield (1994).

5 Webb and Webb (1909, p. 291).

6 For a good account of the pre-war mass strikes, see Holton (1976).

7 See, for example, Tanner (1990, pp. 352–5); and McKibben (1974, pp. 238–40).

5 More problems with capitalism – but new ideas are slow to gain traction

Introduction

After a short and chaotic euphoria accompanying the cessation of hostilities at the end of 1918, the British economy fell into depression, just as it had after the Napoleonic Wars a century earlier as a consequence of the abrupt curtailment in demand for industrial production. Once again, large numbers of now surplus military personnel returned home looking for jobs; but the situation was exacerbated by the large numbers of women who, having been employed during the war in jobs not normally available to them, were not keen to return to the kitchen – and some of them would soon be able to vote. Whilst one outcome of a now more egalitarian society that was emerging from the trenches and factories of the First World War would be further extension of the franchise in 1928, the two decades before the Second World War would also see many more fundamental changes.

The war had not only witnessed the overthrow of the Russian monarchy by the Bolsheviks in 1917; it had also resulted in the fall of the German, Austro-Hungarian and Ottoman empires. This destruction of pre-war power structures, led, in turn, to a series of revolutions in Europe and elsewhere, many of which were communist or socialist in nature, with the support and encouragement of the Communist International (Comintern). Whilst this might have generated fears of a more confident British communist party, a more pressing concern was the 1919–21 Irish war of independence. The communists, meanwhile, had problems of their own. Not only were there a number of counter-revolutions, but fascist parties with little affection for socialism were also on the rise – especially in Italy.

But things could have been worse. The post war slump, which was not evenly spread across the country, was concentrated in the regions where the traditional heavy industries were located – such as coal mining and steel in the northwest of England, central Scotland and Wales. In these regions, unemployment and poverty levels were very high. By contrast, the English Midlands, and especially the southeast benefited from the growth of new industries. These included expanding car manufacturers such as Morris and Austin, that had been set up only a few years before the war; other new and prosperous industries included electrics and, especially, house building. This produced improving standards of living in these regions, further contributing to a polarisation of politics and party alignment.

As Lloyd George had feared, this polarisation would have dire consequences for the Liberal Party, in which the party split ultimately proved fatal. Many on the right – in particular, the burgeoning middle class – shifted their support to the Conservatives, whilst those on the left gravitated towards the new Labour Party. Whilst the Liberals would never govern again, Lloyd George initiated a major house-building programme as well as the Unemployment Insurance Act of 1920; and his efforts to mitigate unemployment drew support from perhaps the defining figure of the inter-war years in Britain – John Maynard Keynes – who co-authored *Can Lloyd George Do It? An Examination of the Liberal Pledge* in 1929.

Perhaps the greatest catalyst for change during the inter-war years would be almost two decades of sustained and apparently intractable pressure on the British economy. Traditional ideas about how to operate a capitalist economy would be seen to either fail or generate counter-productive outcomes, with some going so far as to predict the imminent demise of capitalism, an idea that was only reinforced by the 1917 Bolshevik Revolution, the success of the fascists in Italy and the political and economic chaos elsewhere.

But rather than radical social or political change, the inter-war decades in Britain would witness a rapid expansion in the apparatus of the state. This involved not only assuming progressively greater responsibility for the welfare of the population in terms of both housing and unemployment, but also actively engaging with economists for the development of policy – eventually resulting in their more direct involvement. Whether politicians actually took their advice, stuck with what they thought they knew, or chose to side with those economists whose views happened to coincide with their own, is debatable. Whilst Keynes's ideas were not initially formally espoused, the economic "force majeure" provided by preparations for the Second World War would effectively represent the first experiment with "Keynesian" policies.

The defining feature of the inter-war years, then, was perhaps not so much the images of sustained unemployment and the poverty that accompanied it, but the wide range of new ideas it gave rise to – and in many cases, their sharp polarisation. Not only would there be a clear divide between the Conservatives and Labour in mainstream politics, but at the extremes, there would also be a divide between the new fascist and communist factions. In the rapidly developing field of economics, neo-classical economic arguments continued to be expounded by both the Treasury and the Bank of England, supported by economists including Friedrich von Hayek and economists at the London School of Economics. But these would be strongly challenged by the new economic ideas of John Maynard Keynes and the Cambridge economists. A similarly adversarial relationship between labour and employers in the north and west of Britain would eventually spill over into the 1926

General Strike; and there would be a lively debate about the alternative policies of appeasement and re-armament. This would be decided by an extensive programme of re-armament, followed by another major war, that ultimately provided a clear verdict on the effectiveness of Keynes's radical new ideas.

From the point of view of the insecurity cycle, there would be no shortage of chronic crises or democratic pressure; and there was an abundance of new ideas. But what of political leadership? Towering figures such as David Lloyd George were to be in short supply between the wars, until his old ally, Winston Churchill, emerged as Britain's wartime leader. Ramsay MacDonald largely failed to impress as Labour's first ever Prime Minister – especially following his expulsion from the party. The Conservatives fared somewhat better, dominating politics for most of the inter-war years. But the strength of the Treasury and the Bank of England would prove more influential still, allowing old ideas and values to persist.

This is not to say that politicians were an unimportant part of the equation – in many ways they were as much the victims of circumstance as the master. This perhaps provides some mitigation for the appearance of Ramsay Mac-Donald, Stanley Baldwin and Neville Chamberlain among the "Guilty Men" – accused of the attempted appeasement of Hitler and failing to adequately prepare the country for war ("Cato" 1940). The end of that war, though, would bring into play a significant politician who both espoused and consciously implemented new "Keynesian" ideas – in the person of the apparently mild mannered Clement Attlee.

Welfare between the wars

The situation facing many British workers – although by no means all – between the wars in Britain was not dissimilar to that of their predecessors during the nineteenth century. The Liberal reforms preceding the First World War had gone some way towards alleviating the extreme deprivation of the poor; but these had not produced the step change that many had anticipated (Hill 1985, pp. 260–3). This served as a catalyst for further expansion of the labour movement and successive social reforms initiated by other parties both to alleviate the short-term consequences of poverty and unemployment and to attract some of the increasingly important new popular votes. It would soon become apparent that whilst politicians could bring about short-term change, a paradigm shift would require someone with much more fundamental and far-reaching ideas – as well as a relatively tenuous connection to both politics and the establishment, with far fewer vested interests.

In the meantime, short-term fixes were becoming more and more significant. In contrast to the challenges of extending the franchise during the century before the First World War, the more egalitarian society that emerged from the war and its supporting factories meant that further extension of suffrage was almost inevitable – and the legislation passed with remarkably little opposition – especially by comparison to that experienced earlier. Prior to the 1918 Representation of the People Act, only about 60 per cent of men could vote, whilst women remained excluded (Cook 2005, p. 68). After its passage, almost all men could vote, and significant progress was made with regard to the rights of women. Whilst women over the age of twenty-one but under thirty would have to wait until 1928 before being able to vote, the 1918 Act added about 5.6 million men and 8.5 million women to the franchise.[1]

This process of steady expansion of the electorate had two main effects. First, it helped to sharply polarise politics, instituting a clear division between right- and left-wing policy aims. It also made securing the votes of the middle and working classes a priority for both the Labour and Conservative parties – which meant that major issues concerning either of these segments could no longer be ignored without detrimental effects on the party. Moreover, the presence of factions to the extreme right and left – the fascists and the communists – added to the pressure on governments of the time to be seen to be doing their utmost to address the most pressing issues.

The first inter-war social legislation – which also passed with surprisingly little opposition – was the Unemployment Insurance Act of 1920 that built upon the 1911 National Insurance Act of the pre-war Liberal reforms. Only a year later, the 1920 Act would probably have met with far greater opposition, as unemployment rose sharply with the drop in demand following the war. Nevertheless, the new Act provided some degree of cover for around 11 million workers, although those working in agriculture, railways, domestic and the civil service were excluded, presumably on the grounds that unemployment was a far less likely prospect in these sectors (Garside 1990, pp. 37–9). The weekly payment of 15 shillings for men was available for only fifteen weeks, whilst unemployed women had to make do with 12 shillings, funded by contributions from the state, the workers and the employers. The impact of both significant and persistent unemployment is demonstrated by the passing of no less than twenty-four further Unemployment Acts before 1940 was out, including three in 1930 alone, following the Wall Street Crash.

The other main strand in welfare development was the rapid expansion of housing stock, following Lloyd George's Housing and Town Planning Act of 1919. This, often referred to as the "Addison Act", required each local authority to assess its local housing needs, and to build accordingly – replacing the now notorious slums in the process. Not only did this produce more accommodation, it also established design criteria developed from the Tudor Walters report of 1918 for both the houses themselves, and the structure of the neighbourhoods that were created. The result was an unprecedented rate of expansion of good quality, affordable housing stocks. Before the war, in 1911, the total housing stock in England and Wales had stood at 7.6 million units. By 1921, it had risen to 8.0 million; and, undeterred by the effects of either unemployment or the Great Depression, it passed 9.4 million in 1931, reaching 11.3 million by the beginning of the Second World War (Ruben-stein 2003, p. 122).

This exponential increase in the housing stock clearly demonstrates that not only were there sharp divisions in employment opportunities within Britain; during the inter-war years as a whole, the living standards of some 3.3 million households – a considerable proportion of the population – were significantly improved by the new housing stock.

The polarisation of politics

A combination of the successive increases in the franchise, dissatisfaction within the labour movement about the speed and extent of reforms, along with distrust of the Liberal-Labour pact of the earlier period, was about to confirm Lloyd George's worst fears. The house-building programme and changes to the unemployment benefit system would be the last contributions of the Liberal Party, before their replacement by the nascent Labour Party as the main opposition to the Conservatives. Not only would this sharply polar-ise the electorate's options, it would also reflect their contrasting views.

But neither of the first two Labour governments – both minority adminis-trations – delivered a stellar performance; and, initially at least, the Labour Party fared little better than the Liberals had.

1924 Labour minority government

Following Lloyd George's resignation in 1922, the Conservatives looked to have a solid hold on Parliament; but following the death of Bonar Law, Stanley Baldwin, the new Conservative leader, felt that he needed an elect-oral mandate for his proposed protectionist policies. Although the result was indecisive on the individual party front, between then, those parties opposed to protectionism scored a decisive victory; and since the Labour Party had secured more seats than Asquith's Liberals, it was they who formed a minority government, led by Ramsay MacDonald.

The first Labour government was hardly a radical administration. But given its insecure hold on power, a radical agenda was never a realistic option; and a restrained approach served to demonstrate that the new party could indeed administer the apparatus of conventional government. Nor would it be true to say that Labour's first term in office achieved little or nothing. The Wheatley Housing Act in particular, which focused on the construction of council houses for rent at controlled prices, was a significant piece of legis-lation, resulting in the construction of 521,700 council homes, before the subsidy for building them was withdrawn in 1933 (Harmer 2014, p. 63).

MacDonald's brief administration also made improvements to the unem-ployment benefit system, including raising the weekly amount for men to 18s and women to 15s, and abolishing both the gap between claiming periods and the unpopular household means test. There were also efforts to support pension provision, better education and improved public health, notably by creating more sports facilities and improving public parks and open spaces. G.D.H. Cole, an historian for the Labour Party, summed-up the efforts of the first, brief Labour government:

> What it could do and did achieve, was to undo a good many of the administrative effects of the "Geddes Axe", to pass several valuable measures of social reform, and to make a somewhat faint hearted attempt at coping with the unemployment situation by the institution of public works.
>
> (Cole 1948)

The labour movement was, however, having some difficulty in differentiating itself from the active Communist movement; and with the October Revolution still fresh in the memory, there was plenty of concern – real or imagined – that something similar might happen in Britain. The demise of the first Labour administration clearly demonstrates the risk of even appearing to be associated with the Communist Party of Great Britain (CPGB). The government's downfall was largely brought about by events following publication of "An Open Letter to the Armed Forces" by J.R. Campbell, editor of the *Workers Weekly*, the newspaper of the CPGB, on 25 July 1924, resulting in the "Campbell Case". The letter read in part:

> Comrades: You never joined the Army or Navy because you were in love with warfare, or because you were attracted to the glamour of the uniform. In nine cases out of ten you were compelled to join the services after a long fight against poverty and misery caused by prolonged unemployment … Repressive regulations and irksome restrictions are intentionally imposed upon you. And when war is declared you are supposed to be filled with a longing to "beat the enemy". The enemy consists of working men like yourselves, living under the same slave conditions … Soldiers, sailors, airmen, flesh of our flesh and bone of our bone, the Communist Party calls upon you to begin the task of not only organising passive resistance when war is declared, or when an industrial dispute involves you, but to definitely and categorically let it be known that, neither in the class war nor a military war, will you turn your guns on your fellow workers, but instead will line up with your fellow workers in an attack upon the exploiters and capitalists, and will use your arms on the side of your own class. Refuse to shoot down your fellow workers! Refuse to fight for profits!
>
> (Quoted in Klugmann 1968, pp. 366–7)

The problem lay not so much in the contents of the article, which encouraged members of the armed forces to support their fellow workers instead of fighting them. But it was highly inflammatory; and charges were brought against Campbell for alleged "incitement to mutiny". The subsequent decision of the Labour government to suspend prosecution of the case was seen as being tantamount to support for communism – and a clear demonstration of the influence of the "Red Menace" over the party leadership.

Asquith called for a vote on a Committee of Inquiry, which offered MacDonald a way out of the imbroglio, whilst still saving face. Inexplicably, he refused – adding that if Members of Parliament (MPs) voted in favour of such an inquiry, he and his government would resign. The large majority in favour thus bought MacDonald's – and Labour's – first administration to an end within a scant nine months of taking office.

But Labour's apparent problems with the communists were not yet over. That same year, during the general election campaign, the *Daily Mail* published a letter allegedly written by Grigory Zinoviev, head of the Comintern in Moscow, just four days prior to the ballot.[2] The letter was addressed to the CPGB, exhorting it to indulge in all kinds of revolutionary activities. The actual effect of this letter is subject to debate; and it has, as long suspected, been proven to be a forgery. In all likelihood, whilst the Labour vote in the 1924 general election was not seriously undermined, the letter probably helped to turn more of the previously Liberal vote towards the Conservatives, contributing to a Tory landslide. What is certain is that it would not have made Labour's feelings towards the communists any warmer, which, amongst other things, would have an influence on the outcome of the 1926 General Strike two years later.

Such is the persistence of feelings that support the insecurity cycle, that even after almost a century – and the fall of the Soviet Union – Labour's leader, Ed Miliband, was also haunted by the "Red Menace" by some factions of the media; and the present party leader, Jeremy Corbyn is not only experiencing this from much of the media, but also from within his own party.

1929 Labour minority government

Labour's second minority government, which took office in May 1929, could hardly have arrived at a worse time. Following the Wall Street Crash in October of that year, the already sluggish economy was further slowed by the resulting depression in world trade, the erection of tariff barriers and the abrupt slowing of American credit.

The reaction of the working-class component of the electorate was already conspicuous, characterised by regular – and often dauntingly large – "hunger marches", many of which were organised by the Labour Party's old nemesis, the CPGB. Whilst the budget was under pressure and sterling overvalued, this situation had arisen without the assistance of austerity policies – so far. But MacDonald's government – perhaps fearing the effects of any radical or unusual economic policies on Labour's electability, worrying about accusations of renewed influence by the communists, or perhaps because of a genuine belief in the conventional wisdom of the time – took a conventional view of the crisis, especially the financial crisis of 1931 (Skidelsky 1994). With the unemployment rate in Britain having already more than doubled, reaching 2.5 million by the end of 1930, there was significant pressure on the budget; but the financial crisis the following year would prove to be a turning point in a number of respects.

The collapse of the Austrian bank, Creditanstalt, in 1931 made things considerably worse, resulting in a significant and sustained withdrawal of gold from London. Both the Treasury and the Bank of England insisted that it was essential to support confidence in the currency; and they advocated raising interest rates to attract new capital and reducing the deficit through fiscal consolidation aimed at balancing the budget. But this conventional way of thinking was doomed from the start, as interest rates were already punitively high, at over 8 per cent, as a consequence of previous attempts to maintain the value of sterling. It was also clear that during a recession of such severity, there could be no major fiscal consolidation without serious social and economic consequences.

But MacDonald was convinced enough by the conventional wisdom in support of the Treasury's argument to propose a package of austerity measures, including deep cuts in both unemployment benefits and public sector wages. This had dire consequences for both himself and his immediate allies. A deeply entrenched and bitter split in the government resulted in MacDonald being expelled from the Labour Party; and he was labelled a "traitor" and a "rat" for supporting the austerity measures (Dickenson 2006, pp. 3–4). Despite all this, MacDonald was able to remain as Prime Minister in the first of the national governments that would last Britain until the wartime coalition.

MacDonald's adherence to the conventional view thus earned him little in terms of his political career and the desired economic outcomes. But the ill-advised policies did – indirectly – lead to a recovery of sorts in the British economy. The futility of attempting to maintain sterling on the gold standard at an inflated rate of exchange rapidly became apparent; and by September 1931, Britain was forced off the gold standard and the currency was devalued. This permitted a sharp reduction in interest rates, and a steady increase in the money supply, which supported a house-building and consumer durables boom, especially around London and in the southeast of England.

MacDonald did, however, implement at least one significant change with regard to economic management, by setting up the Economic Advisory Council – which included Keynes and Josiah Stamp – to be the Prime Minister's "eyes and ears on economic questions" (Howson and Winch 1977, p. 1). This was the first attempt in Britain to recruit economists into government on a full-time basis, and to create a mechanism whereby the government could regularly and formally call upon a wide range of outside experts for advice. Stamp – who was reputed to be the second richest man in Britain during the 1930s (Fine 2012, p. 52) – was widely regarded Britain's leading expert on taxation; and he was appointed as a director of the Bank of England in 1928, as well as serving on the Economic Advisory Council from 1930 to 1939. If his views on the nature of banking and bankers were representative of those held by others of his time, they reflect a very different perspective to that which led up to the 2008 financial crisis nearly eighty years later. According to Stamp:

> Banking was conceived in iniquity and born in sin. The bankers own the earth. Take it away from them, but leave them the power to create money, and with the flick of a pen they will create enough deposits to buy it back again. However, take away from them the power to create money and all the great fortunes like mine will disappear and they ought to disappear, for this would be a happier and better world to live in. But, if you wish to remain the slaves of bankers and pay the cost of your slavery, let them continue to create money.
>
> (Quoted in Fine 2012, p. 52)

Although the committee itself largely failed to live up to its lofty aims, and exerted little influence one way or the other, it would serve as the first of a series of similar – progressively more ambitious – initiatives, including the Committee on Economic Information which was the "first body at the centre of the government consisting preponderantly of economists and concerned exclusively with economic advice" (quoted in Howson and Winch 1977, p. 2). This Committee would serve as an important predecessor to the ambitious advisory system that was evolved during the early stages of the Second World War, when it was transformed into Stamp's Survey of War Plans, and ultimately the Economic Section of the Cabinet Office. However, Sir Arthur Salter's somewhat depressing assessment of the process of attempting to feed advice into the policy-making process suggests that politics were still far more influential than economics:

> All the relevant information was at our disposal. We were over a great range of controversial questions to make unanimous recommendations which would, if adopted, have profoundly changed the policy of the time. In retrospect they can, I think, be seen to have anticipated much that later became orthodox in Whitehall as elsewhere. But in fact we had little practical effect. Our reports were secret and could be and were rejected by any department which disliked them, without explanation in public, or even in private to ourselves.
>
> (Quoted in Howson and Winch 1977, p. 3)

Thus, although there were already those, who like Keynes, were evolving ideas about the *actual* causes of the economic challenges of the inter-war years – and the policies that were appropriate for addressing their root causes – the conventional wisdom of neo-classical economics proved difficult to shake. As a result, implementation of these new ideas would have to wait.

Whilst the north and west of the country continued to suffer badly during the 1920s and 1930s, the more prosperous new industries – and the house-building boom – located in the south and Midlands contributed to economic prosperity in these regions. This worked to the benefit of their skilled work-force and underpinned the growth of a larger middle class, which in turn generated significant support for the Conservative Party. In the year follow-ing Lloyd George's resignation in 1922, Noel Skelton coined the phrase "property owning democracy" (Torrance 2010), a concept that will re-appear more than once in the context of the insecurity cycle. These proved to be solid times for the Conservatives, with Stanley Baldwin being the last British political leader to win over 50 per cent of the vote in a general election.

Insecurity in the north

That hostilities between labour and employers would resume, after those on the Western Front had ceased, was almost inevitable. Both sides had insisted that the more cooperative – and conspicuously successful – approach to wartime industrial production (and relations) would last only as long as the war. The slump that followed it was almost guaranteed to return relations between workers and employers to their pre-war state, and in the process, to re-create the chronic crisis that accompanied it. But to suggest that economic conditions were universally bleak is a significant over-statement, given the reality of the developing north/south divide.

The new industries in the Midlands and the south, saw considerable growth, with their employees enjoying significant benefits in terms of wages and living standards; and when preparations for re-armament for the Second World War eventually began, these industries – the car manufacturers, in par-ticular – were in a good position to diversify into aircraft manufacturing, with companies like Austin, eventually building Lancaster bombers as well.

Meanwhile, in the more traditional heavy industries – such as coal, steel and ship building – located in the north, Wales and Scotland, it was a com-pletely different story. These industries were in decline and under ever-increasing pressure. The war had done little to maintain their export markets, which were soon dominated by lower cost competitors; and alternative fuels – especially oil – were rapidly replacing coal, which consequently experi-enced a significant reduction in demand. The situation had been made considerably worse by the Bank of England's success in persuading Churchill to restore sterling to the gold standard at pre-war parity in 1925, overvaluing the currency and undermining the price competitiveness of British exports. This caused Keynes to follow up his *Economic Consequences of the Peace* with his own view of the decision – summed up in his *Economic Consequences of Mr. Churchill*.

Many employers, especially those in the now highly competitive coal mining industry, tried to compensate for their falling profits in the usual manner – with lower wages and longer working hours for their workers. This "internal devaluation" inevitably made things worse, resulting in significant unrest, and the union mantra "not a penny off the pay, not a minute on the day". With the support of the Trades Union Congress (TUC), the miners were able to get some apparent relief from the Conservative government, which not only set up a Royal Commission under Sir Herbert Samuel to review the situation in the coal industry, but also provided a subsidy to underwrite the miners' wages for nine months whilst it was carried out. This commission also included Beveridge, who, although he would not accept the model of nationalisation suggested by the CPGB, was a strong supporter of family allowances; and his proposals on this were mostly accepted by the Family Endowment Council. Beveridge would also go on to chair the Unemployment Insurance Statutory Committee from 1934.

However, the Prime Minister, Stanley Baldwin, was acutely aware of the damage a strike could inflict; and he had used the nine-month review and subsidy to buy time – and prepare for the inevitable:

> We were confronted last week by a great alliance of Trade unions. If we are again confronted by a challenge of that nature, let me say that no minority in a free country has ever yet coerced the whole community.
>
> (Quoted in Marxist Internet Archive 2007)

Following the Bolshevik Revolution in 1917, the subsequent creation of the CPGB – and the highly public "Campbell Case" and "Zinoviev letter" of 1924 – the Baldwin government was acutely aware of the potential for communist involvement, as well as the high levels of public suspicion surrounding the possibility of nefarious activities on the part of the Comintern in Moscow. This view was not confined to the government, but was shared by the TUC and much of the labour movement as well.

The CPGB did indeed press for a strike involving 100 per cent of the trade union membership, supported by the creation of its own "defence corps" to counteract any involvement by the police or armed forces, like that which had followed the 1919 "Battle of George Square" in Glasgow. But this was rejected by the unions, as was the CPGB's suggestion of carrying its message to the members of the armed forces – in a remarkably similar manner to that of Campbell's open letter in the *Workers' Weekly* two years earlier. Thus, neither the press, nor the government, nor indeed the trade union movement, liked the look of the communist strategy, interpreting it as preparation for armed revolution. The CPGB's proposals were therefore firmly rejected by the unions who also, at their Liverpool Conference, expelled many communists from the Labour Party. But as a consequence of trying to distance themselves from the communists, the unions were probably insufficiently prepared for sustaining a major strike.

The government, on the other hand, had recognised both the impending acute crisis and the need to deal with it quickly; and it prepared accordingly. Preparatory actions involved the imprisonment of twelve of the CPGB's executive, as well as the setting-up of the "Organisation for the Maintenance of Supplies" (OMS) and – in a move that would be copied by Margaret Thatcher sixty years later – the stockpiling of a sufficient amount of coal to keep essential services operating.

The OMS was an organisation made up of newly recruited "special constables" to prevent disorder on the streets. Because the government's distrust of extremists also extended to the fascists, they were not allowed to join the OMS without first "giving up their political beliefs" – although how exactly this was to have been policed remains a mystery. One member of the OMS later painted a grim picture of the plight of the mine workers in the *Nottinghamshire Examiner*:

> It was not hard to understand the strikers' attitude toward us. After a few days, I found my sympathy with them, rather than with the employers. For one thing, I had never realised the appalling poverty which existed. If I had been aware of all the facts, I should not have joined up as a special constable.
>
> (Quoted in Internationalist Communist Union 2001)

When it was finally published, the Commission's report did not make pleasant reading for the miners. Unlike its predecessor, the Sankey Commission, it did not recommend nationalisation of the industry, an idea already previously rejected by Lloyd George; it settled instead for large-scale reorganisation; the subsidy was withdrawn and miners' wages were cut by 13.5 per cent. This predictably triggered a general strike a few weeks later in May 1926.

In the event, as a consequence of the combination of distrust of the "Red Menace" on the part of many in both the labour movement and the general public, along with the low level of violence and absence of evidence of capitulation on the part of either the state or pit owners, the strike was less comprehensive than it might otherwise have been. Support for the miners came mainly from the transport unions. This, and the significant numbers of middle-class volunteers, along with the military stepping into transport roles, meant that the employers could hold their ground; and the strike was relatively easily broken.

The result, as the TUC had feared, was the swift implementation of anti-union legislation, in the form of the 1927 Trade Disputes and Trade Unions Act, which militated against the threat of further general strikes by making both mass picketing and sympathy strikes illegal. In the long run, the Act did relatively little to limit organised labour in practice.

Nevertheless, the General Strike is important in a number of respects. First, it clearly demonstrated both awareness and nervousness on the part of the communist and fascist groups in Britain. In the case of the communists, this extended to the government, the unions – which had undermined preparations for the strike – and the media, since the *Daily Mail* had been only too happy to publish the Zinoviev letter. Second, the General Strike showed that, in terms of economic thought and employment conditions, not very much had changed since the previous century – in coal mining at least. This was in spite of the further development of the 1911 national insurance scheme just four years earlier, which did not provide much relief. The failure of the 1926 General Strike also did little to improve matters for the affected workers.

Even by 1936, with re-armament well under way, 200 unemployed workers were sufficiently desperate to walk from Jarrow to Parliament, to try to bring work back to Tyneside.[3] This was not the first time that Parliament had experienced the arrival of a "hunger march" since they had been going on throughout most of the 1920s. But in a further display of the nervousness of any association with the communists on the part of both the trade union movement and the Labour Party, neither associated themselves with the Jarrow March or, indeed, any of its predecessors. Disassociation with earlier marches was because many of them had been organised by the National Unemployed Workers Movement – a communist organisation. The Jarrow March, however, was organised by the local council, with no apparent connections to the far left.

The polarisation of economics

The inter-war years saw for the first time, the emergence of economists who were prepared to publicly advocate differing approaches to policy in the most high-profile media of their day, as well as directly within government. The relative ease with which any policy suggestion put forward by mechanisms such as the Economic Advisory Council could be mired in civil service red tape and buried has already been discussed. Some of the council's membership, however, were not content to let the matter rest there, and instead looked to take their ideas to a wider audience.

This new approach of publicly setting out opinions on current economic problems started immediately after the war, which had helped establish the reputation of John Maynard Keynes as one of the Treasury's most able men. He had also acted as advisor to the British government at the Versailles Conference, a position from which he resigned in frustration on 26 May 1919, retiring to Cambridge to write *The Economic Consequences of the Peace*. In it, Keynes (2010 [1919]) points to the material violation of the terms regarding reparations, territorial adjustments and an equitable economic settlement, as a blot on the honour of the Western allies – and probably the primary cause of a future war. Given that he was writing in 1919, his prediction that the next war would begin twenty years hence had an uncanny accuracy; and the success of this book cemented Keynes's public reputation as a leading economist.

Britain's economic problems during the inter-war years provided Keynes with many issues to address, as neo-classical economic orthodoxy and policy either failed to resolve them – or made them worse. The economic problems of this period were commonly taken as evidence by critics of capitalism that it was approaching its end. But Keynes, having started out as a neo-classical economist, came to the (for some, at least) disturbing conclusion that this school of thought was incorrect in a number of key areas.

In this, Keynes was not entirely alone. In 1920, the Lloyd George Liberal government, assuming that the post-war rise in unemployment would be temporary, set up an Unemployment Grants Committee to encourage public works schemes. However, the cost of the schemes raised doubts about the government's ability to meet the interest payments on the 1917 war loan – and thus retain the confidence of its creditors – reinforcing the deflationary bias in government policy. In 1922, Stanley Baldwin, the Conservative Chancellor of the Exchequer, warned that "money taken for government purposes is money taken away from trade, and borrowing will thus tend to depress trade and increase unemployment" (Middlemas and Barnes 1969, p. 127). The theoretical justification for this "Treasury View" was provided by Ralph Hawtrey, the Treasury's economist, who argued:

> [t]he original contention that the public works themselves give additional employment is radically fallacious. When employment is improved, this is the result of some reaction on credit, and the true remedy for unemployment is to be found in a direct regulation of credit on sound lines.
>
> (Hawtrey 1925, p. 48)

The British Government had thus decisively reverted to pre-war laissez faire economic and financial orthodoxy. Public expenditure was reduced in an attempt to balance the budget; an effort was made to re-pay wartime loans; and monetary policy was targeted at defending sterling. Persistent high unemployment and deficits in the balance of payments were initially attributed to the ongoing effects of the war, which had disrupted export markets and radically increased production costs. The Treasury therefore reasoned that a return to economic "normality" required wage reductions to restore prices to their pre-war levels. However, efforts to cut wages met fierce resistance from the trade unions; and militancy intensified, stoking fear of socialism – especially when the Treasury restored the gold standard, re-valuing sterling at its 1914 parity. The resulting price deflation squeezed British manufacturers even further, who predictably tried to limit their own losses by reducing labour costs, thereby precipitating the 1926 General Strike.

But despite the ensuing economic, social and political unrest, high unemployment and a persistent balance of payments deficit, the Treasury continued to single-mindedly pursue its restrictive economic policy, with very little success as far as reducing the national debt was concerned.[4] This strategy would again be adopted by the coalition government of 2010, following the 2008 financial crisis – with comparable results.

The theory behind the "Treasury View" rested on the belief – held by Keynes himself, at the time he wrote his *Treatise on Money*, published in 1930 – that savings determines the level of investment and that monetary policy is appropriate for countering economic fluctuations (Laidler 1999, pp. 148–9).

Keynes later modified his position, arguing that the solution to Britain's economic problems lay in increasing home demand to compensate for shrinking exports. In 1924, he had published "Does Unemployment Need a Drastic Remedy?" arguing that the cure for unemployment was not only in monetary reform but also in "the diversion of national savings from relatively barren foreign investment into state encouraged constructive enterprises at home". In 1928, in "How to Organize a Wave of Prosperity", he had again argued for public spending to combat unemployment; and in 1929, with Hubert Henderson, Keynes wrote the pamphlet, *Can Lloyd George Do It?*, in support of Lloyd George's campaign pledge to reduce unemployment by major public works expenditure, financed by borrowing.[5]

However, the British Treasury refuted this contention in its 1929 White Paper and Winston Churchill re-iterated the orthodox Treasury view in his 1929 budget speech:

> Let us, first of all, by way of preliminary digression, address ourselves to the burning question of whether national prosperity can be restored or enhanced by the Government borrowing money and spending it on making more work. The orthodox Treasury view ... is that when the Government borrow[s] in the money market it becomes a new competitor with industry and engrosses to itself resources which would otherwise have been employed by private enterprise, and in the process it raises the rent of money to all who have need of it.
>
> (Churchill 1929)

During the late 1920s and 1930s, Keynes had often been accused of ignoring the need to maintain confidence in both Britain's financial policies and its position in the international community (Middleton 1982, p. 55). Keynes, however, was also opposed to fiscal profligacy, and his critics misunderstood the fact that in Keynes's analysis, austerity was indeed necessary – but only to be applied during a boom, to avert inflation or the risk of financial collapse. This is why, following the 1931 financial crisis, Keynes "wrote to Prime Minister (MacDonald) to say that a crisis of confidence was 'very near' and the budget must be balanced" (Middleton 1982, p. 175).

As unemployment continued to climb, Keynes and colleagues at the University of Cambridge sparked a public debate about the economics of government stimulus and austerity. In response to the editor of *The Times*, who had sought economists' opinions about the problem of inadequate private spending, they stressed the importance of *both* private *and* public spending to address unemployment caused by insufficient effective demand.[6] The idea behind proposing government spending during a slump was to mobilise unused – and especially human – resources. This, in turn, expands aggregate demand, mobilising further resources. The result is a virtuous cycle with multiplier effects since the total increase in economic activity is greater than the increase in government spending that set it off.

Meanwhile, the neo-classical view of economics was not without its equally vocal proponents, with Hayek and his colleagues at the London School of Economics (LSE) responding with the alternative, orthodox position. These were "of the opinion that many of the troubles of the world at the present time are due to imprudent borrowing and spending on the part of public authorities". They also argued that any public spending should take the form of investment in the securities of private businesses and set out their case for fiscal austerity and the freeing-up of markets.[7]

The debates between these two opposing views were lively and at times, little quarter was asked or given, with Keynes describing Hayek's "Prices and Production [as] one of the most frightful muddles I've read", and adding "it is an extraordinary example of how, starting with a mistake, a remorseless logician can end up in Bedlam" (quoted in BBC 2011).

By attributing the crisis to differing causes – insufficient effective demand as opposed to insufficient funds for private investment – the Cambridge and LSE economists advocated contrasting policy solutions. The Cambridge economists argued for government borrowing from the public to spend on public works to close the gap between actual and potential demand whilst the LSE economists argued for government austerity to make space for private investors in the market for finance.

In *The Means to Prosperity*, Keynes (1933) continued to call for fiscal stimulus; and in 1935, Lloyd George again proposed government borrowing and public works to address the problem of persistent unemployment. By then, "public support was sufficient to make ministers feel that they ought to be seen as doing something" (Peden 1984, p. 176) and the Treasury relaxed its resistance. By 1935, however, recovery was well underway – but it had come *not* from fiscal policy but from monetary policy designed for an entirely different purpose. Speculation during the 1931 financial crisis had forced sterling off the gold standard. The resulting depreciation allowed interest rates to be very significantly lowered, which not only reduced the cost of financing the 1917 war loan, but also triggered a house-building boom which led the economy out of recession.

However, the economic picture was not uniformly positive. Unemployment remained high in the north and the west; Keynes recognised this[8] – as well as the need to prevent other parts of the economy from over-heating. So in 1937, he wrote a series of articles in *The Times* on "How to Avoid a Slump": In "The Problem of the Steady Level", he urged that any new productive capacity be located in Britain's distressed regions; and in "The Right Time for Austerity", he argued that the time had now come for austerity, "to protect us from the excesses of the boom and, at the same time, put us in good trim to ward off the cumulative dangers of the slump when the reaction comes, as come it surely will". Keynes thus made explicit the point that – whilst during the slump, the cure for unemployment is stimulus – once the recovery is established, austerity is required to prevent the economy from over-heating and triggering inflationary pressures.

During the inter-war years, neo-classical economics – the then dominant orthodoxy – was incapable of explaining the persistence of high levels of involuntary unemployment and the failure of markets to clear. Whilst this might have constituted a "massive onslaught of circumstances" to clear the way for new ideas to challenge the conventional wisdom, as John Kenneth Galbraith (1999) also observed, "it is a far, far better thing to have a firm anchor in nonsense, than to put out on the troubled seas of thought" (p. 131). Consequently, it was the economic recovery generated by the massive stimulus to aggregate demand dictated by the Second World War, rather than a conscious change of economic orthodoxy, that seemed to justify Keynes's ideas about the role of the state in the economy. It also re-established confidence in the West that capitalism could be restored. Once again, in the words of Galbraith "one could not have had a better demonstration of the Keynesian ideas" (quoted in Yergin and Stanislaw 2002).

Even when Keynes's ideas were gaining significant ground, however, his old adversary, Hayek, remained unconvinced. His book, *The Road to Serfdom* was written during the Second World War, between 1940 and 1943, and warned against the perils of government involvement in the economy – suggesting that this would sooner or later lead to totalitarianism, of the type experienced in Fascist Germany and Italy, or in Stalin's Communist Russia. The book was a moderate success in Britain, where the print run was small, due to the strict rationing of paper; but it also had a successful run in the USA.

Hayek would later move from the LSE to the University of Chicago, where he would influence Milton Friedman, and contribute to the development of the "Chicago Boys". He was also among the founders of the Mont Pelerin Society, and as a result Hayek helped to keep "laissez faire" ideas alive, to power the next major movement in the insecurity cycle. Indeed, it has often been argued that *The Road to Serfdom* was amongst the more indispensable items within Margaret Thatcher's famous handbag.

Both Hayek and Keynes were therefore amongst the first economists to adopt a public, political and technical role in their attempts to promote alternative ideas and to influence economic policy. Whilst Seebohm Rowntree had had to rely largely on his friendship with Lloyd George for his influence, Keynes was well connected in finance, civil service, society and academia – with a solid reputation in all of these areas. As a journalist and author, he was not only well connected, but also highly productive, as a short list of some of his publications between the wars illustrates. Keynes did not content himself with a single tract on theory, but was also happy to weigh in with an opinion on individual issues, including *A Tract on Monetary Reform* (1923), *The Economic Consequences of Mr. Churchill* and *The End of Laissez Faire* (1926), *A Treatise on Money* (1930), *The Means to Prosperity* (1933), *The General Theory of Employment, Interest and Money* (1936) and *How to Pay for the War* (1940), to name but a few.

Communism versus fascism

The polarisation of economic thought, party politics and relations between employers and workers were not the only issues produced by Britain's travails during the inter-war years. Aside from the question of what to do about the highly militaristic new Germany, there was also the matter of the new and more extreme systems evolving in Communist Russia, as well as Fascist Italy and subsequently Hitler's Germany.

The idea of socialism in its various forms was hardly a new one; Marx's *Das Kapital*, predicting both revolution and the inevitable demise of capitalism, had been in print for half a century. But the 1917 Bolshevik Revolution – even though it took place within a largely agrarian context instead of an industrial society – had lent weight to this possibility. Even more concerning, was the fact that the communist movement was intended to be an international one, encouraging a similar process of revolution elsewhere. This meant that communist parties in other countries – including the CPGB, which had been established in 1920 – took their policy lead from the Comintern in Moscow.

This would, in many ways, be as much of a handicap as an asset. In addition to abrupt policy changes produced by doctrinal debate (such as whether to support parliamentarianism, as advocated by Vladimir Lenin, or to work towards a revolution instead) or actual events elsewhere (such as Hitler's invasion of the Soviet Union (USSR) which abruptly reversed the party's pacifist stance), it also raised suspicions about these worrying external influences. This extended to the Labour Party, which although happy to affiliate with other socialist organisations in Britain, pointedly and repeatedly refused to do so with the CPGB. But it did not stop individual communists from joining the Labour Party and even, on occasion, being elected as MPs.

This suspicion is amply illustrated by the affair of the Zinoviev letter, published just before the 1924 general election by the *Daily Mail*, which appeared to contain instructions from the head of the Comintern for its British subsidiary to indulge itself in all manner of disruptive behaviour. The fact that this letter is now generally agreed to have been a forgery is significant because if it was considered worthwhile to fan the suspicion of troublesome foreign influences at work, it is hard to avoid the conclusion that there was clearly already significant concern about the possibility.

From the British point of view, once the brief post-war boom had come to an end, it appeared that an industrial economy might prove to have irresolvable problems. As already discussed, these were concentrated for the most part in the ageing industries of the north of England, Wales and central Scotland, where the first signs of trouble appeared almost as soon as the guns on the Western Front had fallen silent. What would come to be known as the "Battle of George Square" – or "Bloody Friday" – took place at the end of January 1919, following the November armistice.

What began as a strike for a shorter working week ended up as a full-scale riot, with running battles between police and some of the estimated

40,000–60,000 strikers. When it became clear that the Glasgow police were unable to quell the riot, by now openly described by its leadership as a "socialist revolution", the then Secretary of State for War, Winston Churchill dispatched 10,000 troops, with tanks, machine guns and a howitzer, in a clear show of force. But the strikers won a ten-hour reduction in their working week.[9]

Whilst many of the members of extreme socialist organisations would be concentrated in areas dominated by the ageing heavy industries, such as Clydeside, this did not prevent a number of them – including some of the leaders of the strike that precipitated the George Square riot – being elected to Parliament. In the 1922 general election, Emanuel Shinwell and David Kirkwood – both of whom had been sentenced to several months in prison following the riot – were elected as Labour MPs; and, in 1935, William Gallacher (who had also spent time in jail after the riot) was elected MP for West Fife, openly representing the CPGB.

Although the CPGB had a presence within the trade union movement, the labour movement, Parliament and even the House of Lords (in the form of Wogan Philipps, 2nd Baron Mitford),[10] the movement never really appeared to be capable of precipitating revolutionary change. There are a number of likely reasons for this, particularly in relation to the drivers for the insecurity cycle. With little clear and credible leadership – and with the steady stream of directives from Moscow – the requisite political support is conspicuous by its absence. Second, the chronic crisis that underpinned the democratic pressure for change was limited to specific parts of the country; by contrast, the experience of those in more prosperous parts of the country was more positive, thereby limiting overall support for revolutionary change.

The "threat" of communism, however, would prove to be a long-term political factor. Not only were the Zinoviev letter and the Campbell affair both perceived as useful weapons against the labour movement in 1924; even after the dissolution of the Soviet Union in 1991 – and the winding up of the CPGB shortly afterwards – the "Red Menace" has still been regularly resurrected for use against Labour Party politicians, few of whom would have come close to the level of commitment to communist principles espoused by William Gallacher.

Britain's fascists, although arguably less conspicuous than their communist counterparts, certainly influenced the debate. According to Hayek, they were considered by many in British academia to be an almost inevitable capitalist response to the threat of socialism or communism – which is one of his reasons for writing *The Road to Serfdom* and for his firm view that government involvement in the economy from either perspective was not something to be desired.

However, Keynes – Hayek's chief protagonist – whilst not having any sympathy for fascism, appeared to have attracted a greater level of support from the new regime in Italy than he had so far managed to garner from the British government. His book *The End of Laissez Faire*, which represented perhaps his most unequivocal work in favour of socialism, was listed as required reading by the League for Industrial Democracy and the Rand School of Social Science in the United States, as well as regularly appearing on the reading lists of Harvard economics and sociology courses. But this did not prevent the adoption of Keynes's ideas by noted fascists. Benito Mussolini, himself, personally set his approval – and signature – over James Stratchey Barnes's book, *Universal Aspects of Fascism*, which bears Mussolini's imprimatur. In it, Barnes (1929) contends:

> [f]ascism entirely agrees with Mr. Maynard Keynes, despite the latter's position as a Liberal. In fact, Mr. Keynes' excellent little book, *The End of Laissez-Faire* (1926) might, as far as it goes, serve as a useful introduction to fascist economics. There is scarcely anything to object to in it, and much to applaud.
>
> (pp. 113–14)

However, a major contributing factor to the failure of either extreme – communist or fascist – to gain a real foothold in Britain, in spite of the succession of dire warnings about the imminent end of capitalism emanating from those on both the left and right during the inter-war years, was an unexpected change of economic fortunes. During the 1930s, even before the economic benefits of a large-scale programme of re-armament became apparent, the chronic crisis that had been at the heart of the problems in Britain – as well as those in Germany, Russia and elsewhere – came to an end with the abandonment of the gold standard in 1931. The resulting sharp drop in interest rates unintentionally sparked recovery and set off a house-building and consumer durables boom, especially in the southern and eastern regions of the country.

Appeasement versus re-armament

Whilst there are many aspects of the debate about the policy of appeasement – and its subsequent agreement to the beginnings of Nazi expansion – from an economic perspective, it is in many ways a reprise of the austerity versus stimulus debate. Austerity measures had hit the defence budget hard, not only as a consequence of attempts by the League of Nations to limit armaments following the carnage of the First World War, but also because money was required to fund the increasing cost of unemployment benefit.

Britain had already been forced off the gold standard before the 1932 Disarmament Conference in Geneva. In the end, the conference achieved little; but when it was re-convened the following year, shortly after Hitler's ascent to the post of Chancellor, it soon became apparent that Germany was preparing to re-arm on a very significant scale.

Whatever the rights and wrongs of the appeasement debate from other perspectives, there can be little doubt that Britain was in no position to fight any kind of significant war. The feeling that there should never be another war like that of 1914–18, followed by resulting attempts at dis-armament, meant that at the time of the conference, not only did the Royal Navy have a shortage of ships, the Royal Air Force was still equipping front line fighter units with open cockpit biplanes, such as the Hawker Fury. It was clear that Britain would have to work out both how to fund new equipment and how to develop the new technologies – and manufacturing facilities – required.

At an early stage, it was also clear that any future war would rely heavily on air power; and by late 1934, the Air Ministry ordered the first Hawker Hurricanes, followed closely by approval for the Supermarine Spitfire in 1936. However, this quickly raised the questions of how to build sufficient of these new aircraft – especially the more complex Spitfire – to equip front line squadrons and to replace those which would inevitably be damaged or destroyed in combat.

The solution was found in the renewal of the partnership between the state and the private sector that had worked so well during the First World War; but this time, it was initiated four years in advance of the outbreak of hostilities, rather than a year afterwards. The "Shadow Factory" system was evolved in 1935 to leverage the technologies and manufacturing skills of the new car manufacturing companies in the Midlands – and to adapt them to aircraft production. The idea was for new facilities to "shadow" the existing car plants, effectively increasing productive capacity where the skills and transport hubs were available, should the need arise. Eventually, the three phases of shadow factory development would result in the extension of the scheme beyond the English Midlands – partly, at least, to put them beyond the range of enemy bombers, but also to spread the employment benefits to other regions of the country.

Even so, despite Keynes's long-standing insistence that new industries should be targeted in areas experiencing the decline of older ones, only one new factory – Hillingdon, in Glasgow – made it as far as Scotland. Whilst Scotland would benefit significantly from the process of re-armament, it would be in the form of work for the old, heavy industries – especially ship building and steel, as a result of the commissioning and rapid construction of the King George V class battleships and the Illustrious class aircraft carriers.

The overall outcome of the re-armament process was a progressive recovery from what had hitherto appeared to be intractable economic difficulties; and, almost by accident, this confirmed some of Keynes's theories about the role of the state in managing the economy and about the significance of effective demand in macroeconomic development. This should perhaps not have come as a surprise, since both the Napoleonic Wars and indeed the "War to end all wars" had produced comparable economic stimuli – as well as unemployment and massive war debts in their wake. Whilst the Second World War would generate a similarly large debt, the Cold War and continued fear of the "Red Menace" would mean the continuation of some of the stimulus, dampening the post-war slump.

Conclusions: "laissez faire" overturned by evidence, not dogma

The years between the two world wars in Britain are characterised by almost constant crises, not a little fear and the emergence of many – and frequently diametrically opposed – new ideas. There was also no shortage of democratic pressure; yet from the point of view of the insecurity cycle, whilst there was plenty of insecurity, surprisingly little changed.

One of the main factors militating against a shift in the cycle is the sheer inconsistency of the pattern. Whilst it was necessary to send 10,000 troops, complete with tanks and a howitzer, to Glasgow within two months of the end of the First World War, to quell large-scale union unrest, in the English Midlands, other union members were too busy making cars and building houses to get involved. As a result, in spite of the increasing polarisation of British politics, the limited extent of industrial action made it possible to resolve such acute crises relatively quickly and decisively; and this served to reinforce the insecurity cycle's existing paradigm and to maintain the tendency towards stability for a time. The reactions to the "Battle of George Square" and the 1926 General Strike are good examples of this.

A second factor reinforcing the status quo is the more random element of fear. From the reactions of the TUC to the CPGB's advice prior to the 1926 General Strike, the *Daily Mail*'s reaction to the apparent intervention of the Comintern, and the effect of the Labour Party's reaction to the Campbell Case all suggest that far more people were inclined to be wary of communism than to embrace it. Following the Second World War, this nervousness would continue through the Cold War; and it persists even now, although it is hard to imagine the early membership of the CPGB being impressed by the socialist credentials of Tony Blair, Ed Miliband or Jeremy Corbyn, in spite of the best efforts of the present day media.

The large number of new and competing ideas may also have militated against change. Like the communists, Sir Oswald Mosley's "New Party", and its successor, the British Union of Fascists, managed to acquire some degree of support; but in the case of the fascists, beyond the membership of a small group of the aristocracy, and in the case of the communists, a small number of MPs, neither managed to engage significant political interest. The limited nature of extreme deprivation also militated against expansion of social unrest and protest, and hence the electoral base for any potentially supportive politician who might otherwise be tempted to take up the cause. In the case of the left, its typically de-centralised leadership also tended to limit the possibility of the emergence of a sufficiently credible political focus to drive electoral change, whilst other workers were doing far too well to be interested in a socialist revolution.

But not everyone was interested in new ideas. Free market capitalism's depressing tendency to produce regular crises and lengthy recessions had, after a short intermission during the war, returned to "normal" with a vengeance.

In this context, rather than attempting to address the problem of unemployment, both the Treasury and the Bank of England appeared prepared to do any damage necessary to the real economy, in order to – as they saw it – "maintain confidence in the currency". This reliance on neo-classical ideas and on the imperative to defend the currency – even to the extent of supporting an over-valued sterling with interest rates well above 8 per cent, whilst simultaneously attempting to balance a budget that included items such as unemployment benefit and war debt with austerity – is a clear example of why the insecurity cycle is so named. As often as not, the cycle is driven by the feelings – usually of insecurity – of interest groups, rather than by actual, logical calculation.

This may serve as part of the explanation as to why, eighty years later, the coalition government led by David Cameron adopted a very similar strategy following the 2008 financial crisis – with comparable effects on the British economy. These policies not only made the slump and depression more severe than they would otherwise have been; they also demonstrate the difficulty that new ideas have in gaining traction. As Keynes (1997 [1936]) himself put it, "the difficulty lies, not in the new ideas, but in escaping from the old ones" (p. xii).

Credible political support appears to be a key element in whether or not paradigm and policy change actually takes place. Whilst Keynesian ideas were deliberately tried during the New Deal with the support of President Roosevelt, in Britain they were confirmed by circumstances instead of deliberate policy choices. A combination of sterling being forced off the gold standard and the extensive (and unavoidable) programme of re-armament achieved what Keynes himself, even as a government advisor, could not.

The inter-war years had, like the nineteenth century, brought with them considerable insecurity, but in the process, surprisingly little change. The welfare state had been modestly developed, but still along very similar lines to the Liberal reforms that followed the industrial revolution, with the real improvement being in the quantity and quality of new housing made available. State involvement in both the economy and labour and industrial relations had been deliberately abandoned after the First World War; and despite the scale of carnage during the war, the new ideas being put forward, and the best efforts of both the Treasury and Comintern to cause trouble, Britain did indeed manage to return to "normal".

However, following another world war, proof of the efficacy of state involvement in the economy, the return of large numbers of people with military experience, and the morphing of the Second World War into the Cold War (with a now nuclear-armed USSR), change was surely on its way. This time, it would have political support from the new Prime Minister, Clement Attlee, and a re-energised Labour Party – as well as a new world order.

Notes

1 See, for example, "Electoral Registers through the Years", on electoralregisters. org website.
2 See, for example, Bennett (1999).
3 See, for example, Perry (2005).
4 As a percentage of GDP, public debt had risen from 25 per cent in 1914 to 182 per cent by 1923, as consequence of the cost of the post-war recession. By 1929, it was down to 160 per cent; but it rose again to 178 per cent by 1933 owing to the Great Depression. But as the economy recovered during the 1930s, the national debt steadily fell as a percentage of GDP, reaching 110 per cent by 1940.
5 Keynes favoured borrowing because in his view, during the 1920s and 1930s, potential savings exceeded domestic investment opportunities. The excess either went abroad or was used by some to consume more than they produce. The excess savings could thus be more productively employed to provide a source of funds for public works. He argued against money creation because, according to Moggridge (1992, p. 464), "in existing circumstance, the Bank of England could not increase the volume of credit because an expansion in credit would tend to reduce the rate of interest and lead to an increase in foreign lending with awkward consequences for the balance of payments".
6 Macgregor *et al.* (1932a and 1932b).
7 Gregory *et al.* (1932).
8 Whereas *The General Theory*, published in 1936, had been concerned with nation-wide macroeconomic aggregates, recognition of the uneven nature of the recovery had moved Keynes's thinking on.
9 See, for example, Gallacher (1920); Glasgow Digital Archives (2017); International Socialist Archives (2006).
10 See, for example, Griffiths (2004).

6 A change of ideology – but capital undermines Keynes

Introduction

Free market capitalism in Britain had had a distinctly torrid time during the inter-war years. Much of the economy had been mired in recession, if not depression. The neo-classically informed policies of the Treasury and the Bank of England had only served to deepen the crisis; and it was not until the policies that the conventional wisdom had predicted would bring financial Armageddon were forced upon Britain that things began to improve.

This had started to move economic thinking in favour of Keynes's ideas – although by no means decisively, as Hayek and his colleagues at the London School of Economics stoutly resisted them. But both the Second World War and the new post-war world order that had been planned for its aftermath eventually settled the matter – for a time.

There had also been little relief for the various interest groups between the wars. Politically, the Liberals had entered a terminal decline, whilst the Labour Party, which had nudged them aside, had problems of its own. A combination of Labour's ill-defined relationship with the Communist Party of Great Britain (CPGB) and an equally ill-advised leaning towards orthodox financial thinking when the pressure was on, had shifted the support of many of the previously Liberal Party voters towards the Conservatives, at least initially.

The workforce had also experienced mixed fortunes, with those employed in the new manufacturing industries in the south and east doing very well. But in large parts of the rest of Britain, where the traditional heavy industries were located, unemployment and poverty were standard fare. The result was a north/south divide and a polarisation in political leanings, with workers who were doing better opting for political leaders and parties likely to provide stability, whilst those in the north of England, Wales and parts of Scotland looking for altogether more radical policies. This would not only bring their unions into conflict with employers – and frequently the government as well – but the CPGB would also continue to find backing.

As a result, on the eve of war, the competing and frequently fractious interest groups that keep the insecurity cycle moving were eying each other warily. However, the imperative – for most, at least – of winning another "industrial" war would, just as it had before, result in a much higher degree of cooperation than usual. This approach, along with Keynesian policies, would prove effective in managing the war effort; but whether it was as effective a driver of change as the depressing days of the inter-war period – which had produced a "we're not going back to that!" attitude on the part of the electorate that would ultimately result in the replacement of Britain's inspirational wartime leader, Churchill, with one that aimed to win the peace – would be a moot point.

But no matter how good one or more interest groups might believe life to be, there is always at least one that feels otherwise. So whilst it may appear that the insecurity cycle is approaching its point of stability, it is not likely to linger there for long.

The Second World War: social, political and economic management of the crisis

As the Second World War approached, there was greater consensus than there had been in 1914 that this was a justifiable war against fascism, with the main opposition coming from the communists – until Hitler's invasion of Russia in 1941. This consensus – and the general fear of invasion and defeat – contributed to an unprecedented tolerance of state direction and control; and by the time the war broke out in 1939, it was clear that the government had learned many of the lessons of the First World War. Conscription was operating even before the outbreak of war; and the TUC General Council had been consulted about which workers should be granted reserved occupation status.

The events of the inter-war years meant that Britain entered the Second World War with substantial economic and financial regulations already in place; and industries which were to prove central to the war effort had been revitalised by the 1930s recovery. This was built upon by the wartime government – a coalition of the Conservative, Labour and Liberal parties led by Winston Churchill, on which Neville Chamberlain, Clement Attlee and Archibald Sinclair were invited to serve. Widespread controls over productive capability and industrial production were instituted. Restrictions were imposed on civilian trade and consumption, both to ensure that all necessary supplies were directed to the war effort and to avoid the levels of price inflation that had caused so much tension during the First World War; and rationing of food and other basic consumer goods was introduced to ensure fair distribution. Labour and capital movements were restricted; and dilution agreements in key industries were worked out very early on.

Ernest Bevin, Minister of Labour – and the unions

In 1940, upon Clement Attlee's advice, Churchill appointed Ernest Bevin, a founding member of the powerful Transport and General Workers' Union (TGWU), to the post of Minister for Labour and National Service. Although having been a trade union representative, in his new role, Bevin did not see himself as such; and he readily consulted his counterparts in government as well as employers and managers. He negotiated with other ministries about food subsidies, rationing and price controls; and persuaded the Treasury to raise the excess profits tax to 100 per cent (Middlemas 1986, p. 20).

Under the Emergency Powers (Defence) Act, Bevin was assigned complete control over the labour force and allocation of manpower; and he was determined to use this authority not only to help win the war but also to improve wages and working conditions and to strengthen the bargaining position of trade unions in the post-war future (Borth 1945, p. 74). This was quite different from the aims of Lloyd George and the unions during the First World War, where both owners and trade unions had looked forward to the lifting of wartime labour regulations and a "return to normal" upon the war's end. Although the coercive powers of the 1940–5 wartime government were greater than they had been during the First World War, the basis of cooperation was similar, including a ban on strikes and lockouts, which was not lifted until 1951, strict penalties for unofficial strikes and compulsory arbitration. These powers though, were rarely exercised due to a strong preference for avoiding disputes (Fraser 1999, p. 187).

Direction of labour to "essential work" and restrictions on leaving work were among the first policies Bevin introduced; but instead of assigning control over these decisions to employers, he put them into the hands of national service officers (Fraser 1999, p. 185). Bevin also set up the Factory and Welfare Advisory Board to assist in the delivery of significant improvements in wages and working conditions, with particular attention to sanitation, health and safety and employee welfare in factories. Canteens and personnel departments were set up; and money was provided to local authorities to develop day nurseries (McIvor 2000). Bevin also turned his attention to dealing with the problem of casual work in the docks; and in 1940, compulsory registration of a permanent dock labour force with a guaranteed minimum amount of pay was introduced, and dockers were required to move between ports as required.

Bevin demanded – and was granted – powers for the Ministry of Labour and National Service (MLNS) to assist in organising production (Middlemas 1986, p. 20); and out of the largely advisory National Joint Advisory Council (NJAC), he constructed his active governing body, the Joint Consultative Committee (JCC), which was composed of seven representatives each from management and the trade unions (Middlemas 1986, p. 21). Labour-management cooperation was encouraged in finding ways of improving efficiencies in the use of machinery, materials and work methods; and trade union members became heavily involved in productivity committees, the first of which were organised in Woolwich Arsenal at the initiative of the shop stewards. Organised workers' direct involvement in increasing output was given a boost when Germany attacked Russia and the Communist Party of Great Britain committed itself fully to higher efficiency and increased production. By 1944, over

4,500 Joint Production Committees had been set up to deal with questions of production, working conditions and work discipline (Harling 2001, p. 158).

In this context, shop stewards again emerged as key figures in dealing with shop floor reorganisation and over-seeing the improved working and welfare conditions which were being introduced. But given the way that many of the drivers of the insecurity cycle function, many workers were inevitably suspicious of their representatives becoming spokesmen for management, rather than the shop floor, giving rise to a feeling that management would be the primary beneficiaries of these ideas (Fraser 1999, p. 188).

Although strikes and lock-outs were legally prohibited under statutory Order 1305, both trade unions and collective bargaining were actively encouraged. Employers that had previously resisted unions came under pressure to recognise them – and trade unions began to appear in traditionally unorganised sectors, including the smaller engineering works. Trade union organisation and orderly industrial relations were fostered by the setting up of the National Arbitration Tribunal, to which unresolved disputes could be referred, and whose settlements were legally binding. No official attempts were made to directly control wages, but moderation in wage demands was voluntarily accepted by the trade unions. In return, prices of items heavily weighted in the index of retail prices were controlled and subsidies were used to keep down the cost of living (Jones 1987). Wages and prices did rise between 1939 and 1945, but by much less than during the First World War.

However, Order 1305 did not stop strikes, with both these and absenteeism remaining a problem throughout the war – in fact there were more strikes in the eleven years during which the order operated than the previous twenty. There were almost as many strikes in 1940 as 1939; and the number continued to rise year upon year. But they were of short duration, with the days lost being fewer than ever before – roughly one-third of those lost during the First World War – and only 109 prosecutions (Fraser 1999, p. 186; Middlemas 1986, p. 31). There was a strong view – which Bevin himself held – that communists and Trotskyists were behind the disputes, especially those on Clydeside and among the miners (Fraser 1999, p. 189). This served as the motivation for Regulation 1AA, instituted in April 1944 with the support of the TUC, making incitement to strike an offence. But it was never used and immediately repealed upon the war's end.

The TUC's General Council – in return for Bevin's "political charter, to carry the assent of 'labour' " – approved all Ministry of Labour orders (Middlemas 1986, p. 20). According to Middlemas (1986):

> Here was a golden age of industrial relations, when the TUC's goodwill could be taken for granted, when a Minister ruled who did not need educating, when officials would oversee and control the national labour market as never before or since – an age to which subsequent officials looked back with nostalgia, even longing.
>
> (p. 45)

Labour, finance and industry

To assist the war effort, a "quasi-corporatist" structure quickly developed, in which a dense consultative network of industrialists, trade unionists and state officials negotiated issues relating to production, working conditions and discipline at work (Harling 2001, pp. 157–8). But – in contrast to the trade unions, which had access to a single minister in the MLNS, and City institutions, which directed themselves to the Treasury – British industry was fragmented along functional lines, between the Ministries of Supply, Aircraft Production, Transport, Trade, Food and Defence (Middlemas 1986, pp. 29–30).

The trade union movement was thus fully incorporated into the war effort, in a role mirroring that of industry and finance; but in many respects it was in a privileged position. Manpower was designated *the* essential resource – above industrial production and finance. According to Middlemas (1986): "In order of priority – and priorities were essential – manpower came first, followed by production, then finance; an exact inversion of the 1930s pecking order which was soon reflected in the machine of government itself" (p. 20). In this context, the TUC had a direct link to the War Council and the main department of state.

However, political organisations were largely excluded from the wartime system, particularly during the extreme crisis, from May 1940 through early 1943. As a consequence, the tri-partite relationship between the trade unions, industry and the state tended to downgrade the Labour Party relative to the TUC; and during the war "Bevin was deputy Prime Minister in all but name, with greater authority than Attlee, the Party leader" (Middlemas 1986, p. 42).

Wartime finance

Britain's need to survive dictated the pattern of wartime finance; and by 1939, it was agreed that this would be a "cheap money" war, with high levels of taxation instead of war loans (Middlemas 1986, p. 26). Both direct and indirect taxes were increased, with taxes roughly trebling over the course of the war (Harling 2001, p. 158) and many wage earners paying income tax for the first time. But the tax system was steeply progressive, and the heaviest burden fell upon the wealthiest members of society. The result was to increase revenues whilst at the same time reducing inflation.

The war was also financed by the issue of Treasury Bills, making the banks potentially highly liquid. Thus, to secure monetary control, the government required the banks to deposit investible funds not committed to the war effort with the Treasury. This measure was also designed to reduce demand pressure on scarce resources, thereby stifling inflationary pressure.

The sterling area – a group of countries that either pegged their currencies to the pound sterling (instead of gold) or used the pound as their own currency – was another important pillar of wartime finance. The sterling area had developed informally during the 1930s, following Britain's abandonment of the gold standard in 1931. But early in the war, emergency legislation united the bloc (except Hong Kong) into a single exchange control area with the objective of protecting the value of the pound. In this context, the Bank of England guided the coordination of monetary policy; all internal transactions were free, all external transactions were tightly controlled and capital outflow was forbidden. According to Middlemas (1986):

> this financial and diplomatic achievement was remarkable. Its value to Britain's survival can scarcely be measured: the monetary union minimised Britain's dependence on dollar reserves, and helped hold the pound until 1949, after its initial fall to $4.03 at the outbreak of war.
>
> (p. 27)

Shortages of dollars had been endemic from the start; and Britain soon became dependent upon the US for supplies, but did not have the foreign exchange to pay for them. The means of maintaining the flow of food, oil and materiel (including warships, warplanes and other weaponry) from America was found in "lend-lease" – "the provision of supplies to Britain not in exchange for money but acknowledged by some 'consideration' to be negotiated later" (Moggridge 1992, p. 652);[1] and it was agreed that the bill for lend-lease would not become payable until the war's end.

Britain also accumulated substantial wartime debts with countries of the Commonwealth, which were held as off-shore holdings of inconvertible sterling both to protect Britain's gold and currency reserves, and to prevent them being used to buy imports from Britain, whose productive capacity was fully engaged in the war effort.

Fiscal policy

The greatly increased tax burden, introduced to help finance the war, also had the effect of limiting inflation by reducing consumer demand. The commitment to fighting inflation encouraged the coalition government to pioneer the "Keynesian" strategy of using the national budget to regulate both investment and consumption. In *How to Pay for the War*, John Maynard Keynes (1940) argued that the war effort should be financed largely through increased taxation and compulsory saving, rather than deficit spending. Both could be expected to dampen demand, thereby limiting inflation and helping to channel output to the war effort – with compulsory saving having the additional benefit of boosting demand at the end of the war, when savings could be withdrawn, thereby helping to mitigate a post-war slump.

In September 1941, Keynes's name was put forward to join the Bank of England's Court of Directors; and he subsequently became a member of the Chancellor of the Exchequer's consultative council, carrying out a full term from the following April (Mynors 1941 and 1942). With Keynes fully installed at the Bank of England, the Treasury began to experiment with demand management techniques, using the 1941 budget to regulate prices and spending, thereby supporting industrial production and employment (Middlemas 1986, pp. 32–3). Although compulsory savings and an excess earnings tax were discussed, the budget instead introduced post-war credits as recognition for the higher taxes paid by the public in support of the war effort. By using the budget to attempt to manage the general level of demand during the war, the British state assumed greater responsibility for the direction of the economy than ever before; and it was able to test Keynes's ideas about the ability of the government to manage the economy successfully.

Wartime planning for the welfare state

As the war progressed, enthusiasm for planning extended well beyond economic management – to the idea that the state also had a role to play in improving the quality of life for its citizens (Harling 2001, pp. 159–60); and from early on, not only did all three political parties form reconstruction committees, professional and other groups developed schemes of their own.

Despite severe resource constraints, significant social service provisions were instituted during the Second World War. These included school meals, nurseries for working mothers, cheap milk for children and nursing mothers, and the introduction of canteens, doctors and welfare workers into factories. Looking back, Richard Titmuss wrote in 1950:

> It would, in any relative sense, be true to say that by the end of the war the government had, through the agency newly established or existing services, assumed a measure of direct concern for the health and well-being of the population which, by contrast with the role of the government in the nineteen thirties, was little short of remarkable.
>
> (p. 506)

The 1942 Beveridge report on *Social Insurance and Allied Services* looked forward to a significantly improved national health service and social security system during the post-war period, with the explicit aims of avoiding mass unemployment and eradicating poverty. William Beveridge, the committee's chairman – who had been a researcher for the Webb's Royal Commission on the Poor Laws before the First World War – played a central role in researching and writing the report, which proved to be enormously popular. Within the first month of publication, over 100,000 copies were sold and it was widely discussed at public meetings throughout the country, with a special edition being published for the armed forces (Harling 2001, p. 160). The Beveridge Report was followed in 1944 by the White Paper on Employment which committed the post-war government to Keynesian demand management and dedicated itself to a radical reform of education (Morgan 2001, pp. 5, 6 and 14).

The welfare state programme and commitment to full employment proved very popular and the Labour Party actively campaigned for its introduction immediately after the war. The Conservative Party, concerned about the cost of Beveridge's and other social reforms – and more generally about increased state intervention in the economy – was more cautious. Early in 1943, Churchill laid down the principle of "all for the war, and nothing not for the war", to prevent the debate about post-war reconstruction from hindering the war effort (Middlemas 1986, p. 32); and he ruled that while plans for social reform could be developed, decisions would have to wait until the first post-war general election. As a result, a series of White Papers on post-war policy was issued by the coalition government, but very little legislation was passed.

Nevertheless, full employment and the promise of radically improved social services, a start to which had been made despite wartime stringencies, were no doubt of major importance in motivating the war effort, as were the "we are all in this together" spirit they engendered. An important part of this was the high level of cooperation at the shop floor to increase productivity, which closely involved union shop stewards, especially after the Soviet Union joined the war against Germany.

But it would be wrong to suppose that the high levels of wartime cooperation and worker involvement meant that bitter memories of the inter-war years had been forgotten. The broad consensus within the working class was that "we are not going back to how it had been before the war". This revealed itself in inter-party differences within the wartime coalition government about the direction of post-war social and economic policy, and by the unpopularity of the Conservatives despite the very high rating given to Churchill as a war leader.

The scepticism about the Conservative Party was revealed by the significant fall in their share of the vote in successive wartime by-elections, and the four seats they lost between 1943 and 1945 (Addison 1994, p. 249). It also emerged in attitudes of the rank and file of the victorious British Army in North Africa expressed in proceedings of the Cairo Parliament. This was organised by the Army Bureau of Current Affairs, to keep the soldiers "abreast of currents affairs" (Baker 1989, p. 15). A mock election was held, with individuals standing as candidates for political parties. The Labour Party won an absolute majority and proposed a radical socialist programme for post-war Britain; this included plans to nationalise the Bank of England and financial institutions, increased pensions, equality of opportunity in education, the building of 4 million houses over the next ten years, and an Atlantic Charter together with an Anglo Soviet Alliance. As a consequence of the radicalism of the debate and the resolution, the Cairo Parliament was suppressed by the Army High Command; and Leo Abse, a left-wing activist in the Cairo Parliament, who had made the offending proposals, was arrested and posted out of Egypt.[2] But news of this was leaked to London and raised in Parliament.

There is also evidence that despite the appearance of social solidarity, some were getting weary of the sacrifices of war and losing patience with having to suffer them for the "public good". Harling (2001) draws attention to "widespread efforts to sidestep wartime rationing restrictions, growing popular resentment of bureaucratic interference in daily life, the gradual rise in the frequency of unofficial strikes, [and] surging resentment within the military about the growing pay differentials between civilians and members of the armed services" (pp. 160–1), suggesting that these lend support to the idea that the vision within society for major post-war social reform may have been exaggerated.

The 1945 general election – Clement Attlee as an "electable socialist"

With the Second World War approaching its end in Europe, the Labour Party pulled out of the wartime coalition government in May 1945; and King George VI dissolved Parliament, which had been sitting without an election for the preceding ten years. Churchill thus returned to lead a "caretaker" government for the duration of the election campaign.

Many observers at the time believed that the Conservatives, under the leadership of the war hero Churchill, would be unbeatable – as David Lloyd George had been in 1918. This is despite the publication of opinion polls showing a Labour lead. As it turned out, the position of the Labour Party had changed dramatically during the war. Labour MPs had served as ministers for key ministries within the national government; and Attlee was Churchill's Deputy Prime Minister. As a consequence, Labour had gained valuable experience in government and was seen by voters to have performed with considerable competence.

The Labour manifesto, *Let Us Face the Future*, proposed a radical departure from the past, including comprehensive social security, a national health service and the nationalisation of major industries. By contrast, the Conservatives' campaign – under the slogan "Vote National – Help him finish the job" – revolved around Churchill's personal popularity. Much of its rhetoric focused on the alleged threat that Labour's proposals posed to Britain's democratic institutions, even though the policies outlined in the Conservative manifesto, *A Declaration of Policy to the Electors*, were very similar to Labour's, with their chief differences revolving around the issues of nationalisation and maintenance of wartime controls.

Voting took place on 5 July 1945, but to allow time for the collection of ballot boxes from servicemen overseas, the votes were not counted until 25 July. When Labour's victory was announced the following day, it took the country – Attlee and Churchill included – by surprise. Labour won by a landslide – with 393 seats and an overall majority of 183 in the House of Commons. The Conservatives lost nearly 200 seats in the House of Commons, dropping from 387 to 197. The Liberal Party also lost badly, with

Sinclair, the party leader, losing his seat and the number of Liberal seats being reduced to just twelve.

Whilst the vote probably represented a rejection of the Conservative Party rather than Churchill as a war leader, war weariness among civilians and the armed forces was also likely to have played a role – as did memories of the inter-war years, which had been dominated by Conservative governments – and to which no one wanted to return. According to Harling (2001, pp. 161–2), "there was a widespread perception that the Conservatives were the 'guilty men' who had presided over the appeasement and economic stagnation of the 1930s, a perception that trumped Churchill's popularity".

By contrast, Labour's success was almost certainly related to confidence in its ability to build the optimistic and hope-filled post-war world to which so many had looked forward during the darkest days of war.

The country's popular mood with the cessation of hostilities thus found its expression in the Labour Party's landslide election victory in the 1945 general election, in which the armed forces' vote played an important part. The Labour party came to power fully committed to Keynesian full employment policies and the creation of the welfare state. However, as the insecurity cycle is dynamic, rather tending towards equilibrium, it too would soon face severe challenges, not least being the very high level of Government debt.

The state steps in again – with wide political and democratic support

The Labour governments of 1945–50 and 1950–1 took advantage of the buoyant post-war atmosphere – which presented an unparalleled opportunity to commit the state's expanded capacity to the provision of a broad range of social services – and they ultimately proved themselves successful in implementing the most ambitious interventionist programme in British history.

The National Insurance Act of 1946 embodied most of Beveridge's proposals; this, together with the introduction of a modest family allowance, came close to providing the "national minimum standard" that had been the objective of the Liberal social reformers, nearly four decades earlier. In line with earlier reforms, it was a contributory scheme; but it was also universal, based on Beveridge's contention that social insurance should be a right of citizenship.

The universal right to tax-supported medical services accompanied the establishment of the National Health Service (NHS) in 1948. In this, Aneurin Bevan, Labour's Minister of Health, had struck a compromise with the British Medical Association (BMA) by which the professional autonomy and relative pay of doctors would be protected – at the same time as the government got most of its objectives. The NHS would be funded by a contributory scheme, with the Exchequer playing a central role; hospitals would be nationalised; and regional boards and councils as well as municipally run health centres would be set-up. Not only would the NHS be the "world's most comprehensive health service, [it would be] the *only* one expressly committed to achieving equality in the distribution and use of health care" (Harling 2001, p. 163, emphasis in the original).

Labour was also committed to a significant expansion of public housing; and local authorities were given sizeable Exchequer subsidies to support the government's ambitious campaign. Unfortunately, this fell short of Bevan's vision due to persistent bad weather and shortages of labour, material and credit; and only 800,000 dwellings were constructed by 1951. But by dedicating local and central government to this plan in a difficult fiscal and economic environment, Labour provided what would turn out to be the beginning of a long-term effort to improve the quality of life for British citizens by increasing and improving the country's stock of housing (Pelling 1984, pp. 110–13; Morgan 1985, pp. 163–70).

Another long-standing objective of the Labour Party, which was achieved under the 1945–51 Attlee governments was a programme of nationalisation – and this period saw state management of industry rise to about a fifth of the economy with nationalisation of the Bank of England; coal, electricity and gas; cable and wireless; civil aviation, railways, road and transport; and iron and steel. The government also delivered on its commitment to create jobs throughout the country, supported by the 1945 Distribution of Industry Act, which provided financial incentives to set up new plants in less prosperous regions, including Scotland and the northeast.

Despite these impressive achievements, and the improvements in longer-term social security they delivered – *and* the economic recovery that had been realised as a consequence of the government's strict containment of the consumer-goods sector of the economy and maintenance of wartime levels of taxation – there is evidence that many had grown weary of the self-sacrifice required by state-imposed austerity. According to Philip Harling (2001): "Despite its legislative and rhetorical efforts, Labour in power was unable to mould the electorate into community-spirited citizens who were willing to tolerate long-term discomfort for the sake of a rather vague notion of the public good" (p. 165).

The Labour government was also beginning to lose many of its original cabinet ministers, including Ernest Bevin, to old age; at the same time, the Conservatives – due to the 1950 general election that had returned the Labour Party to government by a slim majority – appeared fresher, with an influx of new MPs.

The 1951 general election was held just twenty months after the 1950 general election, following the King's expression of concern about leaving the country for his 1952 Commonwealth tour due to the danger of a change of government in his absence (Judd 2012, p. 238). In response – and in the hope of increasing the Party's Parliamentary majority – Attlee called the election. But despite winning the popular vote, the Labour Party lost to the Conservatives, who won the most seats; and Churchill became Prime Minister.

However, despite disagreements about the details of economic management and taxation, the Conservatives largely perpetuated the policy direction that had been initiated by the Labour governments of 1945–1. The government continued its commitment to full employment and accepted responsibility for fostering and controlling economic growth; it also committed itself to strengthening social security. However, as Harling (2001) points out, the post-war state

> did not attempt to reshape the structure of British society on radically egalitarian terms. The Labour governments and their successors greatly shored up the basis of social security, but neither they nor most of their constituents were interested in using the powers of the state to transform what was still a markedly class-conscious and hierarchical society.
>
> (p. 170)

Post-war economics: "Keynesianism" in action

The lessons in economic theory and policy learned by failures to counter the social and economic costs of unrestricted markets during the inter-war years led to a commitment by the 1945 Labour government to full employment and a welfare state; initiatives which laid the foundations for post-war prosperity. Following Keynes, expanding government expenditure and increased state intervention in the labour market found wide acceptance amongst economists. Expanded education and training, improved social welfare provision, greater job security and higher labour standards were welcomed because they contributed to human capital formation, effective job search and more efficient labour utilisation. It was also recognised that general well-being enhanced economic performance by not only increasing the quantity and quality of labour input; it also underpinned economic progress from the demand side by enhancing the standard of life and encouraging the development and diffusion of new products. At both the individual and economy-wide levels expanding resources and improving capabilities interacted in a virtuous cycle of rising economic performance. In turn, the viability of the welfare state was guaranteed as the necessary redistribution could be made with minimal political risk as real incomes rose, and as full employment reduced social welfare dependency.

The importance of trade unions to effectively represent workers' interests and to counter the monopoly power of employers was also acknowledged. The Attlee government acted quickly to repeal the 1927 Trade Disputes and Trade Union Act; and the 1945 Wages Council Act provided better protection for poorly organised workers. But Order 1305 was continued and the restoration of pre-war activities was delayed. The new government also perpetuated the tri-partite system of joint consultation with employers and trade unions; and the unions were increasingly involved in policy-making and integrated into the organisations and institutions which were charged with developing and improving the working of the economy and the welfare state. In turn, economic, social and democratic pressures combined in the upgrading of the labour force, a process that particularly benefited those in the lower ranks of the labour market.

External economic relations

Although Keynesianism and the welfare state promised greater social and industrial accord, the immediate post-war period soon revealed problems with the delivery of wartime aspirations. The most immediate problem facing the 1945 Labour government was that the wartime effort had virtually bankrupted Britain. Keynes estimated that Britain's overseas deficit during the post-war transition period would be between £1,500 and £2,250 million (plus the bill for lend-lease), and he argued that the most economically effective way of bridging this gap was by securing a loan from America. Meanwhile, the ending of hostilities bought the lease-lend to an end, so that the bill for it became due immediately.

Much of the deficit was in US dollars for payments due for lend-lease and other means by which US supplies had been financed during the war. Britain had also accumulated substantial wartime debts with countries of the Commonwealth; and after the war, the pressure on Britain to repay its wartime debts mounted as exchange controls were relaxed and the Commonwealth countries became more independent.

Temporary measures thus needed to be put into place to bridge this balance of payments chasm whilst a permanent solution could be found. The major sticking point in the subsequent negotiations was the US's insistence on a rapid return to financial orthodoxy in international relations, requiring full convertibility of currencies and an end to trade and currency restrictions – an insistence that paid scant regard to the run-down state of Britain's post-war economy.

After protracted negotiations, a £3.75 billion US loan was agreed in November 1945, together with a scheme to repay the lend-lease debt. But this deal also committed Britain to trade liberalisation and the restoration of sterling convertibility by July 1947. The implementation of these conditions in 1947 triggered a major foreign exchange crisis and a massive run on sterling with significant depletion of Britain's gold and foreign currency reserves. The crisis was ended by a suspension of convertibility in July 1947, accompanied by substantial cuts in British public expenditure.[3]

The 1947 international financial crisis was a harbinger of Britain's major post-war economic problems. The large holdings of sterling abroad that had been accumulated to pay for the war were liberated; and together with gold and dollars they became widely used as an international currency, both as a means of exchange in foreign trade and as a reserve currency. With the liberalisation of international trade and payments, international currency speculation was revived, posing a significant threat to the stability of the US and the

UK, whose currencies were used as an international means of exchange and held as reserves by other countries. Concerns about the economic and/or financial performance of either country resulted in speculation against their currency and a threat to their fixed exchange rate. It became standard practice for a country whose currency was under speculative threat to turn to other counties and/or the IMF for support, which almost inevitably brought requirements that the recipient take measures to reduce pressure on their economy by deflating effective demand. As a consequence, growth in the British economy followed a "stop/go" pattern, around a long-term path of relative decline.

Economic performance

The British economy was also badly run-down by the war effort. In the early years of the war, production had expanded at an unprecedented rate; and by 1943 real GDP was a third higher than it had been in 1938. However, by then Britain had reached the limit of its capability. In 1945, when the war ended, real GDP was 90 per cent of its 1943 level; by 1947 real GDP had fallen further to 86 per cent of its 1943 high; and it was not until 1953 that real GDP returned to its 1943 level.

Notwithstanding the difficulties it faced, the Attlee government established principles followed by all British governments until the 1970s. It introduced the welfare state, adopted Keynesianism by using monetary and fiscal policies to secure full employment and to counter demand inflation, and introduced incomes policies to counter wage cost inflation. The most pressing problem in the post-war period remained the need to generate sufficient foreign exchange to meet the bill for essential imports – a continuation, if more pressing, of the difficulties faced in the 1930s. Nevertheless, by the late 1940s the trade balance had improved from −2.9 per cent of GDP in 1947 to +2.6 per cent in 1950 as a consequence of an export drive, the control of demand (and especially imports) by the continuation of wartime consumer goods rationing which became more stringent after than during the war, and a 30 per cent devaluation of the pound from $4.00 to $2.80.

Inflation was officially regarded as the major threat to economic stability during the years immediately after the war. The rate of increase in earnings accelerated from 4 per cent in 1946 to 9 per cent in 1948; and this wage pressure was intensified by the 1949 devaluation of sterling against the dollar by 30 per cent. This triggered a rise in sterling import prices which was passed on to domestic prices. In response, the Attlee Labour government, facing increasing inflationary pressure, opted to counter it by restricting wages increases.[4]

Post-war wage restraint evolved as the inflationary pressure intensified: Stage 1 (1945 to 1948) saw the publication by the government of *A Statement on the Economic Considerations Affecting the Relationship between Employers and Workers*, although little in the way of active policy was initiated beyond regular government exhortations for moderation in wage bargaining. Stage 2 (1948–9) began with publication of the *Statement on Personal, Costs and Price* and a government call for a voluntary freeze of both wage rates and incomes from profit, rents and other sources. At the insistence of the TUC, exceptions to the wage freeze were extended to particularly low wages and to those required for the maintenance of customary wage differentials. Stage 3 (1949–50), in the context of a devaluation of the pound, began with a request by the government for a six-month extension of the pay freeze and a widening of its scope to preserve the cost advantage of the sterling devaluation and free up resources for the export drive. Stage 4 (1950–1) was rather more ambitious. The government requested a long-term wage freeze on the grounds that inflation had replaced unemployment as the main economic problem. Therefore, wage control needed to become a permanent feature of full employment economic strategies. Proposals were made for setting up a Wage Advisory Body; but the TUC refused to sanction any advisory committee on wages and did not think that formal wage restraint was acceptable without rigid price control. Stage 5 (1951) consisted of a proposal for the strengthening of price control and the announcement of a statutory limitation of company dividends in the hope that this would create the right atmosphere for wage restraint. The Attlee wage policy proved successful in bringing down the rate of inflation from 9 per cent in 1948 to 5 per cent in 1950.

The return of a Conservative government in 1951 bought to an end these developments in incomes policies, although the Attlee wage policy provided both a template for future developments of incomes policies by proposing the need for statutory control of wage determination, and an institutional framework to oversee wage and price policy. It also signalled a switch from unemployment to inflation as the primary focus of macroeconomic policy, and the phasing out of rationing, which finally ended in 1954.

The 1950s consolidated Keynesianism as the dominant influence on British macroeconomic policy. Inflation became less of a problem as world prices fell after 1952, and by the end of the 1950s retail prices were more or less stable. For much of the 1950s and 1960s Keynesian inspired macroeconomic policy was dominated by hands-on government management of the economy – using various combinations of fiscal, monetary and income policies designed to secure non-inflationary, full employment growth. Experiments were also made with economic planning designed to restructure the economy and stimulate output growth.

Keynesian economics offered the possibility of managing the economy in such a way as to secure, generalise and advance prosperity; and both Conservative and Labour governments used a mix of policies to *fine tune* the economy to secure non-inflationary, full employment growth. However, this prized objective proved difficult to achieve as attempts to improve economic performance were brought to a halt by accelerating inflation and unsupportable balance of payment deficits. Economic retrenchment usually secured the objectives of slowing inflation and improving the external balance; but only at the cost of politically unacceptable levels of unemployment which prompted policy reversal. The *stop stage* in this stop/go cycle included variable packages of policy measures, including raising the bank rate,[5] hire purchase restrictions,[6] increases in taxation and cuts in public sector expenditure, restrictions on bank lending to the private sector, and restriction in wage and price increase. These policies were reversed, usually more piecemeal than they had been introduced, in the *go stage* of the policy cycle (Radcliffe Committee 1959, chapter IV; Kaldor 1986). Nevertheless, by historical and more recent standards, joblessness remained low. Between 1951 and 1960 unemployment rates ranged from 1.8 to 3.0 per cent averaging 2.4 per cent; and between 1961 and 1970 they ranged from 2.1 to 3.7 per cent averaging 2.9 per cent.

During this period, especially 1952–60, macroeconomic performance was characterised by full-employment, non-inflationary growth and rapidly rising living standards; and this was considered "the golden age" of post-war economic history. It is nevertheless important to recognise that the successes of post-war governments in delivering economic prosperity were in part a consequence of external factors, including aid delivered by the Marshall Plan and the strength of the American post-war boom; whilst the avoidance of a post-war slump can be attributed to the continuation of defence spending as the Second World War morphed into the Cold War. In retrospect, Britain's golden age was perhaps less lustrous than it seemed at the time, especially when set against what was happening in other industrial countries. But for the majority of British people, relative stability and contentment compared well with the turbulent inter-war years and the traumas of the Second World War.

Meanwhile, back in the City...

Like the rest of the British economy, the City of London emerged from the war into a changed world. Quite apart from the rapid dissolution of the British Empire, the Bretton Woods system established a restrictive and closely regulated system for international finance and ushered in an era of managed currencies. Its chief architects, John Maynard Keynes and Harry Dexter White, had been key witnesses to the destabilising effects of what Keynes described as the "massive, sweeping and highly capricious transfers of short-term funds" (quoted in Burn 2006, p. 51) that had precipitated the international financial crises of the 1930s and brought an end to the gold standard. The Attlee government, too, recognised the importance of a stable financial system and had set out its plan for domestic finance more closely focused on economic requirements: "The Bank of England with its financial powers must be brought under public ownership, and the operations of the other banks harmonised with industrial needs" (Labour Party Manifesto 1945).

However, in spite of all of this, London's financial sector would show both agility and inventiveness that would make its industrial counterparts look positively leaden-footed. It would also demonstrate the ability to side-step any symbiotic relationship between finance and industry. This dynamism may well explain why pragmatic politicians, with a view to quick results, tended in practice to prioritise the interests of finance over those of industry, with perhaps unintended but nevertheless far-reaching consequences.

The 1929 stock market crash had produced a more sceptical approach to financial services, with the Treasury assuming greater control over monetary affairs. Since the financial community was held responsible for the turmoil, reform focused on stricter control of domestic financial markets and on limiting the power of financiers and the Bank of England (Helleiner 1994, p. 32). As US Treasury Department Secretary, Henry Morgenthau, told the conference at Bretton Woods, the objective was "to drive the usurious money lenders from the temple of international finance ... [and] move the financial centre of the world from London and Wall Street to the US [and HM] Treasury" (quoted in Gardner 1980, p. 76). The Treasury thus assumed responsibility for monetary policy and for regulating building societies, friendly societies and trustee savings banks; the Board of Trade was made responsible for securities and insurance regulation; and the newly nationalised Bank of England was given the task of keeping the banks in order. However, according to Morgan (1985), nationalisation of the Bank of England was a great "non-event", with little real effect on its traditional relationship with the City.

As memories of the stock market crash and Great Depression faded, and as high levels of employment and rising living standards were achieved, the atmosphere of caution gave way to one of confidence and innovation, which gradually overwhelmed concerns about the need for regulating and stabilising finance. During the 1950s, a number of developments, facilitated by the Conservative Macmillan government's desire to return to peace-time normality, progressively loosened restrictions on financial markets (Reid 1982). Credit controls were eased; and in October 1958, hire purchase controls were eliminated, paving the way for the emergence of an effectively unregulated shadow banking system and fuelling a credit-funded consumer boom.

The City was also quick to exploit international opportunities. The 1950s saw the emergence and rapid growth of the unregulated London Eurodollar and sterling wholesale money markets, which provided a means of circumventing the Bretton Woods system (Burn 2006). The Eurodollar market was regulation-free, created by merchant and overseas bankers in London, for the exchange of foreign currencies, primarily US dollars. The Marshall Plan for rebuilding post-war Europe had resulted in an enormous increase in US dollars (Eurodollars) held by foreign companies and countries, creating the need for a market for their exchange. During the Cold War, London became the preferred centre for Eurodollar activities – especially for the Soviet Union (Helleiner 1994, pp. 81–100).

When the Midland Bank first began bidding for Eurodollar deposits in 1955, discussions took place about possible violations of the spirit of exchange control legislation (Schenk 2004). However, since such dealings were not illegal, attracted dollars to London (helping to alleviate the balance of payments deficit) and helped raise the status of sterling as an international currency, they were welcomed by the Bank of England. But as the Eurodollar market expanded, concerns were raised about possible risks. When Sir Charles Hambro of Hambros Bank approached the Bank of England to express his disquiet in 1963, the Bank bluntly responded:

> It is par excellence an example of the kind of business which London ought to be able to do both well and profitably. That is why we, at the Bank, have never seen any reason to place any obstacles in the way of London taking its full and increasing share … If we were to stop the business here, it would move to other countries with a consequent loss of earnings for London.
>
> (Burn 1999, p. 241)

The absence of regulation of the Eurodollar and sterling wholesale markets encouraged the migration of foreign banks and bankers to London as the City internationalised (Schenk 2004). It also set precedents for other unregulated markets. The growth of wholesale money markets, attracting funds from industrial and commercial institutions, served to further augment London's standing as an international centre of finance. Not only was it attractive to established merchant and international banks; it also gave rise to new British secondary and fringe banks, which also operated beyond the reach of the regulators.

During the 1950s, there was an "almost complete agreement … that the City depends on its open and international character and that Britain depends on the City" (Schenk 2004, p. 339). Moreover, it was widely held that City prospects depended on the strength of sterling. As a result, both Conservative and Labour governments favoured City interests over those of industry. The policy response to successive sterling crises during the 1950s and 1960s was to support sterling by raising interest rates and cutting public sector expenditure, although this raised borrowing costs, reduced growth and increased unemployment. In the end, the main effect of the Eurodollar market was to encourage the ascent of the US dollar as the main international currency. However, by then, the City had learned that it could operate very effectively – and profitably – whatever the status of sterling.

The end of "laissez faire" – for now

Despite its challenges, the post-war period delivered a shift in ideology; and during the 1950s, Anthony Crosland (1956) observed that in place of the doctrine of laissez faire, "even conservatives and businessmen … subscribe to the doctrine of collective government responsibility for the state of the economy" (p. 65).

With the outbreak of the Second World War, close cooperation between the government and the institutions representing the trade unions, industry and finance was seen to be vital to winning the war; and these institutions were integrated into the apparatus of the state. In this context, political harmony and efficiency emerged as key features of the wartime system. Following the war, based on an assessment of the problems experienced during the inter-war years, the post-war settlement represented a break from the past. In this context, there was great confidence in the ability of the state to deliver on its promises; and "ideal solutions rejected older models of state activity based on market forces and the lower levels of corporatist activity prevalent before 1940" (Middlemas 1986, p. 341). The government committed itself to social security and a high and stable level of employment; and the 1944 White Paper on employment policy laid out the framework that conditioned the policies of both Labour and Conservative governments after 1945.

But despite the general consistency in the direction of policy pursued by both Labour and Conservative governments from 1945 onward through the 1950s, tensions were also building – within the labour movement and society more generally. By 1951, when the Conservatives returned to power, 7,740,000 men and women were members of trade unions – one of every two men and one of every four women – and trade union membership had risen by a million since the war's end (Fraser 1999, p. 198). With the outbreak of the Korean War during the summer of 1950, the bargaining position of the trade unions strengthened further.

Although labour relations appeared to be relatively peaceful, internal frictions and inter-union rivalries were simmering beneath the surface. Among many other issues, skilled workers were troubled by the narrowing of pay differentials between skilled and non-craft workers; many workers resented the extension of the closed shop; others took exception to the refusal of non-union workers to support strikes; and there was strong resistance to innovation with respect to union organisation. In 1955, the "years of peace" came to an end, with the number of strikes reaching their highest level on record (excepting 1944). The number of disputes continued to rise, year on year, with the number of days lost to industrial action peaking at over 8 million in 1958 (Fraser 1999, p. 200). As a consequence, by the late 1950s, the trade unions and their membership were coming under increasing attack by both the public and the media, with particularly hostile publicity focusing on communist activities, especially after the 1956 Soviet attack on Hungary.

Within society more broadly, different groups were complaining that such policies as stop/go, wage restraint, exchange controls and industrial discipline were frustrating the contributions they might make. People still supported the policy objectives of full employment and the welfare state; and there was no sense that their frustrations could not be resolved to the satisfaction of competing groups if only they could agree upon a set of mutually attractive incentives (Middlemas 1986, p. 336). But polls were beginning to reveal fears of unemployment, inflation and deteriorating living standards.[7]

All of this fed into a general sense of dissatisfaction with the post-war state; and by the 1960s, it would come under criticism by those on both the political right and left, for wasting taxpayers' money and failing to eradicate poverty. At the same time, as Britain's relative decline – particularly in relation to its European counterparts – became increasingly apparent, the state's explicit commitment to economic growth, full employment and price stability would make it vulnerable to further criticism and disillusionment.

Conclusions

The unprecedented levels of cooperation that characterised both the wartime years and the decade or so afterwards were – initially, at least – more the result of necessity than choice. Whilst the "Keynesian" policy direction had proven effective, in the absence of financial crisis and, especially, a major war, it might never have been given the opportunity.

It is possible that Keynes's ideas and policies might have endured rather longer, had he not suffered a heart attack so soon after publication of his 1936 *General Theory of Employment, Interest and Money*. Not only did this limit his participation in the subsequent debate about economic theory and policy; it also gave those neo-classical economists who felt the study lacked sufficient maths and formulae to add some of their own. The result, dismissively described by Joan Robinson as "Bastard Keynesianism", watered-down Keynes's concern about economic equality and his advocacy of the use of public spending to support effective demand. The importance of time in Keynesian theory was also played down by adoption of the more static Hicksian IS-LM representation of the *General Theory*, which reduced the Keynesian system to one of comparative statics and lost crucial elements of Keynes's analysis, including uncertainty, expectations, speculation and animal spirits.[8] Thus, not only were Keynes's ideas taken in a very different direction; this "brand" of Keynesianism is the one that would be seen to have failed when the stagflationary crises of the 1960s and 1970s arrived.

However, more tellingly for the insecurity cycle, not all of the interest groups were happy with the new spirit of cooperation that characterised the post-war consensus. Whilst returning finance to its position as the servant of the economy suited most of the other groups in society, regulation in place of speculation did not sit well with finance – and Josiah Stamp's observations about the nature of banking and finance would come back to haunt Britain more than once during the next half century. Whilst Stamp's "flick of a pen" would become a click on a mouse, the speed of innovation, global reach and ability to evade effective regulation would eventually return finance to its position as the most powerful interest group of all. But the dynamic movement of the insecurity cycle suggests that this state of affairs is unlikely to be permanent.

Notes

1 For details see Pollard (1992, pp. 181–2).
2 See Baker (1989, especially section 1).
3 For a detailed account of these negotiations and Keynes's central role in them see Moggridge (1992, especially chapter 29 "In the shadow of the debt").
4 Attlee's policy advisors were not united in their views about the relevance of incomes policy for wage control:

> James Meade and others in the Economic Section of the Cabinet Office were convinced that "peculiar difficulties of wage policy were due in large measure to general inflationary pressures, and that it was essential to do everything feasible to move towards a condition of greater balance between supply and demand, including reducing food subsidies".
>
> (Jones 1987, p. 35)

5 The Treasury and the Bank of England jointly fixed the *official* interest rate at which the latter would lend to commercial banks, and which was designed to regulate the level and cost of bank lending.
6 The regulation of hire purchase was centrally important in the fine tuning of consumers' demand in the three decades after 1946. Hire purchase was controlled by adjustments to the proportion of the purchase price required as a down payment, and by changes in the interest rates and the length of the repayment periods which determined the size of the monthly repayments. These proved effective counter-cyclical measures, but they concentrated the burden of cuts on a narrow range of industries.
7 In 1961, a Gallup poll concluded that there was

> considerable support for the belief that Britain needs "more government planning and control of industry". Today, 45 percent [in contrast to 15 per cent in 1956] believe that there should be more planning ... Only one in every four believes that the proper remedy for the present situation is to cut down on [government] expenditure.
>
> (Quoted in Middlemas 1986, p. 390)

8 See, for example, Kahn (1984); Robinson (1973, 1978 and 1979).

7   Keynes versus "Keynesianism"
Liberalism resurrected

Introduction

By the first half of the 1950s, the post-war settlement appeared to be delivering on its promises. Living standards were rising and the problem of generalised poverty had all but disappeared; unemployment and inflation were low; industrial output and productivity were increasing faster than ever before; and the rate of economic growth was higher than during any period previously (Pollard 1983, p. 274; Salter and Reddaway 1966, p. 198). In July 1957, the Conservative Prime Minister Harold Macmillan felt comfortable enough to observe that "most of our people have never had it so good" (quoted in Hill 1985, p. 293).

But this "golden age" was as much the result of external factors, as it was the general agreement and unprecedented cooperation – during peace time, at least – between the opposing interest groups representing labour, industry, finance and the state. The conditions within which it existed were remarkably benign from Britain's point of view, especially given the sharply reduced level of international industrial competition.

But post-war governments – as well as private industry – had failed to take advantage of the respite caused by the almost complete destruction of both European and Japanese industry. When they should have been investing in modern plant, technologies and processes, the focus was on social welfare and industrial peace. Worse still, the industries that had been nationalised consisted largely of the troublesome coal mining, ship building and steel making sectors that had not only been uncompetitive before the war, but were also the source of the most militant trade union activity. Rather than investing in the future, the state had opted for the consolidation of decline and appeasement – this time of the working population – and they had set themselves up to fail.

The post-war consensus thus carried with it the seeds of its own demise; and by the second half of the 1960s, with far less benign external conditions, it was becoming increasingly clear that the performance of both the British economy as a whole – and industry, in particular – were well below that of other industrial economies, particularly those of the re-emergent nations which had been faced with little alternative to re-building and investing in the latest industrial processes (Pollard 1983, p. 346).

Problems were also apparent on the domestic front. Consumer and house prices were rising; and there were recurring balance of payments deficits due to an increased appetite for relatively inexpensive imports. Failure to correctly divine the causes of Britain's economic problems – and to apply appropriate policies to ameliorate them – has often been regarded as a major failure of post-war Keynesian economics. But this is to overlook the very significant and increasing influence of "neoliberal" ideas and policy – not infrequently branded as "Keynesian" – that not only lay behind some of the more damaging attempts to address the issues but also motivated repeated experiments with monetarist policy.

Keynes had died in 1946; and attempts to retrospectively incorporate more "science" into his ideas would result in a number of questionable policies that – whilst sometimes labelled "Keynesian" by their proponents – would likely have been found of dubious merit by Keynes, himself. Moreover, although inflation is an undeniably important problem, Keynes had relatively little to say about it in *The General Theory*, particularly by comparison to his emphasis on full employment; and the policies subsequently used to address it were, at best, only mildly Keynesian.

More significantly, though, the failure to address the obvious problems of industry produced a strong sense of chronic crisis. These problems also set labour against the state and – since the state was now an employer – against industry as well. Finance also crossed swords with industry; and, in some respects, through ill-advised re-organisation, so did the state. With all of these adversaries at home, let alone the increased competition abroad, it is little wonder that industry suffered the most. Of all of the interest groups in the insecurity cycle, perhaps the most successful during this period was the poor, with absolute poverty having all but disappeared – at least for now. Restoring these adversarial relationships between the interest groups would ultimately provide the preconditions for another shift in the insecurity cycle.

Whilst all of the interest groups would play their part in the collapse of the post-war settlement, finance not only managed to play a significant part in the decline of industry, but also to lay the foundations for its present dominance – in spite of some spectacular failures of its own. The re-emergence of financial actors as short-term speculators, rather than the long-term servants of the "real" economy, would also contribute to inflationary difficulties and lengthening dole queues. But it was not just the home-grown speculators that would play a role; the collapse of the Bretton Woods international monetary system during the early 1970s would expose an over-valued sterling to renewed speculation, forcing James Callaghan to ask the IMF for the largest loan ever requested – and seriously damaging the Labour Party's financial reputation in the process.

As the gap between what the government promised and what it was able to deliver widened, confidence in its ability to steer the economy declined;

and by the end of the crisis-ridden 1970s, the stage was almost set for a funda-mental shift in the insecurity cycle and a return to pre-Keynesian liberal eco-nomic policies – "neoliberalism". All it needed was a final acute crisis and strong political backing – both of which were to come.

The role and responsibilities of the post-war state

The Second World War had transformed thinking about the role of the state in economic and societal affairs. Confidence in the government's ability to manage the economy and to ameliorate the problems that had plagued the inter-war years was initially very high (Middlemas 1990, chapter 1). Having won the war, most British people expected to be rewarded; and whatever their political leaning, they believed that the government had a role to play in providing essential social services, maintaining full employment, expanding exports and ensuring a favourable balance of trade – all whilst supporting the value of sterling and a fair distribution of wages and incomes (Hill 1985, p. 283; Youngson 1967, p. 159).

These new ideas, along with the state's wartime record, meant that the relationship between industry, labour, finance and the state was, for the first time, carried on into peacetime (Harling 2001, p. 168). Even the importance of trade unions as an effective countervailing force against the monopsony power of employers was acknowledged. As a result, trade unions were involved in policy-making; and they were integrated into the organisations and institutions charged with improving the working of both the economy and the welfare state (Moore 1982). According to Middlemas (1990),

> [the post-war political] regime was intended to change behaviour pat-terns by associating the institutions, together with their members, in a common endeavour in which each gained enough materially to offset the sacrifices made as obligations, yet retained sufficient continuing influence over the definition of final national objectives to prevent any one of them destabilising the implied political equilibrium, or breaking out of their political contract into free and unrestrained competition, where new participants might intrude or old, recognised ones be excluded.
>
> [But] discussions of the most difficult problems such as productivity, efficiency, investment or industrial relations, attempts to lay down more precisely how improvements could be induced generated such com-petitive confusion that they were abandoned or buried until the political contract should be in working order. Large elements of the past, includ-ing outmoded attitudes and habits also intruded. More time and effort was spent on preparing for crisis management than for crisis resolution.
>
> (p. 3)

Thus, the post-war government – which had often found itself in an awkward position vis-à-vis these institutions – typically chose to leave thorny issues to the parties involved, focusing instead on the electorally less sensitive fiscal and monetary policy instruments of demand management.

This, however, would eventually come home to roost as its consequences became progressively more obvious. In this context, most damaging was the effect of the prioritisation of social security enhancement over industrial modernisation; and by the mid-1960s, the resulting productivity, efficiency and competitiveness deficits which lay behind many of the domestic economic problems were becoming increasingly apparent. But even so, there remained a marked reluctance to challenge the unions when wage agreements outpaced improvements in productivity. This continued timidity in negotiation would do little to help with the inflationary pressures of the late 1960s and 1970s; it would also result in a failure to regulate finance and to curb those practices that had produced financial crises before the war. Both of these things, they would come to regret.

The investment in welfare also meant that government expenditure as a proportion of gross national product (GNP) – which had already increased significantly during the war – never returned to its pre-war level so taxes also remained high (Pollard 1992, p. 342). As a proportion of GNP, spending on social welfare rose from 12.5 per cent under the Conservatives in 1951, to 16.1 per cent under Labour in 1964, 23.1 per cent under the Conservatives in 1970 and 27.1 per cent in 1979 (ibid., p. 343). Substantial funding was also devoted to armaments, in an effort to both preserve Britain's "great-power" status and its position as a key ally of the United States during the Cold War. Although this fell from 8.6 per cent of GNP in 1951 to 5.4 per cent in 1979, Britain still spent a higher proportion of its GNP on military expenditure than any other advanced capitalist country aside from the United States.[1] The third major component of public expenditure was the financing of debts from the two world wars, which accounted for an annual average of 4.5 per cent of GNP between 1951 and 1971 before rising during the 1970s as a consequence of increased borrowing and interest rates (Pollard 1992, p. 343).

Higher levels of public spending on defence and debt financing meant that fewer resources were available for other purposes, such as major infrastructure development or large-scale modernisation – of the nationalised industries, in particular. According to Middlemas (1990),

> Defence spending and the strategic and political world responsibilities … permanently skewed the British's economy's balance of payments and domestic priorities accorded to defence-related industry, to the long-term detriment of general industrial and financial development on which the post-war settlement ultimately rested.
>
> (p. 14)[2]

The government did belatedly attempt to address both the chronic regional disparities and weaknesses in industrial competitiveness, primarily through nationalisation but also (largely unsuccessful) experiments with economic planning and attempts to produce large competitive corporations from groups of smaller struggling businesses without additional investment (Pollard 1992, pp. 345–54). But these efforts would be continuously interrupted by recurring crises, themselves often the result of failure to achieve stability in wages, the balance of payments, inflation or indeed, all three. This would in turn contribute to the abandonment of the fundamental post-war policy aim of full employment.

During the 1950s and 1960s, at least one problem was largely conspicuous by its absence. The Bretton Woods international monetary system effectively militated against currency speculation, resulting in a refreshing lack of financial crises. But the influence of Bretton Woods would be clearly illustrated by the events following hard on its collapse after Richard Nixon's withdrawal of gold backing for the US dollar in 1971. This too, would add significantly to the travails of the British government.

Finance versus government

A major issue in the immediate post-war period was the high dependency on imports, the lack of exports earnings to pay for them, and the threat this posed to Britain's already seriously depleted gold and foreign currency (especially dollar) reserves. During the war, the means of maintaining the flow of imports of food and material from the US had been found in lend-lease, causing Britain to become heavily indebted internationally. Britain also accumulated substantial wartime debts with countries of the Commonwealth, which were held as off-shore holdings of inconvertible sterling until the end of the war to protect Britain's gold and currency reserves. This meant that Commonwealth holders of sterling could not use them to buy exports from Britain, whose productive capacity was fully engaged in the war effort; nor could they convert them into dollars to spend in the US.

After the war, together with gold and dollars, sterling became widely used as an international currency, both as a means of exchange in foreign trade and as a reserve currency. As exchange controls were relaxed, Britain's outstanding debts became freely traded, as the large holdings of sterling abroad were liberated. This caused the value of sterling to become increasingly influenced by speculation in foreign exchange markets, challenging the ability of the government to maintain a fixed exchange rate – the then preferred policy option.

Defending the fixed exchange rate depended upon the Bank of England's willingness and ability (determined by its gold and foreign currency reserves) to intervene in the foreign exchange market. In these circumstances, it became standard practice for British monetary authorities, when sterling was under pressure, to seek support from other central banks and/or the IMF, the price of which was a requirement on Britain to adopt austere economic measures to placate the speculators.

The chronic weakness of sterling was to a significant extent a consequence of the British economy's supply side problems. Since demand tended to grow more rapidly than supply during the upswing of the trade cycle, in an increasingly free trade world, this sucked in imports, creating a balance of payments deficit that put pressure on sterling by stimulating speculation against it. In this context, when intervention in the foreign exchange market to support sterling depleted Bank of England reserves, international support – which was conditional on the implementation of a restrictive domestic macroeconomic policy – was required. The effect of the resulting economic downturn was a tightening of the supply constraint and a further undermining of British competitiveness.

The way out of this impasse was to improve the competitiveness of the British economy. But this, in the face of the determination to repeatedly defend the value of sterling – and the failure to sustain the long-term economic growth necessary to sufficiently increase productivity – meant a reduction in the rate of increase of British prices relative to those of its competitors, thus putting the onus on lowering price inflation.

Keynes, "post Keynesians", "neo Keynesians" and "neoliberals"

Ideas inspired to varying degrees by Keynes, were by now the dominant influence on British macroeconomic policy; and for much of the 1950s and 1960s, macroeconomic policy was characterised by government "fine-tuning", using various combinations of fiscal, monetary and income policies. Keynes, however, had advocated intervention *only* when the economy was "stuck" in a state generating either excessive involuntary unemployment or risking financial crisis. But both Conservative and Labour governments intervened far more frequently, using tools intended primarily for coarse adjustment to secure non-inflationary, full employment growth. Since Keynes had died shortly after negotiating the US war loan in 1946, he was unable to challenge either this or the more obviously inappropriate policies that would be implemented in his name.

By the late 1960s, non-inflationary, full employment growth was becoming increasingly difficult to achieve and even harder to maintain. Attempts to improve economic performance resulted in accelerating inflation and often the spectre of an unsupportable balance of payments deficit. In this context, although economic retrenchment (austerity) had the potential to reduce inflation and improve the balance of payments, it also created unacceptable levels of unemployment, which damaged trade union relations and prompted another abrupt policy reversal. The "stop" stage of what came to be known as the "stop/go" cycle included such measures as reductions in public sector expenditure, wage and price controls, hire purchase restrictions,[3] increases in the bank rate[4] and cuts in bank lending – all of which were reversed in the "go" stage of the policy cycle (Radcliffe Committee Report 1959, chapter VI; Kaldor 1986).

Nevertheless, by most standards at least, joblessness remained low. Between 1951 and 1960 unemployment rates ranged from 1.8 to 3.0 per cent averaging

2.4 per cent; between 1961 and 1970 they increased, ranging from 2.1 to 3.7 per cent averaging 2.9 per cent. During the stormy 1970s they jumped again, varying between 3.6 and 5.6 per cent, averaging 4.7 per cent. GDP, meanwhile, grew between 1951 and 1979 at an annual average rate of 2.5 per cent – only falling in 1974 and 1975, and then by just −1.3 and −0.6 per cent, respectively.

How do you solve a problem like inflation?

Although in his *General Theory*, Keynes devotes remarkably little attention to the subject of inflation, the causes of the inflation of the 1960s – and even those of the dreaded "stagflation" – should have been clear enough; and they were indeed correctly identified by the inheritors of Keynes's work at Cambridge, the so-called "post Keynesians". Indeed, both before the First World War and during the inter-war years, Britain had already experienced simultaneously rising food prices and high unemployment. During the 1970s, rising commodity prices – in particular that of oil – combined with an increasing excess of imports over exports, meaning that imports brought with them powerful inflationary forces. But no policy solution was targeted at these problems.

The gap left by Keynes was quickly filled by subsequent "Keynesian" thinking, which offered two possible causes for inflation: "demand pull" and "cost push". Demand pull inflation was attributed to the excess of monetary demand over supply at – or close to – full employment, with the cause of inflation being pressure from demand in the product market. Thus, when demand inflation is felt, key to its control is the regulation of effective demand. However, Phillips (1958), himself a so-called "neo-Keynesian" – the dominant American branch of Keynesianism – muddied the waters by ascribing the likely cause to excess demand in the *labour* market, which he explained as a spill-over of excess product market demand into the labour market where it pulled up wages as employers competed for increasingly scarce labour. The main impact of the *Phillips curve* in the formulation of theory and policy was that, despite its supposedly Keynesian orientation, it is actually almost a reversal of Keynes's ideas, since it prioritises inflation over full employment, legitimising what would have once been considered unacceptable levels of unemployment in the process.

An alternative explanation for inflation was offered by those arguing that prices are pushed up by *costs* rather than pulled up by demand.[5] Costs at the macroeconomic level include unit wage costs (requiring an increase in wages cost relative to productivity), the profit mark-up, taxes on consumer goods and sterling import prices; and increases in any of these can trigger inflation. Foreign currency prices are outside the range of domestic policy, although their sterling equivalents are influenced by exchange rates. However, the principal target for anti-cost inflation was wages – and especially the system of wage determination – with the policy instrument of choice being incomes policies. This would lead to some tricky relationships with the trade unions, and eventually Edward Heath's question "Who Governs Britain?" Once again, import costs were apparently ignored. Not only was the post war consensus starting to fracture – so was Keynesianism.

Experiments with monetary policy

The choices offered by Keynesians of various persuasions were not, however, the only offerings on the table. Monetary policy was another approach for managing the economy, and with it, inflation.

During the post-war period, responsibility for controlling the money supply lay with the Bank of England, which also operated as "lender of last resort", charging the bank rate for this service. To maintain financial security, banks were required to hold a set proportion of assets as cash and high-quality, highly liquid short-term assets. This reserve requirement was established by the monetary authority as a means of regulating the economy's monetary base. An increase in the bank rate increased costs to banks, inducing them to pass on the increase to their customers, which discouraged additional borrowing. Thus, the bank rate was the main instrument of monetary control, although at times, more direct methods were used.

In November 1951, the newly elected Conservative government opted to prioritise the use of monetary policy in managing the economy; and to curb overheating, the bank rate was raised from the 2 per cent that it had been since 1931 to 2.5 per cent – and to 4 per cent in March 1952. Whilst the economy scarcely grew during that year, it quickly recovered, expanding at over 3 per cent in each of the next three years.

In 1955, in another attempt to rein in the economy, interest rates were raised and more direct interventions were adopted, including hire purchase restraints. Pre-election tax cuts were reversed, public sector investments reduced and the Chancellor of the Exchequer asked banks for a "positive and significant reduction in their advances". But lending continued to rise sharply until the end of 1956 when further direct controls were imposed. This was followed by a series of additional interest rate increases, with the bank rate rising from 3 per cent in 1954 to 7 per cent in 1957.

Since it was clear that monetary policy was not working as the government had hoped, a Royal Commission, chaired by Lord Radcliffe, was set up to look into the working of the monetary and credit system. Its report was highly sceptical about the effectiveness of monetary policy, arguing that it had failed to keep the system in balance. The Radcliffe Committee's view was that the government's monetary policy was "far removed from the smooth and wide spread adjustment sometimes claimed as a virtue of monetary action: this is no gentle hand on the steering wheel which keeps a well driven car in its right place on the road" (Radcliffe Committee Report 1959, para. 473, p. 168). The Committee concluded that "monetary measures cannot alone be relied on to keep in fine balance an economy subject to major strains from both without and within. Monetary measures can help, but that is all" (ibid., para. 514, p. 183).

Despite this signal failure – and the cautionary tone of the Radcliffe Report – monetary policy was given another try during the early 1970s, by an increasingly desperate Edward Heath when the Conservatives returned to power. It had been resuscitated as a result of econometric research by Charles Goodhart, a Bank of England economist, which appeared to contradict the findings of the Radcliffe Report. This suggested that "the demand for money function was stable *and* that there was a significant negative coefficient on interest rates [so that] you could rely on interest rate adjustments – and did not need direct credit controls – to maintain monetary stability" (Goodhart 2003, p. 26).

Preferring Goodhart's comforting reassurance to the Radcliffe Committee's less encouraging view, quantitative controls on bank lending were abandoned and the neo-classically inspired Competition and Credit Control (CCC) policy was introduced in 1971. An inter-bank wholesale money market was created where banks could freely compete; and the bank rate was replaced by the Minimum Lending Rate (MLR), linked to the average discount rate for Treasury Bills at the weekly tender by inter-bank competition. This then became the discount rate used by the Bank of England in its capacity as lender of last resort.

Goodhart predicted that interest rates, determined by the wholesale money markets, would accurately control the credit supply. However, reality was a very different story. The unrestrained banks instead lent freely, balancing their books by borrowing in the inter-bank wholesale market on the strength of these newly created assets – producing an apparently unrestricted supply of credit (Kaldor 1986, pp. 104–5). Later, Goodhart commented rather plaintively: "My demand-for-money function broke down within a couple of years of being estimated! What had gone wrong?" (Goodhart 2003, p. 26). Lord Radcliffe, however, had already answered his question: attempting credit control by interest rates alone would at best cause a "diffused difficulty of borrowing" (Radcliffe Committee Report 1959, para. 472, p. 167; Kaldor 1986, p. 104).

The uncontrolled credit creation fuelled by CCC caused the inaugural round of reckless mortgage lending and with it, the first post-war housing bubble.[6] Prices increased 77 per cent (51 per cent in real terms) between 1971 and 1973 – despite an interest rate hike from 5 per cent at the end of 1971 (the bank rate) to 13 per cent at the end of 1973 (the MLR) – revealing the extent to which demand for mortgages had been dampened by lending controls rather than interest rates. At the end of 1973, the government sharply reined in credit creation, removing the life support system of the secondary banking sector – which had evolved to circumvent official controls on bank lending – in the process. This precipitated a Bank of England coordinated bail-out – the "lifeboat" – to forestall a "financial panic of nineteenth-century style" (Kaldor 1986, p. 106). Unlike the bail-outs of 2008, the lifeboat was funded by the banks, rather than the public purse; but nonetheless, the familiar financial crisis was back.

The policy reaction to this debacle was the imposition of the Special Supplementary Deposits Scheme, better known as the "corset". This required those issuing interest-bearing deposits in excess of the level prescribed by the government to lodge equivalent special deposits with the Bank of England, upon which no interest would be paid. The corset was activated three times during the 1970s, effectively impeding the credit-generating capabilities of the banking sector (Stephens 2007, p. 203).

Whilst the corset had no direct effect on building societies – then the main provider of mortgages, but officially outside the banking sector as defined by the Bank of England – they were not spared policy intervention. In 1973, a Joint Advisory Committee was set up to prevent another housing bubble by ensuring that funds available for house purchase more closely matched housing supply. Non-legally binding guidelines for lending were set, that the Building Society Association agreed to monitor. However, research suggested that levels of funds remained more important than official guidelines in determining how much building societies lent; and in 1978, when a house price bubble again threatened, a curb on lending was agreed.

But monetary policy – this time revived by Milton Friedman and the Chicago School economists (the "Chicago Boys") – would make yet another appearance a decade later. Whether or not Margaret Thatcher was surprised by the results being remarkably similar to those achieved by Edward Heath, is not recorded.

The government is seen to struggle with the economy

The British economy had had a relatively prosperous 1950s. But the consequences of failing to modernise industry soon became apparent with the re-emergence of Japan and the continental European countries as leading competitors and the rapid increase in low-cost manufacturing in developing countries. The subsequent relaxation of exchange rate controls fuelled the growing importance of multi-national firms, with globalisation accelerating as they relocated production to escape the higher labour and social welfare costs in industrial countries – encouraged by both tax breaks and the more docile labour offered by developing countries. This contributed to de-industrialisation in long-established industrial regions – especially the least competitive.

But reality was not proving to be a problem for industry only. The Phillips curve analysis had claimed that – in spite of it having happened before – prices and unemployment could not rise together. However, it was increasingly clear that this was precisely what was happening. Speaking in the House of Commons on 17 November 1965, Shadow Chancellor Iain Macleod said:

> we now have the worst of both worlds – not just inflation on the one side or stagnation on the other, but both of them together. We have a

sort of "stagflation" situation. And history, in modern terms, is indeed being made.

(Hansard 1965, p. 1165)

But things would soon get even worse, with the return of the old fashioned financial crisis. In 1971, in response to the first US trade deficit since before the First World War, President Nixon announced that the US would no longer provide gold backing for the American dollar.[7] This automatically decoupled the other Bretton Woods currencies from gold. Restrictions on international capital movements and fixed currency relationships were thus eliminated, as were controls on government borrowing, increasing exposure to highly liquid – and potentially hostile – global financial markets, which ultimately determined the terms on which states could borrow.

This was especially unhelpful from an inflationary point of view, since it not only diverted speculative funds into commodity markets (Robinson and Wilkinson 1977, p. 11), driving up both industrial and consumer prices (Kaldor 1976), but also resulted in speculation against a clearly overvalued sterling. The effect of the increase in commodity prices was made still more damaging by exponentially increasing oil prices. Meanwhile, the usual deflationary policy response gave rise to recession and rising unemployment, which further increased the welfare bill, whilst lower tax revenues and the costs of mass redundancies and failing industries put pressure on the balance of payments. It was definitely not a good time to also be faced with regular demands for significant wage increases from trade unions in the now even less competitive nationalised industries. Something had to be done – but what?

A crisis – but of Keynes, "Keynesianism" or emergent "neoliberalism"?

The return to economic liberalism – "neoliberalism" – was strongly influenced by the work of Friedrich von Hayek, Milton Friedman and the Chicago School economists, who certainly had a view on what should be done. They had not only been keeping liberal economic ideas alive but also developing them further in well-funded right-wing think tanks since the late 1930s, waiting for a crisis that might help to undermine the foundations of Keynesianism (Cockett 1995; Denham and Garnett 1998; Desai 1994). In Friedman's view,

[o]nly a crisis – actual or perceived – produces real change. When that crisis occurs, the actions that are taken depend on the ideas that are lying around. That, I believe, is our basic function: to develop alternatives to existing policies, to keep them alive and available until the politically impossible becomes politically inevitable.

(Friedman 1962, pp. viii–ix)

Once the crisis occurred, Friedman believed that it was crucial to act swiftly, before the moment was overtaken by the "tyranny of the status quo" (Friedman and Friedman 1984, p. 3). Events in Britain certainly looked very much like the crisis of Keynesianism that the neoliberals had been waiting for.

Resurrecting monetary theory once again, Friedman (1977) argued that inflation is a purely monetary phenomenon, caused by an increase in the money supply. The level of unemployment, he went on, is determined by supply and demand in the labour market; and there is a level of unemployment at which inflation is stable – a *natural* level determined by labour market inflexibility and imperfections. He accepted that an increase in the money supply could cause unemployment to rise above the natural level, but only whilst inflationary expectations, expressed in wage claims, adjusted upwards to the higher level of prices. This was the exact opposite of Keynes's view that unemployment could be *involuntary*, and was thus a clear attack on the conventional wisdom.

But this *adaptive expectations* view was not the only new idea on offer, and was, itself, challenged by *rational expectations* theorists who argued that by experiencing inflation, individuals come to understand the process and what triggers it, ruling out unanticipated inflation and the possibility of any deviation of unemployment from the natural rate. They thus fully embraced the pre-Keynesian orthodoxy of the primacy of the money supply in determining both prices and conditions in the labour market – and thus the level of unemployment. From this, it follows that the cure for inflation is monetary control and the cure for unemployment is supply side measures including labour market deregulation, more effective incentives and training.

Similar non-Keynesian policy conclusions were reached by the "neo-Keynesians" but by a different theoretical route. Meade (1982) argued that for any given increase in total monetary expenditure, the balance between inflation and unemployment is determined by wage pressure from trade unions. He took the wages firms can afford to pay as being determined by diminishing marginal productivity.[8] Therefore, the unemployment rate at which inflation stabilises – the so-called *non-accelerating inflation rate of unemployment* (NAIRU) – is a function of excessive wages negotiated by unions, above the level of marginal revenue product necessary to deliver full employment. A reduction of NAIRU therefore requires a moderation of wage increases,

> first, because less and less output may be added to production as more and more *men* have to work with the given equipment and other resources of the firm[9] and, second, because the employer may be selling his product in an imperfect market so that if he produces and sells more he may have to lower his selling price (or incur greater selling costs) in order to dispose of the increased output.[10]
>
> (Meade 1982, p. 49)

Imperfect competition in the product market is thus seen as driving a wedge between wages and marginal productivity and the extent of this *exploitation*[11] is determined by the degree of monopoly. Neo-Keynesians have further argued that this wedge is widened by employers' taxes, excise tax, real import prices and other non-labour costs (Nickell 1985, p. 101).

For neo-Keynesians, the link between wages and productivity – the hallmark of neo-classical theory – is broken and wages become a residual category to which marginal productivity is only an upper limit. Refusal by workers to accept such limitations then results in unemployment as firms respond to not meeting their target profits by sacking workers. This reserve of the involuntarily unemployed, by increasing competition for jobs, checks real wage growth and increases the amount of *unpaid labour*[12] needed to restore profitability (Carlin and Soskice 1990, p. 138). The neo-Keynesians also broke with the neo-classical traditions by recognising that income distribution is determined by relative power and is therefore a social and political – rather than an economic – phenomenon. However, they did follow the neo-classicists in claiming that the conflict over the distribution of income can be automatically resolved by adjusting the balance of market forces in favour of capital by restricting union activities, lowering labour standards, increasing unemployment and reducing social welfare benefits.

Meanwhile, the Cambridge economists and post-Keynesians offered alternative explanations and cures.[13] They had also accurately identified the most obvious causes of the inflation. In their view, the increase in prices during the 1960s and early 1970s was the result of increasing commodities prices, which had a knock-on effect on producer and consumer price inflation. This was made worse by the wage/price spiral, as workers sought to maintain living standards in the face of falling real incomes, whilst employers tried to protect their profits by raising prices. With incomes policies restraining wages, falling real incomes reduced purchasing power. This, however, had an asymmetric effect, dampening demand for British goods and services – which were relatively more expensive than foreign ones – and encouraging a shift in consumption towards imports. This further dampened home demand, output and employment, adding to the depressive effect of governmental counter-inflationary austerity programmes (Wilkinson 2012). Rising inflation and unemployment therefore interacted to produce stagflation.

However, these ideas fell upon deaf ears as, increasingly, the problems of the crisis-ridden 1970s were attributed to "Keynesian" fallacies, whilst neo-classical ideas gained ground. Amongst economists, this sparked a revival of traditional liberal beliefs in the monetary causes of inflation and the efficacy of unrestricted markets in maximising economic welfare, a revival labelled "neoliberalism"; and during the 1970s, openly neoliberal theories of unemployment supplanted Keynesianism as the conventional wisdom in macroeconomics, shifting responsibility for unemployment from an insufficiency of effective demand to labour market failure. The events of the 1970s also eventually discredited incomes policies.

Trade unions versus government

The Attlee Labour government had flirted with the idea of incomes policies, but never fully implemented them; and when the Conservatives came to power in 1951, the emphasis shifted to experiments with monetarism. However, Attlee's wage policy had nonetheless created a template for future developments by proposing the need for statutory control of wage determination and providing a framework to oversee the process. Thus, as the focus of macroeconomic policy shifted from unemployment to inflation, there was growing interest in the idea of incomes policies, which were operated in various forms until 1979 by both Conservative and Labour administrations, in repeated attempts to control inflation. But rather than forming part of a coordinated low inflation, full employment strategy, they tended to be ad hoc measures, aimed at quickly slowing wage increases relative to rising prices.[14]

In 1956–7, the Conservatives established the Council on Prices, Productivity and Incomes to examine pay settlements. Although it had neither the legal power to intervene in collective bargaining nor the power to enforce its recommendations, voluntary pay restraint was nevertheless encouraged in the light of its findings. The Conservative government took a step closer to compulsion in 1961–2, with a zero-increase wage norm − or wage freeze − in public sector pay settlements and through the decisions of wages councils − requests with which they simply refused to comply. The wage freeze was watered down to a "guiding light" of 2 to 2.5 per cent, which was then further increased to 3 to 3.5 per cent, except for those increases linked to outstanding productivity gains and/or to attract labour where it was scarce.

The incoming Labour government of Harold Wilson in 1964 took a more direct approach to wage and price control. The National Board for Prices and Incomes was set up the following year, in an attempt to target inflation through direct intervention in both wages and prices. This would bring him, as well as the next three prime ministers into an increasingly adversarial relationship with the trade unions, which had become progressively more influential following the war. Even the Board's early skirmishes with the British Road Haulage Association over price fixing brought stiff resistance, whilst the Transport and General Workers' Union had been strongly opposed to the entire principle of state intervention in wage determination from the beginning.

However, a "Statement of Intent" was agreed with the Trades Union Congress (TUC) and the Confederation of British Industry, introducing a 3 to 3.5 per cent wage increase norm − again with some exceptions. But when this failed to slow wage increases, the TUC was persuaded to introduce a "wage-vetting scheme". In 1966, a statutory wage freeze was enacted via the Prices and Incomes Act, which set criminal sanctions for disobedient firms. This was lifted the following year, and voluntary norms were resumed. But some powers were retained, allowing settlements to be referred to the National Board for Prices and Incomes, which could delay implementation for up to six months, later extended to a year. The same year also witnessed the first truly national strike since 1911, by the National Union of Seamen, bringing many of Britain's major ports to a standstill – with significant ramifications: not only did the strike look likely to undermine the 3.5 per cent wage settlement limit; the stoppage of trade moved the balance of payments further into the red, precipitating a sterling crisis.

Wilson was entirely opposed to the strike, even going so far as to accuse "politically motivated men" – by implication, communists – of orchestrating it, and declaring a state of national emergency. Although these powers – one of which was to use the Royal Navy to break the strike – were not used, the strike did lead to an attempt to reduce union power through the White Paper *In Place of Strife*. But Wilson's cabinet was split over this and the idea was eventually dropped, following discussions with the TUC.

But the sterling crisis rumbled on, with Wilson resisting devaluation of the currency; as he himself pointed out: "Whichever party is in office, the Treasury is in power" (quoted in Dernauf and Blume 2008, p. 560). However, once again, attempts to defend the pound were doomed to failure, with eventual devaluation producing something of an economic recovery – but not enough to keep Labour in government.

Heath's Conservative government, which followed in 1970, had taken note of the rocky relationships with the trade unions – and initially took a much more "softly-softly" approach to wage control. The idea was to steadily lower inflation by setting targets for wage increases, each lower than those of the previous year, with the government using its influence in the public sector to implement them. However, the government was forced to revert to compulsion in 1972 with another pay freeze, followed by limits on increases[15] plus alternative flat-rate increases designed to help the lower-paid. A Pay Board was established with the statutory powers to implement this "pay code" and advise the government on pay policy.

Like Wilson, Heath also attempted to rein in the power of the trade unions, using the Industrial Relations Act of 1971. However, this set up a confrontation with the unions that his government – beset by problems with both unemployment and inflation – proved ill-equipped to deal with. The two miners' strikes – the second of which produced the infamous three-day week to save power in 1974 – also saw the organisation of "flying pickets" by Bert Ramelson. Ramelson was the National Industrial Organiser of the Communist Party of Great Britain, who had close relationships with many union leaders, including Jack Jones, General Secretary of the Transport and General Workers' Union (TGWU). In 1973, he contended:

We have more influence on the labour movement than at any time in the life of our party. The Communist Party can float an idea early in the year. It goes to trade union conferences as a resolution and it can become official Labour Party policy by Autumn. A few years ago we were on our own, but not now.

(Quoted in Taylor 2004, p. 70)

This suggests that there might well have been some truth in Wilson's earlier assertion about the influence of "politically motivated men" on the activities of the trade unions during the early 1970s.

Meanwhile, wages and prices continued to rise. This can now be explained, as the Cambridge economists had long argued, by the interaction between increases in world commodity prices – especially oil[16] – and the working of the Heath government's "threshold" agreements.

Threshold agreements were based on the supposition that wage demands depend upon *expectations* of future increases in prices.[17] Following this logic, settlements guaranteeing compensation for future price increases – should they occur – would encourage workers to accept lower current wage increases. Thus, the final stage of Heath's incomes policy included "escalator" clauses – the so-called "threshold agreements" (Wilkinson 1974). If prices increased by more than 7 per cent over their October 1973 level, a 40 pence wage increase would be triggered, with each additional percentage point price increase adding a further 40 pence to weekly earnings.[18] The hope amongst policy makers was that the promise of future pay increases would so reduce the expectations element in wage settlements that the 7 per cent threshold would not be crossed before the agreement expired.

Unfortunately for those hopeful policy makers, since the cause of the inflation had been mis-identified, by April 1974, inflation had easily passed the 7 per cent threshold. Worse still, before the threshold agreements expired in November of that year, eleven further 40 pence wage increases had been triggered, adding around 10 per cent to average earnings. Meanwhile, price inflation, which had been at 9.2 per cent in 1973, passed 16 per cent in 1974, reaching 24 per cent in 1975 – triggering wage increases of 13 per cent, 18 per cent and 27 per cent, respectively – and threatening a major wage/price explosion. This was all too much for Heath, whose manifesto for the 1974 general election enquired, "Who Governs Britain?" But no-one else seemed to know; and the result was a hung Parliament.

Rather than continue the coercive policies attempted by Heath and engage in confrontation with the unions, the following Labour minority government of 1974–9 instead left enforcement of pay norms to the TUC, which thus became responsible for "policing" settlements on the government's behalf. This formed part of the "Social Contract" which had, in essence, committed the Labour Party to a series of statutory measures – including price and rent controls, public control of investment, improved social welfare, legislation on employment and industrial democracy, and measures for the redistribution of income through the tax and social security system – in return for which the unions would exercise voluntary pay restraint.

Phase 1 aimed at pegging wages to increases in prices since the previous annual settlement, continuing the practice of setting a twelve-month interval between wage agreements. The plan this time was to limit price increases through the Price Commission and then let wages follow those prices down. But having failed to correctly identify the cause of the inflation yet again, this plan fared no better than the ill-fated threshold agreements had; and faced with price and wage inflation of over 20 per cent, it was finally abandoned in mid-1975. Ironically, this inflationary crisis was resolved when Jack Jones, General Secretary of the TGWU, put forward a proposal for a general flat-rate increase of no more than £6 per week for the next round, which was carried by a large majority of the TUC at a meeting in September 1976 (Morgan 1990).

However, this proved to be merely a calm in the midst of the storm: a maximum increase of 5 per cent was set for the following year; and within twelve months, the government and the TUC agreed a 10 per cent maximum across the board. However, by the time of its 1977 Congress, the TUC had had enough of wage controls and voted for a return to free collective bar-gaining and an end to the Social Contract. Union-supported pay restraint had reduced average after-tax real earnings by 19 per cent from their 1975 peak and 10 per cent from their 1973 level, when the threshold agreements had come into force, with price inflation dropping from 24.1 per cent in 1974–5, to 7.5 per cent in 1977–8.

The government of James Callaghan, who had led the opposition to Wil-son's *In Place of Strife* – and replaced him as Prime Minister in 1976 – con-fronted the by now familiar problems of high inflation and unemployment, militant trade unions and an especially unhelpful sterling crisis. Britain's wors-ening balance of payments had led to the currency being generally felt to be over-valued. Whilst this would have been bad enough with the Bretton Woods system still in place, Nixon's decoupling of the dollar from gold – and with it the pound – had resurrected the possibility of a speculative attack. The run on sterling was so serious that it was now felt to be under-valued. Whilst this allowed the government to arrange a short-term loan from the US to prop up the pound, by the time repayment was due, there were insufficient funds to cover it. Callaghan was thus forced to apply to the IMF for a loan – the largest ever – to cover the repayment. But the accompanying demands for austerity put even greater pressure on the economy – and left him little room for expansionary policies.

But just as it appeared that the economy was beginning to recover on its own – with the strengthening of sterling and the surplus in the balance of payments resulting from the discovery of North Sea oil – the country was again thrown into crisis. In July 1978, the TUC refused to accept a 5 per cent pay increase for the coming year when inflation had fallen to 7.5 per cent. At around the same time, striking workers at Ford were awarded a large pay increase, causing public sector workers – including many workers in the NHS, the ambulance service, schools, garbage collection and cemeteries – to follow suit. White-collar civil servants – putting in claims for as much as six times the rate of inflation – joined in. The result was the so-called "Winter of Discontent", during which it is claimed that hospitals were picketed, the sick were neglected, schools were closed, rubbish accumulated in the streets and bodies went unburied.[19]

These strikes proved to be the undoing of both Callaghan's government and the trade union movement since they were all too much for the electorate. Callaghan, who had had a comfortable lead in the polls, had been delaying the upcoming general election in the hope of further improved economic performance. But the public sector strikes reversed his lead; and the resulting strong democratic upsurge resulted in a 5.2 per cent swing towards the Conservatives – the largest since the landslide Labour victory in 1945.

The Winter of Discontent would not be made the "glorious summer" by any "sun of York". Instead, it would introduce a "daughter of Grantham" with a copy of Hayek's *The Road to Serfdom* in her handbag. However, whilst they had undoubtedly triggered the shift, the unions may not have been entirely to blame. According to Harling (2001):

> In the end, it is probably fair to say that the authority of the state was being compromised not so much by the unions as it was by the complexities of an international economic situation that left national governments with a limited ability to "steer" their economies in ways that could generate benefits all round.
>
> (p. 187)

The cycles of incomes policy-on and incomes policy-off thus came to an end in 1979, after which macroeconomic policy has been dominated by attempts to control inflation by monetary means, with employment being left to market forces.

Government versus industry

The post-war Labour government's programme of nationalisation had initiated the process of industrial concentration, inspired by American-style Fordist mass-production. The increasing size of highly successful vertically integrated producers – particularly American and German ones – had shifted the conventional wisdom; and it now argued that, rather than large size threatening to distort market outcomes as a consequence of collusion among producers, the tendency in capitalist industrial development was towards large firm dominance.

But this created inconsistencies. Keynesian ideas – which explained unemployment as being *involuntary* when it was the result of insufficient effective demand – were still informing *macroeconomic* policy. But neo-classical *microeconomic* theories – of economies of large-scale production and perfect, imperfect and monopolistic competition – influenced post-war industrial policy, in which nationalisation and the promotion of industrial concentration featured prominently.[20]

In spite of the establishment in 1964 of both the Department of Economic Affairs – primarily to curb the power of the Treasury – and the Ministry of Technology, there was, it seems, a dangerously inadequate understanding of the structure and functioning of large companies. Informed by ideas about the benefits of large-scale production, Harold Wilson's government, in particular, prioritised "size" over modernisation aimed at improving competitiveness and productive efficiency. The assumption was apparently that economies of scale in production were the result of size alone, rather than the modern plant and technology – and organisational and managerial systems – required to achieve them.

This ill-informed view appears to have also rested on the assumption that these new ideas about industrial organisation were universal, and could hence be simply transplanted from one economy to another, regardless of circumstances or culture. An example of this can be found in the government's unsuccessful experimentation with French-style economic planning during the early 1960s through the National Economic Development Council.

Another complication impeding industrial progress may also have been related to existing budget commitments – to social welfare, defence and debt financing, in particular – which made further significant investment in industry unaffordable. Whatever the cause, the result was a policy aimed at producing large companies, without reference to the appropriate structures or modernisation required to deliver productive efficiency. It also had a significantly damaging impact on Britain's smaller firm sector but failed to improve the competitiveness of its now much larger ones to compensate.

The small firm sector contracted sharply: between 1935 and 1963 the number of manufacturing firms employing 200 or fewer workers declined 56 per cent, from 136,000 to 60,000; whilst their share of output fell from 36 to 16 per cent (Pollard 1992, p. 254). By contrast, the large firm sector expanded rapidly. Plants became larger, but less so than firms – which grew by adding further plants than increasing the productive capacity of existing facilities. By 1972, the 100 largest manufacturing firms operated an average of seventy-two plants, compared with twenty-seven in 1958 (ibid.). The growing dominance of large firms included the retail distribution, financial services, transport and communications sectors.

In many sectors, the degree of concentration can be explained at least partly by nationalisation – and the fact that, despite being subsequently privatised, they remained heavily concentrated. However, in all sectors of the economy, the increase in firm size cannot be explained by the benefits of economies of large-scale operation, as suggested by the neo-classical theories of industrial organisation.

Restrictive practices: intended and unintended consequences

Harold Wilson had announced at the Labour Party Conference of 1963:

> We are redefining and restating our socialism in terms of the scientific revolution. But that revolution cannot become a reality unless we are prepared to make far reaching changes in economic and social attitudes

which permeate our whole system of society. The Britain that is going to be forged in the white heat of this revolution will be no place for restrictive practices or for outdated methods on either side of industry.

(Quoted in Matthijs 2011, p. 74)

Alongside industrial concentration, tighter regulation of restrictive practices, monopolies and mergers would form the second strand of industrial policy in an attempt to modernise industry.

In its 1944 *Employment Policy* White Paper, the wartime coalition government had explained:

> 51. An undue increase in price due to causes other than increased wages might similarly frustrate action taken by the Government to maintain employment. If, for example, the manufacturers in a particular industry were in a ring for the purposes of raising prices, additional money made available by Government action for the purposes of maintaining employment might simply be absorbed in increased profit margins and no increase in employment would result...
>
> 54. Workers must examine their trade practices and customs to ensure that they do not constitute a serious impediment to an expansionist economy and so defeat the object of a full employment programme.
>
> Employers, too, must seek in larger output rather than higher prices the reward of enterprise and good management. There has in recent years been a growing tendency towards combines and towards agreements, both national and international, by which manufacturers have sought to control prices and output, to divide markets and to fix conditions of sale. Such agreements or combines do not necessarily operate against the public interest, but the power to do is there. The Government will therefore seek power to inform themselves of the extent and effect of these restrictive agreements, and of the activities of combines, and to take appropriate action to check these practices which may bring advantages to sections of producing interests but work to the detriment of the country as a whole.

(HMSO May 1944, p. 19)

Driven by the idea that market imperfections were likely to cause either under-utilisation of resources or monopoly exploitation, in 1948, Attlee's government had established the Monopolies and Restrictive Practices Commission, which produced a series of influential reports.[21] A general review of restraints on trade was published in May 1955 as *Collective Discrimination: A Report on Exclusive Dealing, Collective Boycotts, Aggregate Rebates, and Other Discriminatory Trade Practices*. The following year, the government gained powers to curb competitive restrictions deemed to be against the public interest, resulting in a decisive shift from enquiry to control in the form of the Restrictive Trade Practices Court.

All restrictive agreements were now required to be registered, with 2,430 being volunteered and 100 more discovered. Of these, the majority were nullified before judgement, scrapped, or abandoned in preference to registration. Of the remainder, most were judged to be against the public interest. However, although collective price fixing among smaller firms was prohibited, the legislation had the effect of encouraging firms to individually fix prices for product they supplied. Consequently, the 1964 Retail Prices Act aligned retail price maintenance with other restrictive practices, prohibiting individual firms from fixing the retail prices of the goods they supplied. But this did not apply to the dealings between the plants and subsidiaries of large multi-plant and multi-national firms.

On paper, the anti-restrictive practices legislation secured notable successes. In retail trades, prices became more flexible, a change which benefitted large retailers with greater buyer power that could pass the cost of their price cutting back to their suppliers. However, the consequential intensification of price competition with the abolition of resale price maintenance contributed greatly to demise of individual retailers and small firms and chains, further increasing the dominance of their larger competitors.[22]

Monopolies and mergers: policies and outcomes

The lack of weight given to the negative effects of power imbalances when the possible consequences of outlawing collective restrictive/protective practices were officially examined is striking. This is particularly true in relation to the much closer attention paid to the multi-faceted nature of market domination when monopolies and mergers were investigated using the powers given the government by the 1948 Monopolies Act.

In the follow-up to the 1948 Monopolies Act, policies were initiated to regulate mergers and takeovers. The 1965 Monopolies and Mergers Act allowed the Board of Trade to refer mergers above a specified size or market share to the Monopolies Commission. Whilst the vast majority of "restrictive agreements" between small firms had been removed, the situation for large companies could hardly have been more different. Between 1965 and 1973, 833 mergers were considered – but only twenty were referred to the Commission. Of these seven were abandoned, seven allowed and three halted. Between 1973 and 1977, only twenty-three of 700 mergers were referred – clear evidence that they were indeed considered the means to beneficial rationalisation – with Tony Benn's Industrial Reorganisation Committee (IRC) being active throughout much of this period, creating corporations such as British Leyland.

Altogether, by the end of the 1970s over sixty monopolies had been investigated by the Monopolies Commission, and several hundred mergers had been screened. Twelve voluntary codes of practice protecting the consumer were introduced and the Office of Fair Trading exacted promises of good behaviour from numerous individual companies. It monitored the Consumer

Act 1974 and carried out the licensing required. Yet, because there were misgivings about the effectiveness of the package of policies as a whole, an Inter-Departmental Committee was set-up in 1978. But this committee did little more than suggest modest reforms. The two main problems proved to be (1) the ineffectiveness of preventing secret or unofficial collusive actions and (2) the weight given to the argument that while increasing firm size might be exploitative, it also had the potential to improve business efficiency and strengthen British firms in foreign competition (Pollard 1992, pp. 258–9).

Thus, although agreements among smaller firms were judged to render competition "imperfect" – and therefore ineffective and exploitative – little was done to restrict either monopolisation or to prevent expansion by take-overs and mergers. According to Pollard (1992):

> [t]he Government's attitudes towards the task of providing a competitive environment for British industry were, in fact, vacillating and ambiguous. In spite of its elaborate provision for "fair trading" and against monopoly it was at times itself enforcing or encouraging the monopolistic organisation of industry, as in the case of British Leyland, the aircraft industry, shipbuilding, computer manufacture, cotton spinning and agricultural marketing: not to mention the nationalised industries. Under the Labour Government the Industrial Reorganisation of 1966–70 had been given the task of actually aiding and initiating mergers, including the spectacular creation of the GEC-AEI-English Electric combine, and British Leyland, all in the interest of efficiency.
>
> (p. 261)

This ignored the reality that there are two dimensions to inter-firm collaboration. By closely working together to improve their technical, organisational, production and marketing performance firms can further their own and their customers' and suppliers' interests. Alternatively, by conspiring together with others, firms can rig markets to their mutual advantage against those of their suppliers, competitors and customers. Similarly, there are two sides to large firms' operations. They can, by securing the economies of large scale operations, lower costs and prices; and they can use their massed resources to both foster technical improvements and develop new products, processes and more efficient forms of organisation. Alternatively, they can exploit their relative market power to fix prices and impose constraints on their competitors, suppliers and customers.

However, the disappearance of large numbers of small firms and their replacement by large ones – a high proportion of which had been created by cobbling together smaller ones instead of seeking the efficiencies of large-scale production – did nothing to address Britain's lack of competitiveness. But even this would not be the biggest problem that British industry would have to face. Worse was to come as another interest group broke with the consensus, and destroyed large sections of manufacturing capacity in the process, adding to the dole queues and ratcheting up the tension between government, employers and trade unions. Finance was back in the business of speculation.

Finance versus industry – and a rude awakening

By the time the problems of British industry were fully apparent, there seemed little room or resource for turning them around quickly. So with the economy slowing, governments opted for ill-informed approaches to industrial re-organisation and actively encouraged expansion of the financial services sector to counter stagnation (Magdoff and Sweezy 1987). Whilst early post-war reforms had prioritised productive over speculative capital, with "national compartments constructed around the Fordist-Welfare-State concept" (Burn 2006, p. 2), the gradual loosening of controls restricting the international movement of financial capital during the 1950s had reversed this, effectively decoupling finance from industry. It also transformed what had, in effect, been a public international monetary order into an essentially private one (ibid., p. 13).

This would have a pivotal effect on the future cohesion of the individual interest groups. Since there were fewer productive investment opportunities within British industry, funds were instead largely aimed at more speculative activities. However, not only was finance abandoning its role as the servant of industry by reducing the flow of capital for productive purposes, it was about to completely reverse the process, by stripping out as much value as possible from a wide range of (in many cases) perfectly viable British companies – and redistributing it to its own speculative shareholders. As a result, ill-informed re-organisation – rather than investment and modernisation – would not be the only destructive force British industry had to contend with during the late 1960s and early 1970s.

By the 1960s, with the post-war boom at its height, recollection of the 1929 stock market crash had largely passed from memory, being replaced by confidence and a renewed appetite for risk – particularly if that risk could be transferred to others. Investors also began to realise the potential power of external shareholders in large, apparently family-owned companies, whose shares were traded on the stock market.

One such investor was James Slater, who, with Peter Walker, formed Slater Walker Securities and engineered his first hostile takeover in 1964, after Cork Manufacturing – having taken into account the property boom caused by low interest rates – increased the valuation of its Chingford office block to £1 million. Prior to this, its shares had been quoted at 13 shillings (£0.65); but after the re-valuation, they should actually have been worth 40 shillings (£2.00) (Slater 1977). Realising that this meant the company was hugely under-valued, Slater built up a 25 per cent share-holding as a prelude to a hostile takeover. Whilst considered "un-gentlemanly" by some in the City – not unlike the Midland Bank's first bids for Eurodollar deposits – this was not in any way illegal; and the realisation of potentially large profits from such under-valued companies rapidly swamped any remaining scruples held by many others.

The hostile takeover, however, was soon lauded as a rational restructuring by investors and government alike, cutting out waste and making the target company more efficient, rather than as a short-term asset-stripping operation purely for profit. The resulting (usually brief) share price increases caused by the sudden spike in demand re-awakened irrational beliefs in the infallibility of the stock market, which typically responded well to takeover announcements. Given the trust placed in its judgements, the price increases of target companies were seen as proof of the efficacy of the formula by many, including the financial press (BBC 1999, Part 2) and even more unfortunately, the British government, who were – until the practice was brought to an abrupt halt by rising interest rates – inclined to support the idea.

It is difficult to quantify the full extent of the resulting industrial carnage. One survey showed that of the 2,126 manufacturing firms (outside the iron and steel industry) quoted on the London stock exchange in 1964, more than 400 (close to one-fifth) had been taken over six years later (Rowley 1974, p. 72). The number increased substantially during the intervening years; and in July 1973, it was revealed that Slater Walker alone owned more than 10 per cent of forty-five leading British companies (ibid., p. 77).

The rising value of the holdings of corporate raiders allowed them to carry out ever more acquisitions, with the stock market not only increasing the vulnerability of target companies but also giving the raiders the means to exploit that vulnerability. The resulting profits then created additional funds with which to carry on the process, as ever larger businesses were stripped of their assets to pay off the debts incurred in their own acquisition.

Neo-classical theorists, too, needed little encouragement to laud the stock exchange as an "efficient market" for managerial control, where poorly managed companies, whose under-performance was reflected in their stock prices, could be acquired by more efficient management teams. According to this logic, hostile takeovers provided evidence that the stock market was functioning effectively, restructuring companies in a way that shareholders were uniquely placed to trigger (Deakin and Slinger 1997). It therefore follows that the prices the stock market delivers must always reliably reflect the value of the underlying productive asset.

On the strength of these ideas, the stock market boom caused by the corporate raiders was initially taken as clear evidence of returning industrial strength, rather than the wholesale destruction of productive capacity – with the brief spike in share prices reinforcing these assumptions. The hostile takeover was thus predicted to also have a beneficial impact on the longer-term performance of the companies concerned (Shleifer and Vishny 1997). This, in turn, convinced politicians that a miracle cure for ailing British industry had just dropped into their laps, so policy was adjusted accordingly.

However, the reality was that most acquisitions performed far less well than before, if indeed they were able to continue at all (Martynova and

Renneboog 2008). But Harold Wilson's Labour government embraced the idea. In his view, the solution to British industry's competitive problems was growth through mergers to achieve economies of large-scale production (Beath 2002, p. 223). The Labour Party pledged to set up the Industrial Reorganisation Corporation (IRC) to "stimulate rationalisation, modernisation and expansion in those fields where British industry at present seems unable to compete with the giant firms of the US and Europe" (Labour Party Manifesto 1966); and the IRC was duly established in 1966.

However, this did the government few favours. The results failed to include the promised industrial nirvana. Instead, large numbers of workers were made redundant, whilst the newly formed conglomerates conspicuously failed to prosper. Problems for those businesses that had been forcibly restructured multiplied (Deakin and Singh 2008); and many were left without the resources to sustain productive activities. The large job losses that typically followed hostile acquisitions further soured relationships between the government – which had strongly espoused the policy – and the trade unions, who were, for the most part, on the receiving end of it (Martynova and Renneboog 2008). The bulk of the "profits" generated by hostile takeovers were in fact coming from asset stripping rather than effective restructuring, resulting in a long-term detrimental effect on corporate performance (Bluestone and Harrison 1982; Lazonick and O'Sullivan 2000).[23] Whilst this reality eluded the government for some time, not only was the heavy industrial sector largely hollowed out; but Wilson's support had also both weakened trade unions and curtailed opportunities for longer-term investment in manufacturing.

The takeover boom was finally ended, not by government, but by rising interest rates following the collapse of Bretton Woods. These not only ended the property boom which had fuelled the takeover spree, but also spelt serious trouble for many secondary banks, reliant on cheap debt finance – including Slater Walker. Slater, himself, was forced to step down in 1975, to be replaced by James Goldsmith – another well-known corporate raider. Correspondence released under the Freedom of Information Act reveals not only a complete change of attitude towards the corporate raiders, but also fierce animosity between the Treasury and the Bank of England. In a briefing to the Chancellor of the Exchequer Denis Healey, a Treasury official admitted that "We asked the Bank for an analysis of the problems underlying the collapse [of Slater Walker] but this has not been forthcoming" (HM Treasury 2005).

Nor was the Treasury impressed by the Bank's approval of James Goldsmith as a replacement for Jim Slater. Brian Unwin, Treasury Undersecretary, wrote:

> Given the history of "City" characters … I hope the Bank, who are up to their neck in the Slater Walker affair, are fully satisfied that Mr. Goldsmith is a proper person … he is hardly a noted banking figure and

indeed his reputation as far as the general public is concerned is that of a playboy and speculator.

(HM Treasury 2005)

Relations between the Bank and the Treasury would remain fraught for some time, a situation scarcely conducive to the effective functioning of Britain's tripartite financial regulatory system.[24] However, although the leveraged buy-out was, for now at least, discredited, British industry struggled to recover; and relationships between finance and the "real" economy would never quite heal either.

This would come back to haunt governments of both persuasions during the following decade, as the damage to the relationship between the state and labour had also been significant. Lengthening dole queues were not meant to have been any part of post-war Britain. It was also clear that as mis-guided as its overall industrial policy had been, the state had once again, as soon as the chips were down, put its faith in finance. The unravelling of the consensus was clearly gathering pace.

In the aftermath of the leveraged buy-out, the Monopolies and Mergers Commission was set up and legislation was passed to require disclosure of all share holdings of 5 per cent or more. Edward Heath, Conservative Prime Minister, belatedly recognised the practice of corporate raiding for what it was, branding it "the unacceptable face of capitalism" (Morgan 2001, p. 319). Corporate raiding, however, had also exacerbated other problems in the British economy, which would soon take Heath's mind off corporate raiders.

Continued demand for imported consumer goods, financed by increased borrowing, resulted in further deterioration in the balance of payments – once again putting pressure on sterling. The now even less competitive British companies, many amongst the largest employers, produced waves of layoffs rather than innovative products at competitive prices, contributing to growing tensions between government and the unions. Worse still, these forces were powerfully inflationary. So not only were the state's employees producing less, they wanted more remuneration, to cushion them against the falling living standards resulting from inflation and incomes policies during the early 1970s (Wilkinson 2012).

Conclusions: power imbalances within the insecurity cycle – ideology reverses after less than four decades

By the late 1970s, Britain had gone from being an imperial power to the "sick man of Europe" in only three decades. This was an intolerable situation as far as Margaret Thatcher – elected Conservative Party leader after Heath's defeat in 1974 – was concerned. With Thatcher came new ideas about the role of the state and its relationship with the economy and society – the so-called "new right" critique (Harling 2001, p. 186).

According to this critique, by habitually conceding to the demands of powerful interest groups – especially the trade unions – the state was seen to have not only compromised its authority but also strengthened these interests, particularly following the public sector strikes of the Winter of Discontent. Voting in the 1979 general election revealed only three clear strongholds for Labour – northwest England, south Wales and central Scotland – all of which were also strongholds of the more militant trade unions and long-outdated staple industries. This clearly demonstrates that the democratic upsurge associated with the insecurity cycle is not by definition left-wing or socialist in nature. In this instance, it led directly to a mandate to emasculate the trade unions, whose creation had driven so many of the previous shifts in the cycle.

Behind the scenes, but centrally important in Britain's return to economic liberalism, were the well-funded right-wing "think tanks", perhaps most significant of which was the Institute for Economic Affairs.[25] Having emerged during the 1950s in response to the shift towards Keynesianism, they remained in the background, churning out books and pamphlets, until the opportunity to influence opinion and policy presented itself (Cockett 1995; Denham and Garnett 1998; Desai 1994). Not only are they credited with preparing the ideological ground for Thatcherism; they would also play a role in seeing that it endured beyond her terms in office through their influence on the "modernisation" of the Labour Party during the 1990s (Pautz 2011).[26]

Neoliberal thought and policy had thus been kept alive – and developed further – during the scant few decades of the Keynesian consensus. This helped to provide a framework for not only criticising Keynesian theory and policy, but also branding some of the old "laissez faire" ideas as new; it also offered an alternative set of ideas and policies to the Keynesian conventional wisdom. The social welfare system was openly criticised for failing to deliver value – for both taxpayers and beneficiaries – and economic planning was condemned as being politically dangerous and economically inefficient.

Evidence of the bankruptcy of Keynesian demand management was found in its failure to maintain full employment and control inflation and in its tendency to generate excessive budget deficits and tax levels that were seen to have crowded out private investment.[27] Even Labour's ideas had shifted towards neoliberalism, with the April 1975 Labour budget being the first post-war budget aimed at deflating the economy. But even before these measures were imposed, in a memorable speech at the 1976 Labour Party Conference, James Callaghan made it clear that his government would no longer attempt to reflate, signalling that it was now prepared to sacrifice jobs to bring inflation under control:

> We used to think that you could just spend your way out of recession and increase employment only by cutting taxes and boosting government expenditure … [But] it only worked by injecting bigger doses of inflation into the economy followed by a higher level of unemployment at the

next step ... The option [of spending your way out of a recession] no longer exists.

(Callahan 1976)

The Cold War – especially in the light of the Communist Party of Great Britain helping to orchestrate union militancy – helped to generate both the fear that helps drive change, and the necessary strong political support for new ideas. In particular, it brought Hayek's ideas back into the debate, with his short polemic against totalitarianism – *The Road to Serfdom* – reportedly finding a home in Margaret Thatcher's handbag.

In the end, whilst it had taken two centuries to finally replace "laissez faire" as the conventional wisdom following the Second World War, it took little more than two decades to begin to reverse that process. Whether this is the result of the apparent failure of Keynesianism, the power imbalance between the two sides of the insecurity cycle – or a combination of the two – is a matter for debate.

Notes

1 See, for example, Bartlett (1972); Cain and Hopkins (1993, pp. 234, 265–6, 275–7, 290–1); Cairncross (1985, pp. 230–1); Chick (1998, p. 39); Kennedy (1988, pp. 367–8); Mann (1988, p. 27); Watt (1984, pp. 149–51); Wilensky (1975, pp. 75–9).

2 See also, Pollard (1982); Strange (1971); and Bartlett (1972).

3 The regulation of hire purchase was centrally important in the fine tuning of consumers' demand in the three decades after 1946. Hire purchase was controlled by adjustments to the proportion of the purchase price required as a down payment, and by changes in the interest rates and the length of the repayment periods which determined the size of the monthly repayments. These proved effective counter-cyclical measures, but they concentrated the burden of cuts on a narrow range of industries.

4 The *official* interest rate fixed jointly by the Treasury and the Bank of England at which the latter would lend to commercial banks when functioning as lender of last resort, and which was designed to regulate the level and cost of bank lending.

5 The question of whether cost inflation is possible without an inflation of demand by a permissive increase in the money supply was resolved (at least to the satisfaction of the cost inflation theorists) by the assumption of endogenous money so that cost inflation generates its own money supply.

6 CCC resulted in an increase in interest-bearing deposits of 112.5 per cent between 1971 and 1973, compared with the previous annual increase of 5–10 per cent (Kaldor 1986, p. 105, footnote 69).

7 Under the Bretton Woods system, most countries sought to maintain an overall balance of trade, settling international trade balances in US dollars, with the US's agreement to redeem other central banks' dollar holdings for gold at a fixed rate of 35 dollars per ounce. The US, however, had not been overly concerned about maintaining a balance in trade since it could pay its export deficits in dollars. Nor had it taken action to prevent the steady loss of American gold. By 1971, under pressure to devalue its currency, due to the decline in US gold reserves, instead of devaluing the dollar, President Nixon removed gold backing from the dollar. (See Helleiner 1994, pp. 115–21, for a further discussion.)

8 That is the marginal product of labour times the price of the product. For the imperfectly competitive firm both marginal product and the price of products decline with output.

9 This is because Meade made the neo-classical assumption of diminishing marginal productivity in production.

10 This is because Meade made the neo-classical assumption of diminishing marginal satisfaction in consumption.

11 Joan Robinson (1969 [1933]) wrote: "We shall say that a group of workers are being exploited when their wage is less than the marginal physical product that they are producing valued at the price at which it is being sold" (p. 283). She also spelled out in detail the conditions under which a reduction in the degree of monopoly, and hence the exploitation of workers, would or would not increase employment.

12 See Marx (2015 [1887], chapter 25 and, especially, pp. 762–72).

13 See, for example, Kaldor (1976).

14 Governments generally did little to control prices, more usually they contributed to price increases by raising indirect taxes.

15 After the initial pay freeze, phase 2 of the policy established a maximum pay increase of £1 plus 4 per cent and at least twelve months between pay settlements; and phase 3 set a limit to weekly pay increases of £2.25 or 7 per cent, whichever was greater.

16 Import price pressure on domestic prices increased during the early 1970s as world prices of food and raw material began to rise sharply under the pressure of growing demand; and this inflation was exacerbated by the trebling of oil prices by OPEC following the Arab/Israeli Yom Kippur War in 1973. During that year, sterling prices of imports in Britain increased by 24 per cent, and by a further 42 per cent in the following year in 1974.

17 For a discussion of wage inflation and expectations, see Coutts *et al.* (1976).

18 In 1974, since average weekly earnings were around £40, 40 pence was approximately 1 per cent.

19 For further detail, see for example Morgan (1990, pp. 382–433); Whitehead (1985, pp. 282–4 and 1987, pp. 241–73); Taylor, R. (1996, pp. 88–121, esp. pp. 108–9); Hall (1986, pp. 94–5).

20 These theories, which had been evolved during the inter-war years, shifted the focus to individual firms competing in particular idealised market structures and away from clusters of firms operating in industrial regions or sectors. Taking a static equilibrium approach based on a priori reasoning and assuming a given market size, capacity utilisation – and hence employment – is theorised to be determined by the "equilibrium" level of output, which only in perfectly competitive markets is at full employment. From this perspective, as in any other market, unemployment is considered *voluntary*; and the solution – as in any other market – is a reduction in the price of labour (see, for example, Sraffa 1926; and Robertson *et al.* 1930).

21 For a detailed account of this, see Hunter (1966).

22 An important example of this was the fresh milk market. The Milk Marketing Board (MMB) was set up in the 1930s to regulate the wholesale milk market. The MMB intermediated between the milk producers and the milk sellers and fixed a guaranteed price for farmers. The MMB had a chequered career and was finally abolished by the EU. This shifted the balance in favour of large milk retailers which were by then overwhelmingly the retail chains who used milk as a loss leader in their competition with each other, and in the process virtually eliminated door to door milk deliveries. The large retail chains could then shift the cost of cheapening milk back to the dairies and ultimately to the milk producers, threatening milk supply.

23 See also Cosh and Hughes (2008), who endorse the earlier conclusions of Singh (1975), p. 954: "insofar as the neoclassical postulate of profit maximization relies on the doctrine of economic natural selection in the capital market (via the take-over mechanism) the empirical base for it is very weak".

24 A more public breach resulted when the Conservative Chancellor, Nigel Lawson, felt that the Bank's intervention in the Johnson Matthey Bankers affair in 1984, had been carried out without his being kept fully informed.

25 The Institute for Economic Affairs (IEA) had been founded in 1955 by Antony Fisher, at the request of Hayek; and it was part of the international network of free market thinkers associated with the Mont Pelerin Society. The "crisis" Thatcher confronted when she came to office seemed to verify the IEA's critique of the Keynesian consensus; it was thus well placed to provide an alternative to the policies that seemed to have failed. In 1974, the Centre for Policy Studies (CPS) was founded by Keith Joseph and Margaret Thatcher, to champion economic liberalism in Britain; and the Adam Smith Institute (ASI), founded by Madsen Pirie and Eamonn Butler in 1977, served as a driving force behind the development and promotion of Thatcher's privatisation, taxation, education and health policies (Denham and Garnett 1998).

26 A number of the ASI's policies were also adopted by the Blair Labour government; and in 1998, with the foundation of the Institute for Public Policy Research (IPPR) (by James Cornford), Labour had its own think tank, which was instrumental in both the Party's modernisation and popularisation of its "Third Way" politics.

27 For a further discussion, see for example, Mishra (1984, chapter 2).

8   Neoliberalism entrenched

Introduction

The latter half of the 1960s and the whole of the following decade had – for the first time since the Second World War – witnessed growing animosity between the government and the unions, both of which had considerable power. Prior to this, there had been few problems. But as it became undeniably clear that Britain had fallen far behind her industrial competitors – and as the resulting negative effects on both inflation and the balance of payments intensified – their objectives began to diverge. Meanwhile, finance and the Treasury had largely continued with "business as usual", despite the consequences for either – or both – of the two warring parties. Together, these three interest groups had already seriously undermined productive industry in Britain, but there was worse to come.

The immediate outcome of these events was to produce greatly heightened insecurity on the part of the unions as well as genuine unease about the threat of socialism on the part of politicians, especially those like Margaret Thatcher. This fear would provide the backdrop for many of her policies; and in spite of the overall economic aim being a return to libertarianism, they would also contain a significant "Hayekian" political dimension. At this point in time, "Keynesian" ideas, although showing some signs of frailty, were still deeply held; and any alternative ideas would experience considerable difficulty in unseating them – just as they would in attempting to topple the neoliberal creed forty years later.

Perhaps surprisingly, in the context of the Cold War – with known communists orchestrating much of the union militancy – during the 1970s, the Labour vote had held up remarkably. This may have been due in part to the high density of union membership at the time. But when the public sector strikes of the Winter of Discontent provided a crisis that directly affected ever more electors, there was a clear change of mood; and the resulting democratic upsurge propelled Margaret Thatcher into office. Inspired by Hayek's ideas, the spectre of socialism, real or imagined, would be Thatcher's primary target, as indeed it had been for another of her formative influences – Augusto Pinochet's Chile.

The chronic crisis of the 1970s and the acute crisis of the Winter of Discontent thus served as a catalyst for a shift in the insecurity cycle. It also provided the context for what Milton Friedman referred to as "shock treatment" (Friedman 1988). The 1979 Conservative government simply took a leaf out of Friedman and the "Chicago Boys'" Chilean playbook, and withdrew the state from much of the economy, selling off not only the nationalised industries, but also vast numbers of public sector houses. This would have lasting effects on the welfare bill, attitudes towards property, debt and consumption, as well as the balances of banks' loan books. It would also eventually produce significant and growing inequality – and the return of mass poverty; and, as in the case of Chile, the trade unions would find themselves in the firing line.

The outcome of Thatcher's policies would be remarkably similar to that experienced by Chile, although she would not go as far as Pinochet in reducing social welfare costs. In Britain, the expense of regulatory systems set-up to monitor the newly privatised industries meant that the state's financial commitment to the economy shifted, rather than shrank. Economic policy included further experimentation with monetarism; and for a short time, the resulting widening deficit, as well as the cost of tax cuts were mitigated by the discovery of oil beneath the North Sea. Whilst in retrospect, it is clear that this could have been better invested, so too could the rapidly expanding resources of the financial sector, which helped to power the nation's shopping spree.

By the time Margaret Thatcher left office, the Winter of Discontent was a distant memory, the unions had been crushed and European growth had slowed sufficiently to allow the UK to catch up. All of this could be presented as success, although Britain's growth was fuelled by new "industries" – house buying and retail – both being funded by steeply rising private debt. The general sense that things were looking up meant a significant reduction of pressures on the insecurity cycle. Thus, no-one, including the Labour Party, saw much benefit in shifting course.

But Labour was not looking forward to being permanently in opposition. Despite evidence during John Major's two terms in office that the Labour Party might well win an election, under Tony Blair, the party opted to move sharply to the right. "New Labour" embraced neoliberalism, whilst claiming it to be a "Third Way" – a nebulous concept that never did crystallise into anything recognisably unique. Unfortunately for New Labour, they would then find themselves in government when the wheels came off the economy. With neoliberalism proving to be at least as problematic as its predecessor, their experiment with neoliberal capitalism would backfire badly.

Thus, by the 2007–8 financial crisis, Britain had experienced more than three decades of neoliberal policies, under five Conservative and three Labour governments, supported by the old Bretton Woods institutions and, increasingly, the European Union. According to its advocates, these policies should have produced higher, more stable growth in GDP and a more competitive economy with greater choice and lower prices. They should also have reduced waste, due to lack of government interference, justifying the supposedly lower taxes. Admittedly, acceptance of the "natural" rate of unemployment had meant an end to full employment; but the "trickle down" effect of the wealthy spending their resources was expected to minimise this. Hayek – and indeed Thatcher – might add that these policies would also fend off socialism. But this last point would be the only issue on which they could not – yet, at least – be seriously challenged.

In the sections ahead, we consider neoliberalism in the context of the four key drivers of the insecurity cycle as well as its contending interest groups. We also explore the additional factors of fear, over-confidence – especially during an extended boom – and the increasing influence of financialisation.

Thatcher, Chile and Britain's "honorary Chicago Boy"

> When General Pinochet came to power in Chile after a military coup in 1973, he unleashed a wave of radical free-market policies that thrilled rightwing observers in Britain. The resulting "economic miracle" in Chile benefited only some and was achieved at a cost of detention, torture and assassination. Nonetheless, it provided an inspiration for the monetarist revolution of the Thatcher years – and echoes of Chile-style economics survive here to this day.
>
> (Beckett 2002)

According to Andy Beckett, the "admission" that Pinochet's – or more precisely, Milton Friedman's – Chile had provided the inspiration for Thatcher's Britain

> came buried in the middle of a paragraph on page 58 of a pamphlet justifying the coup in which he seized power: "This is not the place to describe the details of Chile's new prosperity under Pinochet. Suffice to say that it was Thatcherite before Thatcher, though with a tougher stance towards the trade unions and a more consistent commitment to monetarism and markets".
>
> (Beckett 2002)

The background to this was the 1970 election of Salvador Allende.[1] Aside from being the first (and to date, only) democratically elected Marxist premier, Allende had also earned the ire of the United States by planning to nationalise much of Chile's economy – including significant American interests in both telecommunications and copper. Nor was it just the Americans who were uncomfortable with this new socialist state; Chile's wealthy families and political right, who had previously controlled much of the Chilean economy, also viewed the idea with concern.

However, the roots of the Chilean experiment with neoliberalism went back much further than the CIA-assisted military coup that ended both

Allende's regime and his life in 1973. In line with Friedman's views about the importance of having alternative ideas ready, to quickly take advantage of any crisis that might present itself, the training of Chilean economists at the University of Chicago had begun as early as 1955 – whilst the "Keynesian" consensus was still enjoying its golden age. These "Chicago Boys" studied directly under Friedman and came into contact with Hayek, who during this period was a professor at Chicago's Centre on Social Thought.

The project had been organised by the US Department of State as part of the "Point Four Program", under the 1950 Foreign Economic Assistance Act, which was set up to provide "technical assistance" to developing countries. According to President Harry Truman,

> Communist propaganda holds that the free nations are incapable of pro-viding a decent standard of living for the millions of people in under-developed areas of the earth. The Point Four program will be one of our principal ways of demonstrating the complete falsity of that charge.
>
> (Truman 1950)

Funded by both the Rockefeller and Ford Foundations, this project provided a link between the University of Chicago's Department of Economics and the Catholic University of Chile in Santiago.

But this was not the only significant alliance created for these Chilean economists. Their association with the influential Edwards Group was also a key connection. Highly politicised, strongly ideologically driven and an early adopter of Friedman's radical neoliberal policy matrix, the Edwards Group was closely allied with American economic and political interests; and its membership was strongly rooted in sectors – including finance and the media – likely to be able to exploit and promote such policies. In 1963, the group helped set up the Centre for Social and Economic Studies, the first neoliberal "think tank" in Chile, into which the Chicago Boys were integrated; and it invited them to establish and contribute to an economics section in the group's *El Mercurio*, Chile's leading right-wing daily newspaper (Clark 2017).

All of this put the Chicago "old boys" network into a powerful position, allowing them to present a policy document, the "Program for Economic Development", which was dubbed "The Brick" as a result of its 189-page length. Although this had failed to impress its intended recipient, Jorge Ales-sandri, the right's candidate in the elections that would bring Allende to power, it remained a ready-made economic blueprint following the over-throw of the Marxist leader by a man with little experience of running an economy. The Chicago Boys were thus more than ready for the coming crisis; and the policies they implemented shortly after Pinochet's coup would be all too familiar to those in Thatcher's Britain of a decade later – with noticeably similar results.

Alan Walters, who later served twice as Thatcher's economic adviser, first arrived in Chile two years after the coup, but Milton Friedman's ideas were certainly not new to him. In spite – or perhaps because – of his father having been a radical socialist, Walters followed both Friedman's ideas and his path into academia, whilst also working for the World Bank. Like Friedman, he considered the control of inflation to be the key economic policy objective. The problem, however – amid the still largely dominant post-war Keynesian consensus – had been persuading a government to take such a radical step away from the conventional wisdom of the time. Post-coup Chile therefore provided a valuable opportunity to experiment with Friedman's neoliberal ideas:

> Here was a small economy and society, already quite modern, urbanised, and used to receiving economic prescriptions from abroad. Its new ruler was rightwing but without much of an existing ideology. He faced no elections where bold policies might get him ejected. And he had the authority derived from a complete apparatus of state security. Finally, his predecessor had been overthrown against a backdrop of strikes, shortages and corrosive inflation. Almost any subsequent "reforms" could be made to look like progress.
>
> (Beckett 2002)

Friedman (1988) made no secret of the brutal nature of these reforms, openly describing them as "shock treatment". Nor was this description an over-statement; as a military dictator could treat any resistance harshly, this would be free market economics in its purest form. State spending was cut by over 25 per cent, with immediate and far reaching effects. Hitherto subsidised industries had no time to adapt to their sudden vulnerability to international markets and competition. Import tariffs and any price controls on local products were lifted, causing import prices to plummet and prices of Chilean products to rocket.

As if this were not trouble enough, wages fell to roughly half their level at the time of Allende's election, whilst both interest rates and indirect taxes were increased. This had drastic effects on the workforce. Not only did living standards disintegrate; unemployment spiked with the collapse of businesses suddenly exposed to the new free market economy. There was no funding to support those out of work, many of whom were forced to rely on church-run soup kitchens to keep from starving; and by mid-1976, there were more than 200 of these in the capital alone.

These reforms would be more than familiar to British people during the 1980s where for Margaret Thatcher, large-scale privatisation was a key component of policy. In Chile, this was achieved at fire sale prices, with the beneficiaries often being those who had openly tacitly supported the coup. State assets that were difficult to immediately completely privatise were instead marketised to a significant degree. Among the first organisations to have its budget cut was the state-run health service, with users being actively encouraged, if not coerced, into using private alternatives. State organised pensions were largely dismantled, with individuals being compelled to invest in private funds instead. And the laws restricting trade unions would also have echoes in the UK.

By the lead-in to the 1979 British general election, the radical changes imposed on Chile's economy and society could be presented as "the Chilean economic miracle". Inflation had been sharply reduced and productivity increased, with GDP growth at levels the US and Europe could only dream of. But these measures, characteristic of the neoliberal world view, gauge outcomes that not only matter most to international investors, but also conceal the effects on more vulnerable segments of society. Overall GDP growth, for example, says very little about the distribution of that growth, which tends to be disproportionately allocated to a small segment of society at the top of the income distribution; so unsurprisingly, Chilean society was becoming significantly more unequal.

This was of little consequence for Walters and Friedman, who now believed that they had the "facts" to demonstrate that their ideas worked, and could thus prepare the ground for the 1979 general election – and what was to follow. The British press, particularly its right-wing segment, picked up the story with zeal; the *Daily Telegraph* even went so far as to laud the Chicago Boys as "honest, idealistic and admired". Meanwhile, Walters continued to be a frequent, if low-key, visitor to Latin America. As he put it himself, "It was very exciting. I was an honorary Chicago Boy" (quoted in Beckett 2002).

Whilst the architects of Chile's "shock treatment" were clearly very pleased with themselves, not everyone was convinced by the supposed "facts" emerging from Chile. According to Jean Dreze and Amartya Sen (2002):

> the so called "monetarist experiment", which lasted until 1982 in its pure form, has been the object of much controversy, but few have claimed it to be a success ... The most conspicuous failure of the post 1973 period is that of considerable instability ... no firm and consistent upward trend.
>
> (p. 231)

Data from the UN's Economic Commission for Latin America and the Caribbean sets out the effect on Chilean society. Whereas in 1969, 17 per cent of the population was living in poverty, by 1985, this figure had ballooned to 45 per cent.

But this was not how the idea of neoliberalism would be presented to the British electorate. Its true purpose would, like the experiment in Latin America, be motivated by politics as much as economics. Margaret Thatcher's own words reveal the motivation behind not only a coup of her own against Edward Heath as Conservative Party leader (following the reversal of his own experiment with monetarism in 1973), but also against British socialism. Her memoirs reveal clear distaste for the "hard left", which, in Thatcher's view, "were revolutionaries who sought to impose a Marxist system on Britain, whatever its means and whatever its cost", their power being "entrenched in three institutions: the Labour Party, local government and the trade unions" (Thatcher 1993, p. 339). She was also deeply suspicious of what she considered the "fraternal relations between trade union leaders and the Soviet bloc" as well as the "militants clearly out to bring down the Government" (quoted in Beckett 2002) – all of which foreshadowed the visceral struggle ahead with the National Union of Mineworkers.

For now, though, it was enough to pave the way to government and prepare the electorate for a fundamental change in the conventional wisdom. The political support for a move in the insecurity cycle would soon be in place.

Thatcherism: the state again steps away from the economy

The 1970s had witnessed initial steps towards financial liberalisation with the switch from direct to indirect controls on bank lending under Competition and Credit Control in 1971. This was followed by the shift from fixed to floating exchange rates in 1973, after the collapse of the Bretton Woods system. But by the late 1970s, the government still played an important role in managing the UK economy, with the aim of maintaining both full employment (although this was becoming increasingly difficult to achieve) and a social welfare net. Capital movements, investment, prices and incomes were still tightly regulated; large swathes of industry and housing remained under public ownership and trade unions remained powerful.

When Margaret Thatcher ascended to office in 1979, she viewed the British as "a brave people who were stifled and controlled by a bureaucratic state that penalized the good and rewarded the bad, stifled innovation, while generating feckless welfare dependency" (quoted in Coutts and Gudgin 2015, p. 9). Like the other governments of the 1970s, she was welcomed into office by the now familiar high inflation, high unemployment and restless trade unions. Like Heath, her response leant heavily on Milton Friedman's monetarist ideas, with sharply increased interest rates and equally abrupt cuts in government spending – with predictable results.

By 1981, GDP had fallen by 2.5 per cent whilst unemployment had risen to 13.3 per cent (the highest in Europe), with industrial unrest sharply increasing. Barring a miracle or a rapid change in policy, the Thatcher government appeared to be living on borrowed time, with Sir Ian Gilmour going so far as to dismiss the latest attempt at monetarism as "the uncontrollable in pursuit of the undefinable" (quoted in Young 2013, p. 203). Inevitably – in spite of her now famous response to the idea of policy change at the 1980 Conservative Party Conference: "You turn if you want to; the lady's not for turning" – by 1984, Thatcher's monetary policy had effectively been dropped.

Her real saviour, however, came not in shifts in economic policy, but in the unlikely form of Argentina's General Galtieri and his occupation of the

Falkland Islands, a British overseas territory. Thatcher's response was to declare war in 1982, with support from a number of allies, including Chile.[2] The outcome was a significant distraction from domestic economic problems for much of the electorate – and a decisive victory – giving Thatcher a popular mandate and returning her to power with a large majority.

Meanwhile, although unemployment remained high, inflation had dropped from a peak of 18 per cent to 8 per cent; and there seemed to be a modest recovery under way. The discovery of North Sea oil in 1970, which commenced production during 1975 and peaked in 1979, had helped reduce the balance of payments and budget deficits. It also turned sterling into something of a "petro-currency", although the higher exchange rate was a mixed blessing for the competitiveness of British industry, which already had more than enough problems with which to grapple.

Whilst the monetarist policy experiment had been a failure, this did not deter the implementation of a raft of other neoliberal policy reforms, many being similar to those that had been tried in Chile. One of the first acts of the new government, for example, was to abandon exchange controls, further opening up the UK economy to foreign competition and foreign direct investment. This accelerated the decline in what remained of domestic industry, intensifying industrial unrest in the process (Harvey 2005, p. 59). Despite strong pressure from the labour movement to protect domestic industry and employment, Thatcher believed that this would only preserve inefficiency and competitive weakness. Her industrial strategy thus focused on allowing the "free" market to determine the winners and losers. But like her predecessors, she entirely failed to grasp the underlying causes of Britain's industrial weakness.

One of the stated aims of the re-privatisation of large sectors of the economy was to promote much wider share ownership; and between 1979 and 1995, roughly two-thirds of these were sold off, raising roughly £30 billion for public revenues (Riddel 1991, pp. 87–92), which was largely used to finance tax cuts in 1985 and 1986. The sales also released the government from responsibility for the state of the declining industries; and no attempt was made to help industry evolve. By 1988, over 20 per cent of British adults owned shares, up from 6 per cent in 1984 (Morgan 2001, pp. 566–7). However, in spite of the government's espoused commitment to the "free" market – and unlike the Chicago Boys in Chile – regulatory agencies were set up to protect consumers and promote competition. The cost of this, as well as that of high levels of redundancies, meant that there was no change in the size of the state.

This rapid and substantial increase in share – and especially home – ownership, however, came with a significant down-side: it introduced a new, speculative dimension into both consumer and financial market behaviour. During recurring stock market and housing booms, Keynes's famous "animal spirits" took hold as confidence soared, fuelling asset bubbles, which came to be accepted as legitimate engines for growth. But they all eventually and inevitably collapsed, with a major stock market crash in 1987, followed closely by the bursting of the house price bubble.

Nevertheless, up until this point at least, the Thatcher government appeared on the face of it – as had the Chicago Boys in Chile – to have conquered many of Britain's economic difficulties; and there was even talk of a "British miracle" (Morgan 2001, p. 568). The seeming return to prosperity also boosted confidence in neoliberal economic ideas. Less obvious though, was that a significant shift in relative power was under way, with the private sector – finance in particular – vastly increasing its influence, at the expense of the state. According to Morgan (2001): "the government's continuing popularity rested on its claim to have been the architect of new prosperity, based on finance, credit and consumer pump-priming rather than on mass manufacturing industry as in the past" (p. 471).

Freer trade encouraged a consumer culture, whilst the proliferation of financial institutions had a similar effect with regard to debt. Britain, like Chile and the US, had thus concluded that the experiment with a better overall society – and the state as a key player – was over. It was instead building an economy increasingly favourable to international corporations, with the large increase in financialisation fostering a switch to financial measures of success. Full employment, let alone concern about the type or value of that employment, was now at best a secondary consideration.

Financialisation: a potent weapon against socialism?

Not much of Margaret Thatcher's first government's policy package had been new. A repeat of the monetarist experiment had been tried and failed; nor had the reversal of trade union law and a return to laissez faire offered anything fresh. According to Eric Evans, instead of basing policy on a more or less coherent body of thought or ideology, "Thatcherism ... offers no new insights and, although profoundly ideological on one level, it is better seen as a series of non-negotiable precepts than as a consistent body of thought" (Evans 2004, p. 2). Evans goes on to contend that

> Thatcher had no difficulty identifying what she was against: state interference with individual freedom; state initiatives that encourage an ethos of "dependency"; woolly consensuality; high levels of taxation; the propensity of organized labour and entrenched professional interests to distort market forces; and a reluctance to be "pushed around", either personally or as a nation state.
>
> (Ibid., p. 3)

It is thus perhaps unsurprising that Thatcher's assertion that "we are building a property owning democracy", during an interview with *Time Magazine*, had also been made previously – by her predecessor, Harold Macmillan, in 1951. Nevertheless, this reprise signalled changes designed to re-shape society and encourage working class Conservative – rather than Labour – voters (Ogden and Melville 1987).

The evident power of the trade unions in Britain, along with the clear influence of the Communist Party of Great Britain and a general advance of socialism in Europe, did little for the confidence of those with wealth and influence. Encouraged by the thinking of Hayek, who had seen at first hand some of the effects of state intervention of a rather less than benevolent nature – and of Alan Walters, who had been involved enough in the Chilean project to be considered an "honorary Chicago Boy" – Thatcher's government decided to embark on a counter-revolution of its own. Not only would the ownership of property provide more people with a stake in the economy; it might also change the way those people thought – and by extension, voted. In other words, it might be expected to significantly inhibit any further tendencies towards socialism. As Augusto Pinochet himself had put it, "Chile will be safe from communism, when every Chilean has their own car and house" (quoted in Beckett 2002).

Building this new property-owning democracy demanded three preconditions: sufficient property for the public to buy, the means for them to buy it and something to encourage them to take the leap. Some of the property would be shares in newly privatised companies, but of far more lasting significance, the 1980 Housing Act encouraged large numbers of council tenants to buy their homes – with the encouragement taking the form of heavily discounted prices.

Massively increasing the supply of credit to purchase these new assets was also essential. Building societies, which had hitherto monopolised the residential mortgage market, lost their tax and other advantages, increasing the interest they paid and earned to market rates. By 1983, banks had been allowed to enter the mortgage market and were gaining market share (Wilkinson 2012). Since they had freer access to the wholesale money markets, they had a competitive advantage. This was addressed by the Building Societies Act of 1986, allowing mutuals to increase the proportion of funds that they, too, could now raise in the wholesale money market. This extra competition pushed down interest rates, fuelling a housing boom and driving a substantial increase in personal debt.

The rapid price rises in artificially under-valued ex-council houses produced quick profits (on paper, at least). This, in turn, helped change attitudes towards debt, recasting it as an investment, rather than a burden, and removing the social stigma with which it had previously been associated. Both home ownership and personal debt rose sharply. Whereas in 1961, seven million households owned their own homes, by 1987, this had more than doubled to 14.5 million; in 1981, 56 per cent of British households lived in owner-occupied accommodations and by 1996, the figure was over two-thirds (Morgan 2001, p. 566; ONS 2010; Wilkinson 2012). This mass privatisation of the housing market would eventually prove problematic, with home ownership figures going into reverse and "Generation Rent" adding to a growing feeling that "free" markets might not in fact magically clear after all. But one effect of the selling off of council houses – 500,000 of them during Thatcher's first term alone – would remain, with the increase in personal debt in Britain representing to no small degree the transfer of large amounts of debt from the public to the private sector.

The large increase in home ownership brought with it further opportunities for the financial sector in terms of mortgages, home improvement loans, secured loans for large consumer purchases, insurance products and so on (Wilkinson 2012). From the consumer's point of view, this moved the financial credibility of any prospective government up the list of key voting criteria for the new home-owning segments of the electorate, many of whom were also sufficiently comforted by the rise in the value of their homes – and hence access to further credit – to be less worried by the flat wage growth being experienced by many.

Whilst this has undoubtedly contributed to the resilience of the neoliberal paradigm since the 1980s, it came with a number of drawbacks. Chief amongst these has been the tendency of consumers to act in a similar manner to investment bankers, by using the credit available from an already heavily leveraged asset (their home), to fund further consumption. The result has been vastly higher levels of leverage for both households and financial institutions, and a commensurate increase in exposure to changes in interest rates and the bursting of asset bubbles; and it has made both consumers and the financial sector vulnerable to any interruption in the supply of cheap credit.

The great sell-off and the boom that followed effectively saddled much of the public with significant debt and created the "speculative consumer" – a cultural change that in many ways mirrored that in the City – as many bought property for financial rather than housing needs. This, in turn, meant that governments could now be judged on the basis of new criteria, such as house prices and interest rate levels, rather than employment. Power had shifted decisively towards finance.

Financial de-regulation: extreme risks and rewards

By the mid-1980s, London had fallen behind New York as an international centre for finance – especially since the 1975 "May Day" deregulation in New York. Thatcher, who blamed both excessive regulation and the "old boy's network" for this lack of competitiveness, opted for fundamental change. The result was the "Big Bang" in 1986, which ushered in radical cultural changes and a period of rapid internationalisation, with profound effects on the UK financial sector, and by extension, the wider economy.

Prior to 1986, the City had consisted of small, specialist firms, largely immune from takeover. Stockbrokers could buy or sell particular shares, but not both; the process was mediated by "stock jobbers", through whose books every transaction went, on a fixed-fee basis. Whilst this system could be cumbersome at times, it was transparent and stable. It was also a significant component of the self-regulatory system, then in place. But on 27 October 1986, this regime was abruptly swept away; the buy and sell sides of brokerage were dis-intermediated, much of the transparency was removed and the modern trader was born. Banks and other financial institutions were also now allowed to trade in stocks and shares, and began to acquire brokerage businesses.

City firms suddenly found themselves vulnerable to international competition as well as to the threat of hostile takeover by banks and other financial intermediaries. Reduced regulation, computerised trading and a time zone ideally placed between New York and Tokyo put London back at the centre of the global financial network. The resulting wave of acquisitions, many by non-British institutions, was not restricted to specialist City firms. By 1992, the Hong Kong & Shanghai Bank (HSBC) had acquired the Midland Bank – then the UK's biggest high street bank by market capitalisation – and moved its headquarters to London to take advantage of the new "light touch" regulation.

British banks, however, also pursued growth through acquisition. In 1986, Lloyds acquired the Continental Bank of Canada, adding the Trustee Savings Bank and the Cheltenham and Gloucester in 1995. The Royal Bank of Scotland (RBS) acquired the Citizens Financial Group, which through its own acquisitions, had become the eighth largest bank in America – giving RBS significant representation in the US market. RBS also acquired NatWest during the 1990s, followed by the Dutch bank, ABN Amro. However, whilst this last move would contribute to RBS's undoing in the financial crisis of 2007–8, the process of acquisition created the "Big Four" UK domiciled banks. They were now highly internationalised in their business and complex in terms of management systems, both of which made them vulnerable.

The year 1986 also brought the Financial Services Act. This was due in part to the radical programme of deregulation, as well as to the 1984 collapse of Johnson Matthey Bankers (JMB), which revealed both flaws in the 1979 Banking Act and fault lines in the regulatory system itself. The Bank of England quickly intervened, to prevent a loss of confidence in the gold bullion market, where JMB was a key player.

However, Thatcher's Chancellor, Nigel Lawson, felt that the Bank had not kept him informed, straining relations between the government and the Bank. This tension appears to have increased pressure for a change in regulatory structure, especially of securities, financial markets and insurance. The Financial Services Act was the first UK legislation to regulate the securities industry and markets.[3] Professor Laurence Gower, who had been asked to produce a report on financial regulation, followed by a draft bill, had recommended a stricter, top-down structure. However, his bill was watered down by the government in the light of the more relaxed regulation evolving in New York. The system adopted embraced self-supervision – overseen by the newly created Securities and Investments Board (SIB) – with firms operating in the UK being required to seek either membership of a self-regulatory organisation (SRO) or direct supervision by the SIB. SIB members were appointed by the Treasury, further eroding the regulatory authority of the Bank.

American banks, in particular, had not been slow to see the opportunity to circumvent the second Glass Steagall Act (which had separated commercial and speculative banking operations, in the wake of the 1929 stock market crash) by setting up in London, beyond its jurisdiction. Many of the small, specialised banks were swallowed up, laying the foundations of the global financial behemoths that would ultimately become "too big to fail".

Britain would soon find itself on the receiving end of these newly empowered financial markets. Whilst Chile had experienced a financial crisis a decade previously as a result of pegging the peso to the US dollar, in 1990, shortly after succeeding Margaret Thatcher as Prime Minister, John Major took sterling into the European Exchange Rate Mechanism (ERM), effectively tracking the Deutsche Mark. The ERM was a "semi pegged" system, where currencies had restricted margins within which to float. The 1992 Maastricht Treaty, however, tightened the criteria: inflation could now be no more than 1.5 per cent above the average of the three best performing member states; balance of payments deficits could not exceed 3 per cent of GDP at the end of the preceding fiscal year nor could debt exceed 60 per cent. In addition, the currency must not have been devalued in the two years prior to membership, whilst long-term interest rates must not exceed those of the three best performing states on inflation by more than 2 per cent. This worsened Britain's existing problem of defending a fixed exchange rate, which had kept interest rates high throughout the 1980s – with the predictable detrimental effect on manufactured exports.

Currency speculators soon realised that sterling was over-valued, despite its membership in the ERM; and in early September 1992, to encourage devaluation, speculators sold billions of pounds with the expectation of buying them back at the depreciated rate, and making a large profit on the difference. This put tremendous pressure on sterling, forcing the government to raise interest rates, whilst attempting to buy the pounds now flooding the market. But, as a consequence of deregulation, the Bank of England did not have access to the funds available to the speculators. Finally, on 16 September 1992 – "Black Wednesday" – sterling was forced out of the ERM. The official cost of the debacle – part of the speculators' profit – was, according to government figures, £3.3 billion (HM Treasury 2008).

However, as has so often happened following usually doomed attempts to defend a currency, the resulting devaluation aided Britain's recovery from recession. Sterling was allowed to float, permitting interest rates to be cut to 7.9 per cent in October 1992. By November of the following year, they were 5.4 per cent, causing commentators to revise their description of 16 September 1992 to "White Wednesday" and Norman Tebbit, a minister in Margaret Thatcher's governments, to rebrand the ERM as the "Eternal Recession Machine" (Tebbit 2005).

The City had been unleashed, and its scope for business hugely expanded. Industry, on the other hand, had been very much slimmed down, had largely pacified unions and – following White Wednesday, at least – interest rates were stable. There were few other benefits though; the asymmetry of the British economy was growing, as was a similar asymmetry in government; the power of local authorities had been weakened, with a steady concentration of power in central government.

Trade unions, employers and industry: a shift in the balance of power

Thatcher, inspired by a combination of Hayek's warnings against totalitarianism, the crushing of Allende's Marxist regime in Chile and its replacement by an extreme free market experiment, decided to confront what she saw as one of the UK's main threats – organised labour. Initially, like Stanley Baldwin before the General Strike in 1926, she played for time, using it to prepare for the inevitable. Thus, early in her term in office, Thatcher had settled with the miners, not yet feeling strong enough to win a major confrontation (Thatcher 1993, pp. 139–43).

By 1983, though, the conciliatory approach had vanished. Having built up substantial coal stocks – and with increased authority after the successful Falkland Islands campaign – Thatcher took on "the enemy within" – the National Union of Mineworkers (NUM). The result was a long, bitter and very public fight. In the end, both the strike and the power of the NUM were broken. Again, following the example of Stanley Baldwin in the aftermath of the 1926 General Strike, trade union power was further weakened by a series of legislative changes, bearing a remarkable similarity to those enacted in Pinochet's Chile These included the banning of secondary picketing; the removal of the trade unions' immunity from the liabilities for economic losses caused by strikes; (a nod to the old Taff Vale Decision of 1901); and the imposition of more restrictive conditions for strike balloting, which sharply reduced both union bargaining strength and the independence of shop stewards (Jarley 2002).

The result was a significant shift in the balance of power between the three main interest groups. The state had not only withdrawn from direct involvement in industry as an employer; it had also legislated against many of the key approaches to the orchestration of industrial action by trade unions – significantly strengthening the position of employers in the process. The effect on the unions was dire; membership declined sharply, partly as a result of the run-down in manufacturing and the mass closure of coal mines. Whereas union density had peaked in 1979 at 55.8 per cent of the workforce, by 1990 it had declined to 38.1 per cent and by 1998 to 29.6 per cent (Fairbrother 2002, p. 64). The bulk of the more traditionally militant union membership was now restricted to the public sector, with not only limited room for action, but also little economic influence. Thatcher had thus finally expunged the long uncompetitive and most militant industries – but had nothing to offer in terms of encouraging any replacements – resulting in an increase in both unemployment and social welfare costs.

But things would get even more difficult for the unions. Although the collapse of the Soviet Union in 1992 – and the subsequent disbanding of the Communist Party of Great Britain – had ameliorated one problematic element, the trade union movement would find itself out of step with an evolving Labour Party. Tony Blair's "New" Labour would, rightly or wrongly, blame the party's electoral failure on its perceived links with socialism, in general, and trade unions, in particular. Rather than continue representing labour in Parliament, Blair's party turned right, adopting the neoliberal mantra. Even the newly problematic Clause IV – originally drafted by Sidney Webb, which committed the party to push for socialism and worker ownership of the means of production – would be dropped. The unions would find themselves with sharply reduced economic influence and political power as the party they had played a pivotal role in creating now perceived them as an electoral liability.

Inequality – and the return of the poor

Poverty and inequality in the UK had generally declined during the immediate post-war decades. Rowntree's third survey of poverty in York, published in 1951, found the almost complete elimination of the type of deprivation he had documented in previous studies – an improvement he attributed to government policies of full employment and the welfare state. Thus, by the 1950s, it appeared that absolute poverty was a minor problem. Inequality had also been substantially reduced; whereas the share of the top 1 per cent in gross income had been 19 per cent in 1919, it fell to around 6 per cent by 1979 (Atkinson 2015, p. 20).

However, Brian Abel-Smith and Peter Townsend's seminal study of poverty in post-war Britain – *The Poor and the Poorest*, published in 1965 – found a re-emergence of *relative* poverty during the latter part of the 1950s. Defining poverty as 140 per cent of the current National Assistance level, Abel-Smith and Townsend (1965) employed a definition of poverty that was explicitly relative: "The approach we have adopted follows from the principle that the minimum level of living regarded as acceptable by a society increases with rising national prosperity" (p. 19). This was in line with a series of academic studies from the Department of Social Administration (now Social Policy) at the London School of Economics, which defined poverty in relation to benefit levels; and it marked a break with the earlier "minimum needs approach" that had been the basis of Booth's and Rowntree's poverty surveys, those of the inter-war years and Rowntree's later surveys.

Abel-Smith and Townsend (1965) found that the proportion of households below the poverty line had increased from 10.1 per cent (4 million people) in 1953/4 to 17.9 per cent (7.5 million people) in 1960, with poverty disproportionately concentrated in one-person households (particularly pensioners) and large households with more than six persons (highlighting the problem of child poverty). These findings reinforced those of others, including Townsend (1955) and Cole and Utting (1962), undermining the complacency surrounding the success of the post-war welfare state, with a major impact on the 1960s social policy agenda. This led to the establishment of the Child Poverty Action group in 1965 and strengthened concern about the plight of both children and the elderly in society.

The growth in inequality that would help power the re-emergence of the poor as an interest group, as well as their steady increase in numbers, thus started early. But when Thatcher came to power in 1979, one result was a discernible "inequality turn" (Atkinson 2015, p. 20). The "seven modernisations" visited on Chile by the Chicago Boys had also done little for the cohesion of Chilean society; and by 2006, with a Gini index of 52.0, it had the widest inequality gap within the OECD. Given the close match in policies with those in Britain, it would be surprising indeed if the UK had not also become dramatically more unequal since the end of the post-war consensus.

In spite of – or perhaps more accurately, because of – the frenzied privatisation, house-buying and consumer boom, the gulf between the rich and poor in Britain had indeed become much wider. Between 1977 and 1981, the ratio of the share of income earned by the top to the bottom 20 per cent of British households increased from 3.7 to 4.1, reaching 5.5 by 1988, with the Gini coefficient rising from 0.27 to 0.28 between 1977 and 1981, and reaching 0.35 in 1988 (Atkinson 1991, p. 330). Considering the Thatcher period as a whole, Sidney Pollard (1992) observed:

> the one aim which, curiously, the Government did not stress in its statements of policy, though it clearly played a large part in its programme [was] the transfer of income from the poor, and especially the poorest, to the rich, and especially the richest.
>
> (p. 379)

It did not take the latest incarnation of "laissez faire" policies to create living conditions reminiscent of those leading up to the Liberal reforms of the early twentieth century, either. Indeed, so bad had things become in some urban areas, that the Church of England felt moved to follow in the footsteps of Booth and Rowntree, producing a report during the autumn of 1985, entitled *Faith in the City: A Call to Action by Church and Nation*.[4] This report attempted to raise awareness of the social and economic disparities in British society that had boiled over in the riots of the summers of 1981 and 1985.

During the late 1980s, the sharp rise in relative income poverty was ruthlessly exposed by the Households Below Average Incomes (HBAI) annual survey. By this measure, the increase in poverty that had taken place during the first half of the 1980s more than reversed the gains of the immediate post-war period. But when this came to light, the government's response was to dismiss the concept of relative poverty on which the figures were based altogether (Lansley and Mack 2015, p. 10). Keith Joseph, Margaret Thatcher's first Education Secretary, argued instead, that the needs of the poor should be defined in terms of subsistence needs only:

> An absolute standard means one defined by reference to the *actual* needs of the poor and not by reference to the expenditure of those who are not poor ... By any absolute standard, there is very little poverty in Britain today.
>
> (Joseph and Sumption 1979, pp. 27–8, emphasis added)

This was a widely held view of those on the political right, and within the Conservative Party during the 1980s: what mattered was not the position of the poor relative to those who were better off, but whether the poor were improving in absolute terms, regardless of whether they were falling behind those above them in society (Lansley and Mack 2015, p. 10). In May 1989, John Moore, the Social Security Secretary, launched a high-profile attack. "Relative poverty", he said, was "simply inequality" and could therefore be ignored (quoted in Timmins 1996, pp. 150–1).

The political dividend of this position – if accepted – would have enabled the government to claim that poverty had fallen rather than soared during the 1980s. But Moore's speech was badly received. At odds with the visible evidence, it also ignored an increasing number of reports that revealed the very real problems of hardship facing a growing proportion of the population. It was therefore politically impossible to completely dismiss the reality of relative poverty, even for a government that was so ideologically uneasy with it (Lansley and Mack 2015, p. 11).

The extent and severity of the return of mass poverty after the "inequality turn" of 1979 is evident in Table 8.1, which shows the Gini coefficient[5] and measures of relative poverty[6] for the population as a whole, children and the elderly in 1964 (when the Labour government came to power), 1970 (when the Conservatives replaced them), 1974 (Labour), 1979 (Conservative) and 1997 (New Labour). This reveals the extent of the increase in poverty and inequality that occurred under the Conservative governments of the 1980s and 1990s – and how this compares with earlier periods since the re-discovery of poverty in Britain during the 1950s and 1960s. Between 1979 and the election of New Labour in 1997, the Gini coefficient increased 46 per cent (from 0.261 to 0.380) whilst the ratio of the earnings of the top 10 per cent to the bottom 10 per cent of the population increased nearly 60 per cent (from 3.178 to 5.063). Overall poverty increased 86 per cent, from 7.3 (13.7 per cent) to 13.6 million people (24.4 per cent); the number of children in poverty more than doubled (increasing by 121 per cent), from 1.9 (14.1 per cent) to 4.2 million children (33.2 per cent); and the number of elderly people in poverty increased by around 4 per cent, from 2.8 (31.6 per cent) to 2.9 million people (29.2 per cent).

Table 8.1 Inequality and poverty in the United Kingdom, 1964–97

	Government		Gini	90/10	Population		Children			Elderly		
	Out-going	In-coming			%	# (millions)	%	# (millions)		%	# (millions)	
1964	C	L	0.272	3.265	13.3	6.9	12.2	1.5		40.4	3.1	
1970	L	C	0.268	3.329	13.8	7.2	13.8	1.8		37.7	3.0	
1974	C	L	0.261	3.212	14.7	7.7	16.2	2.1		34.7	3.0	
1979	L	C	0.261	3.178	13.7	7.3	14.1	1.9		31.6	2.8	
1997	C	L	0.380	5.063	24.4	13.6	33.2	4.2		29.2	2.9	

Source: Institute for Fiscal Studies (2017).

If social conditions for many were deteriorating rapidly, the economy was doing little better. By the end of the 1980s, economic conditions were not much different to those of the 1970s. The cost of switching from policy objectives of full employment and stable prices to inflation control and GDP growth resulted in significant increases in unemployment, from 1.4 million in 1979, to 3.3 million in 1985, briefly falling to 1.7 million in 1990 before rising again to reach almost 3 million by 1994 (Denman and McDonald 1996). According to Sidney Pollard (1992),

> the eleven years of the Thatcher experiment ... ended in almost unmitigated failure ... in 1990, Britain had the highest rate of inflation among advanced economies ... [and] correspondingly, the highest interest rates; and it also had high and rising unemployment; large-scale bankruptcies of firms in all sectors of the economy; falling output and declining national income; and the largest deficit on the current balance of payment in history. Over the period as a whole, despite oil, Britain had, unbelievably, a slower rate of growth than in comparable periods before.
>
> (p. 379)

Prosperity in the south and east coincided with continued decline in the north and west; it also became clear that since the consumer boom had been largely financed with credit, the increased debt, with little or no equity remaining in many consumers' main asset, their home, was stifling further consumption-led growth.

"New" Labour

Whilst all this was going on, the Labour Party was not without insecure politicians of its own, with at least two – Tony Blair and Gordon Brown – being also unsure about socialism. Three election defeats since 1979 had convinced some that without a fundamentally changed relationship with the trade unions, the party might indeed be unelectable.

But this was to overlook both the lack-lustre nature of those who had led the party to those defeats and, in particular, how Neil Kinnock had managed to decisively lose an apparently winnable election in 1992. Opinion polls had consistently predicted a hung Parliament, or possibly even a narrow Labour victory, with Kinnock looking a good bet for Prime Minister. There are a number of possible reasons for Kinnock's defeat. Some blame his triumphalist behaviour and the now notorious, "We're alright!" campaign speech at the Sheffield Arena, whilst others put the result down to the *Sun* newspaper swinging its weight behind the Conservatives. At the time, the *Sun* was clear enough in its own opinion, asserting "It's *The Sun* Wot Won It". "New" Labour's Tony Blair would later go to considerable pains to ensure the support of *The Sun* for his own campaigns. It is also possible that the opinion polls got it wrong. However, as it happened, John Major handed Labour a humiliating loss – Kinnock's second – resulting in his resignation shortly afterwards.

Following Thatcher's replacement by the rather less authoritative John Major, a process of gradual modernisation had begun under the latest Labour leader, John Smith. The main development was the removal of the trade union "block" vote, whereby a union leader could effectively wield all the votes of the membership, to a "one man, one vote" system, giving each individual their own vote. This move did not cause as much controversy as might perhaps have been expected; but Smith resisted further moves, in spite of the urgings of the already influential Tony Blair and Gordon Brown.

John Major's second term of office had significant problems of its own. Accusations of "sleaze" in the Conservative Party were hard to shake off and an economic recession delivered a chronic crisis. This was punctuated by an acute crisis, taking the form of the humiliating ejection of sterling from the ERM on – depending on your point of view – "Black" or "White Wednesday", which had also damaged the Conservatives' reputation for financial management.

Thus, by the mid-1990s, Major's government was becoming increasingly unpopular and lagging behind John Smith's Labour Party in the opinion polls. What might have happened at the 1997 general election, had Smith opposed Major, is a matter for speculation. It is reasonable to argue that he had a better chance of winning than any Labour leader since the Winter of Discontent. But it would not be put to the test; Smith's sudden death from a heart attack in May 1994 paved the way for Blair and Brown to take leadership of the Labour Party. With no intention of leaving their election to chance, they took the reform of the party far further, moving decisively to the right and creating "New Labour".

Social changes during the preceding decade, including the steady increase in property ownership, the sharp decline in trade union membership and the immiseration of an increasing proportion of the population had made the concept of a socialist government, based on trade union support, increasingly untenable. Building on the abolition of the union "block vote" and its replacement by "one man, one vote", Blair further distanced the party from both the trade unions and socialism, ultimately abandoning the now largely symbolic "Clause IV" in the Labour Party's constitution (Taylor 2009). New Labour also espoused a "Third Way". Although never satisfactorily defined (and ultimately abandoned), it apparently embraced liberal market capitalism and the private enterprise economy whilst maintaining a commitment to social justice (Finlayson 2003; Wilks-Heeg 2009; Buckler and Dolowitz 2004).

New Labour politics would be guided by pragmatism rather than ideology, by "what works"; and its 1997 election manifesto even conceded, "some of the things the Conservatives got right. We will not change them. It is where they got things wrong that we will make change. We have no intention or desire to replace one set of dogmas by another" (Labour Party Manifesto

1997). Like the Conservatives, New Labour accepted the notion of a "natural rate" of unemployment and rejected the idea that there was a long-term trade-off between inflation and unemployment, prioritising the former over the latter. Its open economy macroeconomic policy focused on monetary policy – interest rates – to control inflation. The role of the state in the economy would be a stance of "fiscal passivity", supporting supply side measures (including the lowering of labour standards) that encouraged market activities, to stimulate growth. New Labour thus prioritised monetary over fiscal policy as a means of stabilising the economy (Hay 2004).

New Labour's economic and social policies

Having won the 1997 general election by a landslide, the new Chancellor, Gordon Brown, identified the economic policy objectives of New Labour as stability, employability, productivity and responsibility; and in his October 1999 Mais lecture, Brown (1999) claimed that *economic stability* is delivered by pro-active monetary policy and a prudent fiscal stance; *employability* by attaching welfare benefits to labour market activity; *productivity* by long-term investment in science, new technology and skills; and *responsibility* by avoiding short-termism in pay bargaining and by building a shared sense of national purpose.

Brown asserted that global capital flows, financial deregulation and technical change had introduced such turbulence into the money markets that hitting monetary targets had proved impossible and the switch to targeting exchange rates had proved no more successful. The price of first adopting but then switching targets was, in Brown's view, "recession, unemployment – and increasing mistrust in the capacity of British institutions to deliver the goals they set". His solution was the direct targeting of inflation, together with creating a monetary and fiscal policy framework capable of commanding public trust, market credibility and attracting investment capital at low costs.

Since the primary requirements for this were seen to be clearly defined long-term policy objectives, maximum transparency and a justifiable division of responsibility, the Bank of England was made independent and given responsibility for hitting the government's inflation target. A Monetary Policy Committee consisting of leading economists was to fix the interest rate, which was still considered the monetary lever for controlling inflation. This was claimed to remove political influence from the business cycle (Hay 2004), but it also distanced the government from responsibility for interest rates, which had become a politically sensitive measure. However, whilst the Bank of England was theoretically free to set its own interest rates, it would have to manage rates to meet the government's established targets for inflation. The publication of the minutes and votes of Monetary Policy Committee would serve to inform markets and enhance policy credibility.

The 2000 Financial Services and Markets Act created the Financial Services Authority (FSA) as a single, unified regulator for financial services, with responsibility for banking supervision and the regulation of investment services, securities, mortgages and insurance (Goodhart 2004, p. 350). It was also responsible for consumer protection and the prevention of market abuse. The Treasury was to have no operational or financial control over the FSA, which was established as a private company, limited by guarantee, to emphasise its independence. There was no formal legislation setting out the respective responsibilities of the three financial authorities; but a memorandum of understanding was established, fitting the Bank's tradition of informality. The memorandum delineated responsibility: the Treasury was responsible for the legal framework, the Bank for the stability of the financial system as a whole, and the FSA for the supervision of individual firms.

The purpose of this first package of measures was to secure the government's first condition for full employment: *credible stability* to encourage people to plan and invest in the long term.

Brown's second condition for full employment was an active labour market policy matching rights and responsibility. This was necessary, he argued, because the existence of high levels of job vacancies alongside high levels of unemployment disproved the notion that joblessness resulted from the absence of job opportunities. From this perspective, the unemployed had failed to fill vacant jobs because of the scarring effects of the 1980s recession on their skills and employability, and from a disparity between the skills and wage expectations of redundant manufacturing workers and those offered by service sector vacancies.

Thus, responsibility for unemployment was shifted away from the state. Abandoning the Keynesian view that unemployment is systemic and a consequence of an insufficient level of effective demand, trade unions were blamed for trying to hold real wages above the value of the marginal product of workers; the unemployed were blamed for being "unemployable" at the wages demanded by workers – and therefore responsible for their own unemployment and poverty – and workers were blamed for poor labour quality. This, combined with family size, was seen to be the explanation for in-work poverty (as opposed to exploitation) (Wilkinson 2001).

The effect of this mismatch on unemployment, Brown argued, was exacerbated by the failure of welfare benefits to *make work pay*. Consequently, NAIRU had shifted upwards raising the level of wage inflation associated with any given rate of unemployment. It was therefore necessary to reform the labour market to reduce NAIRU, so as to create the conditions for a long-term increase in employment without fuelling inflationary pressures. To meet these objectives, working tax credits (first introduced by the Conservatives after 1988) were significantly expanded to top up low pay and to bridge the gap between what employers were willing to pay, determined by worker productivity, and what potential employees were prepared to accept. These incentives for labour market participation were backed up by the threat of benefit withdrawal designed to coerce the unemployed into work.

From this perspective, attaching benefits to work is seen to make the offer of jobs more affordable to employers whilst making work pay for prospective employees. Thus, the cycle of welfare dependency is broken by creating greater incentives for the poor to work by making up the difference between their household needs and the market valuation of their capabilities.

However, the critique of in-work benefits based on the "Speenhamland effect" dates back to the 1980s, when they were first introduced (by a Conservative government). These had been out of policy favour between 1834, when the Poor Law Reform put an end to the Speenhamland system – that had similarly mixed wages and welfare benefits – and 1971, when Family Income Supplement was introduced as an anti-poverty measure. According to Wilkinson (2001), there are important parallels between labour market developments under neoliberalism and "the unfolding of the Speenhamland catastrophe" (p. 119):

> Since the late 1970s the labour market has been progressively restructured with an increasing polarisation of job opportunities, earnings and wealth. This growing divide is widened by the high levels of unemployment, economic decline and growing poverty in the old industrial areas and inner-cities where the poor are trapped by the multiple disadvantages which include the high costs of mobility imposed by regional house price disparities and other costs of relocation. Meanwhile, the reforms of social welfare away from universal rights towards means testing and the greater coercion of the unemployed have progressively stripped the poor of their social citizen right, rendered them *less eligible* and caught them in poverty and employment traps. These symptoms of increasing market segmentation have been partially disguised by periodic economic up-swings which have done nothing to address the underlying problems. As a result, poverty and denial of economic and social opportunity were more entrenched in the early 1990s than the 1980s, and there can be no expectation that the next recession will have any different effects.
>
> (Ibid.)

But his warning fell upon dead ears and the government duly adopted a twin-track strategy rooted in the neoliberal belief in the efficacy of markets – including labour markets.

The expectation was that the delegation of responsibility for interest rates to a committee of independent experts would improve the working of financial markets by increasing the quality of information and by removing political interference. Meanwhile, the payment of welfare benefits as wage subsidies would improve the working of the labour market by lowering the supply price of labour closer to its full employment demand price.

Other policies hinted at a less centralist approach by the new government. In 1999, a national minimum wage was introduced, albeit at such a low level as to make little if any difference; and the Low Pay Commission was set up to advise the government about its level – which remained almost unchanged. The Greater London Council (which had been dissolved by Margaret

Thatcher) was replaced by the Greater London Authority, with its own mayor; and there were devolved powers for Scotland, Wales and Northern Ireland.

Another policy – which came as a surprise, particularly given Brown's position with respect to responsibility for unemployment (and poverty) – had to do with social policy. In 1999, in his *Beveridge Revisited Lecture*, then Prime Minister Tony Blair pledged to reduce child poverty by 50 per cent within ten years and to eliminate it altogether within twenty. Although welcomed, almost no one in attendance had anticipated this; and for the first time, a relative measure of poverty – 60 per cent of household median income – was officially adopted by the British government (Lansley and Mack 2015, p. 4; Brewer *et al.* 2002, p. 2).

In opposition, leading Conservatives also supported the idea that addressing the inter-related socio-economic problems of poverty and inequality should be a government priority. In *The State of the Nation Report: Economic Dependency*, published by the Social Justice Policy Group in 2006, its chairman (and former Conservative Party leader), Iain Duncan Smith, made it clear that "[a]ll forms of poverty – absolute and relative – must be dealt with" (Social Justice Policy Group 2006, p. 3). The same report went on to contend:

> [w]e should now say explicitly: Poverty must be defined in relation to changing social norms. We should reject completely the notion that poverty can be defined in absolute terms alone. Relative poverty matters because it separates the poor from the mainstream of society.
>
> (Ibid., p. 6)

During the same year – 2006 – in his *Scarman Lecture*, the Conservative Party leader David Cameron also pledged support for tackling poverty: "I want this message to go out loud and clear: The Conservative Party recognizes, will measure and will react on poverty" (Cameron 2006a).

Under Gordon Brown, one of New Labour's final legislative acts before it lost office in 2010 was to introduce the Child Poverty Act. Backed by all major parties, the Act made reducing the number of children in poverty a legal duty for the UK government. This was supported by the incoming Conservative-Liberal Democrat coalition government, whose agreement to form a coalition in May 2010 committed the government to the Child Poverty Act's aims: "We will maintain the goal of ending child poverty in the UK by 2020" (The Coalition 2010). According to Lansley and Mack (2015), "The Act was an unambiguous statement, perhaps the most significant of the post-war era, of the societal obligation to tackle poverty. It was passed with all-party support, apparently showing that a new political consensus on poverty had finally emerged" (p. xi). But perhaps unsurprisingly, within weeks of taking office, in a swift political U-turn, senior coalition MPs launched a number of attacks on the central poverty measure; and the new government quickly distanced itself from the Act.

Thus, despite the rhetoric about tackling poverty, New Labour was no pro-trade union or socialist government. Little was done to relax the laws restricting trade unions. Central control was stiffened in some areas, with schools being allowed, under certain circumstances, to opt out of local authority control and instead be funded directly by central government. Privatisation also continued. Although most of the obvious assets had already been disposed of, future government supply contracts were sold off; and there were repeated attempts to at least partially privatise the Royal Mail, which ironically, ran into stiff union opposition. But there was still precious little support for industry, which had to make do with relatively low and stable interest rates and a reasonably competitive currency.

The move from the Conservatives to New Labour thus brought little discernible policy change, with Margaret Thatcher's expectations following her replacement by John Major being belatedly fulfilled. She was, in Malcom Rifkind's words, "the back seat driver" of British politics, even if the seat of the chauffeur was now occupied by a Labour (instead of a Conservative) Prime Minister. Both Blair and Thatcher made complimentary remarks about the other and the overall direction of policy was similar enough to allow the coining of the term "Blatcherism" (Jenkins 2006, p. 233).

This time, the Tories would spend years in the wilderness of opposition, where they in turn learned from Blair's approach. Following two further uninspiring leaders of their own, with no better success than Labour had experienced a decade earlier, the Conservatives adopted a similar route back to office, having no great urge to change the policies that the electorate could still be persuaded to vote for. Given the tendency of long-term leaders to become accident prone, it was only a matter of time before Blair's popularity would wane, whilst the Conservatives produced a "Blair" of their own, in the form of David Cameron. But the 2008 financial crisis would, to some extent change the rules of the game; and there would be no majority for David Cameron until fear – always a powerful force in moving the insecurity cycle – moved him to risk an "in-out" referendum on Britain's membership of the European Union. It was a rash decision.

The financial crisis: the banks' problem – or everyone else's?

The deep recession of the early 1990s was followed by a prolonged expansion and reduced macroeconomic volatility, described as the "Great Moderation".[7] According to Robert Lucas (2003, p. 1), the "central problem of depression prevention [had] been solved". The collapse of the Soviet Union boosted confidence in the supremacy of free market capitalism, encouraging an acceleration in the process of financialisation and risk taking; and with the rapid development and application of communication technologies, the financial system became increasingly international – and complex.

Competition between financial centres intensified, with the tendency of major institutions to practice "regulatory arbitrage" – seeking the most favourable regulatory environments, rather than the more onerous ones – and in the process, undermining effective oversight. In its place came progressively "lighter touch" regulation, aimed at attracting and retaining highly mobile international capital – with London being a willing player.

From the early 1990s, as huge volumes of liquidity flooded into financial markets from the high-saving economies of the East, Saudi Arabia and other oil rich countries, large amounts of cheap credit were made available to businesses, households and governments in the West. Low interest rates encouraged increased spending on credit, especially in the US and UK, resulting in large and expanding trade deficits. The cheap and plentiful credit once again fuelled residential property price bubbles, which increased equity that could then be used as collateral to support additional consumption (Wilkinson 2012).

Financial institutions increased borrowing as well, much of it off balance sheet via increasingly complex financial instruments. Since the low rates of interest failed to satisfy investors, new instruments with higher yields were created. Among these were securitised products which bundle together financial assets, such as mortgages, credit card receivables and automobile loans – and include riskier assets, to boost yields. In this context, one way to mitigate this risk is to pass it on as quickly as possible, encouraging expansion of the "originate to distribute" model of banking, in which financial institutions create "high yield" securitised products and rapidly sell them on, before the riskier assets begin to default (Bord and Santos 2012). The sale of these assets released liquidity with which to create more assets. Despite the risk, according to Alan Greenspan (2002), these developments were "especial contributors to the development of a far more flexible, efficient and resilient financial system than existed just a quarter-century ago".

Apparently successful responses to recurring financial crises during the 1980s, 1990s and 2000s reinforced the view that monetary policy was "well equipped to deal with the financial consequences of asset price busts" (Blanchard *et al.* 2010, p. 7), with bubbles being viewed as legitimate engines for growth (Bellofiore and Halevi 2011). Despite the havoc caused when they burst, the dominant view was that they are difficult to identify, so policy makers need not concern themselves with preventing them. Rather, "it is the job of economic policy makers to mitigate the fall out when it occurs and, hopefully, ease the transition to the next expansion" (Greenspan 1999).

However, over-confidence – especially during an apparently permanent boom – and the relaxation of vigilance that often accompanies it, is another contributor to shifts in the insecurity cycle. Following the collapse of the "dot com" bubble in 2000 and the 9/11 terror attacks in 2001, the American Federal Reserve (Fed) reduced interest rates (to around 2 per cent), fuelling an extended US housing boom. This was already beginning to slow by 2006, when the Fed raised interest rates to curb inflation.

The effect was catastrophic. The boom had generated a massive increase in securitised products built on mortgages, with the higher rates paid on riskier "sub-prime" loans being used to theoretically supercharge the returns to investors. These "sub-prime" home owners were barely able to afford the initial rates on their "NINJA" – No INcome, Job or Assets – loans, with the rate rise causing an immediate spike in defaults, cutting off the income streams for investors in the securitised products that had been built from them. The inability to tell which financial institutions held these assets, and were therefore vulnerable, resulted in banks being too suspicious to lend to each other – slowing the supply of credit from a flood to a trickle.

By September 2007, the crisis had reached the UK, with Northern Rock seeking a bail-out from the Bank of England. Fear, a notable trigger for change, produced the first bank run in over a century, with a knock-on effect on other institutions. In response to the abrupt cessation in the flow of cheap and plentiful credit, the Fed and the UK Treasury flooded the financial markets with liquidity. But the banks which had by now, as Keynes might have put it, swung from unbridled optimism to unreasonable pessimism, were still refusing to lend. As a consequence, Northern Rock had to nationalised to avoid collapse. Then, in September 2008, Lehman Brothers, the fourth largest investment bank in the US, became the first – and only – major financial institution allowed to fail. This created panic in the international markets and more banks looked to their governments for support. Several large British banks, including HBOS and RBS, had to be rescued by the UK government in the autumn of 2008.

Facing this explosive crisis, economists and policy makers briefly re-kindled Keynesian ideas about the stabilising role of fiscal deficits. In his pre-budget report in October 2008, UK Chancellor Alistair Darling declared that "[m]uch of what Keynes wrote still makes sense. You will see us switching our spending priorities to areas that make a difference ... we can allow borrowing to rise". In November, the G20 vowed "to use fiscal measures to stimulate demand to rapid effect". During the autumn of 2008, motivated by the possible collapse of the international financial system, the US and Britain, followed by the G7,[8] announced that they would buy into their major banks and inject capital directly to recapitalise them. Insurance was extended to depositors to prevent bank runs, and – recognising that although financial institutions may be global in life, they are national in death[9] – governments instead bailed out systemically important but failing banks, increasing fiscal deficits and transferring *toxic* assets to government balance sheets.

This was done without any compulsion on the part of the banks to contribute to the cost of their own rescue, as had been the case during the secondary banking crisis, suggesting a significant shift in the balance of relative power of a dominant financial sector and subservient national government. The institutions judged "too big to fail" were allowed, or forced, to merge – resulting in their becoming significantly larger – and more likely to assume that they could rely on further assistance should it prove necessary.

However, this lenient approach to finance would win the public sector no favours. By 2010, with financial collapse apparently averted, but with unemployment still high due to the recession caused by the crisis, policy turned sharply towards austerity, as the markets now expressed concern about high levels of public debt – first in the Eurozone (due to the perceived risk of sovereign debt default by weaker members) and then more broadly. Neoliberal finance had thus re-asserted itself in less than eighteen months. It was also the clearest demonstration yet of the assertion of private means over public interests.

Neoliberalism after four decades: theory versus reality

The 1970s stagflationary crises had aggravated Britain's sectoral and regional problems and led to the widespread destruction of jobs. Problems of high inflation, high unemployment and de-industrialisation were made worse by rapidly rising state expenditure to meet the growing social security costs of mass redundancies and as governments attempted to salvage failing industries. As these problems were attributed to "Keynesian" fallacies, there was a revival of traditional liberal beliefs in the monetary causes of inflation and the efficacy of unrestricted markets in maximising economic and societal welfare. Thus, since 1979, macroeconomic policy has been dominated by attempts to control inflation by monetary means whilst responsibility for increasing employment has been delegated to market forces. In this context, the role of the state has been restricted to the creation and maintenance of an institutional framework conducive to these ends.

For this purpose, regardless of the party in power, markets and businesses have been deregulated, large sections of the public sector privatised, and taxes on the rich cut to encourage enterprise.[10] Trade unions have been weakened, legal control of labour standards relaxed, out-of-work benefits reduced and made subject to more onerous conditions, and wage subsidisation has been introduced with the express purpose of lowering the natural or non-accelerating inflation rate of unemployment (NAIRU), and generating higher levels of employment.

The shift to neoliberal economic policies had three distinct political advantages. First, the idea that inflation is a monetary phenomenon mystifies the inflationary process and helps distance government from responsibility for rising prices.[11] Second, the idea of a natural level of unemployment – or NAIRU – that is determined by market imperfections effectively frees the government from responsibility for unemployment and poverty – and shifts it to the unemployed and the poor. Third, under neoliberalism, the poor and the unemployed are called upon to bear the lion's share of the cost of economic adjustment; but they have little or no political power.

However, whatever may be the political benefits of neoliberalism, by the arrival of the 2008 financial crisis, the economic costs had become only too clear. The pace of inflation has moderated as unemployment increased; but the causal mechanisms were very different from those proposed by neoliberals. Rather than operating directly on prices, the widespread monetary restrictions of the late 1970s and early 1980s triggered a deep global recession which caused primary product prices to collapse. In addition, increased excess capacity due to a lack of effective demand intensified international competition and lowered world prices for manufactured goods. Meanwhile, the buyers' market strengthened the hands of large retail chains and other dominant firms and provided the opportunity to source more widely and to pressure suppliers into price concessions.

In Britain, exchange rates, kept high by restrictive monetary policies, added to the downward pressure on import prices – and hence domestic inflation. But lower import prices put domestic producers at a competitive disadvantage in relation to foreign producers, further accelerating de-industrialisation. Resulting high levels of unemployment coupled with labour market deregulation and social welfare reforms reduced the bargaining power of the least well paid, lowering their relative earnings and the prices of their services (Wilkinson 2001).

The dampening of inflation was therefore not a result of monetary adjustments. Rather, it stemmed from the combined effects of economic depression and unemployment on the balance of power in labour and product markets. This served to redistribute income towards the more powerful groups – both nationally and internationally – allowing their real incomes to rise and reducing the inflationary conflict between them. In the UK, average annual disposable household income (at constant prices) increased from £14,631 in 1977 to £27,370 in 2007, an increase of 87 per cent (Jones *et al.* 2008, p. 24). However, "only the top quintile (20 percent) increased its share of total income, from 36 to 42 percent. The share of each other quintile group declined, in the case of the bottom quintile from 10 to 7 percent" (ibid., p. 21).

But low levels of inflation have been secured at enormous human and material costs. Mass poverty has re-emerged (Dorling *et al.* 2007; Hills 2004) and the fall in primary product prices has had a devastating impact on economies and well-being in Third World counties. Even the IMF – arguably the strongest proponent and promoter of neoliberalism – admitted that it has failed to deliver the measurable outcomes at the centre of the neoliberal agenda – these being economic growth and progress (Ostry *et al.* 2016).

As discussed above, poverty and inequality increased dramatically after the turn to neoliberalism during the 1980s and 1990s, under the Conservative governments of Margaret Thatcher and John Major. Table 8.2 shows the Gini coefficient[12] and measures of relative poverty[13] for the population as a whole, children and the elderly in 1997 (when New Labour came to power) and 2010 (when the Conservative-Liberal Democrat coalition government replaced them). As evident in Table 8.2, although poverty improved somewhat under New Labour – particularly for the elderly and children – inequality did not. Between 1997 and 2010, the Gini coefficient increased slightly, whilst the ratio of the earnings of the top 10 per cent to the bottom

Table 8.2 Inequality and poverty in the United Kingdom, 1997–2010

	Government		Gini	90/10	Population		Children		Elderly	
	Out-going	In-coming			%	# (millions)	%	# (millions)	%	# (millions)
1997	C	L	.380	5.063	24.4	13.6	33.2	4.2	29.2	2.9
2010	L	C-LD	.383	5.063	21.1	13.0	27.3	3.6	14.0	1.8

Source: Institute for Fiscal Studies (2017).

10 per cent of the population remained unchanged. During the same period, overall poverty decreased by 4 per cent, from 13.6 (24.4 per cent) to 13.0 million people (21.1 per cent); the number of children in poverty fell by 14 per cent, from 4.2 (33.2 per cent) to 3.6 million children (27.3 per cent); and the number of elderly people in poverty fell 38 per cent, from 2.9 (29.2 per cent) to 1.8 million people (14.0 per cent).

Assessing the macroeconomic impact of neoliberal economic policies on the UK economy since 1979, Ken Coutts and Graham Gudgin also conclude that neoliberalism has failed to deliver on its promises:

> Even in 2007 government current spending was higher as a percentage of GDP than it had been in 1979. Welfare dependency rose by 50 percent during the Thatcher-Major years and remains at this level today. Attempts to reduce taxation through lower public spending ... did not survive the first post-Thatcher recession in 1990/91. Levels of business investment in the UK have remained low compared with all major competitors. Company formation rates ... [are] not much higher than before 1980. Expenditure on R&D has also remained lower than competitors and ... has been trending downwards relative to GDP. The erosion in manufacturing has left the UK with a permanently lower rate of productivity growth.
>
> (Coutts and Gudgin 2015, p. 9)

Although financial deregulation contributed to increased GDP growth up to 2007, this was in large part due to the enormous (and ultimately unsustainable) expansion in household borrowing to fund consumption and spending on assets, especially houses. The result was a succession of asset bubbles, the collapse of which precipitated recurring financial crises, culminating in the 2008 financial crisis and the deepest and longest recession in over a century.

Moreover, the policy tools used to secure the aims of neoliberalism have adversely affected Britain's ability to maintain the rates of growth necessary to sustain the increase in real incomes underlying the decline in domestic inflation. The overvalued pound serves to keep import prices down and export prices non-competitive; high interest rates targeted at internal inflation have squeezed – and continue to squeeze – manufacturing and the other wealth-creating sectors. As a result, the ability to generate the necessary resources to maintain living standards is threatened and the trend increase in the balance of payment deficit on the current account can be expected to make it increasingly difficult to prevent sterling from depreciating, and the cost of imports rising (Wilkinson 2007).

Neoliberalism has thus reproduced the economic conditions of the inter-war years at which the Keynesian reforms were targeted, including an increasingly stagnating economy with slow growth, low rates of innovation and poverty for many in the midst of plenty for some.

Conclusions

The result of the crisis produced by the Winter of Discontent has been more than three decades of neoliberal policies, maintained by all three of the main political parties in Britain, with the support of what was once the Bretton Woods framework, and increasingly, as we shall see in Chapter 10, the European Union. However, the cumulative effect of these policies has fallen well short of the predicted outcomes in almost all respects.

High and increasing levels of inequality, approached only by other nations which have embraced neoliberalism to a similar degree, suggest that neoliberalism does indeed work well – but only for a select few. For everyone else, the vision offered stands a very high chance of being a mere mirage. So why does it continue to endure after almost forty years?

Whilst financialisation has certainly influenced the way that much of the electorate thinks and votes, this alone cannot account for the remarkable resilience of the neoliberal paradigm. Many of the problems experienced as a result of recurring financial crises since the turn to neoliberalism are ascribed to mysterious global influences, the even more obscure "markets" or even "market imperfections". Much of the success of neoliberalism in terms of its endurance is down to story-telling.

The neoliberal credo sounds as though it ought to be true, even though there is clear evidence to the contrary. For example, austerity is often justified by comparing the national accounts to those of an ordinary household. Whilst on the face of it, this might make sense to many, few householders are, even in this financialised environment, able to set their own interest rates, carry out quantitative easing or devalue the currency.

In terms of controlling this message, there are clear implications from the concentration of media ownership within international corporations, whose interests are more likely to be aligned with shareholders than other groups within society and whose global footprint distances these interests from the lot of any group of electors. It is perhaps not surprising then, that the growing levels of opposition to the present conventional wisdom are more inclined towards social, rather than industrial, media – where they do indeed have some control over the message.

The mixed economy that had taken a century and a half to create lasted less than four decades – partly as a result of a failure to either address the thornier issues, or invest for the future – and partly due to the activities of interest groups, such as finance, and the nurturing of neoliberal ideas. However, one of the key tenets of the insecurity cycle is that nothing is forever. Like the post-war consensus, the neoliberal consensus has consistently failed to resolve its own crises, with the recession following the 2008 financial crisis producing at least as many problems as the 1970s did for "Keynesianism". Both crises produced packages of austerity policies, with generally similar results. It seems unlikely that a challenge to the neoliberal order will wait forever. The next chapter will assess events in Britain since the 2008 financial crisis, and consider whether the drivers of the insecurity cycle are likely to be strong enough to produce another shift.

Notes

1 For various discussions of Chile's neoliberal experiment, see for example, Beckett (2003); Clark (2017); Dreze and Sen (2002); Fischer (2009); Harberger (1985); Ffrench-Davis (1983); Foxley (1983); Corbo (1989); and Edwards and Lederman (1998), among others.

2 For a discussion of the turning point caused by Britain's decision to go to war over the Falkland Islands, see Morgan (2001, pp. 457–61).

3 For further information about the 1986 Financial Services Act, see, for example, Rider *et al.* (1987).

4 *Faith in the City* can be located at: www.churchofengland.org/our-views/home-and-community-affairs/community-urban-affairs/urban-affairs/faith-in-the-city.aspx.

5 The Gini coefficient ranges from 0 (perfect equality) to 1 (maximum inequality).

6 The 90/10 inequality ratio is a measure of the income earned by the top 10 per cent of income earners compared with that earned by the bottom 10 per cent. The poverty rates for the population as a whole, children and the elderly set the poverty line at 60 per cent of the median income level. All income levels are net of taxes and housing costs, and adjusted for inflation.

7 See, for example, Stock and Watson (2002) and Bernanke (2004).

8 The G7 consists of the finance ministers from the US, UK, France, Germany, Italy, Canada and Japan.

9 Quoting the Governor of the Bank of England, Mervyn King (Financial Services Authority 2009, p. 36).

10 Despite the rhetoric about reducing taxes, the overall level of taxation was not reduced; rather there was a switch towards indirect taxes and away from high marginal tax rates.

11 New Labour institutionalised this distancing by setting up the Monetary Committee of the Bank of England with responsibility for determining interest rates – the principal policy instrument for controlling inflation.

12 The Gini coefficient ranges from 0 (perfect equality) to 1 (maximum inequality).

13 The 90/10 inequality ratio is a measure of the income earned by the top 10 per cent of income earners compared with that earned by the bottom 10 per cent. The poverty rates for the population as a whole, children and the elderly set the poverty line at 60 per cent of the median income level. All income levels are net of taxes and housing costs, and adjusted for inflation.

9 The 2008 financial crisis

A crisis of neoliberalism or just another financial crisis?

Introduction

Fear – always an influence in the insecurity cycle – arose from the possibility that the 2008 crisis might cause a complete meltdown in the international financial system. This resulted in a brief Keynesian response in the form of a package of internationally coordinated stimuli, promoted by the then Prime Minister, Gordon Brown. However, as soon as it appeared that financial collapse had been averted – and the underlying fear receded – there was a return to "business as usual".

Finance had acquired an image problem. But despite a continuing litany of rule-breaking (and even outright fraud), it, too, returned to "business as usual" – literally with a vengeance – and threatened the very governments which had rescued it and were now consequently much more heavily indebted. These public debt levels were made still worse by the deep and extended recession that had been precipitated by the financial crisis – itself made worse by the very non-"Keynesian" policies of austerity demanded by the financial "markets". This recession continues at the time of writing, with meaningful GDP growth still at a premium a decade after the onset of the crisis. Thus, in spite of the mayhem resulting from poor risk management, questionable business practices and near bankruptcy, the financial sector largely continues to call the shots.

What then of neoliberalism – the theory and current conventional wisdom – that has for many, once again, clearly failed the reality test? Britain continues to suffer the effects of a major crisis and a decade of recession, with much of the damage being effectively self-inflicted as a result of the government's insistence on continued austerity policies. Austerity also did little for the insecurity cycle. Not only did it undermine the position of those who rely on public services the most – the poor – it created further insecurity by making them wonder where the next cuts might be coming from. This state of affairs may have been expected to have a similarly dire effect on "laissez faire" as the decade of economic under-performance and the "Winter of Discontent" had had on "Keynesianism".

It came close. The landslide election of Jeremy Corbyn as Labour Party leader in 2015 was not only a major shock for those on the party's political right; it also galvanised MPs into open opposition and an official attempt to replace him. This in-fighting continued up to the lead-in to the 2017 general election, where initial opinion polls had given the Conservatives a decisive advantage of around 20 points (YouGov 2017a). But by the day of the ballot, this had shrunk to the point where Labour and the Conservatives were level pegging (YouGov 2017b). What the outcome might have been, had Labour MPs generally supported – instead of opposed – their new leader can only be surmised. But if the record of the insecurity cycle demonstrates anything, it is that no conventional wisdom, regardless of how unassailable it might appear at the time, lasts indefinitely. This clearly implies that sooner or later, neoliberalism, too, will fail to satisfy.

Economics: social science, natural science – or blind faith?

Neoliberal theory has attempted to turn economics into a pure science, rather than a social science. But in this, too, it has clearly failed. In assuming away many of the factors that drive economies in practice – as well as simply ignoring the failures of neoliberal economic theory and policy in this context – neoliberalism has come to resemble a faith, rather than a science, with "markets" – and occasionally, shareholders – doing service as the deity of choice.

The view that economics is more of a hard science than a social science – a view referred to by some as "Physics envy"[1] – has also helped to justify the separation of commercial interests from society, with dire effects. The result has been the impoverishment of society, not only in lowering the quality of life of consumers, but also depriving them of the wherewithal to consume. This has done little to make economic growth any easier to find. Indeed, so desperate have some become to magic growth from anywhere possible, that it has even been argued that illegal activities such as drug dealing and prostitution should be included – with these two activities being added to the UK's national accounts in September 2014, boosting GDP by an estimated £65 billion (nearly 5 per cent) (Allen 2014).

But even now, economists remain divided. Whilst 364 economists signed an open letter against Margaret Thatcher's monetarist plans in 1981, after three decades of neoliberalism, fifty-five economists took a similar route to argue against Corbyn's proposals in the *Financial Times* (Martin 2015) – provoking a rebuttal in the *Guardian* from hundreds more economists and media educators (*Guardian* Letter 2015, 2017a and 2017b). Whilst this is in some ways reminiscent of the duel between Hayek and Keynes during the inter-war years, it clearly demonstrates that whilst there may still be a significant number in support of the current conventional wisdom, there is equally surely a significant faction prepared to take a different view – especially when even economists at the IMF are starting to back-track away from neoliberalism.

Whilst the nature of both economic liberalism and society has evolved over the last two centuries, as this chapter will show, it is difficult to ignore the many echoes of nineteenth-century thinking and policy that have re-appeared in twenty-first-century Britain – with similar consequences. Laissez faire policies have had generally consistent outcomes, as by extension do largely "free" markets. It remains to be seen whether this century will produce similar reactions to the problems they generate, or whether it will take an entirely new tack, founded on genuinely new ideas.

"The economic consequences of Mr Osborne"

In Britain, the 2010 general election delivered a Conservative-Liberal Demo-cratic coalition government led by David Cameron, which defined itself as a "government of austerity". During its first two years in office, the Chancellor of the Exchequer, George Osborne, aggressively pursued this policy, inflict-ing serious – and predictable – damage on both the economy and that part of society most reliant on public services. In 2012, the government continued its austerity rhetoric, defending such policies on the basis of a series of highly spurious alleged beliefs, whilst easing up somewhat on the policies themselves (Chick *et al.* 2016, p. 5).

Most of the attempts at justification were based on the by now familiar neoliberal dogma. By defining the crisis as a "crisis of debt" and "failure of the public sector" – as opposed to a "crisis of growth" (Hay 2013a and 2013b) and of "the financial system and associated *vested interests*" (Chick *et al.* 2016, p. 10, emphasis in the original) – the government insisted that not only did Britain have too much public debt (and so could not afford more); it also argued that monetary policy could effectively resolve the problem. But the reality was that at the start of the crisis, UK government debt relative to GDP was at a record low – close to its lowest in 300 years – and despite having rescued the banking system, Britain still had a debt-to-GDP ratio much lower than its historical long-term average (of 110 per cent).[2] Moreover, with the cost of debt so low (and real interest rates negative), monetary policy on its own was unlikely to be effective. Even the IMF – the once "high priest" of austerity – urged Britain to increase public spending on infrastructure and public works that would generate employment and growth as well as positive real returns (Lagarde 2011).

Another, somewhat questionable claim was that embracing austerity would give the government "financial credibility", which, in turn, would deliver lower long-term interest rates. But long-term interest rates are determined by the state of the economy – *not purely* by the state of public finances – and economic stagnation was unlikely to provide much confidence in the gov-ernment's ability to manage the economy, much less its finances. The gov-ernment also made the old neoliberal argument that higher levels of public investment "crowd-out" private sector spending. But after a financial crisis, private firms are typically reluctant to invest until they see *evidence* of increased demand, whilst consumers are reluctant to spend until they feel confident about employment, often choosing to pay off their debts instead. So if the private sector cannot be expected to lead the recovery, there can be no "crowding out" of private investment by public policy.

The public was thus sold the idea of austerity on the basis of appeals to ethics and morality concerning indebtedness, supported by misleading analogies and ideas about the nature of government finances. One of the earliest and most abiding of *these* is the notion that governments' budgets are analogous to those of firms and households – and that they therefore require balancing. But this comparison is fundamentally flawed because, unlike a private household or firm, a sovereign government with control over its currency and a floating exchange rate is not operationally constrained by its budget. This is because it can both issue and adjust the value of its currency to manage a deficit. Moreover, whilst a household or firm can balance its budget by reducing spending and re-paying its debts, a government cannot. During a slump, government deficits rise as a consequence of falling tax revenues and rising social costs, putting upward pressure on public debt levels at the same time as GDP growth is slowing. In this context, cutting public spending will not only deepen the slump – it will also *add* to public debt.

In short, despite the neoliberal rhetoric, in economic terms, government deficits and increasing public debt-to-GDP ratios were for the most part a consequence of the 2008 financial crisis and the resulting bank bail-outs. But they were made considerably worse by the ensuing economic recession that caused tax receipts to plummet and social costs to soar. In this context, neoliberal policies in general – and austerity in particular – added significantly to the downward pressure on both the economy and social conditions within it.

Labour, "Momentum" and the re-polarisation of politics

Labour's election win in 2005 was to be its last for some time. Tony Blair's questionable – strongly opposed but determined – support for the Iraq War and the spectacular debacle of the 2008 financial crisis were certainly not helpful to Labour. But they were of no help to any other party, either. Although the following general election in 2010 resulted in a swing of more than 5 per cent away from Labour, the outcome was far from decisive. Even with the "first past the post" system, parties other than the usual choices of Conservative or Labour gained around 35 per cent of the vote.

This might perhaps be seen as the beginning of real signs of disillusion with neoliberal ideas and policies. Given the twin crises of the Iraq War and, especially, the financial crisis, vibrations in the insecurity cycle might well be expected. But with few new alternative ideas or policies on offer, the outcome is probably best described as confused. In the event, the general election produced a Conservative-Liberal Democrat coalition government, led by the largest party emerging from the election – Cameron's Conservatives.

The other key outcome was the resignation of Labour's leader, Gordon Brown, and his replacement by Ed Miliband.

Although Miliband did not cut an impressive figure as a media performer – and was not an electoral success – in other ways he had a powerful, if unintended, effect on the Labour Party. This would influence both its sharp return to the left, and some of the key approaches taken by "Momentum", the organisation created to support Jeremy Corbyn. First, Miliband had effectively cleared the way for the election of a potentially radical new leader (McHugh 2015). Until shortly after Thatcher's first election victory, the Labour Party leader had been elected exclusively by Labour MPs. But Miliband's own election as party leader, at the expense of his brother David, was to no small extent the result of trade union influence in the vote. This had taken place under an electoral college system, where party members and MPs had one-third of the votes each, with the balance being held by the trade unions.

This balance was radically shifted by a fundamental rule change in 2014, following accusations that the Unite union had used undue influence in the selection of the replacement for Eric Joyce as MP for Falkirk. Thus, in order to avoid yet more accusations of Labour being controlled by the unions, Miliband set up the Collins Review, which proposed a "one person one vote" system for leadership elections (Collins 2014). Under this system, MPs could be comfortably out-voted by party members – especially if the membership expanded sharply. This change went through largely uncontested, as by now, the principle of "one person, one vote" was well established in other areas of policy-making within the Labour Party. But it would come to have huge implications, especially as the right to vote was also extended to registered "supporters" of the party, who were allowed to join the party via their mobile phones for just £3 (Bale *et al.* 2016).

After Miliband's humiliating defeat in the 2015 general election, eligibility to vote in the leadership contest to replace him required that new members be registered by 12 August 2015. In just three months, 120,000 people had paid £3 to become official supporters, whilst a further 100,000 or so had become full members. In total, just over 600,000 people – about four times the complete membership of the Conservative Party – took part in the election; and almost 60 per cent of them supported Corbyn (Eaton 2015). These two changes would thus not only prove decisive in his election as party leader by an unprecedented margin; they would also be pivotal in crushing the leadership challenge by Owen Smith that followed Corbyn's election – in spite of limits being placed on the ability to vote for some of the new party "supporters".

The other major contribution made by Ed Miliband was also largely accidental. Whilst some incidents during his leadership of the party such as the "bacon roll" affair and the "Ed Stone" resulted in largely self-inflicted wounds, there seems little doubt about the general hostility of the industrial media towards Miliband (Russell 2015). His departures from the neoliberal canon had hardly been sufficient to convincingly earn him the title of "Red Ed"; and it is hard to see how even his election, with the unions as king-maker, could justify it either, given his abrupt changes to the leadership election process (Burnell 2014). But it seems that the futility of trying to either influence a hostile set of industrial media – or for that matter, to try to reach his key target audiences using them as a channel – was not lost on Jon Lansman. Lansman had worked on Corbyn's successful 2015 campaign and subsequently played a key role in founding the pro-Corbyn organisation, "Momentum" – a new kind of political entity with limited financial resources but considerable social media savvy.

Miliband would not have to wait long to see the result of the changes he had initiated. But whilst initially opposing Corbyn's leadership, following Corbyn's unexpected success in capturing votes in the 2017 general election, Miliband experienced something of a conversion, having revised his opinion about serving in a Corbyn cabinet – shadow or otherwise (Maidment 2017).

When Miliband resigned following Labour's defeat in 2015, few people outside of politics had heard of Jeremy Corbyn. Having been a noted left-wing campaigner for many years, Corbyn was only included on the list of candidates to provide an apparently full representation of the spectrum of ideas within the Labour Party. He was never considered to be a serious prospect; nor was it thought that Corbyn would win a record landslide majority – twice.

In many ways, Corbyn's election was the result of a democratic upsurge powering political support, rather than the other way around. In the run-up to the election, Corbyn, himself a member of the party's left-wing grouping, expressed neither ambition nor confidence during interviews with the *Guardian*. In response to the question of why he was the left-wing group's candidate, he replied, "Well, Diane [Abbott] and John [McDonnell] have done it before, so it was my turn ... That's why I'm doing it". But he was quick to add: "At my age I'm not likely to be a long-term contender, am I?" (Hattenstone 2015). Corbyn also implied that he had reservations about running at all:

> All of us felt the leadership contest was not a good idea – there should have been a policy debate first. There wasn't, so we decided somebody should put their hat in the ring in order to promote that debate. And, unfortunately, it's my hat in the ring.
>
> (Ibid.)

However, getting his hat in the ring at all was by no means guaranteed. Many people would help Corbyn to win the party leadership – most of whom he barely knew – and this support started early. Making it onto the candidate list required nomination by thirty-five of his fellow MPs, which under normal circumstances was a big ask; but these were not normal circumstances. John McDonnell was significant in ensuring that Corbyn's name did indeed make it onto the candidate list, arguing that failure to include a representative from the left in the election would drive a wedge between the new leader and the electorate. Corbyn was also supported by Ben Sellers, who encouraged activists from the left-wing Facebook group "Red Labour" to directly urge MPs through social media to nominate Corbyn. Even so, it nearly didn't work, with the final nominations being secured within seconds of the deadline. Corbyn thus made it onto the candidate list by the skin of his teeth; and more than half of those who helped get Corbyn's name onto the ballot paper voted for other candidates.

But it wasn't just those largely responsible for nominating Corbyn that had little to do with him personally; the same went for his most significant supporters during the ensuing campaign. Corbyn had only met Ben Sellers – who was to be one of the most significant figures working for his election and part of Red Labour – once. "New" Labour might have largely purged the official party structure of left-wing supporters had it not been for independent forums, such as Red Labour, appearing on Facebook, away from immediate interference. As the name suggests, this was intended to be a resource for more socialist-minded Labour Party members – and within two years of its creation in 2011, Red Labour had attracted something in the order of 20,000 active followers.

Crucially, this meant that Corbyn's campaign would not have to start from scratch. Not only was there a ready-made group of activists and supporters; those like Ben Sellers, who helped to run Red Labour, had also had several years during which to cut their teeth in terms of political campaign management. One of the insights gained from this experience was an understanding of the fundamental difference in the way that two key social media platforms – Facebook and Twitter – were used, as well as of those who used them.

There appeared to be very little crossover between these two social media. Journalists and politicians tended to rely on Twitter, where threads are easier to follow and soundbites and quotes are a good fit with the limited number of characters available. But for those wanting to communicate at greater length, Facebook is a much better fit, with a rich vein of electors and activists. This facilitated the development of ideas and opinion on Facebook, which could then be launched into Twitter, as appropriate. It also meant that the journalists and MPs almost exclusively using Twitter were effectively blind to the strength, nature and tactics of the campaign in support of Corbyn – and why his support appeared to them to have come out of thin air. As Ben Sellers put it:

> You can put the most controversial things on Facebook, the press won't notice them. Then you repeat them on Twitter and suddenly they're news. I wrote something complaining about journalists' "tittle tattle" when Jeremy didn't stand for the national anthem. It had a huge response on Facebook but the press ignored it. We put the same quote on Twitter and the national press had attributed it to Jeremy and within two hours it was national news.
>
> (Wilson 2016)

With Corbyn's name finally on the candidate list, the primary objective was achieved, and the campaign shifted gear, with Red Labour becoming the driving force behind a new social media project – JeremyCorbyn4Leader. Here, however, things did not go entirely as planned. Whilst JeremyCorbyn-4Leader had been intended as a supporting campaign, its high profile resulted in it becoming almost the de facto official campaign as far as much of the industrial media were concerned, resulting in significant potential for confusion. It also suggests that at that time, any official communication from Corbyn himself was simply not achieving anything like the same sort of cut through as the Red Labour group.

But Ben Sellers wasn't the only significant figure in the effort to elect Corbyn as party leader. Jon Lansman – a friend of Corbyn – would also play a major role, not only in the official campaign but also in the morphing of Jeremy Corbyn Campaign 2015 (Supporters) Ltd into Momentum Campaign (Services) Ltd – now usually referred to simply as "Momentum". Whilst several unsuccessful attempts had been made to produce a coherent left-wing grouping before – including by Lansman himself – the pace of the development of Momentum came as some surprise. But this time, the process seemed to succeed as a consequence of not being planned. As one journalist put it: "It has almost accidentally morphed from a political campaign into a social movement, joining disparate elements of the British left ... On the ground, friendships are being formed out of the campaign, connections made, activists born" (O'Hagan 2015).

This social movement first became apparent at, of all places, the Glastonbury festival, where Red Labour's JeremyCorbyn4Leader stand was queued-out, and appeared to be a bigger draw than the actual entertainment on offer. At this point, Jeremy Corbyn started to become a real – as opposed to just a social media – sensation. Following his performance at a live debate in Nuneaton, where his views, style and audience response all suggested that he had comfortably come out on top, Corbyn stepped decisively into face-to-face politics, by following each subsequent debate with a rally – most producing an audience of sufficient size and mood to suggest that the unthinkable had indeed happened. Britain had produced a charismatic, but above all – viable – left-wing candidate.

Jeremy Corbyn was, however, not simply appealing to an existing left-wing audience. In sharp contrast to Tony Blair's "vacuo-Olympian style" (Jenkins 2006, p. 216), Corbyn came across as genuinely believing in the policies and approach he was espousing; and as a result, he was acquiring a much broader range of supporters. This was something that New Labour had imagined could simply never happen; and even following Corbyn's subsequent election as leader, many within the party openly argued that there could never be sufficient support for a solid showing at a general election – a view that would be tested rather sooner than anticipated. Meanwhile the success of Corbyn's rallies only served to strengthen the online campaign, which continued to ratchet up both attendance and Labour Party membership.

Peter Hitchens of the *Daily Mail* – hardly a natural Corbyn supporter – was one of the 2,000 who went to the Cambridge rally. His assessment of Corbyn's "new kind of politics" is therefore, perhaps, more than a little surprising:

> This was itself a refreshing change from most modern political speeches, crafted by professional experts in blandness, rehearsed and spoken by the "leader" (what a horrible term this is) more for effect than for edification. I simply don't think any of his rivals could have done this, not because they're stupid or bad speakers, but because they don't actually have coherent political positions.
>
> (Hitchens 2015)

Despite these comments, the efforts of the industrial media to support other "moderate" candidates continued. But they clearly fell on deaf ears, with Corbyn winning marginally less than 60 per cent of the vote. Corbyn's support by the party membership, the constituency parties and the trade unions was overwhelming. However, the opposite was true of the Parliamentary party – of which much of the structure and membership was a legacy of Tony Blair. The centralisation of control, as well as the adoption of neoliberal policies, had had a lasting effect on the attitudes of MPs, who now felt that they were justified in directly confronting the party's new leader – in spite of an unassailable democratic mandate. As a result, fewer than two hundred MPs felt that *their* views counted for more than over a quarter of a million party members. This discontent rumbled on, producing very public in-fighting, and finally, a leadership challenge. Whilst this was won by Corbyn as handily as the first ballot, the unedifying display of a party clearly at war with itself was hardly the best preparation for the admittedly unexpected 2017 general election. In spite of a strong showing by the Labour Party on the day, it is a matter for speculation as to how things might have gone, had the party united and turned its attention to policy, rather than to Tony Blair's legacy.

The implications for the insecurity cycle are also significant. New ideas are not restricted to policy. The strategy used to elect Jeremy Corbyn was extremely effective. It had never been seen before, was not seen in time – and there were few obvious ways to counter it. The level – and breadth – of support garnered by a left-wing candidate also suggests that from the point of view of a significant number of British citizens, there is a significant chronic crisis. One of the effects of significant inequality is that policy tends to be made by those in the minority – who are much less likely to perceive a chronic crisis themselves. The election of Jeremy Corbyn as Labour Party leader thus demonstrates what happens when this state of affairs is reversed.

Corbyn was neither a demagogue nor a "rock star" candidate. In many ways, he succeeded by effectively channelling the feelings, views, experiences and perceptions of a sizeable part of the electorate who feel both left behind and left out. Given the high and still growing levels of inequality in Britain, it should not have been surprising that there is a matching growth in support for left-wing politics. In this, there is an echo of the effect of "new unionism" during the nineteenth century, where the impetus for change and the development of a new movement – the Labour Party – was distinctly bottom–up (rather than top–down) in nature. Effectively, a mass movement achieved a change that intellectual socialists such as William Morris failed to inspire. The implication of this is that whilst visible support by a credible politician is essential for a shift in the insecurity cycle, that politician does not have to be the senior partner in the relationship with democratic pressure. Both Thatcher and Blair took the electorate with them; the electorate largely took Corbyn with them.

New ideas, however, have not been restricted to the engagement of the electorate. During much of the leadership and subsequent general election campaign, Labour outlined a process for policy development, as much as actual individual policies. This involves consultation with the electorate, as well as business and academia to generate new policy approaches designed to address specific problems.[3] This not only represents a departure from "New" Labour's centralised approach to both policy development and implementation; it also allows for departure from the neoliberal policy canon.

It is clear that the Labour Party's return to left-wing policies has found significant support. But whilst this has not yet produced a shift in the insecurity cycle, it has certainly produced some wobbles in the neoliberal conventional wisdom. For the time being at least, politics is once again polarised into opposing political offerings.

Fear and the insecurity cycle: the EU referendum

Meanwhile, the Conservatives had problems of their own, particularly over the question of Europe. Edward Heath's decision to take Britain into the European Community during the 1970s had been a controversial one due to concerns by some about the effect that membership might have on Britain's national sovereignty. But divisions within the Conservative Party over Europe would prove to be a persistent theme. Margaret Thatcher's resignation in 1990 had been in part motivated by pressure from opposition within the Conservative Party to her approach to the European Community (Thatcher 1993, p. 830); and John Major's second term in office had been tormented by the political consequences of the UK's forced exit from the European Exchange Rate Mechanism in 1992 and his inability to prevent deepening divisions within the party over the Maastricht Treaty on European integration. According to Patrick Diamond (2016), "[t]hese events created a new political generation of hard-line eurosceptics within the Tory party, which its leaders from John Major to David Cameron have been struggling to contain ever since".

But not only had the question of Europe produced smouldering divisions within the Conservative Party. It also motivated the genesis of a new party, the United Kingdom Independence Party (UKIP). Thus, in an effort to stem the Eurosceptic tide, at the 2006 Conservative Party Conference, David Cameron (2006b) had expressed hope that Conservatives would stop "banging on about Europe". But his plea appears to have fallen on deaf ears. Whilst it is arguable as to whether Harold Macmillan ever said "events dear boy, events" in response to being questioned over what politicians most feared, David Cameron might well have some sympathy with that assessment.

However, it was not only the Conservatives who had reservations about the European Union (EU). Until the recession following the 2008 financial crisis took hold, UKIP were generally thought to appeal to only about 2 per cent of the electorate, increasing to around 3 per cent by the 2010 general election (Hunt 2014). But the combination of sustained high levels of immigration after 2000, notably from eastern European states that had recently joined the EU – followed by recession and austerity after 2008 – things began to change. By 2012, some opinion polls had started to put UKIP support at something closer to 15 per cent (BBC 2015a) – more than enough to give many Conservative MPs sleepless nights. The increased support might not result in many – if any – UKIP MPs; but it might well be enough to reduce the Conservative vote to a point where they could lose seats to Labour. The fear factor was spreading.

Pressure continued to grow, especially from Conservative MPs in seats that might be thus threatened. They were looking for answers – increasing the pressure on Cameron to hold an in/out referendum on EU membership, to "shoot the UKIP fox" (Osborne 2013). Quite what was behind his decision is presently uncertain. But it is more than possible that Cameron did not expect to win an overall majority in the 2015 general election, and subsequently gambled that the election promise could then be safely negotiated away as part of a coalition arrangement. As a result, in January 2013, in what has become known as the Bloomberg speech, the referendum was promised (Cameron 2013). This turned out to be a miscalculation. With UKIP support dropping markedly, whilst that for the Conservatives was rising, the Conservatives had a comfortable working majority – quite possibly the result of promising the referendum to supporters of a "single issue" party. Whatever the reason, the referendum was now inevitable.

The immediate result of the referendum pledge, however, was not to neutralise the European debate. Quite the contrary, in fact. Far from being effectively finished, the "UKIP fox" appeared instead to be running with renewed vigour. Whilst there had indeed been a noticeable surge in support for UKIP, things really came to a head when this democratic upsurge started to acquire conspicuous political support. Up until 28 August 2014, UKIP had never looked like it would gain a single MP at Westminster. However the defection of the Conservative, Douglas Carswell, to the party – and his victory in the subsequent by-election – abruptly removed any remaining complacency, especially when it was followed by the defection of a second Conservative MP, Mark Reckless. At the by-election on 20 November 2014,

Reckless, too, was returned as an MP – representing UKIP. This was followed by considerable media speculation as to how many more Conservatives might join Nigel Farage's party, whilst Farage himself did not fail to exploit the opportunity of unsettling Cameron's party still further.

These events demonstrate some of the subtleties of the insecurity cycle, particularly with regard to political support. Nigel Farage's UKIP was undoubtedly highly influential in the calling of the EU referendum, although Farage himself was never elected an MP – let alone Prime Minister. The party did, however, do more than enough to instil sufficient fear in the Conservative Party to have a very significant influence on its policy. How UKIP might have performed in the 2015 general election had Cameron not called the referendum will always be a matter for speculation – but it is very doubtful that they could have won it, or even have helped Labour to do so. Fear of the unknown thus appears to have played a significant part; and a small party – almost a pressure group – had managed to change the course of national politics.

The defection of Conservative MPs to UKIP following the Bloomberg speech kept the referendum issue at or near the top of the news agenda, as did Cameron's tour of EU capitals in an attempt to produce a deal that would work for his party and the UK electorate. When this failed to produce a convincing result, both the "remain" supporters and those backing the "leave" campaign accused each other of trying to harness fear for their own ends, in campaigns during the run-in to the plebiscite.

Cameron's attempts to steer away from these accusations by describing his campaign as "Project Fact" failed to either remove the idea of "Project Fear" from the media, or indeed convince Boris Johnson, who saw the suggested "facts" rather as "a series of questionable assertions", whilst dismissing Cameron's campaign as simply "baloney" (Stewart *et al.* 2016). Meanwhile, *The Express* newspaper on 6 June 2016 headlined the view that "Now FOUR polls put LEAVE camp ahead as Project Fear sees British voters desert Cameron" (Mansfield 2016). The debate was typically far more emotional than it was factual; and voters would have had a hard time making up their minds on the basis of the arguments offered by either side.

Nevertheless, on 23 June 2016, 51.9 per cent of the participating UK electorate voted to leave the EU, forcing David Cameron's resignation, with Cameron being replaced by Theresa May. On 29 March 2017, the British government invoked Article 50 of the Treaty on the EU, putting the UK on course to leave the EU on Friday, 29 March 2019 (BBC 2017a). One way or another, fear had played a large part in both the genesis of the referendum and its outcome; and it had allowed UKIP to punch far above its political weight – and perhaps achieve its political ends – but without actually having to win political power.

The EU referendum may yet have further implications for the insecurity cycle, as well as perhaps contributing to Labour's distinctly ambivalent approach to the question of EU membership. One of the more eye-catching policies in the Labour Party manifesto for the 2017 general election was a programme of nationalisation of a number of industries – something that many in Labour's leadership believed would be difficult to implement under EU law.

Over-confidence and the insecurity cycle: the 2017 general election

When Theresa May called a snap general election in 2017 in an attempt to secure an electoral mandate for negotiating Britain's departure from the EU (*New Statesman* 2017), the outcome hardly seemed in doubt. Some opinion polls had given the Conservatives a lead of as much as 20 points, whilst the average was still comfortably into double figures (Burn-Murdoch *et al.* 2017). It looked as though May would succeed in her aim of significantly increasing her majority from its existing seventeen seats, whilst Labour would be all but finished as a political force. There was even talk of a split within Labour and as a result, the formation of a new party (Rogers 2017).

Instead, the election resulted in a hung Parliament, with May being forced into an arrangement with Northern Ireland's Democratic Unionist Party. What had happened to so sharply reverse fortunes in just a matter of a few weeks? The Conservatives' election manifesto included some – on the face of it, at least – remarkably non-neoliberal policies, including interventions in industrial strategy, additional commitments to public services and (perhaps most remarkably) very little in the way of promised tax cuts (Conservative Party Manifesto 2017). It looked more like a manifesto designed to capture votes from Labour than a traditional Conservative package. Perhaps for similar reasons, the campaign also differed in other ways, focusing more on May as leader than the party, than on proposed policies. Whilst this may have been due to a feeling that her personal appeal to Labour voters might well be stronger than that of the Conservative Party generally, it did little to unite her cabinet – especially as they were barely consulted on the contents of the manifesto. But most of all, the campaign was meant to be about Brexit – which, given the divisive nature of the EU referendum result, was a high-risk strategy.

The Labour Party, meanwhile, took the view that not only did the effects of almost a decade of austerity on public services need to be addressed, a Labour government would also commit to a programme of nationalisation, specifically of the energy sector, Royal Mail and the Railways (Labour Party Manifesto 2017). Whilst Brexit was also a consideration, it did not dominate the agenda, but would nonetheless remain a factor in the performance of the Labour Party.

The election campaigns revealed a clear difference in the way that the two main party leaders came across. Jeremy Corbyn was able to communicate easily and to generate trust in his "authenticity". By contrast, Theresa May tended to avoid involvement in televised debates, and attempted rigid control of a single message – in the manner that had worked for so long, for so many others. But it did not work well this time, earning her the soubriquet of "The Maybot" and making her seem far more remote than Corbyn (Crace 2017). In short, May's rather technical approach did not stand up well to the more human image of Corbyn, who, rather than being isolated from his supporters and cabinet, had Momentum in his corner. This would prove a decisive advantage, especially in terms of engaging younger voters, both as volunteers and casting their votes on the day.

The Conservatives had, as well as Lynton Crosby – Cameron's campaign manager from 2015 – engaged Jim Messina, who had performed a similar role for the US presidential campaign of Barack Obama. Momentum had also drawn in allies from America. During the contest for the Democratic nomination in 2016, Bernie Sanders's campaign had performed surprising strongly against the much better-funded Hillary Clinton campaign. With fewer financial resources available, the Vermont senator's team had been forced to look for advantage elsewhere; and they found it in innovative approaches to communications and voter engagement. Many of the techniques developed and perfected during the Sanders presidential campaign were subsequently integrated into Momentum's strategy, as were some of the people who had developed them.

Erika Uyterhoeven had been the national out-of-state organising director for Bernie Sanders's campaign; and at thirty, like many within Momentum, she was young. In Sander's campaign, Uyterhoeven's role had been to mobilise activists in borderline states to move to higher-priority states. In an interview with the *Guardian* on 30 May 2017, she suggested that the essential thing as far as Corbyn's campaign was concerned, too, would be to deploy activists in the right places (Khomami 2017). She also helped mobilise what would otherwise be an overwhelming number of people, deploying technology never before used in a UK general election campaign to do so. One such technology was the website "My Nearest Marginal", which helped activists organise door-to-door campaigns in support of Labour, where additional votes really counted. Her assessment of the basis for the strategy developed by the Sanders campaign was stark. "The right can throw money at elections – we throw people" (ibid.).

A combination of Conservative-backed policies – such as what became known as the "Dementia Tax", the replacement of the "triple lock" on pensions with a mere "double lock" and the means testing of winter fuel payments for pensioners – did little to make May appear any warmer. But the election was indeed substantially about Brexit. The referendum had produced a clear result – 52 to 48 per cent of the vote in favour of the "leave" campaign – a result that turned out to be much closer than the difference between the two main parties at the beginning of the election campaign, which was then well into double digits. Also, unlike the referendum, which had been a simple national poll, the general election would be held under the usual "first past the post" system on a constituency basis.

These considerations should have been enough to raise questions in the Conservative Party about the wisdom of campaigning so heavily on Brexit.

Better consultation with May's cabinet might have produced a broader strategy. As it was, according to the British Election Study of August 2017, Brexit was mentioned as the dominant issue by more than a third of respondents. As a result, the UKIP vote collapsed almost completely, with more than half turning to the Conservatives and a further 18 per cent opting for Labour. "Remain" voters, however, tended to favour Labour far more strongly, even if they had previously supported other parties.

Brexit was one factor, but over-confidence was not the only insecurity cycle factor in play during the election. The increase in inequality also played a part, with members of "generation rent", in particular, expressing their feelings strongly. The turnout amongst private renters increased from the previous election two years earlier, moving from 51 to 65 per cent; and in contrast to the Conservatives' 14 point lead amongst home-owners, by the time the 2017 general election arrived, Labour had a 23 point lead among these private renters. Whilst this might be the result of a number of factors, it does suggest that the "broken" UK housing market is starting to make "generation rent" think that something has clearly gone wrong with the "property owning democracy" (Goodwin and Heath 2017).

But perhaps the most telling analysis comes from YouGov research into the reasons for voting either Labour or Conservative in the 2017 general election (YouGov 2017c). At 28 per cent, the most popular reason for voting Labour was "Manifesto/Policies" whilst the most popular reason for voting Conservative, at 21 per cent was "Brexit" – the implication being that many Labour voters felt that Brexit was one of a number of issues, rather than the central one. Another finding in this study suggests that the insecurity cycle is likely to continue for some time yet: the second and third most popular reasons for voting labour, respectively, were "Anti Tory" and "Jeremy Corbyn" – both of which came in just ahead of "provide hope/fairness for the many". Meanwhile, the equivalents for voting Conservative were, predictably, "Anti Labour", "Anti Corbyn", with "Agree with their policies/principles…" following some way behind.

Echoes of the nineteenth century in today's Britain

Real world cycles are not characterised by rigid, predictable movements because complex systems – such as human societies – have many moving parts that are constantly influencing each other. But as Keynes (1924a) observed, to make sense of contemporary socio-economic developments, it is important to "study the present in the light of the past for the purposes of the future" (p. 322). Perhaps Mark Twain's observation – that "History does not repeat itself, but it rhymes" (quoted in Eayrs 1971, p. 21) – is a useful way of thinking about the relationship between current day events and their echoes from nineteenth-century Britain. In this, employment insecurity, social insecurity, the return of mass poverty, demonisation of the poor and popular mass movements stand out.

Employment insecurity

During the nineteenth century, the second industrial revolution was accompanied by rapid population growth, most of which was concentrated in the cities. In search of work, some found solid employment with reliable wages, but many did not – forced to accept casual work, low wages and accommodation that was both over-crowded and of questionable quality. Twenty-first-century Britain, as a consequence of immigration and a failure to put a floor under the labour market has also seen a significant population increase, with much of it again being concentrated in urban areas; and as happened over a century ago, this has had detrimental effects on the labour market, accommodation standards and prices, and the numbers of the urban poor.

The forces that produced the industrial revolution – notably the use of technology to displace humans – continue into the present. As a result, the labour market, especially that for lower- and semi-skilled workers, tends to generate insecure, often casual work – frequently in what has come to be known as the "gig economy", where instead of a regular wage, workers are paid for the "gigs" they do, such as a car journey or a food delivery. In this growing segment of the economy, zero hour contracts, low wages and few – if any – benefits (such as holidays or sickness cover) are commonplace. In other sectors, such as retail, workers are being rapidly displaced by self-service check-outs; and in others, such as transport and distribution, they are likely to be displaced by self-driving vehicles – all in an effort to cut costs.

Transport is just one of the sectors of the gig economy that has already come in for particular criticism. A good example is Uber, an American private car hire and delivery company operating in over 600 cities worldwide, that has recently been the subject of protests and legal actions. Uber's services are booked using a mobile app; and its drivers, who are given no guarantee of "gigs", either use their own cars or rent a car to drive with Uber. Having arrived in London in 2012, within five years, Uber's 40,000 drivers – most of them non-white and many of them immigrants – far outnumbered the city's 21,000 traditional cabbies. Uber fares are 30 to 50 per cent lower than those of black cabs, which appeals to its customers; but its drivers are forced to pay a 25 per cent commission on every fare (Benhold 2017). London's traditional cab drivers have complained from the start that Uber is undermining their ability to compete; and if driver-less cars – in which Uber is investing heavily – become a reality, both traditional cabs and Uber drivers will become a thing of the past (Hern 2015; Edwards 2017).

But employment is not the only issue of concern. In September 2017, due to concerns about "public safety and security" arising from Uber's failure to report criminal offenses and to carry out background checks on drivers, Transport for London (TfL) announced that Uber's London licence would not be renewed upon expiry. According to figures from the Metropolitan Police, there had been forty-eight alleged sexual attacks by Uber drivers during the first two months of 2017 alone, an increase of 50 per cent over the previous year (Saner 2017). Uber's response was to announce that it would appeal the decision and to launch an online petition against it, to which the response in support of Uber's continued presence in London has been enormous (BBC 2017b).

Employment terms and conditions in the gig economy are reminiscent of the casual, insecure and poorly paid labour arrangements that resulted in the 1889 London Dock Strike. Like the dock and wharf companies of the time, gig economy companies justify their actions on basis of the need for competitive advantage, with the added "benefit" of offering their workers "flexibility and choice". But the description of the casual dock workers prior to the strike in 1889 suggests that whatever the flexibility and choice offered them, it was far from welcome.

Social insecurity and sub-standard accommodation

The problems of poor conditions and insecurity are not restricted to jobs, as the accommodation workers in casual employment are likely to go home to is also under pressure. With much of the public sector housing stock having been sold off by the Thatcher government, privately owned and/or managed accommodation has been playing an ever larger role. Accommodation in the private sector is more likely than its dwindling public sector equivalent, to put margins before quality; and it tends to mitigate in favour of higher rents and lower standards.

Data from the 2015–16 English Housing Survey reveal the scale of the difficulties facing those forced to find a home within the private rental sector. In 2015–16, 14.3 million households in England (63 per cent) were owner-occupiers, down from a peak of 71 per cent in 2003; 4.5 million households (20 per cent) were private renters and 3.9 million (17 per cent) were social renters (Department for Communities and Local Government 2017, p. 1). Of renters, from a decade earlier, the proportion of households with children living in private rented accommodation increased from 30 to 36 per cent (945,000 more households) whereas those living in social rented accommodation decreased from 36 to 32 per cent (123,000 fewer households) (ibid., p. 2).

Unlike local authorities or housing associations, private landlords are under far less pressure to ensure that their properties meet the required standard, with additional regulation of the market being strongly resisted by both the coalition and Conservative governments. According to John Healey, Labour's Shadow Housing Secretary:

> Renters too often don't have the basic consumer rights that we take for granted in other areas. In practice, you have fewer rights renting a family home than you do buying a fridge-freezer. As a result, too many are forced to put up with poor quality and sometimes downright dangerous housing.
>
> (Quoted in Singh 2017)

Thus, almost a century and a half after the bleak assessment by Dr Alfred Hill, Birmingham's first Medical Officer, of properties available to rent in 1880 (Chinn 1995), the situation for low-income renters is not much better, with almost a third (28 per cent) of private renter homes (6.6 million) failing to meet the Decent Homes Standard. This compares with 18 per cent (4.2 million homes) in the owner-occupier and 13 per cent (3 million homes) in the social renter sectors (Department for Communities and Local Government 2017, pp. 29–30). The same study revealed that 1.4 million households were living in unsuitable – or even unsafe – accommodation, with approximately 17 per cent of the total number of homes rented from private landlords (795,000 homes) containing the "the most dangerous kind of safety hazard", such as "dangerous boilers, exposed wiring, overloaded electricity sockets and vermin infestations" (Kentish 2017).

Despite these sub-standard and deteriorating conditions, rents have been increasing. According to a report from Your Move and Reeds Rains, rents increased by nearly a quarter (24 per cent) between 2010 and 2015, far outpacing consumer price inflation, which rose by 14 per cent, at the same time as wages for most have fallen in real terms (Jones 2015). In 2015–16, the proportion of household income being spent on accommodation was highest for private renters, who, on average, spent 35 per cent of their household income on rent, compared with 28 per cent for social renters, with owner-occupiers spending 18 per cent of their income on mortgage payments (Department for Communities and Local Government 2017, p. 2).

Renters are also increasingly vulnerable to eviction. A report by the Joseph Rowntree Foundation[4] found that in 2015, over 40,000 renters in the UK were evicted from their homes (up 20 per cent over 2003), with an increasing rate of evictions in the private rented sector, 83 per cent of which was due to "no fault" evictions, using Section 21 of the 1988 Housing Act (Clarke *et al.* 2017, p. 1). Of those not evicted, many were being forced to move as a consequence of unaffordability, sub-standard property conditions or disputes with the landlord. These trends in evictions and forced moves were strongly correlated with expansion of the private rented sector and cuts to Local Housing Allowances.

However, although conditions in general are somewhat better for social than private renters, this is not always the case. The devastating fire at Grenfell Tower – managed by the Kensington and Chelsea Tenant Management Organisation, an arms-length management organisation responsible for the entire housing stock of the Royal Borough of Kensington and Chelsea – is presently the subject of a major inquiry. Whilst it is difficult to speculate on the outcome, it seems unlikely that it will bring much good news to less well-off urban renters.

In short, the effect of either flat or falling real wage levels, combined with steadily rising property prices – some of it underpinned through market interventions by the government – has been to fundamentally undermine the housing market. Whilst "generation rent" – a large group of people with sharply reduced prospects of entering the property market, and therefore forced to rent their homes – forms one side of the new equation; much of the housing stock has been acquired by private landlords, providing the other. The rise of the "buy to let" property market highlights another problem – a loss of confidence in pension arrangements, which may well be inadequate to meet pensioners' needs – if indeed, they can afford to make any arrangement at all. As a result of insecurity about future retirement incomes, many have chosen to invest in property, fuelling the growth of the private rented buy to let segment of the property market.

With these kinds of insecure wages, employment and accommodation conditions continuing to developing, pressure for a shift in the insecurity cycle will only increase.

The return of mass poverty

As during the nineteenth century, competition for lower- and semi-skilled employment has put downward pressure on wages and conditions, increasing employment insecurity. At the same time, competition for accommodation has put upward pressure on rents, which does not always result in adequately maintained accommodation. These two factors have contributed to the growth of the urban poor, and with it, an expanded role for both charities and the church – who had also taken up much of the slack prior to the evolution of the welfare state.

Not only has the twenty-first century brought a dramatic increase in poverty, inequality has also increased. The downward pressure on the wages of those in casual and lower- or semi-skilled sectors, however, does not apply to those in the City or those in higher income sectors, whose earnings – as well as standards of living and accommodation – head strongly in the opposite direction. This has been accelerated by the reduction of taxes for the highest income earners and by an increasing reliance on secondary or indirect forms of taxation that place a disproportionate amount of the tax burden on the less well-off.

Institute for Fiscal Studies data show that between 2010 and 2015 – under the coalition and Conservative governments – inequality increased even further than it had under New Labour, which according to Peter Mandelson, a theoretician of New Labour, was "intensely relaxed about people getting filthy rich" on condition only that they paid the taxes a (largely sympathetic) government chose to levy on them (quoted in Mishra 2017). The Gini coefficient, which ranges from 0 (perfect equality) to 1 (maximum inequality) rose from 0.380 in 1997, when New Labour came to power, to 0.383 in 2010 and to 0.397 in 2015 (Institute for Fiscal Studies 2017). At the same time, the 90/10 income inequality ratio – comparing the income earned by the top 10 per cent with that earned by the bottom 10 per cent – increased from 5.063 in 1997 to 5.233 in 2015 (ibid.).

Whilst the poor were growing in number, New Labour's move to the right meant that there has been very little – if any – Parliamentary representation for the poor, urban or otherwise. This is also true of those who as a result of recession, stagnant wages, inflation or austerity – or all four at once – are at a significant risk of joining the poor. These include the latest in a string of newly recognised groups, the "Just About Managing" families (JAMs). Whilst Ed Miliband worried about the "squeezed middle" and Nick Clegg referred to "alarm clock Britain", the situation for many – "the bleary-eyed grafters struggling to raise families, while getting out to work, with little money left over to pay for luxuries" (Parkinson 2016) – is all too reminiscent of Seebohm Rowntree's description of life on the poverty line over a century earlier. The Conservative Chancellor George Osborne used the term "hard-working families" to describe the same people (ibid.). But whatever they are called, like the JAMs, they had and have very little to spare.

According to the Resolution Foundation think tank,[5] JAM families consist of some 6 million working households and 10 million adults, in the bottom half of the income distribution but above the lowest decile, who receive less than 20 per cent of their income from means-tested benefits. Around 80 per cent of these households have at least one person in full-time employment. They are not, however, always "low-income" households. Those with an annual income of as much as £50,000 a year could qualify as JAM, if they have several children to feed and clothe. Whilst most JAM incomes come from work, they are often topped up by welfare support, with JAM families accounting for around two-thirds of all families with children receiving tax credits. Two-thirds of JAM families have less than a month's income in savings (Bell 2016); and with so little in reserve, the balance between JAM and poverty is easily tipped by inflation or stagnation in either wages or benefits – or both.

Theresa May's inaccurate assessment of this group's situation reveals just how acute their vulnerability actually is, as well as how quickly their fortunes can change. During a speech intended for their ears, she said:

> You have your own home, but you worry about paying a mortgage. You can just about manage but you worry about the cost of living and getting your kids into a good school. If you're one of those families, if you're just managing, I want to address you directly.
>
> (May 2016)

However, at the time of May's speech, Resolution Foundation data suggested that home ownership among the "just managing" had actually fallen by more than half, from 59 per cent in 1995 to 26 per cent in 2016, whilst private renting had increased by roughly the same amount from 22 to 56 per cent (Resolution Foundation 2016). This will have further long-term effects on their household budgets, as they will frequently be forced to continue paying rent into old age. According to David Finch, the Resolution Foundation's senior economic analyst: "This switch from owning to renting means that 'just managing' families are now having to set aside a quarter of their income on housing. As a result they have suffered over a decade of lost income growth" (ibid.).

Just About Managing families weren't the only ones with problems; many were not in fact managing at all. In May of 2015, the BBC reported ONS data showing that whilst 7.8 per cent of the UK population was in "persistent" poverty in 2013, nearly one-third had fallen below the official poverty line, at some point between 2010 and 2013 (BBC 2015b). According to the Institute for Fiscal Studies' (IFS) poverty data, 21.8 per cent of the British population (14 million people) were living below the poverty line in 2015, with 29.7 per cent of children (4 million) and 15.6 per cent of the elderly (1.9 million) in poverty (Institute for Fiscal Studies 2017).[6] Given differences in both the definition of poverty, as well as the means of data collection, an accurate comparison between the ONS and IFS data from 2015 and Seebohm Rowntree's York study in 1899 would be problematic. But it is impossible to ignore that fact that whilst in 1899, 27.8 per cent of York's population was in primary or secondary poverty – a problem that had been largely eliminated from Britain under the post-war consensus – by 2015, poverty had returned to levels comparable to those observed by Rowntree.

But not only are the numbers of people living in poverty reminiscent of nineteenth-century Britain. Based on data from the four sets of national surveys into poverty in Britain since the 1980s – the 2012 and 1999 Poverty and Social Exclusion surveys, and the 1990 and 1983 Breadline Britain surveys – Lansley and Mack (2015) report that:

> In 2012, nearly three out of every ten people in Britain fell below the minimum living standard set by society as a whole, twice as many as did so in 1983. One-in-ten households lived in a damp home, a thirty-year high. The number of those who could not afford to heat their home adequately had trebled since the 1990s, rising from three to nine percent. The numbers of those who had skimped on meals from time to time over the previous year had doubled since 1983 – up from thirteen to twenty-eight percent.
>
> (p. ix)

They go on to explain that "[t]he reality for people on low incomes today is one of a constant struggle to get by, of endless worry about how to pay the next bill, of parents cutting back for themselves to prioritise the kids, and of young people left with few hopes for the future" (ibid.).

In 2013, a number of reports on poverty – and in particular the use of food banks – by charities including the Red Cross, Church Action on Poverty, Oxfam and the Trussell Trust, were largely suppressed or ignored by the coalition government and Tory ministers. This is in spite of the fact that during the winter of 2013, for the first time since the Second World War, the Red Cross collected and distributed food aid to the needy in Britain, which came as a surprise to many (McDonald-Gibson 2013). Chris Johnes, Oxfam's

UK poverty director, for example, said that he was "genuinely shocked" that the Red Cross was getting involved in providing food aid: "They don't do things for reasons of grandstanding ... The fact that they are doing this ... is a clear signal how serious things have become" (quoted in BBC 2013).

Moreover, all of these reports identify austerity and cuts to benefits and social safety nets – singling out the universal credit system, the government's flagship welfare overhaul, as leaving claimants unable to afford meals as a consequence of benefits delays – along with unemployment and the increased cost of living as causal factors in the growing numbers of people finding themselves in poverty and in need of emergency food. Identifying the level of food poverty in the UK a "national disgrace", the Church Action on Poverty and Oxfam report makes the point that

> up to half of all people turning to food banks are doing so as a direct result of having benefit payments delayed, reduced, or withdrawn altogether ... [and] changes to the benefit system are the most common reasons for people using food banks.
>
> (Cooper and Dumpleton 2013, p. 3)

However, the government's initial response was entirely dismissive. In October 2013, in response to the Red Cross Report, a spokesman for the Department of Work and Pensions said that there was no "robust evidence" that welfare reforms were linked to the increased use of food banks (BBC 2013). But in April 2014, the All-Party Parliamentary Group on Hunger commissioned an inquiry into the extent and causes of hunger in the United Kingdom. The inquiry's report, *Feeding Britain: A Strategy for Zero Hunger in England, Wales, Scotland and Northern Ireland*, was published in December 2014.

But attitudes on the part of the government to both the inquiry's report on food poverty and those finding themselves reliant on food aid suggest that things have changed very little during the intervening century or so since Booth and Rowntree's surveys – and they would have been all too familiar to both. For example, Iain Duncan Smith, the Work and Pensions Secretary, contended that

> [t]he report itself today and other reports ... show there are often people with very dysfunctional lives, people who have been caught in drug addiction, family breakdown, people who have gone into serious illness that aren't claiming benefits and come into difficulty. All of these have to be ultimately dealt with by the department.
>
> (Quoted in Holehouse 2014)

And Baroness Jenkin of Kennington, who sits on the House of Lords refreshment committee – which itself has been criticised for refusing "to merge catering services with the House of Commons, because, according to a former Commons clerk, it would mean peers drinking inferior Champagne" (ibid.) – went so far as to suggest that a lack of cooking skills (especially relating to porridge) was a major part of the food poverty problem.

Attitudes about the poor

Attitudes towards those struggling to make ends meet have also returned to a distinctly Victorian character. Walker (2014) documents the social and psychological dimensions of poverty, which have intensified since the 1980s:

> Accompanying the secular trend towards increased income targeting, greater conditionality, and more residual provision, the tone of the public debate has fluctuated, with peaks of negativity in the 1980s, the late 1990s, and late 2000s ... [when the poor were associated with] the concept of "broken Britain": worklessness, lack of effort, people receiving "something for nothing", large families, bad parenting, and antisocial behavior.
>
> (p. 178)

This is supported by Owen Jones's (2016) study of the "unjust distribution of wealth and power" in contemporary British society (p. xxi). Although the amount of public money spent on unemployed people represents a relatively small proportion of the social security budget, since the Conservatives returned to power in 2010, the government has set about reducing it even further, "rolling back the state in an effort to complete Thatcher's work" (Jones 2016, p. ix). Jones goes on to demonstrate how demonisation has become a powerful means of gaining electoral support for such policies, with "the recipients of social security [being portrayed] as workshy, feckless free-loaders ... Rather than helping the poor, Tory ministers have openly condemned them as 'skivers' and 'shirkers' to exploit divisions within the working class" (ibid., pp. x–xi).

Further evidence of this can be found in comments by then Prime Minister, David Cameron, and then Chancellor, George Osborne, in 2012. Echoing Margaret Thatcher's speech at the Young Conservative Conference in February 1975,[7] Cameron (2012) announced during Prime Minister's Question Time: "*We* back the workers, *they* back the shirkers" (emphasis added). In October of the same year, in a speech at the Conservative Party Conference, Osborne asked "Where is the fairness ... for the shift worker, leaving home in the dark hours of the early morning, who looks up at the closed blinds on their next door neighbour sleeping off a life on benefits?" (Osborne 2012).

These viewpoints by the more prosperous certainly seem to support the assessment of William Lucas Sargent, writing in the 1850s that "[n]othing was more common than to hear denunciations of the wasteful spending of the working people, of the imprudence of their early marriages, of their lack of frugality, and of their drunkenness" (quoted in Chinn 1995, p. 40). Thus, the idea that poverty is not necessarily the fault of the poor themselves – an idea that both the Booth and Rowntree studies had made clear – has been dismissed and the poor are again being blamed for their plight.

It would also appear that working to Rowntree's admittedly rather bleak "physical efficiency" budget is not getting any easier, either. According to the report of the government's inquiry into the causes and extent of hunger in the UK, "[a]s well as lacking resources, ... [the poor] may have difficulties budgeting for a week's worth of shopping, ... as whatever income there might be is devoted to other, non-essential items of expenditure or to paying off debt" (All-Party Parliamentary Group 2014). The All-Party Parliamentary Group's Report drew another telling comment from the coalition government, with Cameron appearing to ignore the large numbers of working poor, when he announced that "it (the report) comes at a time when the economy is growing and we are lifting people into work and out of poverty" (quoted in Holehouse 2014).

George Osborne, however, appeared to have few illusions about this; and his plans for further austerity included reform of the tax credit system – a measure that would directly impact the working poor, including a significant number of Just About Managing households. Whilst the nature of the House of Lords has clearly changed since the days of the Liberal reforms and the 1909 "People's Budget", responses to their actions have not necessarily followed suit. When the House of Lords voted to delay Osborne's measures – mostly due to a lack of clarity on the transitional arrangements – Cameron, like Lloyd George before him, threatened to flood the Lords with new peers in order to get his way (Wheeler 2015).

Popular mass movements

Large numbers of people experiencing similar problems and frustrations are likely, if these difficulties are not being addressed, to organise popular mass movements. This was the case in the nineteenth century with Chartism, various other movements pressing for a much extended franchise and new unionism. It was also the case during the Second World War, with the strengthening of a collective determination that post-war Britain would be a world worth fighting for. Within the armed forces, the Army Bureau for Current Affairs led compulsory discussions about Britain after the war; and among civilians, there was "a strong sense that it was time for a new beginning" (Marr 2007, p. 4). Recognition of the problem of mass poverty motivated leaders of the Roman Catholic, Anglican and Free Churches to write a letter to *The Times* of 21 December 1940; in it, they made a number of proposals, foremost among which was that extreme inequality of wealth and possessions should be abolished. One of the signatories, William Temple, soon to be the Archbishop of Canterbury, initiated a church-led campaign for social reforms, which linked with other secular movements, ultimately resulting in the welfare state and a better post-war society than Britain had ever experienced.

Since the "inequality turn" in 1979, however, pressures have mounted within UK society. But following Britain's extensive de-industrialisation, significant anti-union legislation and the dwindling of organised labour, mass movements have tended to be community and socially based – not all of them constructive. The four days of rioting of early August 2011 – which started in London and spread to other cities, including Birmingham, Manchester, Salford, Nottingham and Liverpool – are one such example. What began as a small-scale peaceful protest in Tottenham, North London, against the police shooting of a local black man, Mark Duggan, two days earlier, quickly turned into serious violence.

Although the causes of the riots were hotly debated, the contributory role of the coalition government's programme of austerity cannot be denied.[8] Yet from officialdom and the mainstream media, there was a general denial that the civil unrest was in any way part of a response to the worsening social and economic conditions experienced by a growing segment of the population (Abbas and Croft 2011). Rather, in a speech to the House of Commons responding to the riots, then Prime Minister David Cameron (2011) asserted that they were nothing but "criminality, pure and simple"; and Ken Clarke, then Secretary of State for Justice, dismissed those taking part as the "feral underclass" (Clarke 2011).

A collaborative social research inquiry conducted by the *Guardian* and the London School of Economics (2011), funded by the Joseph Rowntree Foundation and the Open Society Foundations, provides powerful evidence refuting the government's claims. Based on in-depth interviews with rioters, the study found:

> They expressed it in different ways, but at heart what the rioters talked about was a pervasive sense of injustice. For some, this was economic – the lack of a job, money or opportunity. For others, it was more broadly social, not just the absence of material things but how they felt they were treated compared with others.
>
> (*Guardian* and London School of Economics 2011, p. 24)

The sense of hopelessness is apparent in the response of a nineteen-year-old unemployed man in Birmingham, when asked what he would like to see changed: "Fuck knows. Dunno. Don't really care about that no more. I've gone past caring. Just think there's no point in me wishing, wanting things to happen" (ibid., p. 26). The report goes on: "In the face of such hopelessness, it is perhaps unsurprising that many of those we interviewed thought that further riots were likely. Not least, it seems, because many felt that little was likely to change" (ibid.).

The general sense of outrage at the effect of austerity programmes in increasing inequality also found an increasingly influential voice in the world-wide

"Occupy" movement.[9] The Occupy protests were a societal reaction to a popular recognition that society's economic problems were attributable to profligacy of the financial sector and consequential social and economic disparities. However, the Occupy protesters initially found it difficult to find a credible media outlet for their message. In the late autumn of 2011, this began to change, especially when they protested outside St Paul's Cathedral in the City of London. As had been the case during the Second World War, an important agent for change – in both share of voice and eloquence of the protest – came, perhaps unexpectedly, from the Roman Catholic and Anglican Churches.[10] The Vatican's Pontifical Council for Justice and Peace (2011) called for the creation of a global system for managing a global economy and strongly backed the introduction of a Financial Transaction Tax; and in a letter to the *Financial Times* the Archbishop of Canterbury, Rowan Williams (2011), argued that the societal unrest, evident in the Occupy protests, had deeply social, moral and economic causes. He went further to suggest that:

> The protest at St. Paul's was seen by an unexpectedly large number of people as the expression of a widespread and deep exasperation with the financial establishment that shows no signs of diminishing. There is still a powerful sense around – fair or not – of a whole society paying for the errors and irresponsibility of bankers; of impatience with a return to "business as usual" ... It isn't easy to say what we should do differently. It is time we tried to be more specific.
>
> (Williams 2011)

Whilst the financial sector chided the Church for its involvement, it is well worth noting that, unlike politicians, the influence of the financial sector over the Church is relatively weak; and it is hard to dismiss the Church's overall objectives and policy proposals.

More recently, the emergence of Jeremy Corbyn – as a political representative of the interests of those feeling some of the pressures that gave rise to these earlier protests – has offered hope and a voice. And in the Momentum movement, many have found renewed and potentially powerful political representation in the form of the Labour Party, since its decisive move towards the left. The pressure exerted by new unionism and a wider franchise during the nineteenth century had to wait half a century – five decades which included two world wars, a financial crash and a global depression – before there was a change in the conventional wisdom. It remains to be seen what kinds of crises it might take to produce a comparable shift in the future.

Twenty-first-century influences

Whilst there are many things about twenty-first-century Britain that might have been familiar to our Victorian and Edwardian predecessors, there are also many things that they would have found surprising, if not downright shocking.

The financialisation of all interest groups – including the poor – rather than just employers and the middle classes, would be likely to be one such difference. The result has been much higher levels of private debt, to a point where a poor credit score – and consequently limited access to further debt – is now considered to be almost a form of poverty in itself (Mitchell *et al.* 2005). This led to the creation of specific financial services for those finding themselves in this kind of financial position. The less well-off are thus not only forced to borrow; they frequently go further into debt as a result of extortionate interest rates, sometimes known to exceed 4,000 per cent APR (Jones, R. 2013). Access to credit at reasonable terms, if available at all, has also been undermined by the growth of the gig economy, where zero hour contracts mean that income streams are unpredictable; and borrowers are likely to have few reserves available to smooth out the peaks and troughs.

This asymmetry in access to credit – as well as an ability to service it – has other implications. Not only has it increased the cost of owner-occupied homes and under-pinned the growth of the privately rented accommodation market; it has also contributed to significant and growing inequality. Those who cannot afford a home of their own are barred from one of the most consistent stores of wealth and security available in Britain. With wages not only remaining flat – or even in reverse – but also being irregular, this is unlikely to change. Meanwhile, prospects for the diminishing number of those with the wealth, income and material resilience to ride out any challenging economic times tell a very different story.

Computers and information technology represent another fundamental difference from nineteenth-century Britain, with significant implications for the insecurity cycle. The explosion in both the numbers and distribution of personal computers, along with their processing power, is partly what lies behind the globalisation of the financial sector – as well as the reliance on neoliberal economists and their mathematical modelling.

However, there is a clear and developing divergence between industrial and social media – and this is already having an impact on the insecurity cycle. The consolidation of many previously independent organisations into large corporations has included much of the communications sector, and with it many news channels. Whilst it is hardly unusual for newspapers to have had a discernible political alignment – which was certainly the case in the nineteenth century – consolidation of titles has often meant consolidation of alignment; and this has tended to reinforce the conventional wisdom.

Until recently, this has meant that promoting an alternative point of view has been difficult. The media's regular characterisation of the Labour Party leader, Ed Miliband, as "Red Ed" would hardly have stood up to serious comparison with other figures in the socialist movement; and such a description might well have put a smile on the faces of the likes of Annie Besant.

However, social media played a large part in the rise of Jeremy Corbyn to the position of Labour Party leader; and the party's shift to the left is producing a much more radical agenda. Not only does this use of social media represent something of a lack of interest in industrial media, it allows people in similar situations, with similar problems and views to both communicate and organise directly. Following the de-industrialisation of Britain and the emasculation of British trade unions, social media-based groups have effectively taken over much of the role of the trade unions, in terms of organisation and policy development, creating what has been termed a "social union" or "community unionism" (Dibben 2004; Wills 2001).

This shift in media consumption and usage has also allowed new social unions to extend their footprint, and consequently their influence, internationally. This can be seen in the cooperation between the American Bernie Sanders and British Jeremy Corbyn campaigns. It may even be that this is the beginning of a "life support system" to rival that which the neoliberals have put so much effort and resource into building.

Whilst the conventional wisdom has largely dominated the industrial media with regard to economics and politics, the role of the poor has shifted. Reports by the likes of the British Red Cross on poverty and the use of food banks have been largely ignored or downplayed, and the less well-off have now been recast as entertainment (Tyler 2015), rather than being the subject of Booth and Rowntree-like reports. Television programmes – like Channel 4's *Benefits Street*, Channel 5's *Can't Pay, We'll Take It Away* and *Nightmare Tenants, Slum Landlords* – cast the problems of the poor in a very different light to that chosen by the nineteenth- and twentieth-century reformers.

Another aspect of day-to-day life that might surprise a time traveller from Victorian or Edwardian Britain would be the level of public services available. Under-funded and under pressure as they might be, social welfare services still represent a major improvement over those available to nineteenth-century casual workers. But perhaps of greatest significance is the fact that many still believe in the principle of these public services, whilst some can still remember them in better days. Thus their main legacy may well be in demonstrating that there are problems that need to be ameliorated – and that the phrase "free market" is not in fact a silver bullet solution to every policy problem.

Conclusions

Britain has spent more than half of the last 217 years in recession, with numerous financial crises. But in spite of this track record, free market capitalism has only faced one serious, existential challenge. It took almost a century and a half before the arrival of the "Keynesian" revolution, albeit with short-term welfare reforms along the way – yet it took less than thirty-five years to reverse it. This suggests a critical gulf in power between the two sides of the insecurity cycle; and it underlines the short-term nature of politics.

With the fall of the Soviet Union in 1992, not only was seventy-five years of communist threat removed. Free market capitalism could then argue that it had proven itself to be the only viable model of the economy. However, considering the background to the insecurity cycle, it is clear that the opposing Cold War models helped to maintain the cycle – and that both systems have significant failings. Whilst there is truth in Joan Robinson's identification of "Bastard Keynesianism" resulting from attempts to incorporate Keynes's ideas into neoclassical economics and to build in more mathematics, simply turning back the clock to a "truer" Keynesianism would be unlikely to represent any better a way forward, than continuing with laissez faire – although Keynes might well prove a more fertile starting point for new ideas aimed at today's problems.

Perhaps the main question is identifying and addressing the right problem. The collapse of the post-war consensus was a consequence of a number of factors, of which the failure to develop and maintain competitive industries is significant; not only did this put pressure on national accounts, it also contributed to today's unbalanced economy. Poor and adversarial relationships between employers/government and the trade unions were an inevitable result of the ensuing pressure on industry, re-igniting the insecurity cycle in the process. The failure of the Bretton Woods framework and institutions to maintain international order was also a major contributing factor, especially with a growing global over-supply of certain manufactured durables – as well as credit – causing ever slimmer profit margins.

Laissez faire has been persistent for a number of reasons; the message is simple and, on the face of it at least, reasonably convincing. From a corporate perspective, the objectives are common – producing widespread and sustained commitment to the concept; consequently networks and resources are extensive and maintained over time. These networks and resources include both media and finance, and the long-term nature of the objectives contrasts strikingly with the more divided, shorter-term, more poorly resourced groups such as the state, labour and, in particular, the poor. This is what lies behind the power imbalance that has maintained liberalism for so long, and undermines the role of the nation state.

Shifts in the insecurity cycle are produced by the key drivers already identified: a crisis, either chronic or acute (often both), new ideas, democratic pressure and significant political support. Fear, over-confidence and perhaps Friedman's "tyranny of the status quo" can variously super-charge or inhibit movements in the cycle. But without all the main drivers being in place, a movement is very unlikely to occur.

Notes

1 See, for example, BBC (2016); Clark and Primo (2012); Lo and Mueller (2010, pp. 3–4); Mirowski (1992, 1999); Schabas (1993).
2 See, for example, Abbas *et al.* (2010).
3 See, for example, Economists for Rational Economic Policies (EREP) www.primeeconomics.org/erep/; Progressive Economics Group (PEG) https://peg.primeeconomics.org/; and Policy Research in Macroeconomics (PRIME) www.primeeconomics.org/.

4 Clarke *et al.* (2017).
5 Finch (2016).
6 The poverty line is set at 60 per cent of the median annual income, net of taxes and housing costs.
7 Quoted in Chesshyre (1975).
8 See for example, Briggs (2012); *Guardian* and London School of Economics (2011); Kawalerowics and Biggs (2015); Roberts (2011).
9 For further information, see www.occupytogether.org.
10 It is interesting to note that there is a precedent for the Church's response. During the 1980s, the effect of Thatcherite policies served to aggravate the plight of those in "Urban Priority Areas" who were suffering the immediate effects of reductions in public spending and taxation and the withdrawal of state welfare provisions. The Anglican Church's response was the 1985 *Faith in the City* report (Archbishop of Canterbury 1985). Financial deregulation took place the following year, with "Big Bang" liberalisation.

10 Britain and the European Union

Introduction

The Brexit referendum of June 2016 delivered a small majority (51.9 per cent to 48.1 per cent) in favour of the United Kingdom leaving the European Union (EU).[1] As discussed earlier in Chapter 2, much in the UK's constitution is unclear; but no-one doubts that a referendum vote does not create new law. For a short while after the vote, it was not obvious how Brexit should be initiated: was this a matter for the executive branch of government? Or was legislative approval required?

In January 2017, the UK Supreme Court ruled in the *Miller* case that an Act of Parliament was required;[2] and in March 2017, the Westminster Parliament passed the European Union (Notification of Withdrawal) Act, authorising the government to give notice to the EU of the UK's intention to leave the Union. The notice was duly given on 29 March 2017. Under Article 50 of the Treaty on the European Union, the UK will cease to be a member of the EU two years from the date of this notice. Article 50 envisages that, in this two-year interval, negotiations between the Union and the departing member state will be conducted, with a view to settling the terms of the separation.[3] At the time of writing in the winter of 2017-18, these negotiations are continuing (if not exactly progressing).

So much, at least, is clear. But what is not at all clear is how Brexit will affect the British economy and polity. To answer this question requires us to consider a number of prior ones.

The first set of these questions concerns the nature of the institution – the European Union – which the UK has been a member of since 1973, and is now set to leave. What is the European Union trying to achieve? What precisely did the UK sign up to when it joined and how did this commitment evolve over time? What constraints did EU membership involve, and what benefits did it bring?

A second set of questions concerns Brexit itself. On what terms will the UK leave, and how will its future relationship with the Union be constituted? What new opportunities will the UK acquire to make its own policies, once it is free (to whatever extent) of EU influence? What will be the implications of Brexit for Britain's trading relations with the rest of the world and how will these, in their turn, affect domestic policy-making in the years to come?

Brexit also poses a deeper conundrum. The referendum vote threw into sharp relief certain features of the British political and economic system which seemed to set it apart from European neighbours with which it should, on the face of it, have much in common. After all, Britain, like them, is a market economy which claims to observe the principles of liberal democracy and the rule of law, with a welfare state that cushions some of the effects of the market and seeks to guarantee basic social protections. Brexit was not preordained; and it is possible that it will be postponed, perhaps for some indefinite period, or reversed. However, the Brexit referendum changed not just Britain's future, but the understanding of its past. We now need to ask: what exactly was it that made Britain's relationship with the European Union so problematic throughout the forty-plus years of its membership? How powerful are the forces pulling Britain away from the rest of Europe, and how will they shape the options available to British policy makers in the years to come?

The idea of the European Union

In addressing the question "What is the European Union?" we need to distinguish between the technical features of institutions such as the single market, which we shall explore shortly, and the wider project which underpins them. For its adherents, the European Union is less a set of mechanisms or institutions, and more an idea which is in the process of being realised.

At the core of this idea is the principle of economic and political cooperation between independent states. The EU has never professed to have the goal of creating a new state, a "United States of Europe". In terms of its formal structure, it has more in common with other institutions for international cooperation, such as the United Nations or World Trade Organization, than it does with a nation state such as the United Kingdom.

But this is only part of the story. The European Union has developed a deep form of inter-state cooperation which has, over time, achieved a high degree of transnational economic integration. Economic integration, in turn, has served a greater purpose, which motivated the formation of the Union at its outset and continues to provide its reason for being: this is the preservation of peace and democracy in Europe. The Union is a project born out of the experience of the two world wars, which, from the perspective of its founders, were akin to European civil wars (Griffiths 2012). It is easily forgotten, from a British perspective, that virtually every part of the rest of the European continent has experienced authoritarian rule or foreign occupation at some point in the past century.

Underlying the idea of the European Union are conceptions of the state, and of its relation to society and the economy, which have deep historical roots. The first of these is the concept of the *rule of law state* or *Rechtstaat*. All liberal democracies recognise some version of the rule of law, understanding it to mean the principle that laws governing social and economic life should be publicly enunciated, consistently implemented and of general application (Bingham 2010). From these precepts it is possible to derive a number of additional principles. One is the notion of citizenship, with its implication that all members of the polity are entitled to the equal protection of the law. Another is the idea of constitutional limits to the power of the government: the state is not the source of law but is subject to a higher legal authority, and so is, itself, rule-governed.

These ideas are by no means unfamiliar in a British context. However, there is a divergence between the mainstream British understanding of the "rule of law" and the continental conception of the "rule of law *state*". British legal and political theory, following Dicey (1885), who in this regard was synthesising some long-standing elements of political thought and constitutional practice, sees the rule of law as an emergent practice, one which reflects a political understanding of the origins of legitimate government, and of the limits to it. The continental tradition, by contrast, tends to see the rule of law as actively instituted by the state. Seeing the rule of law this way is characteristic of the formal constitutions and codified private law systems of the French and German legal traditions (Chen and Deakin 2014).

This might be thought of as a distinction without a difference, or at least as one with no real substance to it. Surely what counts is the way government operates in practice, and not how it is described. But ideas can matter, and the cognitive gap between mainland European and British conceptions of the rule of law has had real consequences. The European Union is a law-driven project to a degree which has no obvious counterpart in British constitutional experience. To many of its British critics, it is this "teleological" or "constructivist" aspect of the European Union which makes the UK's participation in it problematic. For others, one of the benefits of the UK's membership is precisely the opportunity it has provided to modernise the British legal and constitutional system.

A second idea which finds expression in the practices and institutions of the European Union is that of the *social market economy*. At its simplest, this means that the operations of a market economy can co-exist with social protection. In a more extended sense, it implies that a welfare state is not only compatible with the functioning of a capitalist market, but is in a more active way complementary to it, in the sense of providing an institutional underpinning for participation of the general population in production and exchange.

The expression "social market economy" has its recent roots in the experience of economic reconstruction in post-1945 Germany (Nörr 1998). The term was used by politicians of the German social democratic party, the SPD, in the 1950s, to signify social democratic acceptance of the role of the market in Germany's post-war revival. In that context, it implied an acknowledgement of the limits to state control of the economy and a rejection of collective ownership of the means of production. But it also had the converse effect of emphasising the intertwining of certain social protections, in the form of collective bargaining, codetermination and employment rights, with the German growth model, which was (and is) focused on the need for industrial stability and social peace to support its large manufacturing sector.

The idea of the social market economy has come to have wider resonance in the context of European Union law and practice. The phrase "competitive social market economy" appears prominently in the European Treaties and is more than just a rhetorical device. As we shall see, European Union law does not set out anything like a comprehensive labour code; nor does it mandate a particular kind of welfare state. However, the Union has significant competences in the social policy field; and social and economic rights find concrete expression, alongside civil and political ones, in the EU Charter of Fundamental Rights, which, following the Treaty of Lisbon, was fully integrated into the Union's legal order. However far it takes the idea of the market as the principal mechanism of economic governance – and it sometimes seems to take it a very long way indeed – the Union does so in a framework which sees social rights and market freedoms as two sides of the same coin (Damjanovic 2013).

For many in the right wing of the British political class – and in the neoliberal think tanks which act as a conduit for the transmission of economic theory into government – the idea of a social market economy is at best a contradiction. And most likely, it is a dangerous delusion, a version of the "fatal conceit" which Hayek (1982) identified with socialist thought. But the British left has also been resistant to the social market concept, seeing it as an unnecessary concession to free market capitalism. In the British context, nationalisation of the means of production and direct government delivery of social welfare were the preferred means for achieving social democracy for most of the twentieth century. Support from British trade unions for the EU's social policy agenda was a pragmatic response to the absence, from the late 1970s onwards, of an elected government which was sympathetic to their interests. Prior to the speech given by the EU Commission President Jacques Delors to the Trades Union Congress in 1988, outlining plans for a "social dimension" to the single market, British trade unions had been sceptical towards the European project. So here again, there is something of a cognitive gap between Britain and the mainland.

The third concept which needs to be understood as underlying and informing the structures and practices of the EU is *ordoliberalism* (Peck 2010). This is the idea that the state should actively support the market economy and play a proactive role in constituting the conditions for its operation. In this sense, ordoliberalism is a variant of neoliberal thought. Some of its adherents were members of the Mont Pelerin Society in the middle decades of the twentieth century, alongside Friedrich von Hayek and Milton Friedman. Ordoliberal thought has roots in the inter-war period and its doctrines were first formulated in opposition to the command economy operated by the Nazi government after 1933. After 1945, ordoliberal economists played a prominent role in Germany's reconstruction and were influential in the drafting in the competition law provisions of the EU's founding legal instrument, the Treaty of Rome of 1957 (Ptak 2009).

But ordoliberalism is distinct from the libertarian strand of neoliberal theory which is prominent in British and American political economy (Schnyder and Siems 2013). Libertarian thinking sees the market as largely self-constituting. In so far as it needs the state for support, it depends upon private law which is, itself, a "spontaneous order", to be distinguished from the "made order" of regulatory legislation (Rothbard 1978; Hayek 1982).

The distinction between these two strands of thought has practical consequences. Libertarians see little justification for antitrust law, regarding private monopolies or restrictive practices as liable to disintegrate of their own accord, under the pressure of market forces. Ordoliberals, by contrast, see capitalism as tending naturally towards the concentration of economic resources, and so regard an active competition policy, enforced by the state, as essential to the preservation of the market, as well as a guarantor of political freedoms that would be put at risk by corporate power. It was this ordoliberal view which came to be reflected in the competition policy provisions of the Treaty of Rome. It was also to inform the design of the single currency and its implementation following the Treaty of Maastricht in 1992.

The distinction between ordoliberal and libertarian versions of neoliberal thought needs to be borne in mind when assessing British responses to the European Union. Many contemporary British critics of the Union, such as the Economists for Brexit group and their political allies in think tanks including the recently created Institute for Free Trade, adopt a position which is more consistent with libertarian thinking than with ordoliberal precepts.[4] For these groups, leaving the EU is an opportunity for Britain to adopt a minimalist trading regime, with few or ideally no tariffs on imported goods, and a chance to initiate a programme of deregulatory reform on matters of worker and consumer protection (Hannan 2016; Bootle 2017). From this perspective, allowing the market to work is preferable to attempting to manage it via antitrust law.

For some on the British left, ordoliberalism, or at least some manifestations of it, such as the Union's recent response to the Eurozone debt crisis, exemplify the sense of the EU as a pro-market project. And it can indeed seem that the EU is acting as nothing more or less than a transnational competition authority, denying the governments of member states a strategic role in economic planning. But close examination of the EU's antitrust and state aids policies suggests that its position is more nuanced than this description allows (Damjanovic 2013). It is nevertheless the case that at the level of EU practice, ordoliberal values coexist uneasily with those of the social market.[5] This tension has implications for British policy-making in the light of Brexit.

Institutions of European economic cooperation and integration

We now drill down into a closer examination of European institutions. The European Union is about more than economic cooperation and integration. It articulates a range of fundamental human rights and has, over time, assumed competences beyond economic policy, including in the areas of security, justice and foreign affairs. However, economic integration is the principal means by which the Union seeks to achieve its wider political goals. Three sets of institutions are particularly important for understanding how the EU works and how it has influenced UK social and economic policy: these are the customs union, the single market and the single currency.

The customs union

The simplest form of economic cooperation instituted by the European Union, and the first to be established in its formative years of the 1950s and 1960s, is its *customs union* (Egan 2012). A customs union is an arrangement between states which governs the basis upon which they trade with each other and with the outside world ("third countries"). It generally has three aspects: (1) the abolition of internal tariffs, enabling goods to move freely across national borders within the union; (2) a common external tariff, according to which all states in the union impose the same customs duties on goods entering from third countries; and (3) common rules of origin, according to which states agree to allow goods to circulate within the internal economic space of the union only if they comply with certain standards, for example relating to consumer safety or product specifications. The principal economic benefit of a customs union is the elimination of tariffs and related processing costs on goods which are internally traded. A related benefit is the reduction of transaction costs which is achieved by having common rules of origin for traded goods.

The single market

The EU's *single market* both extends and deepens the model of economic cooperation inherent in the customs union (Bulmer and Armstrong 1998; Pelkmans *et al.* 2008; Egan 2001, 2012). It extends it in the sense that while the customs union is concerned with the trading of goods, the single market covers other factors of production, including labour, services and capital. It deepens it in the sense that it requires member states to do more than simply remove tariffs and other formal barriers to trade. By participating in the single market, the EU's member states agree to adjust their laws with a view to removing indirect or "non-tariff" barriers to trade. This can mean removing regulations on production and exchange which tend to restrict inter-state trade; but it also means creating new rules to ensure equal market access for goods and other factors of production, regardless of their national origin.

A concept with foundational importance for the European single market is that of *mutual recognition*. According to this idea, goods and services produced according to standards applying in one member state should, within certain generally agreed limits, be accepted as tradable in all the others. Mutual recognition, so stated, is a powerful mechanism for convergence, as it puts not just goods and services, but national rules themselves, into competition with each other. It creates the risk of a "race to the bottom" as goods in states with stricter standards on matters such as safety and quality can be undercut by those produced in states with looser rules on these matters.

For this reason, the principle of mutual recognition is qualified by exemptions which allow member states to preserve regulations they consider essential for reasons of national social and economic policy. The scope of these exemptions varies according to context. Some originate in Treaty provisions and legislation; others derive from case law of the Court of Justice. Their effect is to allow member states to maintain a certain degree of autonomy in the making of regulations which may have an effect on access to their national markets.

The principle of mutual recognition is also qualified by rules made centrally, that is by the EU institutions, which set common standards to which all member states must conform. These harmonising rules generally set a floor of regulation below which no member state can go; but they may also operate as a "ceiling" or in some instances a uniform rule. They thereby place a limit on how far member states can undercut each other by engaging in regulatory arbitrage. Over time, there has been extensive harmonisation in such matters as product safety, environmental regulation and consumer protection. And as we shall see in more detail below, labour market and financial market rules are also subject to this form of EU-level regulation.

The process of constructing the single market has been a slow and gradual one. It did not come into being overnight; and it has been an exercise in compromise. It is a highly political process, requiring member states to identify and articulate their national interests and to put them into play in European-level negotiations and deliberations (Moravcsik 1998).

At the same time, the construction of the single market has been an exercise in "integration through law" (Cappelletti *et al.* 1986). European Union law has evolved to frame the project of economic integration (Weatherill 1995). A new legal order has emerged which is neither entirely akin to the national legal systems of sovereign states, nor is it in the nature of international law – that is, the law governing relations between sovereign states – at least as conventionally understood.

The European Union can trace its origins to an international legal instrument, a treaty, which in 1957 established the forerunner of the EU, the European Economic Community (EEC). The Treaty of Rome (as it became known) was agreed by the original six member states (Belgium, France, Germany, Italy, Luxembourg and the Netherlands). The Treaty itself set out the legal foundations of what was to become the single market (then more normally referred to as the "common market"). These included (1) the so-called "four freedoms" guaranteeing the free circulation of goods, labour, enterprise ("services" and "establishment") and capital; (2) a uniform competition policy, aimed at overcoming restrictive practices, monopolies and related barriers to market entry; and (3) the prohibition of unfair government subsidies to industry ("state aids").

It was understood at the outset that these legal provisions would not be self-executing. Thus provision was made in the Treaty of Rome for the establishment of institutions to advance the project of integration, including: (1) an executive branch – the Commission – tasked, among other things, with preparing new regulatory measures (Schmidt and Wonka 2012); (2) a rule-making body – the Council – consisting of representatives of the governments of the member states (Pollack 2012); (3) a Parliament consisting of national representatives whose role was initially consultative but has since acquired co-decision making powers (Raunio 2012); and (4) a Court charged with arriving at authoritative interpretations of Treaty provisions along with secondary legislation made principally by the Council, including "directives" which member states were to implement in domestic legislation, and "regulations" which were to be directly applicable in national law (Azoulai and Dehousse 2012).

In creating these new institutions, the fledgling Union was to some degree following an existing template. Thus it drew on earlier models such as that of the European Steel and Coal Community, the organisation which had preceded the EEC, and elements of practice drawn from agencies of the United Nations, such as the International Labour Organization. In time, however, the EEC was to depart radically from these earlier models.

The first critical steps in this direction were taken by the Court. Within a few years of its formation, the Court had developed, through case law, principles which were to ensure that EU law (as it became) would be unlike previous instances of international legal cooperation. These principles were that (1) EU law took priority over domestic (national) law in the event of any conflict between them ("supremacy"), and (2) EU law could, in certain instances, take effect in the national legal order of a member state, that is, without the state in question taking steps, or sufficient steps, to incorporate it into its legal system ("direct effect").

These principles were implicit, at best, in the Rome Treaty, and their assertion by the Court represented a bold articulation of its own role. But when, in the course of time, that assertion was accepted, not only by the other European institutions but by the national courts of the member states, the scene was set for EU law to become the principal mechanism of transnational economic integration. This was because a member state failing to implement an EU-level standard, or to do so adequately, was liable to find its national laws being displaced or disapplied in favour of the relevant European standard. As a result, the member states had good reason to ensure that legal measures adopted by the Union were implemented in a timely way and subsequently observed. They also had strong incentives to invest resources in the processes of negotiation and deliberation which led to new laws being adopted by the Union, since in doing so they were, in effect, making laws for themselves.

To begin with, the impact of EU law on domestic legal systems was relatively marginal. In the course of the 1960s and 1970s, the legal instruments adopted by the Council were mostly directed to removing direct barriers to market access, including measures on the rights of migrant workers, the activities of state monopolies and the harmonisation of technical standards relating to goods and services. In 1986, the then nine member states, including the UK, agreed a new treaty, the Single European Act, which gave fresh impetus to the integration process. This was achieved by extending the range of matters over which the Council could adopt new laws by a "qualified majority", so that even a large member state, with voting rights roughly proportionate to its population, could find itself outvoted over an increasing number of issues. The Single European Act also clarified and widened the authority of the Union to act as a transnational regulator in areas which included labour markets and financial markets (Green Cowles 2012). The 1992 Treaty of Maastricht, while of primary importance for paving the way for the single currency, also made significant additions to the Union's single market competences (Laursen 2012).

Over time, partly as a result of the proliferation of new Treaty provisions and secondary laws, and also by virtue of the Court's expansive and dynamic approach to legal interpretation, EU law aimed at constituting and protecting the single market has penetrated further into the core of national policymaking. It is no longer concerned only with the removal of formal barriers to trade, but extends its reach to the harmonisation of national laws and regulations which indirectly affect market access. This takes the form of "positive harmonisation" in those areas where the Union has acquired the competence to set common standards. A substantial body of law in areas including labour law, consumer protection and environmental regulation has developed by these means. New regulatory techniques have been developed, allowing member states greater discretion in the way they implement and enforce directives; and the substance of regulation has evolved to meet new needs, as in the development, for example, of the precautionary principle as a foundational precept of European environmental regulation (Burns and Carter 2012).

Single market law can also take the form of "negative harmonisation" in instances where the Court has ruled that national-level regulations unduly restrict the cross-border movement of economic resources. This approach has led the Court to intervene in areas of social and economic policy which on first impression (and indeed on further inspection) have little connection to the goal of economic integration. It was by these means, for example, that the UK's Sunday trading laws came under challenge in the early 1990s (Maher 1995). These laws did not discriminate between goods produced in the UK and those imported from elsewhere in the Union; nor did they apply differentially to companies registered in the UK and those operating as subsidiaries or branches of overseas firms. However, the Court's case law developed to the point where it was argued that restrictions on retail operations based in the UK had the effect of reducing the volume of goods likely to be imported for resale, and thereby acted as a barrier to trade. This legal interpretation was never less than controversial and was eventually discarded by the Court in favour of a narrower reading of the relevant Treaty provisions, but in the confusion created by the Court's rulings, the UK's Sunday trading laws became a dead letter and their repeal soon followed.

Another controversial interpretation was the Court's ruling in the *Viking* case, delivered in December 2007 (Freedland and Prassl 2015). There is no EU directive directly regulating the right to strike; and the Union has no power to adopt one, as collective labour law matters are mostly excluded from its social policy competences. In *Viking*, however, the Court ruled that strike action designed to stop the reflagging of a passenger vessel, the *Rossella*, from Finnish to Estonian law – a move which would have undercut the terms of a Finnish collective agreement – was contrary to one of the "four freedoms" forming the core of single market law, namely the freedom of establishment. Freedom of establishment is a right conferred on enterprises to move their seat of operation or, in some instances, registration, from one member state to another. The reflagging of the *Rossella* came under the scope of this right. The Court ruled that the collective action in question, as it was designed to frustrate the reflagging of the ship – or at any rate to counter its effects – was unlawful. In reaching this conclusion, the Court ruled that the collective action did not strike a "proportionate" balance between the interests of the workers concerned and the principle of free movement. It was irrelevant that it was permitted by Finnish law. Partly because of its explicit adoption of such a heavily value-orientated test of proportionality in an area previously thought to fall outside the competence of the Union altogether, the Court's ruling prompted a considerable push-back in the form of adverse legal and political reactions; but it has not been overturned or significantly qualified, and continues to place severe restrictions on industrial action with a transnational element.

This, then, is the nature of the single market: no longer confined to facilitating cross-border trade in goods and services, EU law, in the name of promoting economic integration, has significantly qualified the law-making capacity of the member states. According to the logic of cases such as *Viking*, there is, in principle, no area of regulation that is beyond the reach of single market law. And by virtue of the continued operation of the doctrines of supremacy and direct effect, single market law has the power to override domestic laws of all types, even to the extent of disapplying constitutional norms.

The single currency and the Eurozone

Deepening still further the process of European economic and political integration is the institution of the single currency, the euro, and the process of governance surrounding and supporting it, which comes under the broad heading of economic and monetary union (EMU) (Dyson 2012). EMU has led to the creation of a structure within a structure – the Eurozone – which encompasses the nineteen member states signed up to the single currency, while affecting, in varying degrees according to context, those intending to adopt it at some future point (currently all the others except for the UK and Denmark).

Currency unions between sovereign states have existed in the past; and precedents for some aspects of Eurozone governance can be found in the system of fixed exchange rates which operated under the gold standard between the middle of the nineteenth century and the 1930s. However, there are features of the EU's monetary union which make it distinct, in particular in the degree to which arrangements for the management of monetary policy have spilled over into the conduct of economic and social policy.

As in the case of the single market, the Eurozone depends for its operation on a regulatory framework set out initially in the principal European Treaties, and then detailed in various subsidiary regulations. Under the Treaties, monetary policy is made an exclusive competence of the Union. The power to conduct monetary policy is in principle shared between the European Central Bank (ECB) and the national central banks of the member states which make up the Eurozone. This "Eurosystem" is, in practice, focused on the ECB, whose founding statute contains its mandate to set and implement the Union's monetary policy, with the overriding aim of maintaining price stability. In this context, the ECB's principal task is to set a single interest rate for the Eurozone economies. In the course of the sovereign debt crisis which began in 2009, the Bank assumed a wider role as guarantor of the single currency. In performing this role it provided liquidity and related forms of support to the national banking systems of several Eurozone countries. The Bank maintained that its actions were consistent with its original mandate, a position eventually upheld, not without challenge, by the Court of Justice. A less formalistic interpretation of the Bank's mandate would be that it evolved to meet the extraordinary circumstances of the crisis, and received the retrospective validation of the Court at a point when any other result would most likely have led to the unravelling of the single currency (Deakin 2014).

The logic of a currency union is that the states within it cede the conduct of monetary policy to a central authority. This is done not just in order to reduce transaction costs associated with foreign exchange dealings, although that is one of its more immediate effects. It also locks national economies into a fixed relationship with each other. It does this by removing the possibility of individual countries engaging in competitive devaluations, that is to say, taking steps to reduce the value of their currencies in order to give locally produced goods and services an advantage in international markets. This was a principal motivation behind the initiation of the EMU process at Maastricht in 1991; and it can be understood as complementary to the effort, going on in parallel at this time, to construct a single market based on the principle that the circulation of goods and services should reflect economic rather than political interests.

At the same time, some openly political motivations influenced the drafting of the Maastricht Treaty (Laursen 2012). One was the concern that a newly unified Germany would exercise a disproportionate degree of economic influence inside the wider Union. The vesting of the power to conduct monetary policy in a central authority was meant to counterbalance this influence. The quid pro quo for this move was the embedding of some long-standing features of German monetary policy in the institutional design of the European Central Bank. These include the priority given to price stability as the goal of monetary policy and the inclusion in the European Treaties of provisions formally restricting the powers of the Bank to provide financial support to national governments or to the Union itself. The so-called "no bail out clause" did not, in the end, prevent the Bank initiating a programme of quantitative easing to support the single currency from 2010 onwards; but the delay in its intervention – other central banks, including the US Federal Reserve and the Bank of England, had responded more quickly – worsened the effects of the crisis for the debtor states.

In principle, the institutional structure agreed at Maastricht envisages a division between monetary policy, which is now exclusively a Union competence, and economic policy, which is shared between the Union and the member states (Hinarejos 2015). In practice, monetary policy has come to overshadow economic policy, and thereby to limit the autonomy of the member states in the economic sphere.

The Maastricht Treaty also set targets for fiscal stability – "convergence criteria" – the formal justification for which was that member states running persistent budget deficits and thereby accumulating sovereign debt would in effect be transferring an element of liquidity risk to those with budgetary surpluses. A programme for maintaining fiscal equilibrium was set out in greater detail in a subsidiary legal measure, the Stability and Growth Pact, which was agreed by the Eurozone states in 1998, in anticipation of the introduction of the single currency the following year (Deakin and Reed 2000). As it turned out, Germany was among the member states (France was another) to breach the Maastricht Treaty's convergence criteria in the years immediately following the implementation of the euro, with the result that the Pact was effectively left unenforced.

This was, however, the least of the problems attending the operation of the new regime. Far from bringing about economic convergence, the single interest rate encouraged widely divergent outcomes across the Eurozone (Palley 2013; Stiglitz 2016). For states in which the single interest rate implied a form of monetary loosening, policies of credit expansion were initiated, leading to asset-price inflation, real wage increases and a property bubble. Other member states, following Germany's lead, were meanwhile following policies of credit restriction and wage repression with a view to enhancing the competitiveness of their traded goods and services, while exporting capital abroad, mostly to other Eurozone states, thereby feeding the bubble further. With the onset of the global financial crisis in September 2008 (the origins of which lay elsewhere, in the financial liberalisation pursued by the Anglo Saxon countries), the full implications of the divergence between debtor states (principally Greece, Ireland, Portugal and Spain, and to a lesser extent Italy) and their creditors (Germany and states influenced by its economic model including Austria, Finland, the Netherlands and Sweden) became clear. During 2009 a sovereign default on the part of one or more of the debtor states – and with it, the likely disintegration of the Eurozone – became a real possibility.

That this has been avoided owes practically nothing to the original institutional design of the EMU, and everything to the flexibility shown, if belatedly, by the ECB in its response to the crisis. Sovereign defaults were averted when in July 2012 the governor of the Bank, Mario Draghi, publicly undertook to do "whatever it takes" to ward off currency speculation by making an open-ended commitment to buying bonds issued by the debtor states on the secondary market. The Bank's Open Market Transactions (OMT) programme began a few weeks later. Despite its necessity, the OMT programme was the subject of serial legal challenges, which were only resolved when the Court ruled in the Bank's favour in June 2015 (Deakin 2017b).

The longer-term effect of the crisis has been to reset the terms of European integration. The Bank, acting in a "troika" together with the Commission and the International Monetary Fund, organised a programme of financial assistance for the debtor states, on condition that they enacted cuts to social security provision and initiated programmes of "structural reform" in the labour market, reducing employment protection and limiting the effects of collective bargaining. These deregulatory social policy measures were initially contained in Memoranda of Understanding agreed between the troika and the debtor states, and later made an explicit condition of the liquidity which the ECB was providing to national banking systems (Armingeon and Baccaro 2012). In July 2015, the Bank threatened Greece's newly elected Syriza government with the withdrawal of liquidity if it did not end its policy of reversing the deregulatory labour market measures of its predecessor. It took only a few days for the Greek government to abandon its position and resume the policy of austerity-related reforms which the troika had made a condition of continuing financial relief (Varoufakis 2015, 2017).

At the onset of the crisis, Eurozone governance reflected a view that the plight of the debtor states was caused by profligate social spending. The solution to the problem therefore lay in a strengthening of the model of fiscal discipline first set out in the 1998 Stability and Growth Pact. To this end, a series of regulations was adopted with the aim of reinforcing budgetary surveillance from the centre and penalising member states running fiscal deficits. The Treaty on Stability, Coordination and Governance (the "fiscal compact"), agreed by the member states in 2012 but not yet part of EU law (although its eventual incorporation into the Treaties is envisaged), requires member states to introduce constitutional amendments, formally ruling out deficit spending across the economic cycle. Because this is intended to have the effect of preventing the use of fiscal stabilisers as a response to recession, in practice, it is likely to lead to states seeking to restore their competiveness through wage repression and cuts to social welfare (Obendorfer 2014).

But as the crisis has continued, there has been a shift in emphasis (Deakin 2017b). The decision of the ECB to initiate its OMT programme, and its subsequent validation by the Court, removed the immediate threat of a sovereign default, stabilising the single currency. The conditionality inherent in the Memoranda of Understanding continues after challenges to its legality were rebuffed. But the limits of austerity policies have been recognised, with the IMF calling publicly for the restructuring of Greek debt. Meanwhile, the Commission has been rediscovering the importance of the social dimension of EMU, launching, from 2015, a new initiative to embed social policy in Eurozone governance, the European Pillar of Social Rights, and in 2017 beginning a discussion on the merits of an agency to enforce transnational labour standards, the European Labour Authority. These developments, which might look like a radical departure, given the emphasis on austerity in the fiscal compact and Memoranda of Understanding, are not so surprising when seen in the long run of the Union's evolution, within which social policy has consistently had a role in economic and political integration (Barnard and Deakin 2012).

In short, the sovereign debt crisis has prompted the emergence of new forms of governance associated with the process of economic and monetary union. As an outsider to the Eurozone, the UK has not been directly affected by these policies in the same way that it has by the evolution of the single market. But even prior to Brexit, the UK's decision to opt out of monetary union meant that it was increasingly sidelined from the core of EU decision-making (Hinarejos 2015). As Eurozone governance continues to evolve, the UK's marginalisation becomes more complete, whatever the upshot of Brexit.

The impact of the European Union on British economic and social policy

There are few areas of British economic and social policy, or related practice, which have remained untouched by EU membership. However, EU law is not a comprehensive code of economic governance. The EU has limited competences and its programme of integration does not equally affect all areas of economic life. In the case of competition policy, virtually the whole of UK domestic law and practice has been reshaped by EU-level norms. By contrast, very few aspects of Britain's welfare state are the subject of direct EU interventions. The Union has no general competence to make rules in the area of social security law; and its interventions in this field are in essence limited to protecting the rights of migrant workers from other EU member states.

On matters of market regulation, there is a mixed picture. In relation to labour markets, the EU has had considerable impact on some issues, such as working time, and virtually none on closely related questions, such as the minimum wage (Barnard and Deakin 2012). On the politically charged issue of migration, choices made by successive UK governments determined how EU principles on freedom of movement played out in practice (Deakin 2016). In the area of company law and financial markets, the UK has been an exporter of laws and practices to the rest of the EU, rather than, as in labour law, a recipient of norms originating on the continent (Grundmann 2011). Thus, rather than there being a single, over-arching answer to the question of how EU membership has affected UK industry and finance, a varied picture emerges with significant differences according to the sector or context being considered.

The wider conduct of economic policy largely lies outside the remit of EU law. Decisions on levels of taxation and public expenditure are, in principle, matters for the member states. But as we have seen, the Eurozone is not just a currency area, it is also emerging as a regulatory order; and its member states no longer have full autonomy in the conduct of economic policy. While the UK remains outside the Eurozone, it is not directly affected by this process; but its indirect impact may be hard to avoid whatever form is eventually taken by Brexit.

Labour law and collective bargaining

In contrast to the clear position it took on the "four freedoms", competition policy and state aids, the Treaty of Rome was almost silent on labour law and social policy. This omission was deliberate. At the Messina summit, which paved the way for the founding of the EEC, the six member states adopted the Spaak Report (1956), a blueprint for the model of economic integration which informed the Rome Treaty. Drawing in part on advice offered by the International Labour Office (ILO) (Ohlin Report 1956), Spaak concluded that there was no need for the transnational harmonisation of labour standards.

This was for two reasons. First, the ILO economists, echoed by Spaak, argued that wages and living standards would tend to level-up as the common market was gradually established. Workers would have an incentive to move to states with more generous welfare provision, whilst firms would have an interest in locating in countries and regions with workers who were well trained and supported by the infrastructure of the welfare state. No empirical evidence was provided to support this claim, and as levels of labour migration remained at very low levels up to the point when central and eastern European countries joined the EU during the 2000s, there is no basis for supposing that the ILO experts were right in the assumption that worker mobility would pressure states to maintain social standards.

The second reason given by the ILO experts had more traction. This was that, at the time of the Rome Treaty, each of the six founding member states was committed to maintaining social rights and a generous welfare state, to the point of embedding a number of labour market protections in their constitutional laws. They were all signatories to relevant ILO Conventions and, through the Council of Europe, were in the process of negotiating a new international treaty, the European Social Charter, which would reinforce this commitment. In adopting this argument, Spaak was accepting that social policy had a role to play in shaping the formation of the common (and later, single) market; and he was not advocating deregulation. However, social policy was to be a matter for each of the member states to decide in the light of their national priorities, rather than an issue for centralised rule-making.

This compromise was embedded in the design of the Rome Treaty (Barnard and Deakin 2012). It contained a number of provisions that encouraged cooperation between the member states on social policy issues and gave the central institutions a role in encouraging the "approximation" of labour standards; but it did not envisage the formal harmonisation of labour laws through directives or regulations. Although an isolated reference to the right of women to equal pay with men was included in Article 119 of the Treaty, no means were provided for its implementation.

Over the following decades, the competences of the Union on issues of social policy were incrementally extended at various points, without ever quite maturing into a comprehensive labour code. In the mid-1970s, Article 119 was given an expansive reading by the Court, which stressed its far-reaching direct effect in national law. In 1975, the Council adopted a directive on equal pay for women and men, and followed this up in 1976 with one on equality of treatment between the sexes in employment more generally. Changes made in later Treaties expanded the power of the Union to legislate in the general area of anti-discrimination law; and by the early 2000s, it had adopted measures on equality in relation to race, sexual orientation, transgender rights, age and disability. Each of these measures had a significant impact on UK employment law; and EU standards in this area currently underpin the UK's general anti-discrimination statute, the Equality Act 2010.

Health and safety is another area in which EU law standards have had a tangible effect on UK law and practice. The Single European Act of 1986 included provisions expanding the then European Community's powers to adopt measures in this area. It seems that the British Prime Minister at the time, Margaret Thatcher, was prepared to accept the legitimacy of health and safety regulation on the grounds that Hayek had considered it a permissible intervention in the otherwise spontaneous order of the market (Hayek had also approved of anti-discrimination laws). Following the adoption of the

1986 Treaty, a number of directives governing health and safety were agreed; and as these were transposed, they led to a significant strengthening and modernisation of UK law. However, the UK balked at the use of the Single European Act to support a measure harmonising working time laws; and, after failing to prevent the adoption of the Working Time Directive of 1993, the UK embarked on a futile attempt to have the Court strike it down. The Directive was eventually implemented in the UK via regulations adopted in 1998 and had a tangible effect in mitigating the UK's long hours culture. But its impact was limited by derogations which the UK had negotiated while the directive was in draft, including a controversial provision for individual opt-outs from the maximum forty-eight-hour working week (Barnard *et al.* 2003).

A further area in which EU law influenced UK labour markets was that of transfers of undertakings. A directive dating from 1977 aimed to ensure preservation of employment and continuity of terms and conditions when businesses were transferred from one employer to another. Through case law of the Court, this principle was extended to cover the outsourcing of labour services. At around the same time, during the early 1980s, the Thatcher government was initiating a programme of competitive tendering with a view to forcing local governments to divest themselves of services which did not meet an external market test. EU law altered the context of this process by requiring contractors to take on existing staff and respect existing terms and conditions of employment in cases where there was a relevant transfer. By these means it provided some protection against the use of competitive tendering to erode labour standards. The scope of this protection has varied over time and more recent decisions of the Court have seen a retreat from the position that collective agreements are fully entrenched against a change of employer (Prassl 2013). It nevertheless remains a significant source of worker protection.

More generally, EU law has served as a conduit for the adoption, in the UK, of modes of labour market regulation which originated in aspects of continental practice. One example is the principle that workers employed in part-time, fixed term or agency work should enjoy equivalent protections to those working in a full-time, indeterminate or direct relationship with their employer. This type of regulation originated in national practices in French, German and Italian law, before being incorporated into EU-wide standards from the late 1990s onwards. Another example is the law governing the rights of working parents to time off and flexible working; in this case aspects of the Nordic model of "working environment" legislation were the basis for directives which were then implemented across the member states, including the UK, from the second half of the 1990s.

The importance of EU social policy for UK labour law during this period can be understood by considering those areas from which EU standards were absent. Although the Maastricht Treaty enlarged the social policy competences of the Union, it also resulted in the explicit exclusion of any power to adopt new directives on pay and on most issues of collective labour law, including freedom of association and the right to strike. The UK adopted a minimum wage of its own accord following the election of the Labour government in 1997, as well as a law encouraging union recognition. So the absence of EU law was not necessarily a critical factor in the presence or absence of labour law reform. However, the Blair government did nothing to encourage a revival of sector-level collective bargaining, nor did it restore an effective right to strike. In both of these areas of law, in the absence of common EU standards, the UK remained an outlier by reference to the domestic laws of most of the other member states.

Migration and posting of workers

In the course of the 2000s, the major issue in British labour market policy became the treatment of migrant workers and the related question of the regulation of supply chains through which workers were assigned or "posted" to work in the UK from other member states. Here, we need to consider the two distinct types of labour migration which are envisaged by EU law.

Under the first, a citizen of an EU member state has the right to enter another member state to seek or take up paid employment. This is the concrete form of the right to free movement of persons which, in one form or another, has been protected by EU law since the time of the Treaty of Rome. The European Treaties, together with subsidiary laws in the form of directives and regulations, protect not just the right to enter and reside for the purposes of work, but also provide for a right of equal treatment of migrant workers with citizens of the "host" state, which covers both equality in employment and access to social security entitlements and fiscal benefits, such as tax credits (Barnard 2013).

The second form of labour migration is that associated with "posting". EU law protects the right of an employer established in one member state to assign or post labour to work in another. This can take the form, among others, of a parent company based in one state posting its workers to a subsidiary based in another one, or an agency assigning workers to a client, again on a cross-border basis. As long as the assignment is temporary – a concept which is loosely interpreted – EU law takes the view that the employment conditions of the home state (the state in which the parent or agency is based), and not those of the host (the state of the subsidiary or client), prevail.

This, then, is the reverse of the principle which applies in the case of a worker exercising the right of free movement. The posted worker is not entitled, as the migrant worker is, to equal terms and conditions with those generally prevailing in the host state, and in principle has no access to the host state's social security system. EU law limits the power of the host state to regulate the terms and conditions of posted workers. It is both permitted and required to apply its statutory minimum wage to these workers (if it has one) and certain other basic labour standards; but it is not allowed to apply the full range of protective labour laws to them, the justification being that to do so would distort the market for the cross-border supply of services. Nor may trade unions take steps to apply local collective agreements to posted labour, for example by organising strike action to that end.

Posting thereby provides employers with a means of under-cutting the normal, territorial application of worker-protective labour laws. The principles underlying this area of law were established by the Court in a decision, *Laval*, arrived at in the same month as the *Viking* case in 2007, and relying on the same controversial reasoning (Freedland and Prassl 2015). Attempts to reverse or mitigate *Laval* through court challenges and legislative initiatives have not had much success, although the Commission continues to review the issue of posting. For the UK – and for the debate over its place in the EU – its effects were far reaching.

From 2004, with the accession of central and eastern European countries to the EU, migration from these countries (the "EU-8") into the rest of the Union became an issue. Most of the existing member states took advantage of a temporary derogation from the law on free movement, enabling them to defer the entry of migrants from the accession states for a transitional period. The UK government decided not to take advantage of this opt-out but to allow full freedom of movement for labour from the point of accession of the EU-8.

This was done for a combination of reasons (Consterdine and Hampshire 2013). One was to indicate the UK's support for the political and economic integration of the new member states, a position it had advocated throughout the accession negotiations. Other motivations were driven by considerations of domestic policy. Because the Blair government believed that labour migration was likely to both reduce domestic pressures for wage inflation and meet a growing skills gap, it viewed immediate EU-8 migration as making a positive contribution to macroeconomic and labour market policy. At the same time, the government did not consider inward migration likely to reach significant levels and planned for an annual net inflow of no more than a few thousand workers from the accession states. This proved to be an extreme under-estimate, as annual numbers quickly reached the tens of thousands, with nearly 300,000 EU-8 migrants entering the UK between May 2004 and September 2005.

To understand why migration from the accession states became such a contentious issue in the run-up to the Brexit referendum – and one which probably tilted the outcome of the vote in favour of Leave (Goodwin and Heath 2016) – it is necessary to understand the context in which it took place, and to disentangle the role played by EU law, on the one hand, and domestic UK regulation, on the other (Deakin 2016). In principle, because EU law guaranteed the free movement rights of citizens of the new member states, they had the right to enter the UK in search of work, to be employed there on equal terms with UK citizens, and to reside there, with their dependants, while employed. They also had the equal right to access tax credits and welfare state entitlements, including use of the National Health

Service. These were all features of the right of equal treatment under EU law. To this extent, EU law provided the legal framework within which large-scale migration took place after 2003.

However, EU law provided only the background conditions to growing labour migration into the UK during the course of the 2000s. The British government could have chosen to defer the free movement rights of citizens of the EU-8 from 2004, as did almost all other member states. Even without going this far, it could have taken other steps to mitigate the impact of migration on public services and employment conditions. From 2005, the Labour government operated a scheme to provide additional funding for schools and other local services in areas of high inward migration. This scheme was ended by the Conservative-Liberal Democrat coalition government in 2010. The coalition government also initiated the abolition, from 2013, of the Agricultural Wages Board, which had been responsible for setting and enforcing minimum wages in the farming sector. Thus at this point, far from protecting wages and employment conditions from the impact of an increasing labour supply, the British government was removing protective legislation in one of the industries most affected by increases in migration flows.

The treatment of posting also turned on the interaction between EU law and UK regulation. Following *Laval*, few domestic labour standards could be consistently applied to workers posted into the UK from another member state. In principle, those that did apply included the national minimum wage. The practical enforcement of the minimum wage was another matter again. Because the UK does not operate a national identity card scheme or parallel registration system for migrant workers (again, unlike other EU member states), there was no effective means of tracking the extent of posting and hence of regulating it.

There is some evidence of the use of overseas labour intermediaries to supply workers from the accession states to work in the construction, agricultural and retail sectors from the mid-2000s onwards, but there are few reliable estimates of its extent. However, there is no evidence that the British government was trying to regulate labour posting at the time. When an industrial dispute broke out in 2009 over the application of a local collective agreement to posted workers employed at the Lindsey oil refinery in Humberside, the government's response was limited to attempting to arrange a settlement through the conciliation service, ACAS (Barnard 2009).

What is clear is that organised migration involving cross-border supply chains had a major impact on certain towns and regions, including areas of Lincolnshire and East Anglia, where it was connected to agriculture (Lawrence 2016), and parts of the east Midlands, where it was connected to the retail sector (including the Sports Direct warehouse at Shirebrook, where serial labour law infringements were publicly documented around the time of the referendum (House of Commons Business, Skills and Innovation Committee 2016)). Although regions experiencing a high level of EU migration were not, in general, those which recorded a high Leave vote in the 2016 referendum – indeed, the opposite was the case – there is a correlation between voting patterns and downwards pressure on wages and employment conditions in areas affected by organised migration, with the northeast Midlands, and the agricultural towns of Boston and Wisbech recording some of the highest Leave votes in the country (Deakin 2016).

It is less clear that EU migration in general has contributed to a deterioration in wages and conditions since the mid-2000s. There is no doubt that there was a significant change in the composition of the UK labour force from that point. Prior to the accession of the EU-8 in 2004, net migration into the UK from the rest of the EU consisted of only a few thousand people a year. By 2006 this figure had risen to 100,000 persons, and in 2015 it peaked at over 150,000. However, throughout this period, net migration from outside the EU was running at a higher level than that for EU migration (ONS, 2017).

Following the onset of the global financial crisis in 2008, real wages of workers in the UK fell by around 10 per cent, an unprecedented decrease. But this cannot be attributed to EU migration, which was continuing at more or less the same rate as it had during a period of rising real wages from the early 2000s. The immediate cause of falling real wages after 2008 was the financial crisis and resulting recession (Wadsworth *et al.* 2016). The deeper cause was the policy of austerity pursued by the coalition from 2010 and continued by the Conservative government elected in 2017, for which the Brexit referendum was to prove a welcome distraction.

Financial markets, company law and corporate governance

If, in the area of labour market regulation, the UK has been a net importer of EU laws, many of which it has implemented imperfectly or adjusted to with difficulty, the position is the reverse with respect to company law and financial markets. Here, the UK is not only a clear beneficiary of the single market rules; it has been a net exporter of company law and corporate governance standards, putting it in the unusual position, for once, of influencing the rest of the EU.

The UK was one of the first countries in the modern era to abolish capital controls, this being one of the first acts of the Thatcher government on taking office in 1979. Since that point – and with the further deregulation of its capital markets and stock exchange trading rules in the mid-1980s – the UK has experienced a high rate of both inflows and outflows of capital; and the City of London has increased its standing as global financial entrepôt. The UK did not need EU law to encourage it to observe the principle of free movement of capital; and London's position as a financial centre owes little to EU regulation as such. However, single market rules helped to confirm London's attractiveness as a location for international banking and financial activities by enabling City-based banks to trade into the rest of the EU on a non-discriminatory basis. This "financial passporting" is an example of the application of the principle of mutual recognition. The UK's self-exclusion from the single currency also had little impact on the City, at least once the Court of Justice ruled that the Commission's plans to restrict trading in euros to locations based inside the Eurozone was contrary to Union law, although a number of challenges mounted by the UK government to Eurozone financial regulations which it saw as contrary to its interests were not successful (Hinarejos 2015). London is currently the principal centre for trading in euro-denominated bonds and related securities, but this position is put at risk by Brexit.

During the 1970s and into the 1980s, the UK successfully resisted attempts to adopt company law directives mandating board-level worker representation or other forms of codetermination, along the lines of German law. When, during the 1990s, an element of worker voice was written into EU measures governing transnational enterprises, in the form of the directives on European works councils and European companies, a shift in regulatory style towards allowing member states to choose from a range of options when implementing EU law ensured that few British-based companies found these measures burdensome. A directive designed to encourage works councils in domestic companies was opposed by the Labour government up to the point of its adoption in 2002 and was so weakened as to be practically ineffective following its formal implementation two years later.

With the adoption of the Cadbury Code in 1992, the UK had a model of flexible corporate governance compliance which soon proved attractive elsewhere. Partly as a result of the growing popularity of the Cadbury model outside the UK, the shareholder-friendly orientation of UK corporate governance began to emerge as a global template, a process validated by the OECD's corporate governance guidelines of 1999. Against this background, EU policy makers began to look to UK practice as a basis for company law harmonisation.

This process reached a high point with the conclusion of the Thirteenth Company Law Directive in 2004 (Johnston 2011). This essentially borrowed the City of London Code on Takeovers and Mergers as a basis for the regulation of takeover bids. A report of a high-level group of experts validated the UK approach by arguing that hostile takeovers should be encouraged as a mechanism for disciplining managers and reducing agency costs. Features of City practice, such as the principle of proportionality between investments and voting rights, the restriction of takeover defences and the affirmation of shareholder sovereignty in decisions over change of control, all found their way into the Thirteenth Directive. Because of its provenance, the measure had little impact on the UK other than requiring the City Code to be put on a more or less nominal statutory basis. It continued, as before, to be administered through a form of City self-regulation, via the Takeover Panel. The Directive's impact on the rest of the EU was also somewhat blunted by the inclusion of provisions allowing member states to opt back into measures allowing weighted voting and poison-pill type defences. The Commission has recently been trying to have the Directive revised with a view to bringing it more into line with its original intention to embed the UK's shareholder-friendly approach as a Union-wide norm.

While the UK was exporting rules, with some success, it was also attracting a growing number of incorporations from other member states, as small and medium-sized companies took advantage of the Court's single market jurisprudence to relocate virtually into the UK. Under the Court's *Centros* ruling (1999), freedom of establishment protected the right of a company to opt in to access the law of another member state by reincorporation, even if their main site of operations remained unchanged. This was another application of the mutual recognition principle. It is estimated that over 20,000 companies from other EU member states, mostly Germany and the Netherlands, had opted into UK company law through this route by the mid-2000s (Becht *et al.* 2008). Prior to the Brexit vote, which puts the legal status of these companies in jeopardy, the UK was beginning to play the role of the jurisdiction of choice for corporate registrations, a position similar to that occupied by Delaware in the United States.

Taxation, public expenditure and macroeconomic policy

As we have seen, issues of taxation and public expenditure, along with the conduct of macroeconomic policy more generally, fall outside the competences of the European Union. There are some exceptions to this: value added tax is regulated directly by EU law, and tax law more generally is subject to single market case law, which regulates the use of measures which would have the effect of restricting capital flows or otherwise distorting cross-border flows of economic resources (Ghosh 2007). State aids law can also be invoked to control fiscal subsidies, as in the recent high-profile action taken by the Commission against Ireland in respect of its taxation arrangements with the technology company Apple.

For the most part, however, member states can set taxes and public expenditure at levels which they consider appropriate in the light of national interests. Whilst member states of the Eurozone must observe the convergence criteria set out initially in the Maastricht Treaty, these mandate fiscal *balance* rather than setting an upper limit to state expenditure as such (Dyson 2012).

Following the sovereign debt crisis, the emergence of new forms of Eurozone governance has the potential to reshape the relationship between the member states and the Union's central institutions in the area of macroeconomic management. It is now widely understood that the crisis was triggered by the divergence of economic policies across Eurozone states, and the resulting macroeconomic imbalances, in the years following the implementation of the currency union in 1999 (Stiglitz 2016). As a result, growing attention is being paid to the development of central level mechanisms for the coordination of economic policy. But this is unlikely to take the form of proposals for a single fiscal authority, or the reallocation of public expenditure decisions to the centre. It is possible that the European semester process, through which member states engage in a process of mutual reporting and monitoring on economic policy measures and outcomes, will be extended in scope to cover a wider range of fiscal and social indicators, and that closer alignment of public expenditure decisions will be encouraged as a result (Deakin 2017b).

Although this process mostly lies in the future, it has implications for UK policy-making regardless of the precise form of Brexit. This is because UK economic policy-making cannot sensibly be undertaken in isolation from developments in the continental economies which are likely to remain its principal trading partners for the foreseeable future. Since the UK's departure from the European monetary system (the precursor of the Eurozone) in 1992 – a decision which was effectively forced on it by a combination of currency speculation and its own economic weakness, which necessitated a competitive devaluation – the UK has used its autonomy to follow its own path in macro-economic policy (Keegan *et al.* 2017). The UK stayed outside the Eurozone for reasons of national economic self-interest throughout the 1990s and 2000s, but whilst still a member of the Union, it used its veto to counter proposals it regarded as contrary to those interests, including measures intended to bring about greater coordination of policy-making in the rest of the EU (Hinarejos 2015). This was the context in which the then UK Prime Minister, David Cameron, blocked agreement on the "fiscal compact", more properly, the Treaty on Stability, Coordination and Governance, in 2012. The other member states went ahead with the Treaty anyway, but as an intergovernmental measure, outside the framework of EU law, which limited its impact (Deakin 2014). Following Brexit, this strategy of selective blocking of centralising initiatives will no longer be feasible for the UK, with the paradoxical result that it may find itself more susceptible than before to the drift of decision-making in the remaining member states. But this is only one of many paradoxes of Brexit, as we shall now explore.

Britain's post-Brexit options and their implications for policy-making

To assess how the Brexit process will affect policy-making in Britain, it is necessary firstly to consider the legal and institutional options which will face the country when (or conceivably if) Britain's departure from the EU is confirmed, which is currently planned for March 2019. For our purposes, two dimensions of the UK's post-Brexit status need to be considered: (1) its international trading position, which is a function of rules governing tariffs, market access and non-discrimination; and (2) the laws and regulations governing its domestic economy. In practice, the two are linked since even after leaving the EU, the UK will not be trading in a vacuum. If it does not agree a new trade deal with the EU, or replace those which, through EU membership, it currently has with third countries, the UK will still be trading under the residual regime of the World Trade Organization (WTO), unless it takes the implausible decision to opt out of these rules too; and this has implications of its own for domestic policy.

The European Economic Area and the European Free Trade Association

One option is to participate in the European Economic Area (EEA). The EEA is essentially an extension of the EU's single market. Under the EEA Agreement, which in form is an international treaty, the member states of the EU, together with three other European countries (Norway, Iceland and Lichtenstein), agree to observe the single market rules on free movement, market access and non-discrimination. In practice, this means that the three non-EU countries accept the rules made by the EU member states for the circulation of goods and persons, in return for gaining access to the wider economic area of the single market.

The EEA needs to be distinguished from the European Free Trade Association (EFTA), to which it is nevertheless closely related. EFTA includes the three non-EU members of the EEA, as well as Switzerland, which is not a party to the EEA but has agreed a number of bespoke trade agreements which reproduce most of its features. EFTA dates from 1960, when the UK was one of its founding members; the UK ceased to be a member when it joined the EEC in 1973. The current EFTA Convention, dating from 2001, provides for the abolition of internal tariffs and contains rules on non-discrimination, market access, state aids and competition policy which are similar to those operating within the EU's single market. These rules and related aspects of the EEA Agreements are interpreted by the EFTA Court, which in this respect tends to follow the lead of the EU Court of Justice, although it is not strictly bound to. Unlike in the case of EU law, EFTA rules do not automatically take effect in the national legal systems of its member states.

The EFTA states are not parties to the EU's customs union and do not operate its common external tariff. This means that when goods circulate between the EFTA states and the EU, they are subject to customs checks. It also means that the EFTA states are not parties to trade agreements between the EU and third countries, but can negotiate their own. EFTA currently has twenty-seven such free trade agreements (the EU has over fifty).

If the UK were to participate in the EEA Agreement, the impact of Brexit on both the British economy and on UK policy-making would be minimal, but not entirely insignificant. UK goods and services would continue to be traded much as before within the single market. However, they would face additional customs checks, as is currently the case with those traded between the EFTA states and the EU. In return, the UK would have to accept the rules of the single market, including those made by the EU after it left. In contrast to the current position, it would have no say over the making of those rules. Thus, the principal effect of the UK's EEA membership would be to devolve large parts of its regulatory policy-making to the EU. As we have seen, many aspects of social and economic policy lie outside EU competences; and in these respects, the UK would retain its current autonomy. However, it would not be in a position to preserve that autonomy against new regulations decided on the EU-27 after it left.

The main attraction of EEA membership for UK policy makers is that, in the short-run, any negative impact of Brexit on the economy would be mitigated by comparison to the effects of the main alternative which is to default to WTO rules, discussed below. There would be no tariffs on goods traded between Britain and other EEA countries and the principle of non-discrimination would ensure that UK services could continue to access continental markets as before. But it would not exactly be a continuation of the status quo. As it would be outside the EU's customs union, the UK would have to put in place border checks, which would affect, among other things, the politically sensitive land border between Northern Ireland and the Irish Republic.

EEA membership would also alter the UK's trading position with regard to the rest of the world. If it rejoins EFTA, which is likely to be a requirement for accessing the EEA, the UK would then become a party to EFTA's trade agreements with third countries. These are significantly fewer in number than those to which the UK is currently a party through its membership of the EU. Moreover, as a member of the EFTA, the UK would not be able to negotiate its own trade agreements with the rest of the world.

The EEA Agreement was put in place during the early 1990s, in parallel with the deepening of the single market project at that time, which was given a major impetus by the Maastricht Treaty. The intention behind the EEA Agreement was to give the EFTA states, principally Norway, a close association with the Union, which would facilitate their entry at some future point. Since then, Norway has rejected accession whilst remaining within the EEA and so aligning many of its economic and social regulations with those of the single market.

If the UK were to participate in the EEA after Brexit, it is unlikely to be doing so with the aim of rejoining the EU at some future point. If this were the aim, it would be simpler not to leave in the first place, an option which probably remains legally open to it,[6] if politically problematic at least in the immediate term. Instead, the EEA route is only likely to be used as part of a "transitional" arrangement, under which the UK retains single market access for a period of time, whilst negotiating a new trade agreement with the EU (Deakin, 2017c).

A new UK-EU Free Trade Agreement

The preferred option of the UK government is to replace EU membership with a new free trade agreement (FTA) with the EU. The likely contours of such an agreement are, at present, a matter for speculation; but it is likely to contain elements of FTAs which the EU currently has with third countries.

Thus a possible model is the EU–Canada Comprehensive Economic and Trade Agreement (CETA), which was concluded in 2014. CETA envisages the elimination of tariffs on a range of manufactured goods and the reduction of most of those affecting agriculture. It provides a framework for mutual recognition of professional standards. CETA also contains commitments for the harmonisation of intellectual property rules and technical standards, and for the implementation of environmental and labour protections. But it does not replicate the single market's non-discrimination rule with respect to services. Thus, if CETA became the model for a future UK-EU agreement, there would be a reduction in market access for the UK's service industries, including its financial sector. On the other hand, the UK would have greater scope to set its own regulatory policies.

Because an FTA along the lines of CETA would not avoid the need for customs checks, a possible variant of – or addition to – a CETA-style FTA would be a bespoke customs union of the kind which operates between Turkey and the EU. Under this arrangement, which covers goods but not services, Turkey agrees to apply the EU's common external tariff and to observe the EU's common rules of origin on traded goods. For the UK, a similar agreement would have the advantage of removing transaction costs associated with customs processing, but would limit the degree of control it would have over domestic regulatory policy.

The World Trade Organization option

It is very unlikely that a new FTA between the UK and the EU can be agreed and implemented by March 2019. By way of comparison, the deliberations which culminated in CETA began in 2004, when the EU and Canada agreed a framework for their future trading relations. Negotiations were formally launched in 2009; and an agreement was reached between the two sides in 2014. At that point, a court ruling was sought on whether the individual EU member states were required to ratify the agreement. The EU Court of Justice ruled in 2016 that this was the case. A number of ratifications have yet to take place; but aspects of the agreement are being provisionally applied. However, CETA cannot come fully into force until a further court case is settled, this time on the validity of the agreement's dispute resolution system. Meanwhile, the Transatlantic Trade and Investment Partnership (TTIP) remains under negotiation more than two decades after the first initiatives for an EU-US FTA were initiated.

In the practically inevitable absence of a new UK-EU FTA at the point of Brexit, the UK government will probably seek to have in place a transitional arrangement of some kind. This could involve participation in the EEA Agreement or an equivalent to it, which may be the only arrangement on offer (Deakin, 2017c). If there is no interim or final agreement on UK-EU trading arrangements, the likely result is that the UK will fall back on WTO rules. The UK would cease to be bound by single market regulations; but, conversely, it would no longer have preferential access to EU markets. The FTAs which the UK currently has with over fifty third countries would also fall away at this point (Bartels 2016).

As far as the EU is concerned, the UK would then be in the position of being a third country. This means that the EU would apply its common external tariff to the UK, implying customs duties of around 10 per cent for certain manufactured goods, including motor vehicles, and rates of up to 50 per cent for agricultural goods. It is likely that the UK would also adopt, at least to begin with, the EU's tariffs in its dealings with third countries because the UK would be bound by the WTO's "most-favoured nation" (MFN) rule, a version of the non-discrimination principle, under which the UK would not be able to offer more, or less, advantageous terms of trade to those which it operated with the EU.

The UK would be able to negotiate new FTAs with third countries and, as long as these covered "substantially all trade", they would allow it an exemption from the MFN rule. Negotiating a new FTA could take up to a decade or more if the experience of CETA is repeated, during which time the UK would be operating under the WTO's default regime. However, the UK would have the leeway to set its own regulatory policies which was an objective for some of the groups supporting Brexit.

For those on the political right, this opens up the possibility of convergence with the US. According to a blog published on the website of the Institute for Free Trade, a think tank set up in 2017,

> There is now the prospect of a tie-up between the world's largest and fifth-largest economies. Unofficial talks began in July [2017] between US Trade Representative Robert Lighthizer and the British Trade Secretary, Liam Fox. The potential gain is vast. Here are two countries linked by language and law, habit and history. Each is the other's main investor. Every day, a million Americans turn up for work for British-owned companies; and every day, a million Brits clock on to work for American-owned companies. But, until now, London has not been free to negotiate its own trade deals.
>
> (Hannan 2017)

In more concrete terms, this would imply a mutual recognition arrangement under which goods and services validated by the legal system of one country would circulate freely in the other, but without the floor of regulation which operates in the single market to prevent a race to the bottom. Contrasting mutual recognition with TTIP, the Institute's president argues:

> We now have the opportunity to do something bolder and better [than TTIP]. We can negotiate a trade deal based on the principle that what is legal in one country is legal in the other country. If a drug is approved by the FDA, that should be good enough for Britain. If a trader is qualified

to operate in the City of London, that should be good enough for Wall Street. And so on.

(Hannan 2017)

Whether US trade representatives would be willing to accept mutual recognition without any agreement on core standards remains to be seen. In practice, the most likely outcome for the UK of a US trade deal is that it will move Britain closer to US standards and away from those of the EU's single market. But it is not clear that this will necessarily result in a liberalised regulatory regime for the UK. The US does not recognise the precautionary principle as a basis for environmental regulation, but generally requires its trading partners to enter into legally binding commitments, for example, to observe relevant international labour standards.

A further option with traction for the political right in Britain is unilateral free trade. This route has been proposed by the group known as Economists for Free Trade – which during the referendum campaign was known as Economists for Brexit – and which is associated with the Institute for Free Trade (Minford 2017). It would involve the unilateral removal of all tariffs on goods entering the UK; and since WTO rules only set maximum tariffs, this would not be incompatible with the UK's WTO membership. But the UK would have to apply the rule globally, as any discrimination would be ruled out by the MFN rule.

If the UK went down this route, there is no guarantee that other countries would reciprocate. This is not just because they might want to protect their own industries and services but also because WTO rules would prevent them applying tariff abolitions selectively.

However, adherents of tariff abolition argue that "the biggest gains from free trade come from a country eliminating its own trade barriers against imports from the rest of the world" (Minford 2017, p. 3). The removal of barriers on the movement of goods would

> reduce the prices of imports to consumers, and this creates both a gain to them and more competition with our home producers, forcing them to raise productivity. This is a most definite and permanent gain to our economy – a rise in consumer welfare and in GDP.

(Ibid.)

In other words, the stimulation of competition would be sufficient to achieve a one-off improvement in productivity of the kind needed to restore the competitiveness of British goods and services.

However, tariff abolition would not bring about mutual recognition of trading standards; nor would it eliminate non-tariff barriers to trade. Thus, it would not restore to UK producers the market access they currently have under the single market rules, in the case of European markets, or the preferential arrangements they enjoy under the FTAs the EU has with third countries.

According to Economists for Free Trade, tariff abolition would give the UK leverage for trade deals with the EU and third countries

> on broader issues where there are subtle barriers and general issues of competition in all markets – such as removal of other trade distortions on goods, facilitating trade in services, enabling competitive public procurement, guaranteeing full legal protection for foreign direct investment, improving protection of intellectual and other property rights, and so on.
>
> (Minford 2017, p. 4)

The logic of this position is that tariff abolition, by lowering prices of UK imports, would threaten the economic interests of overseas producers, mainly in the EU but also in third countries, currently dependent on access to the UK market. Zero tariffs would be a "threat that will force the EU to do a trade deal" (ibid.).

Thus, as in the case of expectations surrounding a possible UK-US trade deal, this argument involves second-guessing the intentions and interests of the EU. To date, the EU-27 have shown no sign of moving from their publicly stated position of support for the existing framework of single market law. If the UK uses Brexit to "revise highly damaging EU climate change, labour, financial, and clinical trial regulations" (Bourne 2017), the chances of the EU aligning itself with this libertarian economic model do not look very good. More likely is that the UK and EU will drift apart.

It is not just parts of the political right which have been enthused by the possibility of a no-deal Brexit. A left-wing Brexit involving renationalisation and a more prominent role for the state in setting industrial policy has also been mooted. On the one hand, it is not clear how far this is currently ruled out by EU membership (Tarrant and Biondi 2017). As we have seen, the conduct of macroeconomic policy is mostly a matter for the states. The Treaties recognise the possibility of state ownership and direction of public services. State aid rules do not, for the most part, prohibit industrial subsidies, but seek to regulate them, often in the interests of developing a common approach to capacity reductions, as in the case of the steel industry, or coordinating national-level services, as in rail. Emergency subsidies for industries in crisis are generally allowed, under supervision. Thus, the support provided by the UK government for the banking sector following the financial crisis of 2008 was agreed by the Commission, although with some conditions, including the return of the banks to private ownership once their financial stability was restored.

Nor is it the case that a "no deal" option would restore full regulatory autonomy to the UK. WTO membership entails compliance with a version of state aid rules, which would rule out industrial subsidies aimed at achieving a competitive advantage. WTO law does not – as EU law does – form part of domestic law; and so it would operate as a less direct constraint on government action. But trading partners harmed by unlawful subsidies would, at some point, have sanctions available to them, including blocking market access for UK goods.

Both sides of the British political divide have seen the opportunity to recast immigration policy in the light of Brexit. But here, too, the position is less than clear cut. EU migrants who have settled in the UK by exercising the right of free movement are likely to have the legal right to remain, not least because to deprive them of residence would most likely infringe the UK's commitments under the European Convention of Human Rights, which would be unaffected by Brexit (Hughes 2016). Thus, the reimposition of immigration controls is unlikely to bring about a complete shift in conditions of labour supply.

Nor would a no-deal Brexit solve all problems associated with posting of workers. There is likely to be pressure on government to allow migration to continue in sectors where UK-based producers have become reliant on foreign labour. Thus a likely outcome is that the UK will introduce schemes to allow foreign workers to enter the UK to work in specific sectors which, if the practice of other countries is followed, would include agriculture and construction. But after a no-deal Brexit, it would no longer be mandatory for the UK to apply its basic labour standards to posted workers, for example in relation to the statutory minimum wage, as it is currently required to do under EU law. Nor would foreign workers entering the UK under sector-specific arrangements any longer have the EU-protected right to change employers while continuing to work in the UK.

The UK could, of course, choose to impose stringent labour standards of its own for the protection of workers posted from overseas. However, WTO rules, which would apply in the "no-deal" scenario, place limits on how far this can be done without creating a fresh barrier to entry (Novitz 2017).

Conclusions: Brexit and the insecurity cycle

"Blame austerity not immigration for the inequality underlying the referendum decision" was the verdict of the economic geographer and statistician Danny Dorling in the aftermath of the Brexit vote. In the year prior to the referendum, British mortality rates were rising, an unprecedented development. These additional deaths were the result of chronic diseases, such as Alzheimer's and dementia, and illnesses, such as influenza, whose incidences are linked to poverty and the failure of preventive medicine. Britain spends less proportionately on health and other public goods than virtually all other European countries; and it has a higher degree of earnings inequality. But as Dorling (2016) suggests, "to distract us from these national failings, we have been encouraged to blame immigration and the EU".

There is no doubt that part of the Brexit vote reflected disenchantment with the economic and social model which has prevailed in the UK since the late 1970s. Immigration was the lightning rod for much of this discontent, and in some contexts – in particular, the agricultural towns of East Anglia and former mining communities in the Midlands and north of England – it was a factor behind the Leave vote. But for the most part, EU migration into the UK was not a zero sum game. Migrants are mostly young; and many work in sectors where their skills benefit other UK residents, such as health and education (Wadsworth *et al.* 2016). Areas with the largest levels of migration also recorded high Remain votes.

We should also be cautious in describing Brexit as the response of a "left behind" working class. Nearly 60 per cent of Leave voters were in the middle classes – so-called A, B or C1 groups – and a majority lived in the relatively prosperous south of England. Only 24 per cent of Leave voters were in the two poorest social groups (D and E). Most working-class voters abstained (Dorling 2016).

However, given the narrowness of the Leave majority, there would almost certainly have been a different outcome if a stronger case had been made for the EU by the British left. Migration, in particular, and the European Union, in general, might have been a lightning rod for wider discontents. But this does not explain why the EU was not regarded more positively. Here, what stands out is the failure of the EU to do anything more than mitigate, in a minor way, some of the more negative consequences of the UK's neoliberal policy choices. In part thanks to the UK's own role in shaping EU policy, the project of a "social Europe" remained incomplete. Far from placing limits on the programme of austerity initiated by the coalition government after 2010, the EU embarked on one of its own, with punitive and socially regressive effects for states caught up in the crisis over sovereign debt. The example of Greece was hardly going to inspire the British left to support the European project in the months and weeks prior to the referendum.

For most of its supporters in the British political classes, Brexit is a libertarian project which will complete the work begun by Mrs Thatcher and her governments of the 1980s. In 2008, Douglas Carswell, then a Conservative MP who later represented UKIP, and Daniel Hannan, a Conservative MEP who in 2017 became the founding president of the Institute for Free Trade, published a list of laws that would be removed in a "Great Repeal Bill". The list included not just targets familiar from neoliberal critiques of labour legislation – including rules on dismissal procedures, works councils, part-time employment and health and safety at work – but also regulations on money laundering, gambling, data protection, criminal records, fire safety, dangerous animals and gun control. As Carswell and Hannan recognised, most of these proposals were incompatible with the UK's EU membership. Thus, the last measure on their list of repeals was the European Communities Act itself (Carswell and Hannan 2008).

For this influential group, the Brexit referendum provides the opportunity to reshape the British state and society. It is less clear that Brexit helps the political left in Britain. There is nothing of substance in the idea that EU membership prevents the UK from adopting a more collectivist approach to public ownership and management of the economy. At the same time, parts of the British left have never been reconciled to the EU's social market ethos. Its support for the idea of a social Europe was mostly opportunistic and has recently been qualified by an awareness of the potential of EU law to undermine collective bargaining and the right to strike.

As long as the UK remains an active member of the European Union, EU laws and institutions counterbalance some of the more extreme effects of the insecurity cycle. But even before Brexit is completed, the UK is being marginalised – or to be more precise, is marginalising itself – within the wider European project. The UK's decision not to participate in the currency union inevitably means that it will be outside the mainstream of European policy-making. The Eurozone is a structure within a structure, one which will gradually subsume the wider Union. Reversing Brexit (an uncertain prospect at the time of writing) would not resolve this deeper rift in UK-EU relations.

Notes

1 Thirteen million registered voters did not vote and 7 million voting age adults were not registered. These were disproportionately the young and ethnic minorities, groups which tended towards Remain (see Dorling 2016). EU citizens resident in the UK at the time of the referendum, other than those from Ireland, Gibraltar and Malta, were ineligible to vote as were UK citizens living in mainland Europe for more than five years.
2 See our discussion of *Miller* in Chapter 2.
3 Under Article 50(2) TEU,

> A Member State which decides to withdraw shall notify the European Council of its intention. In the light of the guidelines provided by the European Council, the Union shall negotiate and conclude an agreement with that State, setting out the arrangements for its withdrawal, taking account of the framework for its future relationship with the Union.

4 See our further discussion in the section of this chapter titled "Britain's post-Brexit options and their implications for policy-making".
5 See our discussion of the *Viking* case, below.
6 This is because, as a matter of UK domestic law, Parliament could enact legislation authorising the executive to revoke the Article 50 notice (reversing, in effect, the Withdrawal Act), whilst under EU law, the notice given under Article 50 is, in principle, reversible. In October 2017, it was reported that the UK government had received legal advice to this effect, although this remains unpublished (Simor 2017). The matter is not beyond doubt and would probably have to be resolved by the Court of Justice in the event of any dispute.

11 Conclusions

When might the insecurity cycle move again?

Introduction

The track record of neoliberalism in Britain since the election of Margaret Thatcher has been, at best, chequered. For a few, it has worked very well indeed; but for the vast majority, rather less so. The immediate increase in both inequality and poverty was initially masked by the illusion of prosperity produced by debt-fuelled consumption during the following decades. However, the 2008 financial crisis – the consequences of which have been worsened by the austerity policies that followed it – has revealed the underlying reality. Those struggling to remain above the poverty line – as well as those who have already succumbed – are becoming increasingly difficult to either deny or placate.

This chronic crisis forms the basis for a significant democratic upsurge. The term "upsurge" is used deliberately, as much of the impetus for democratic change requires either demand from the electorate, or at least its tacit approval. At the time of writing, much of the democratic upsurge in Britain has coalesced around Jeremy Corbyn's vision; but it also includes elements such as the Green Party as well as, at times, the United Kingdom Independence Party (UKIP). The larger, more focused groups tend to be most influential; so at present, the people supporting Corbyn seem the most likely to precipitate change. Indeed, since the 2017 general election and the resulting hung Parliament – along with the continuing travails of the Conservative Party – a shift in the insecurity cycle may even be underway.

Many have already predicted the imminent end of neoliberalism, with even such institutions as the International Monetary Fund (IMF) – hitherto amongst its strongest proponents – publishing "Neoliberalism: Oversold?" (Ostry et al. 2016). In spite of this, the current conventional wisdom is proving remarkably resilient. Whilst it is possible to argue that the main elements required for a shift in the insecurity cycle are in place – especially with regard to a chronic crisis, democratic upsurge and political support – another key element, alternative policy ideas, is at present weaker. As Margaret Thatcher's governments revealed, sometimes, old ideas that haven't been tried for a long period of time can be enough to support change, especially when they are championed by significant elements of the media and business.

These same elements of business and, especially, the industrial media, can also inhibit ideas which they are opposed to, with fear – as we have seen, a routine influence on the insecurity cycle – often playing a key role in their strategy. Both Ed Miliband's – and now Jeremy Corbyn's – policies have been the subject of campaigns based on this kind of strategy; but with Momentum's successful bypassing of the industrial media, it is possible that this asset has been to some degree negated. However, there is far more to the "life support system" that has kept free market capitalism in place for such a long time than the attitude of large segments of the media.

First, neoliberalism has created and maintained an environment that is favourable to both the neoliberal ideology, itself, and those with the power to sustain it. Also, unlike the ideas behind the post-war "Keynesian" consensus, few additions to the canon – "Keynesian" or otherwise – have been allowed. Nor did those promoting free market capitalism fail to plan for the future; many university economics programmes do not include economic history, Keynes's ideas – or indeed any other non-mainstream body of economic thought – in their curricula; and the track record of neoliberalism, when its theories and models are applied to real world situations, is rarely examined. As a result, these seats of learning are geared up to produce economists and business people predisposed to assume the veracity and efficacy of neoliberal theory and policy.

At the same time, organisations such as the Mont Pelerin Society and a network of well-funded, politically right-wing "think tanks", whilst less obviously suppressing alternative economic ideas, have nonetheless actively promoted the concept of "free" markets, since shortly after the Second World War. These organisations and think tanks are often funded by large corporations, and are intended to help produce the most favourable global environment possible for their sponsors.

As a result, rather than the blame for the 2008 crisis remaining squarely on the shoulders of the financial sector, since the turn to austerity in 2010, it has been argued instead that the main cause of the debacle was a failure of state regulation. The government's rescue of collapsing financial institutions – a clear intervention by the state – has for some reason received little or no criticism in this line of reasoning. Perhaps even more surprisingly, the Labour Party under Ed Miliband actually appeared to *accept* responsibility, shouldering much of the blame for the crisis, probably because it occurred at a time when the Labour Party had already been in government for more than a decade.

The most obvious gap in the pre-conditions for a shift in the insecurity cycle has been a shortage of new ideas, re-fried old ones and the media to support them. As Friedman pointed out long ago, when the opportunity arises, it is essential to act quickly, before the all-too-brief window for alternative ideas to gain traction is overtaken by the "tyranny of the status quo" (Friedman and Friedman 1984). Although emergency "Keynesian" stimulus was used to deal with the immediate crisis in 2008, this was quickly abandoned when it appeared that financial collapse had been averted – and the associated fear and uncertainty subsided. So from the point of view of the insecurity cycle, the opportunity was missed. The status quo appears to be more than capable of hanging on – at least for now. So what might cause the insecurity cycle to shift again?

This chapter considers the development and extent of the neoliberal life support system that any new or alternative ideas will be required to either negate or bypass, and traces the means by which the pre-neoliberal "Keynesian" synthesis – the earlier equally dominant conventional wisdom – was displaced. It then examines the state of play in the other factors likely to catalyse a shift in the insecurity cycle – including crises, democratic movements and political representation and support – before speculating on the most likely developments ahead.

Neoliberal "life support"

Whilst recent economic and political events in Britain show clear signs of the presence of three of the four major factors that have historically been associated with a shift in the insecurity cycle, the remaining element – alternative policy ideas – has yet to gain traction. Since Margaret Thatcher – and especially Tony Blair – the emphasis of politics has been on personality and numbers, rather than society and socio-economic policies; and the state's response to most problems has typically been to make reference to the amount of money being spent on addressing them, rather than what that money was actually going to be spent *on*. Consequently, Jeremy Corbyn's ideas, as well as his vision for society and politics – few of which are demonstrably new – stand in clear contrast to the rather arid and de-humanising neoliberal ideology and policy packages previously on offer.

Nevertheless, there is considerable scope for the development of alternative policy ideas. Following the 2017 general election, the Progressive Economics Group (PEG) was established to seek, discuss and perhaps ultimately support new and alternative economic policy ideas. "[D]edicated to the development of policy solutions to economic problems and issues, based on social democratic principles",[1] PEG has no *formal* link to the Labour Party; and its policy ideas are freely available to all political parties, organisations and individuals. However, under Jeremy Corbyn's leadership, the Labour Party – in line with its new "grass roots" approach – has been actively exploring the policy ideas being generated by PEG. But why has it taken so long for such an organisation to emerge?

The return to economic liberalism was strongly influenced by the work of Friedrich von Hayek and Milton Friedman, who had been nurturing these ideas since the late 1930s, in anticipation of a crisis that would shake confidence in the conventional wisdom of Keynesianism. In Friedman's view, it was important "to develop alternatives to existing policies [and] to keep them alive and available until the politically impossible becomes politically inevitable" (Friedman 1962, pp. viii–ix). Hayek, too, believed that the cultivation of alternative policy ideas was key, and that "the decisive influence in the great battle of ideas and policy was wielded by intellectuals whom he characterized as the 'second hand dealers in ideas'" (Fisher 1978, p. 79). But he felt that it would take at least a generation to win this battle, not only against Marxism but also against socialism, state planning and Keynesian interventionism (Harvey 2005).

After the Second World War, the defenders of economic liberalism sought to organise a response to state interventionism and socialism, with the three main centres of resistance being the London School of Economics (LSE), where Hayek was teaching, the University of Chicago, where Friedman was based, and the Institut Universitaire de Hautes Etudes Internationales (IUHEI) in Geneva (Toussaint 2009). In 1947, Hayek was influential in founding the Mont Pelerin Society, dedicated to disseminating the neoliberal creed and hosting regular international gatherings. The first of these took place in April 1947 at the Hotel du Parc at Mont Pelerin in Switzerland, bringing together thirty-six right-wing economists and philosophers from different schools of thought within liberalism. The meeting was covered by major media outlets, including the American publications *Fortune, Newsweek* and *Reader's Digest* (which had just published an abridged version of Hayek's *Road to Serfdom*); and it was funded by Swiss industrialists and financiers.

The Mont Pelerin Society quickly became a centre for the neoliberal counter-offensive, from which other right-wing think tanks were eventually spun off. The first of these was the Institute of Economic Affairs (IEA), established in London in 1955. The driving force behind the IEA was Antony Fisher, an entrepreneur and strong believer in free markets, who had first attended a Mont Pelerin Society gathering in 1951.

Fisher had met with Hayek after reading the *Reader's Digest* version of *The Road to Serfdom*. He shared Hayek's concern about what they both viewed as "the rise of socialist totalitarianism in Britain" (Peck 2010, p. 134) and was advised by Hayek to "join with others in forming a scholarly research organization to supply intellectuals in universities, schools, journalism and broadcasting with authoritative studies of economic theory of markets and its application to practical affairs" (Fisher 1978, p. 80). Taking this advice to heart, Fisher met with "Baldy" Harper, an agricultural economist who, having been driven out of Cornell for teaching Hayek's ideas, moved to the Foundation for Economic Education, which had been founded in 1946 by Leonard E. Read in upstate New York to promote free market ideas.

Returning to London, Fisher engaged Ralph Harris and Anthony Seldon – alleged to be "the last two economists who believed in free markets" (Blundell 2003, p. 41) – and founded the Institute of Economic Affairs. During the next twenty years, the IEA would grow, but hardly prosper, kept alive by the tireless work of Harris and Seldon – as Fisher became increasingly convinced that the primary challenge was the *retailing* (as opposed to production) of free market ideas (Peck 2010, p. 135). According to Keith Tribe (2009),

The work of the Institute was chiefly in the field of economic journalism, publishing pamphlets and seeking influence on public opinion, opinion formers and politicians ... [foreshadowing] the emergence of a new wave of journalists and commentators with connections to government, the prime example being Nigel Lawson, Thatcher's Chancellor during the 1980s, whose career had begun during the 1950s in financial journalism.

(p. 89)

Disheartened, in 1975 – at the invitation of Patrick Boyle, a Canadian industrialist – Fisher left England to help establish the Fraser Institute; and a year later, he met with Wall Street financier, William Casey, to help set up New York City's first free market think tank, the Manhattan Institute.

However, as the stagflationary crises of the 1970s intensified – and the free market movement began to swing from the margins to the mainstream of economic policy – Fisher would find himself in high demand, helping to set up the Adam Smith Institute, a downstream complement to the IEA, in London in 1976, and the Pacific Research Institute (PRI) in San Francisco in 1979. In 1981, he also founded the Atlas Economic Research Foundation to institutionalise the process of helping start up new think tanks, replicating the IEA model on a global scale. This international network of right-wing think tanks would ultimately play a significant role in not only keeping free market ideas alive during the "Keynesian" consensus but also promoting them far and wide when the opportunities presented themselves.

Although long embraced, supported and financed by a powerful group of very wealthy individuals and corporate leaders – who also funded academic positions and departments – the neoliberal movement had initially remained at the margins of both political and academic influence. But when the crisis-ridden 1970s arrived, neoliberal think tanks began to move centre-stage, particularly in the US and Britain. During the mid-1970s, neoliberal theory also gained in academic respectability when Hayek was awarded the Nobel Prize in Economics in 1974, with Friedman achieving the same accolade in 1976.

However, in Britain, neoliberalism evolved as a body of thought that had been nurtured outside the academy and was not taken seriously within it (Tribe 2009, p. 88). Thus, following the Conservative Party's defeat in 1974, with Fisher's blessing, Keith Joseph – a very active and committed publicist and politician with strong connections to the IEA – worked with Margaret Thatcher to set up the Centre for Policy Studies (CPS). This somewhat anonymous title was adopted instead of other, rather more revealing possibilities, including the Hayek Foundation (Bourne 2013).

It would not be long before the CPS began to exert an influence. When Thatcher came to power in 1979 with a strong mandate for reforming the economy, she perceived the academic establishment as being located along a spectrum ranging from left-liberal to socialist. Thus, Thatcher turned to individuals associated with the CPS and IEA, along with other such think tanks such as the Adam Smith Institute, for advice. The influence of these institutions – and Thatcher's high regard for them – is evident in her letters to Fisher and Harris upon entering Downing Street. To Fisher she wrote: You "created the climate of opinion which made our victory possible"; and to Harris: "It is primarily your foundation work which enabled us to rebuild the philosophy upon which our Party succeeded" (quoted in Blundell 2013). In an interview for the American Public Broadcasting System (PBS) series, *Commanding Heights*, Thatcher said: "It started with Sir Keith and me, with the Centre for Policy Studies, and Lord Harris at the Institute for Economic Affairs. Yes, it started with ideas, with beliefs" (ibid.).

From this point on, "think tanks and external advisers became a fixture in public administration, cutting out academic economists and diminishing their authority" (Tribe 2009, p. 90). This polarisation of university and government was further hardened in March 1981, when a letter to *The Times*, signed by 364 academic economists, argued that the Thatcher government's policy would accelerate the rate of increase in factory closures and unemployment. This side-lining of the academy from economic policy coincided with a transition "into formalized neoclassical economic orthodoxy" which came to dominate academic research and teaching, but "whose purchase on public argument was increasingly at a discount" (Tribe 2009, p. 90).[2]

However, the progressive distancing of economic theory from reality had begun much earlier. During the inter-war years, static equilibrium microeconomic theories of perfect, imperfect and monopolistic competition had replaced Marshall's dynamic analysis of industrial organisation and development, which had been based on careful empirical observation.[3] At the same time, Keynes's (1997 [1936]) *General Theory* was advancing a dynamic approach to understanding macroeconomic development, based on observation of the economic challenges experienced during the 1920s and 1930s. But almost immediately, Keynes's ideas were absorbed into the static "Hicksian" IS/LM framework.[4]

According to Geoff Harcourt (1987), the IS/LM model represented "[t]he attempt to confine Keynes' contributions within a small general equilibrium model" (p. 204). In doing so, it paved the way for the "neoclassical synthesis" – the incorporation of Keynes's ideas about macroeconomic dynamics into static neoclassical economics – which Joan Robinson (1962) would later brand "bastard Keynesianism". From Robinson's perspective,

> The bastard-Keynesian model is not only silly. It is seriously defective in logic. Any arbitrarily fixed quantity of money … is compatible with full employment, in conditions of short period equilibrium, at some level of money-wage rates, the level being lower the smaller the postulated quantity of money, and the larger the labour force to be employed. This is supposed, in the bastard-Keynesian argument, to justify the contention that falling wages and prices are good for trade.
>
> (Robinson, 1965, pp. 100–1)

She also objected to the disregard for key features of Keynes's theory – including its attention to the structure of society, its sense of historical time and the dynamic nature of economic life, and the existence of fundamental uncertainty and instability – all of which could be expected to mitigate against the possibility that there are equilibrating forces that will deliver the economy to full employment.

Nevertheless, by the 1950s, the neoclassical synthesis had become the consensus view in macroeconomics, especially in the United States (Blanchard 1987). When the stagflationary crises of the late 1960s and 1970s arrived, however, this hybrid theory proved ill-equipped to explain events, much less to offer policy prescriptions for addressing them. Advocates of the competing "new classical synthesis" were quick to condemn it, with Lucas and Sargent (1979) contending that not only did the predictions of the neoclassical synthesis represent an "econometric failure on a grand scale" (p. 6); "the doctrine on which [these predictions] were based is fundamentally flawed" (p. 1) as a consequence of lacking a foundation in microeconomics.

Geoff Harcourt (1987), however, had a different assessment of the situation:

> [B]ecause the neoclassical synthesis ... dominated [Keynesianism] when the monetarist counter-revolution came to prominence in the late 1960s and early 1970s, Keynesians were weakened in their fight back because they had already, unnecessarily and illegitimately, conceded the framework of the approach within which the battle was to be fought.
>
> (p. 204)

Economics education: the suppression of alternative ideas

The term "neoclassical synthesis" is generally attributed to Paul Samuelson, whose *Economics* – first published in 1948 and followed by a further eighteen editions, the last of which appeared in 2009 – ranked among the most successful textbooks in its field until 1985, when its twelfth edition, co-authored with William Nordhouse, was published (Skousen 1997). In its third edition, published in 1955, Samuelson wrote:

> In recent years, 90 percent of American Economists have stopped being "Keynesian economists" or "anti-Keynesian economists". Instead, they have worked towards a synthesis of whatever is valuable in older economics and in modern theories of income determination. The result might be called neoclassical economics and is accepted in its broad outlines by all but about 5 percent of extreme left wing and right wing writers.
>
> (Samuelson 1955, p. 212)

According to Mark Skousen (1997), "Samuelson's desire to homogenize mainstream economics into one grand 'neoclassical synthesis' is evident in his 'family of economics'" (p. 146). This was introduced in the fourth edition of *Economics*, published in 1958, advancing a simplified view of alternative schools of economic thought, which Samuelson contended could be reduced to only two – the socialism of Marx and Lenin and the "neoclassical synthesis" of Marshall and Keynes – by the arrival of the twentieth century. From this perspective, "economics" was effectively synonymous with "neoclassical economics"; and for the next thirty years, this narrowing of theoretical approaches dominated the economics curriculum at most universities around the world. The distinction between "micro" and "macro" economics also first appeared in the 1958 edition of Samuelson's *Economics* (Varian 1987, p. 462).

According to Daniel Rogers (2012), the shift in economic thinking and policy towards faith in markets was "accelerated by the US production of graduate-trained economists" (p. 74). However, until the early 1990s, despite a narrowing of the range of alternative theories covered, students were traditionally introduced to the study of economics with analysis of "the real-world complexities of the aggregate institution-thick 'mixed' state-and-private economy" (Rogers 2012, p. 76). Keynes's "fallacy of composition" – that what is true of parts of the economy and of individual actors and markets may not be true of the economic system as a whole – was also acknowledged. The abstract microeconomic theories of individual consumer choice, of the firm and of the markets within which they interact, were generally taught afterward.

The absence of a clear connection between micro- and macroeconomics – the "micro-foundations" of macroeconomics – had long been a source of intellectual disquiet among economists. The neoclassical synthesis had reconciled general equilibrium theory with Keynesian macroeconomics by giving them each their own domain of applicability. Keynesian macroeconomics was seen to apply to the short run, when temporary fluctuations around equilibrium were possible; with general equilibrium theory being seen to apply to the long run, when the economy was assumed to settle at its equilibrium state. But by the 1960s, the logical consistency of this division was being questioned (Howitt 1987, p. 279).

With Keynesianism in decline, the rational expectations revolution brought new classical economics – seeking to construct all macroeconomics upon microeconomic principles – to dominance. Accompanying the new emphasis on the micro-foundations of macroeconomics – and the view that microeconomics is intellectually prior to macroeconomics – was the "metaphor" of "the market". According to Rogers (2012):

Most novel about the new market metaphors was their detachment from history and institutions and from questions of power ... To imagine the market now was to imagine a socially detached array of economic actors, free to choose and optimize, unconstrained by power and inequalities, governed not by their common deliberative action but only by the impersonal laws of the market.

(p. 176)

The 1980s also brought a significant change in the criteria for allocating funding to UK universities. Prior to the Research Assessment Exercise (RAE), introduced by the Thatcher government in 1986, university funding was primarily based on the number of students taught. Under the RAE (replaced by the Research Excellence Framework (REF) in 2014), the mechanism for allocating funding shifted to "research quality", measured by RAE (later REF) scores. Universities quickly learned that to gain high research rankings – and to thereby maintain funding and prestige – they needed to hire and promote economists who had published (or were likely to publish) in the top ranked (mostly American) neoclassical journals. This served to reinforce the position of neoclassical economics within the curriculum of most British universities – at the expense of alternative ideas.

This also precipitated a shift in the teaching of economics, which is illustrated by the reorganisation of the content of Samuelson's *Economics*. Between the thirteenth and the fourteenth editions – published in 1989 and 1992, respectively – microeconomics was moved to the beginning, with a new emphasis on abstract and de-contextualised general equilibrium models of economic behaviour. The Preface of the fourteenth edition celebrated capitalism's victory over socialism and its spread to the eastern European countries that were formerly part of the Soviet Union. Samuelson describes the accompanying events as the "end of history" – "parallel to placing microeconomics first in the sequence", with the publisher advertising the "leitmotif" of the new edition being the "re-discovery of the market" (quoted in Rogers 2012, p. 76).

Thus, by the early 1990s, economics education – and economics as a discipline – had largely become "a series of elaborations and qualifications of the idea of perfect competition" (Rogers 2012, p. 76). Neoclassical economics was typically taught as though it was the only theory of economics; mathematical models came to dominate economic analysis, with mathematics often being an end in itself, instead of a tool for making sense of economic reality. Economic History and the History of Economic Thought – which would have exposed students to alternative approaches to economic thinking – along with courses in areas of economics considered outside of the mainstream were quietly dropped. As economics became increasingly separated from real world events, even recurring financial crises were dismissed due to confidence in the theory of rational expectations and the efficient markets hypothesis – until the arrival of the 2008 financial crisis.

But the narrowing of economics did not occur without resistance. In 1992, forty-four leading economists – including four Nobel Laureates, one of whom was Paul Samuelson – signed "A Plea for Pluralistic and Rigorous

Economics", published as an advertisement in the May issue of the *American Economic Review* (AER). Expressing concern about "the threat to economic science posed by intellectual monopoly ... of method or core assumptions", they called for "a new spirit of pluralism in economics, involving critical conversation and tolerant communication between different approaches" (AER 1992, p. xxv). They went on to contend that "the new pluralism should be reflected in the character of scientific debate, the range of contributions in its journals, and in the training and hiring of economists" (ibid.). But their plea fell upon deaf ears.

Eight years later, in June 2000, a group of (mostly PhD) students at the Ecole Normale Supérieure in Paris, launched a web-based petition calling for economic pluralism. This represented the first attempt by students to articulate the flaws in their education; and it highlighted the gap between their expectations and what they were actually taught about economics, particularly in relation to real world events:

> Most of us have chosen to study economics so as to acquire a deep understanding of the economic phenomena with which the citizens of today are confronted. But the teaching that is offered, that is to say for the most part neoclassical theory or approaches derived from it, does not generally answer this expectation. Indeed, even when the theory legitimately detaches itself from contingencies in the first instance, it rarely carries out the necessary return to the facts. The empirical side (historical facts, functioning of institutions, study of the behaviors and strategies of the agents...) is almost nonexistent. Furthermore, this gap in the teaching, this disregard for concrete realities, poses an enormous problem for those who would like to render themselves useful to economic and social actors ... We no longer want to have this autistic science imposed upon us.
>
> (*Le Monde* 2000)

Some of their teachers launched a petition in support; and the French media gave extensive coverage to these events. In response, students across France signed the petition and the Minister of Education set up a high-level commission to look into the students' complaints.

As news spread via the internet, this "Post-Autistic Economics" movement found wide support internationally; and the Real World Economics Association was established. In June 2001, twenty-seven Cambridge PhD candidates launched their own petition, "Opening Up Economics":

> This debate is important because in our view the status quo is harmful in at least four respects. Firstly, it is harmful to students who are taught the "tools" of mainstream economics without learning their domain of applicability. The source and evolution of these ideas is ignored, as is the existence and status of competing theories. Secondly, it disadvantages a

society that ought to be benefiting from what economists can tell us about the world. Economics is a social science with enormous potential for making a difference through its impact on policy debates. In its present form its effectiveness in this arena is limited by the uncritical application of mainstream methods. Thirdly, progress towards a deeper understanding of many important aspects of economic life is being held back. By restricting research done in economics to that based on one approach only, the development of competing research programs is seriously hampered or prevented altogether. Fourth and finally, in the current situation an economist who does not do economics in the prescribed way finds it very difficult to get recognition for her research.

(The Cambridge 27 2001)

This was followed closely by a gathering of students, researchers and professors from twenty-two countries at the University of Missouri at Kansas City (UMKC), which published an international open letter to all economics departments in support of the "Post-Autistic Economics" movement and the Cambridge proposal (UMKC 2001). However, when the students involved graduated, many of these movements petered out, highlighting the difficulty of keeping momentum between generations of students.

The arrival of the 2008 financial crisis, however, resulted in renewed pressure for economic pluralism. By 2011, students in France had re-grouped and founded "PEPS-Economie" ("Pour un Enseignement Pluraliste dans le Supérieur en Economie"); and in Germany, the "Netzwerk Okonomik" was also thriving. Meanwhile in the UK, the Bank of England hosted a 2011 conference under the banner: "Are Economics Graduates Fit for Purpose?". In 2013, students at the University of Manchester set up the "Post-Crash Economics Society". They also made contact with other British student groups, who themselves were in the process of setting up "Re-thinking Economics" to create an international network, connecting like-minded students and citizens around the world. Since then, other student groups calling for and promoting pluralism in economics have been established at an increasing number of universities across the country.

In response to student demands for change, an open-access platform, "CORE Economics Education", was set-up as a registered charity in England and Wales "for the public benefit, the advancement of education in economics and related fields and to raise public awareness, through the provision of teaching and learning materials and associated activities".[5] Providing resources, including an open-access textbook, designed as part of a revised economics curriculum, aimed at grounding economics education in interdisciplinary, real world and historical knowledge, CORE has already been trialled in a number of universities around the world. Whether CORE will be a game changer – and whether the current momentum driving the movement for economic pluralism will last – remains to be seen; but the signs are promising.

The pressures for a shift in the insecurity cycle

Since the emergence of the interest groups driving the insecurity cycle during Britain's industrial revolution, the four main factors governing the cycle's movements – crisis, democratic upsurge, alternative policy ideas and political support – have been relatively consistent in their effects. Historically, whilst combinations of two or three of the four have produced comparatively small changes that could be accommodated within an existing conventional wisdom, it has usually taken all four – including an exceptionally significant crisis – to produce a decisive shift in the conventional wisdom and the policy paradigm accompanying it.

The shift from market liberalism to "Keynesian" interventionism following the Second World War was the cumulative result of considerable industrial and social unrest, a lengthy economic depression, two world wars, the radical ideas of John Maynard Keynes, a large increase in the franchise, and political support from the Labour Party. The shift back again – a scant thirty-five years later – was the result of more social and industrial unrest, driven by seriously deteriorating industrial performance and the re-emergence of unfettered financial markets, the crisis-ridden "stagflationary" 1970s, the (old) ideas of Milton Friedman and Friedrich von Hayek, and political support from the Conservative Party. Both shifts thus involved democratic upsurge, alternative policy ideas, strong political support – in the form of Clement Attlee and Margaret Thatcher, respectively – and, above all, a significant and sustained sense of "crisis".

We now consider the current state of these four factors, and the degree to which they appear to be potentially capable of generating a change either *within* the conventional wisdom of neoliberalism or perhaps even a change *of* the conventional wisdom.

Inequality and crisis

Since the nineteenth century, the inequality, poverty and inadequate public services that have typically accompanied economic liberalism have long provided a basis for the chronic crisis experienced by an ever-increasing number of people. Combined with political support and propelled by a very well-organised democratic upsurge during the Second World War, the first radical Labour government came to power in 1945. These same factors also brought a second radical labour movement to the brink of power in the general election of 2017.

At the time of writing, the Conservative Party remains in power as a minority government, led by an embattled Theresa May. However, opinion polls suggest that the Labour Party offers an electable alternative. Although a Conservative Party leadership challenge might not result in an immediate significant shift in the insecurity cycle, there are a number of possible bases for an acute crisis – including an escalation of the current chronic crisis – with the potential to tip the balance, perhaps producing the first non-neoliberal government in almost forty years.

With regard to a potential escalation of the present situation into an acute crisis, among others, the IMF, Oxfam, and World Economic Forum (WEF) have all recently drawn attention to high and rising inequality, with potentially serious adverse consequences for social cohesion, economic growth and perhaps the financial sector itself.

Research carried out at the IMF by Andrew Berg and Jonathon Ostry (2011) identifies income equality as by far the most significant factor contributing to sustainable economic growth, with such growth being "possible only when its benefits are widely shared" (p. 15). Their research shows that whilst the benefits derived from lower levels of inequality are shared by most income groups, extreme inequality has historically given rise to crises, with the current rise in inequality being "strikingly similar" to that of the turbulent inter-war years. Noting that "[i]n both cases there was a boom in the financial sector, poor people borrowed a lot, and a huge financial crisis ensued" (ibid., p. 13), Berg and Ostry conclude that "the recent global economic crisis, with its roots in US financial markets, may have resulted, in part at least, from the increase in inequality" (ibid.). What might happen as a result of the continuing increase in inequality and financialisation in the context of a low-growth, stagnant economy is not hard to guess at.

Examining the negative effects of extreme wealth and income inequality – and calling for their elimination by 2025 – Oxfam (2013) notes that during the past thirty years, wealth and inequality, that have both risen to "levels never before seen ... are getting worse" (p. 1). By this account, extreme wealth and inequality are "economically inefficient", "politically corrosive" and "socially divisive": because the rich do not spend as high a proportion of their income as those at the bottom of the income distribution, excessive inequality of wealth and income depresses demand, with adverse effects on economic development and growth. It can also be used to secure political influence to the advantage of the rich, through lobbying or corruption; and it is socially divisive as a consequence of the rich buying private access to services that the majority depend upon the state to provide, and then seeking the withdrawal of support for public provision of those services. The Oxfam report also makes the case that wealth and income inequality are "environmentally destructive" and "unethical". But it concludes that they are "not inevitable".

The World Economic Forum's (WEF) 2012 and 2013 annual surveys of leaders in business, government, academia, NGOs and other institutions, also point to the potential for extreme inequality to precipitate a crisis. Assessing the likelihood of occurrence of fifty global risks during the coming decade – and the degree of impact – respondents of the WEF's 2012 and 2013 Global Risks Perception Survey ranked extreme income disparity as not only the highest likelihood but also the highest impact risk. On the basis of these results, WEF (2012) warns of a "potentially potent combination of chronic labour market imbalances, chronic fiscal imbalances and severe income disparity" (p. 18); and it goes on to argue:

> When amplified by extreme demographic pressures, these conditions could lead to a retrenchment from globalization and the emergence of a new type of critical fragile states – formerly wealthy countries that descend into a spiral of decay as they become increasingly unable to meet their social and fiscal obligations
>
> (Ibid.)

Describing the impact of widening income inequality – evident in the wave of riots that swept Britain in early August 2011 – WEF (2012) explains:

> When social mobility is widely perceived as attainable, income disparity can spur people to reach for success. However, when ambitious and industrious young people start to feel that, no matter how hard they work, their prospects are constrained, then feelings of powerlessness, disconnectedness and disengagement can take root. The social unrest that occurred in 2011, from the United States to the Middle East, demonstrated how governments everywhere need to address the causes of discontent before it becomes a violent, destabilizing force.
>
> (p. 19)

The sense of hopelessness expressed by those involved in the violence of the 2011 riots in Britain was an indication that failure to halt, if not reverse, the trend of increasing inequality has the potential to result in not only continued unrest but also crisis. The consequences of being on the receiving end of increasing inequality – and subsequently falling into poverty, especially when there is insufficient to eat – are difficult to ignore.

At the time of writing, 2017, things had deteriorated further, with persistent inequality again ranked first in perceived importance in the WEF's Global Risks Perception Survey (WEF 2017, p. 15). According to WEF (2017):

> Growth is now only part of the challenge policymakers need to address. Concerns over income and wealth distribution are becoming more politically disruptive, and much greater emphasis is needed on the increasing financial insecurity that characterizes many people's lives. As socio-economic outcomes are increasingly determined globally, popular frustration is growing at the inability of national politics to provide stability ... The combination of economic inequality and political polarization threatens to amplify global risks, fraying the social solidarity on which the legitimacy of our economic and political systems rests. New economic systems and policy paradigms are urgently needed to address the sources of popular disenchantment.
>
> (Ibid., p. 13)

Food poverty

Since the issue of food poverty was first made public in 2013, an increasing number of reports have been published, all drawing attention to the causal contributing role played by policies of austerity, cuts to social welfare benefits, safety nets and welfare reforms – particularly in relation to delays in benefit payment, due to the roll out of the government's new universal benefit system. However, the government's response has been effectively to demonise the poor by suggesting that their condition is largely the result of their own activities – a view also current in the nineteenth century – and to try to turn the working-class electorate against those most in need.

Although the government denies that cuts to the benefits system – and the introduction of the universal credit system in particular – are responsible for food poverty, according to a 2017 report by the Trussell Trust, the UK's largest food bank network, "[f]ood banks in areas of full universal credit rollout ... have seen a 16.85 percent average increase in referrals for emergency food, more than double the national average of 6.64 percent" (Trussell Trust 2017a, p. 2).

Data from the Trussell Trust reveals the extent of the problem. Table 11.1 shows the number of people receiving three-day emergency food parcels from the Trussell Trust, and the number of food banks within this network. Since the 2008 financial crisis, and especially since the turn to austerity in 2010, the numbers of those reliant on food banks – as well as the number of food banks themselves – has steadily and significantly increased, with the most dramatic rises coinciding with the arrival of the coalition government in 2010 and the introduction of universal credit in 2013. Between 2010–11 and 2011–12, the number of people reliant on food banks more than doubled, from 61,000 to 128,697; increasing even further in each of the next two years, to 346,992 people (170 per cent) and 913,138 (163 per cent), respectively, after which it continued to increase, with well over a million people relying on emergency food aid.

Table 11.1 Food poverty and provision by the Trussell Trust

	Number of people	*Percentage increase*	*Number of food banks*
2008–9	26,000		29
2009–10	41,000	58	56
2010–11	61,000	49	90
2011–12	128,697	111	185
2012–13	346,992	170	328
2013–14	913,138	163	423
2014–15	1,084,604	19	445
2015–16	1,109,309	2	424
2016–17	1,182,954	7	427

Source: The Trussell Trust (2017b).

But not only are the numbers themselves significant. The findings of a major study of people receiving food assistance from the Trussell Trust supports existing research, which suggests that they tend to be among the most vulnerable groups within society, which have also been subject to changes in welfare support (Hood and Johnson 2016; Equality and Human Rights Commission 2017) and/or increased benefits conditionality (Watts *et al.* 2014). Moreover, new benefit changes introduced in 2017 are expected to make things even worse, in terms of their financial vulnerability (Hood *et al.* 2017). The Trussell Trust report concludes that this raises a number of questions:

> Firstly, are levels of benefit support sufficient to ensure that all households relying on this income can always meet their basic needs? Our data suggest that this is not the case, especially for people who have disabilities and are relying on benefits. Secondly, for people in work, does this promise an income which meets their basic needs and that of their dependents? Our data suggests that insecurity and unsteadiness in income means even those in work can experience not having enough money for food.
>
> (Loopstra and Lalor 2017, p. xi)

The government's failure to even acknowledge the problem, or to accept responsibility for addressing it, has not only made the situation ever more difficult for those in poverty – and those trying to help; it has also created a significant divide between those in poverty, and those in mainstream politics. With the numbers of those in poverty increasing, this divide clearly represents an expanding potential source of crisis.

Predictably, in the light of the insecurity cycle, this has been problematic before. The hunger marches of the 1920s and 1930s in Britain – and particularly the 1932 Great National Hunger March against the Means Test – revealed the potential of both food shortages and poverty for both crisis and democratic upsurge. Reactions to them also appear to have similarities; upon the protesters' arrival at Hyde Park on 27 October 1932, "they met an almost blanket condemnation as a threat to public order, verging on the hysterical in the case of some of the more conservative press" (Waddington 1992, p. 31). They were also met by a deployment of 70,000 Metropolitan Police, resulting in significant violence which lasted for several days, causing some seventy-five serious injuries. The petition intended for Parliament – said to carry a million signatures – was also confiscated by the police. But this did not stop the hunger marches, with another following in 1934, and perhaps the most well-known – the Jarrow March – in 1936.

The most obvious lasting legacy of the violence that accompanied the 1932 march and gathering at Hyde Park was the creation of the National Council for Civil Liberties. This was formed by Ronald Kidd, due to concerns about the use of *agents provocateurs* by the police, to provide an excuse for breaking-up the demonstration. However, it is also worth bearing in mind that the marches only really came to an end with the increase in employment that accompanied re-armament and the Second World War – after which, Attlee's Labour government won a landslide election victory.

Growth in personal debt

There are other potential triggers for an acute crisis, many of which are also linked to inequality. The classic neoliberal policy response to inequality – expansion of the amount of credit available to the less well-off – offers one such possibility. Over the course of the insecurity cycle so far, free market capitalism's track record in generating regular financial crises certainly suggests that it would be unwise to ignore the likelihood of another at some point in the not too distant future; and there are already some indications as to what might cause the next one. National debt is made up of four main components: government debt, the balance of payments (if it is in deficit), personal debt and corporate debt. Of these, aside from corporate debt – where many organisations are hoarding cash – debt is significant and rising everywhere.

The hoarding of cash and short-term investments by businesses can be traced to the early 1990s, with increasing competition in R&D-intensive sectors – such as information technology and pharmaceuticals – and the acceleration of globalisation (Davidson 2017; Dorfman 2014). More recently, particularly since the 2008 financial crisis, this has become a politically charged topic, with corporations coming in for criticism for *not* using these funds for productive purposes – such as maintaining or expanding the business – which would contribute to economic growth and increased employment (Burke 2013).

However, the reasons for holding cash reserves are not necessarily so sinister. According to a study by the Federal Reserve Bank of Saint Louis, "[t]here are two main reasons why firms find it beneficial to hold cash: precautionary motive and repatriation taxes" (Sánchez and Yurdagul 2013, p. 6). Precautionary motives stem from uncertainty and credit constraints – and are more likely to drive cash hoarding by smaller firms. From this perspective, cash reserves might be held to meet pension shortfalls or to have emergency funds available for investment in new, unanticipated opportunities (such as acquisitions, intangibles and R&D), protection against market risks and uncertainty and share buy-backs; they might also be held if firms find it difficult to obtain credit when funds become necessary.

By contrast, "tax efficiency" objectives – to avoid paying repatriation tax on foreign earnings – are an important motivator for the accumulation of large cash reserves by multi-nationals. But whatever the reason, it is impossible to escape the conclusion that neoliberalism has created an environment designed to suit large global corporations – even at the expense of their country of origin's fiscal balance – whilst simultaneously limiting the influence and earning power of the other interest groups in the insecurity cycle.

Meanwhile, since the arrival of the 2008 financial crisis, public debt has been used to justify austerity – which in turn, has put ever-increasing pressure on many within society to accumulate personal debt of their own, to make-up for cuts in public services and welfare benefits. As of early 2017, UK consumer debt – including credit card debt, personal loans and motor finance – was growing rapidly, much faster than household income, and approaching levels not reached since immediately prior to the 2008 financial crisis (Harari 2017a). This, in combination with stagnant wages and low savings rates, is increasing the vulnerability of the "just about managing" (JAMS) and other less well-off groups; it is also increasing the vulnerability of a significant part of the financial services sector involved in extending credit to them.

Over-confidence as a factor in the insecurity cycle is typically associated with booms and bubbles, when both lenders and borrowers feel certain that the upward trend in asset prices will continue. However, the current increase in borrowing, with the possible exception of motor finance, does not appear to be the result of an obvious boom. Instead, the re-emergence of the poor as an interest group, combined with austerity policies and rising inequality, suggest that much of the borrowing is driven by necessity, rather than enthusiasm. The increase in inequality has tightened the market for "prime" loans whilst at the same time significantly increasing the number of potential "sub-prime" borrowers. This, in turn, has created incentives on the part of lenders, to loosen under-writing standards, just as it did during the lead in to the American sub-prime mortgage crisis – which, in turn, precipitated the 2008 financial crisis.

Whilst benign conditions, especially in the form of sustained, ultra-low interest rates, have contributed to the up-take of debt, those with patchy or non-existent credit histories do not pay the most competitive rates; some short-term "pay day" loan rates exceed 4,000 per cent APR whilst a personal loan rate for a "prime" customer would typically be less than 10 per cent (Jones, R. 2013). This has encouraged lenders to develop new products to compensate for low returns, but has done little to inhibit the resulting increase in risk. In this context, one of the most frequent underlying causes of a financial crisis has been an increase in interest rates. But whilst the Bank of England has signalled that this is indeed likely to be the case, it is not the only possible source of an acute crisis.

In June 2017, supported by the Bank of England's Financial Policy Committee (FPC 2017), a review of lenders in the consumer credit market was conducted by the Bank's Prudential Regulation Authority (PRA) and Financial Conduct Authority (FCA). Reporting on its review of both asset quality and underwriting practices for various kinds of personal debt, the PRA's *Statement on Consumer Credit* revealed some obvious reasons for concern. In general terms, the report noted a reduction in the quality of consumer credit assets held on financial institutions' loan books: "Overall, the PRA judges that the resilience of consumer credit portfolios is reducing, due to the combination of continued growth, lower pricing, falling average risk-weights … and some increased lending into higher-risk segments" (PRA 2017, p. 1).

There was also concern about underwriting standards as well as other issues, suggestive of over-confidence.

> While the PRA Review did not find evidence that the growth in consumer credit in recent years has been primarily driven by a material lowering of credit policies or scoring, the aggregate growth plans of PRA-regulated firms may only be achievable with some loosening in underwriting standards, or further reductions in pricing, notwithstanding a likely "optimism-bias" in firms' business-plan projections ... Moreover, the short maturities of consumer credit mean that the asset quality of the stock of lending can deteriorate quickly.
>
> (Ibid.)

The regulator goes on to strike a note of caution on the subject of the overall debt levels of many of those that have been granted extra credit:

> Rising consumer indebtedness and its impact on borrowers' ability to repay their debt in the future was not always fully considered in firms' assessment of risk. For example, underwriting assessments did not always take into account a customer's total debt (including secured), nor was this routinely monitored for existing customers. Further, underwriting assessments rarely assessed how future shocks (for example to housing costs) could affect borrowers' ability to repay.
>
> (Ibid., p. 2)

The PRA also had particular concerns about developments in specific asset classes, as well as the potential risks associated with them, notably, the sharp rise in debt used to fund vehicles – which now accounts for some 30 per cent of all private debt (FPC 2017, p. 18).

The rapid growth in UK motor vehicle finance has a number of features that bear a striking resemblance to the sub-prime element of the American property bubble that led to the 2008 financial crisis. Like American sub-prime mortgages – and the derivative products built from them – UK vehicle finance loans are made on a different basis to previous products; their markets are opaque and no data is available on either the percentage of sub-prime loans or default rates.

Traditional car finance takes the form of a hire purchase agreement, in which the customer pays a fraction of the car's purchase price as a deposit and takes out a loan to cover the rest, which is paid-off with interest in regular monthly payments. By contrast, "personal contract purchase" (PCP) agreements, the idea of which originated in the United States – and which currently account for 80 per cent of UK consumer car finance (PRA 2017, p. 3) – are not used to actually buy a car. Instead, they extend the right to the use of the car for typically three years, at which point the customer has two options: (1) they can pay a single "balloon" payment and keep the car; or (2) they can hand the car back to the dealer and take out another PCP on a replacement new car.

To make the plan as affordable for the customer as possible, rather than the traditional loan-plus-interest arrangement, the customer pays only for the car's depreciation over the period they drive it. After this, if the buyer returns the car, the dealer can resell it – hopefully at a price very close to its forecast residual value. However, there are a number of obvious potential problems with this arrangement. First, the sheer number of cars being sold on PCPs may undermine the value of used cars; why buy a used car, when it is likely to be cheaper to take out a PCP on a new one? Second, the residual value of the asset can be significantly affected by a range of factors. Air pollution legislation, for example, may have a negative effect on the value of cars with diesel engines; and a recession might well involve larger numbers of car buyers than estimated, exercising their option to walk away from both the car and its associated payments. It is then the dealer that is saddled with both the loan costs and potentially not being able to sell the car for its expected residual value in a depressed market.

In the light of the roots of the 2008 financial crisis, these issues beg the questions of how much debt is involved and who is holding it. According to Bank of England figures, in June 2017, total consumer debt stood at £198 billion, of which loans for vehicles accounted for £58 billion (30 per cent). Of this, around half comes from the car dealerships' parent companies and around a quarter from bank lending. The remaining quarter comes from securitisation (FPC 2017, p. 19) – a process similar to that used during the American sub-prime property bubble to sell-on loans in order to create liquidity with which to fund further lending. All of this suggests that the exposure of banks to the PCP market is probably significantly more than the £24 billion suggested. To put that into perspective, the cost of bailing out the Royal Bank of Scotland (RBS) as a result of the 2008 financial crisis was around £45 billion (Treanor 2015).

The Bank of England's PRA has publicly expressed its reservations. However, it is also in something of a cleft stick. As the regulator, it must not only regulate; it must also attempt to maintain confidence in the markets to avoid precipitating a crisis. As a result, the PRA's assessment of the car loan category was typically measured:

> Motor finance has seen the fastest expansion among consumer credit products, where a key factor has been the growing popularity of Personal Contract Purchase (PCP) deals, which now account for around 80% of gross flows for new dealership consumer car finance.... PCP creates explicit risk exposure to the vehicle's residual value for lenders, who typically offer a guaranteed future value (GFV) for the vehicle. Gross GFV exposure is estimated to be around £23 billion across the industry, and GFVs are typically set in the range of 85–95% of the vehicle's expected future value (with a minority higher than that). PCPs written at

the high end of this range are particularly exposed to a significant down-turn in the used car market, possibly outside historic experience (used car prices fell by up to c.20% in the crisis, before recovering). An initial fall in prices could lead to a surplus of used cars coming to the market, which could further weaken prices and cause material losses to lenders through their GFV risk.

(PRA 2017, p. 3)

MPs, however, have felt less restraint in questioning the lack of data published by the Finance and Leasing Association (FLA), on either "sub-prime" loans, arrears or defaults. Rachel Reeves, the Labour MP for Leeds West and a former Shadow Treasury Minister, focused on the consumer side of the equation, commenting:

> Household debt is back at levels seen just before the financial crash. That should send a chill down the spine of the Bank of England and Treasury. In 2008, sub-prime mortgages were a big problem – missed by policy-makers. Today it's car loans and other forms of consumer credit that are accelerating. Car companies are vulnerable to bad debt and defaults while buyers are racking up debt that may well turn out to be unaffordable.
>
> (Quoted in Inman 2017)

Nor was concern limited to the Labour benches. John Penrose, the Conservative MP for Weston, Worle and the Villages, also made comparisons with the last financial crisis:

> Unless we have pitiless transparency in the car loans market, with industry standards to measure and report the risks in this fast-growing area, we won't be able to spot problems in advance, or fix them before customers or banks get hurt. The finance industry has a great opportunity to show it can be responsible here, and that prevention is better than cure.
>
> (Quoted in Inman 2017)

Whilst the FLA says that lenders can calculate the value of depreciation on a car to within a few pounds based on "rich data", it is worth noting that during the US sub-prime housing boom, the outcome of a national – as opposed to a regional – drop in house values was thought to be impossible, since it had never happened before. But financial factors that were national in footprint combined with a property glut to make the apparently impossible, all too real – with devastating global consequences.

John Penrose summed up the difficulty: "Risk managers say the risk that kills you is the one you didn't spot. The 2008 banking crash started because asset prices got out of control without anyone noticing, and we can't let the same thing happen here" (quoted in Inman 2017).

Household wealth and the burden of debt

The use of credit to finance consumption has a disproportionate impact on households, depending upon their stock of wealth and position in the distribution of income. Although a great deal is known about income distribution based on wages and earnings, for many years, the distribution of personal wealth was a neglected topic (Crossley and O'Dea 2016; Alvaredo *et al.* 2016). However, with growing recognition of the problem of income inequality – and the importance of income earned from capital in this measure – there has recently been a surge of interest in household wealth data.

Recent studies documenting long-run trends in wealth inequality have shown that the period of neoliberalism has been accompanied by an increasing concentration of wealth (Atkinson 2015; Piketty 2014; Saez and Zucman 2014). But there is an "increasing consensus" that neoliberal models, such as "representative agent macroeconomic models cannot satisfactorily explain many aggregate phenomena – including the Great Recession" (Crossley and O'Dea 2016, pp. 5–6). Because the distribution of wealth is an important determinant of household responses to economic policy, macroeconomists have been turning their attention to developing models that help to explain the causes of household wealth inequality.[6] This, in turn, has motivated efforts to collect household wealth data in order to assess the performance of such models.

The level of a household's wealth is a crucial determinant of its material well-being. This is because a household with enough wealth can maintain living standards when income falls – unexpectedly (for example, as a consequence of unemployment) or expectedly (for example, due to retirement) – or when needs increase. Household wealth also has implications for the descendants of those who currently hold wealth that can be bequeathed from one generation to the next.

The distribution of wealth in the UK has been the subject of a number of studies since the nineteenth century.[7] However, aside from these, data on wealth in the UK has for many years been very limited. The four main sources from which wealth data can be collected include wealth tax data, estate tax data, investment income data and household survey data. Of these, household survey data provides the most complete and reliable means of measuring population wealth holdings (Crawford *et al.* 2016, p. 36).

However, since the 1990s, household surveys have only occasionally included questions about wealth;[8] and it was not until the 2006 Wealth and Assets Survey (WAS) was launched by the Office of National Statistics (ONS) that the UK started to systematically compile nationally representative comprehensive data on wealth. Since then, there have been four waves of studies, with WAS Wave 1 (2009) covering the period 2006–8, WAS Wave 2 (2011) covering 2008–10, WAS Wave 3 (2013) covering 2010–12 and WAS Wave 4 (2015) covering 2012–14. The provisional release date for WAS Wave 5 (covering 2014–16) is December 2017 or January 2018.

Thus, since 2009, WAS has been a vital source of information about the material well-being of British households and how they are managing economically. A longitudinal household survey, WAS compiles data on, among other things, level of savings and debt, saving for retirement, how wealth is distributed across households and factors that affect financial planning. Because many of the questions ask households how they "feel" about these issues, it is a useful indicator of related pressures for movement of the insecurity cycle.

One question, for example, asks whether households felt that their financial debt burden was "a heavy burden", "somewhat of a burden" or "no burden at all". As evident in Table 11.2, reporting findings covering the period 2012–14, households with lower incomes were much more likely to assess their debt as a heavy burden, with 43 per cent of those in the bottom decile saying so, compared with only 5 per cent in the top decile. However, perhaps more striking is the consistency of the "somewhat of a burden" response throughout all deciles.

But the weight of debt does not only fall disproportionately on less well-off households; it also impacts younger people, in particular. A 2017 survey commissioned by the Young Women's Trust – formerly the Young Women's Christian Association (YWCA), formed during the nineteenth century as a result of growing interest in the welfare of young women at work – found that of a representative sample of 4,010 eighteen-to-thirty-year-olds in England and Wales, 41 per cent of young women and 28 per cent of young men struggled to make their finances last until their next payday; 25 per cent of young women and 23 per cent of young men were in debt "all of the time"; and 51 per cent of young women and 45 per cent of young men regularly resort to the use of borrowing, credit and over-draft as well as working additional hours, skipping meals and selling/pawning items to make their cash last (Young Women's Trust 2017, p. 3).

Table 11.2 Individual financial debt burden by household

Decile	Heavy burden (per cent)	Somewhat of a burden (per cent)	Not a burden at all (per cent)
1st	43	33	24
2nd	35	36	29
3rd	30	31	39
4th	24	31	45
5th	20	33	47
6th	16	35	49
7th	12	34	54
8th	8	29	63
9th	7	27	65
10th	5	20	75

Source: Wealth and Assets Survey (WAS) (ONS 2015, p. 180).

The same survey reported that 30 per cent of young people (33 per cent women and 28 per cent men) have been offered a zero hours contract, with 39 per cent of young women and 36 per cent of young men feeling worried about job security and over half feeling worried about how much their job pays (ibid., p. 4). When asked about the biggest issues facing young people in the UK, the top three were housing costs, unemployment and pay/job security (ibid., p. 7). All of this illustrates the impact of flat wages, the gig economy and rising prices on millennials, with personal loans, the "Bank of Mum and Dad" and credit cards being the most common means of bridging the gap.

It is also possible to discern the potential impact of these levels of inequality, poverty and insecurity on the insecurity cycle. In the 2017 general election, YouGov research shows that this segment of young people – who are clearly under pressure – were far more likely to vote for Jeremy Corbyn's more radical vision for society, than for Theresa May's "business as usual" neoliberalism:

> In electoral terms, age seems to be the new dividing line in British politics. The starkest way to show this is to note that, amongst first time voters (those aged 18 and 19), Labour was forty seven percentage points ahead ... In fact, for every 10 years older a voter is, their chance of voting Tory increases by around nine points and the chance of them voting Labour decreases by nine points. The tipping point, that is the age at which a voter is more likely to have voted Conservative than Labour, is now 47 – up from 34 at the start of the campaign.
>
> (Curtis 2017)

The stagnating wages that many of those in employment have experienced since the financial crisis – especially the JAMs and young people – may also at least partly account for the trend to support Jeremy Corbyn's Labour. In the 2017 general election, when the electorate is broken down by employment status, the Labour vote was not only 45 points ahead of the Conservatives amongst full-time students; it was also four points ahead amongst those working part time and six points ahead amongst full-time workers. By contrast, the Conservatives were 39 points ahead amongst retirees (ibid.).

As well as PCP car loans, the Bank of England report, discussed above, indicates concern about the forms of private debt, such as personal loans and credit cards that many of the people in the above segments use to attempt to smooth over low or irregular wages. The Bank noted, for example, that the increase in interest free balance transfer offers to thirty months and beyond is undermining the margins available to cover defaults (PRA 2017, pp. 2–3). If rising inflation continues to create pressure for an interest rate rise, fear could well re-enter the equation, increasing the cost of debt, spurring default rates and hence putting pressure on banks and support services. Equally, fear of this scenario might result in the delaying of a rate rise to curb inflation – delaying deflation of the bubble and allowing the cost of essentials to rise instead. Neither scenario is likely to reduce the pressure for a shift in the insecurity cycle.

Low pay, precarious work and the evisceration of social security

A major cause of insecurity in contemporary Britain is its dysfunctional labour market. Britain has a higher incidence of low pay than its European neighbours (Deakin 2013), but also lower productivity (Harari 2017b). Both problems are of long standing but have become particularly severe since the onset of the recession following the financial crisis of 2008. With a large incidence of low pay, the burden of ensuring that poorer households receive an adequate income to live on increasingly falls on the state, which has to top up wages through tax credits. This peculiarly toxic combination is the result of policy failures going back to the 1980s, the effects of which have intensified since the beginning of austerity policy with the election of the Conservative-led coalition in 2010.

As we saw in Chapter 6, Beveridge's plan for the post-1945 British economy had seen social security, collective bargaining and macroeconomic policy as interlocking elements of a single policy aimed at maintaining "full employment". Full employment did not just mean that there were "more vacant jobs than unemployed men"; it also implied that "the jobs are at fair wages, of such a kind, and so located that the unemployed men can reasonably be expected to take them". Beveridge thought that the "labour market should always be a seller's market rather than a buyer's market". One justification for this position was ethical: whereas a labour shortage was an "inconvenience" for the employer, prolonged unemployment was a "catastrophe" for the worker. The other justification was efficiency-based: If there was an over-supply of labour, making workers too easily replaceable, employers would lack "stimulus to technical advance", while workers would have no incentive to "cooperate in making the most of all productive resources" (Beveridge 1944, pp. 18–19).

To achieve full employment in conjunction with a living wage and access to fair work for all, Beveridge envisaged, firstly, a comprehensive social insurance system, which would provide security for the entire working population through the operation of the contributory principle.[9] This would be coupled with industry-level collective bargaining, supplemented by statutory wages councils in low-paying sectors, to entrench the living wage, and a demand-led macroeconomic policy which would maintain employment levels across the business cycle. A key part of the programme was the principle that the social security system should support, and not undermine, collective bargaining. Thus reinforcing a principle which went back to legislation of 1911, the 1946 National Insurance Act ensured that unemployment benefits could not be withheld for a refusal to accept work below the "going rate" for a job, which in practice meant the collectively agreed wage (Deakin and Wilkinson 2005, pp. 166–7).

From the early 1980s, each of these mechanisms was dismantled, and the principles underlying them inverted.[10] Now it was state policy to stimulate the labour supply through policies of labour market activation, while treating collective bargaining as an abuse of market power and distortion of competition. Macroeconomic policy rejected the management of effective demand as unrealistic and counter-productive. Instead, fiscal and monetary policies were aligned to achieve price stability and budgetary equilibrium. In the area of social security, the link between contributions and benefits was broken (although contribution levels remained high and operated as a regressive income tax); and strict forms of conditionality were introduced, with claimants facing loss of benefits for failing to take up job offers below collectively bargained rates or outside their normal occupation. In 1995, this process reached a point where unemployment benefit was formally abolished and replaced with the "jobseeker's allowance", a more than purely formal change of name as the orientation of state support shifted from the insurance principle to active management of "welfare to work" transitions.

The goal of this policy revolution was to restore the labour market to what was understood to be its normal, "undistorted" mode of operation. Its supporters may have genuinely believed that they would bring about a more productive economy while helping the unemployed find stable and well paid work. What happened instead was a mushrooming of low-paid and casual jobs and the rise of a new phenomenon, in-work poverty, which could only be partially mitigated by the operation of a much-expanded tax credit system.

Critical decisions were taken firstly in the mid-1980s, when Conservative governments accelerated the dismantling of collective wage determination and instituted the system of tax credits. The statutory powers of the wages councils were firstly cut back (from 1986) before being removed altogether (from 1993). Family credit, introduced from 1988, was seen as the necessary counterpart to the deregulation of pay: the state would meet the gap in household income caused by failing wages. At the same time, it would "make work pay" by providing a rising income as benefit recipients entered employment. This failed to happen, as a result of the poor design of the family credit system: it was not effectively integrated with other social security benefits and, because it was paid in cash to households, was not taken into account by employers in wage setting. Moreover, because of the tapering of the credit, low earners faced punitive marginal tax rates as their incomes rose, discouraging the transition from "welfare to work".

The "New Labour" government which took office in 1997 could have taken steps to restore collective wage determination and revive the contributory principle as the basis of social security. It had a mandate to introduce a statutory minimum wage and was committed to providing legal support for trade union recognition. Instead, it chose to continue the Conservative policy of combining a light-touch approach to labour regulation with wage subsidisation, the difference being that Labour was determined that the system could actually be made to work.

The national minimum wage (NMW), introduced with effect from 1999, was part of this approach. Ostensibly, it put a floor below wages and so made up for the erosion of collective bargaining which had occurred over the preceding two decades. It did have some positive effects: it reversed the rise in earnings equality, which had begun in the late 1970s and continued year on year ever since, and helped to narrow the gender pay gap (Metcalf 2008). However, the NMW was not designed to be a living wage. The setting of the rate, while ultimately in the hands of ministers, was effectively delegated to a tripartite body, the Low Pay Commission, which was tasked with ensuring that the NMW did not have a negative impact on employment. In practice this was interpreted to mean that it had to be set below the living costs of even the poorest working households.

Thus a Treasury paper published in 2000 argued that setting the NMW at a level equivalent to half average household income "could well have adverse consequences for the employment of low-skill workers". Tax credits would continue to be used as, in contrast to the NMW, they did not "raise the direct cost of low-wage workers to employers". The function of the NMW was to ensure that employers did not cut pay *too far*, as the Treasury put it, somewhat euphemistically, the NMW "by setting a floor to wages, is essential to ensure that low-income workers enjoy the full benefit of the tax credit" (HM Treasury 2000, p. 17).

The Low Pay Commission arrived at a figure for the NMW roughly equivalent to 45 per cent of median earnings when it was introduced in 1999. At this point the equivalent measure in France, the "SMIC", operated at a level over 60 per cent of median earnings, near to the "decency threshold" set by the Council of Europe as a benchmark for minimum wages (Adams and Deakin 2016). The 60 per cent median benchmark is also widely used internationally to define household poverty. New Labour's approach, which arrived at its definitive form in the Tax Credits Act 2002, was to use the fiscal system to bring household incomes from the 45 per cent level implied by the NMW up to the 60 per cent benchmark (Deakin 2013). This meant expanding the scale of tax credits and the number of households affected, while curing some of the design defects of the previous regime, so as to ensure that fiscal transfers dovetailed better with other benefits and with wages. Following the implementation of the 2002 Act, expenditure on tax credits rose from just under £6.5 billion to over £13 billion, and the proportion of working households receiving credits jumped from 8 per cent to over 12 per cent. By 2010, the final year of the Labour government, the cost of the tax credit system (direct expenditure and foregone income tax) stood at nearly £30 billion (DWP 2013). In 2014, over 3 million working households with children were receiving tax credit incomes of some kind, out of a total of around 7 million such households (Keen and Turner 2016).

New Labour could have chosen to follow the continental European model of setting a high wage floor through a combination of statutory minimum wages and sector-level collective bargaining. This option, which had been discussed in policy circles in the late 1980s (McNeil and Pond 1988) and informed Labour's minimum wage policy in the 1992 general election, was rejected by the party prior to the 1997 election. Instead, the NMW was to be given the subsidiary role, supplementing tax credits, which fully emerged once Labour took office. As we have seen, the incoming Labour government also rejected calls for the restoration of sector-level collective bargaining. Its union recognition law applied only to employer-level bargaining and even then was a limited measure which proved to have a minimal impact on the framework of wage determination.

In 1997, fully one-third of children in Britain lived in households with an income below 60 per cent of the median. This was three times the number in "relative" poverty, so defined, that there had been in 1979, when Mrs Thatcher's first Conservative administration had taken office. New Labour managed to reduce the poverty rate somewhat, so that by 2004–5, 28 per cent of children were living in poor households. This was achieved by the targeting of tax credits on families with children. However, the trend was reversed from the mid-2000s (Deakin 2013). Even the expanded tax credit system could do no more than alleviate the effects of stagnating earnings and the rise of casualised employment, trends which were reinforced by the recession which began with the onset of the global financial crisis in 2008.

One sign of this has been the rise in very precarious forms of work including zero hours contracts (ZHCs), under which workers are kept on call by employers and paid only for the time they spend working. Statistical estimates suggest that the number of ZHCs surged after 2008, when they stood at 0.5 per cent of the workforce, to over 2 per cent by 2013. ZHC workers are less likely to be unionised than those in regular employment, and they are paid less; in addition, their working hours are shorter and more likely to be varied by the employer. According to a survey conducted by the Chartered Institute for Personnel and Development (CIPD) in 2012, 20 per cent of employers penalised ZHC workers for not accepting work when offered, 30 per cent expected ZHC staff to be available for work despite not offering them any guaranteed hours in return, and 40 per cent had no procedures for giving ZHC workers advance notice of jobs being cancelled or rearranged. But while ZHCs may be highly casualised, they are not all short-term: in 2012, 44 per cent had lasted for two years or more, and 25 per cent for over five years. Nor is their incidence confined to smaller firms, or to sectors with a history of low-paid and insecure work, such as hospitality. Nearly half of the employers surveyed by the CIPD in 2012 reported that ZHCs were part of a long-term business strategy, and prominent users of ZHCs include numerous listed companies and multi-nationals (Adams and Deakin 2014a).

ZHCs account for a relatively small segment of the whole workforce, and even when account is taken of recent increases in the incidence of other, similarly precarious forms of work, such as agency work and false self-employment (Behling and Harvey 2015), we are far from seeing the end of the contract of employment as the predominant legal model of the work relationship (Adams and Deakin 2014b). Even the rise of the so-called "gig economy" is not so much a sign of deep structural change in the nature of work, as an instance of employers finding new ways to avoid fiscal and regulatory responsibilities through digital platforms and other "intermediary" structures, while continuing to exercise control over workers (Deakin and Markou 2017; Prassl 2018).

The ZHC phenomenon is more important than its relatively small impact on the overall economy implies, however, as it exemplifies the way in which an under-regulated labour market operates to embed precarious work, and is a harbinger of the negative, wider consequences which this process will inevitably have if it continues. ZHCs are a product of the removal of any effective safety net in social security, along with the elimination of union presence or any effective alternative, by way of state regulation, in many companies and workplaces.

From 2010, the coalition government tightened the rules relating to conditionality in the operation of social security and introduced various forms of workfare, under which employers receive the labour of benefit recipients for free in return for providing work "experience". By 2014 disqualifications from benefit for refusing low-paid work or workfare were running at over 1 million a year. There is evidence that the threat of disqualification was being used at this point to encourage benefit recipients to accept precarious employment even where it did not guarantee a regular wage, as in the case of ZHCs (Adams and Deakin 2014a).

The effect of over twenty years of legislative changes following the Jobseekers Act of 1995 has been to leave the UK with one of the least generous systems of unemployment compensation in the developed world. In 2011 the replacement rate for jobseeker's allowance (the ratio between unemployment benefit and the average wage) was below 0.2. At the same time it was around 0.7 in the Netherlands and Sweden. Even a developing economy such as Taiwan had a replacement rate over 0.5. In a group of fifty-one high- and middle-income countries, only Brazil, Estonia, Lithuania, Chile and Georgia ranked below the UK (Adams and Deakin 2014a).

In 2012 the coalition government introduced the Welfare Reform Act. This paves the way for the introduction of universal credit (UC), a new system combining social security law and tax credits which was planned while the Conservative Party was in opposition with the aid of the think tank somewhat counter-intuitively known as the Centre for Social Justice. UC has been presented as a revolutionary measure with the potential to solve once and for all the problem of how to organise welfare to work transitions, while simultaneously bringing long-overdue simplification to social security law. In reality, it is just the latest and most extreme form of the labour market activation policy, coupling conditionality with wage subsidisation, which began with family credit in the 1980s and continued with New Labour's tax credits into the 2000s, and has older antecedents in the ill-fated Speenhamland systems of the eighteenth and early nineteenth centuries.

Universal credit is the purest form so far adopted in the UK of Milton Friedman's proposal for a 'negative income tax' (a more accurate if less attractive-sounding phrase) under which tax credits are completely dovetailed with wages. Critically, UC will extend the principle of conditionality to the payment of tax credits in any case where an earner is receiving less than the equivalent of the statutory minimum wage for a normal full-time working week (which for this purpose is deemed to be 35 hours). This "in-work conditionality" means applying sanctions and penalties, previously applied to the unemployed, to those in low-paid employment (Puttick 2018). The subsidy effect of tax credits will be extended to jobs providing employment for only a few hours a week and offering very low weekly earnings. It is therefore likely to lead to a further rise in the incidence of zero hours contracts and other highly casualised forms of employment (Adams and Deakin 2014a).

In the autumn of 2017 a political row enveloped UC as it became clear that, as it was being rolled out across the country, increasing numbers of households with one or more members receiving benefits or tax credits were being left without support for weeks on end, thanks to a rule delaying the first UC payment for a period of up to six weeks after a claim is first made. The basis for this rule is nothing more or less than the revival of the Benthamite principle of "less eligibility", or the idea that those receiving state support must never be better off than those in "independent" employment: since wage-earners are generally paid monthly in arrears, benefit recipients must not be "advantaged" by receiving payments up front.

The six-week rule was slightly modified under political pressure. But many policy makers continue to believe that once "glitches" like this are cured, and UC works as intended, it will finally solve the problem of how to manage labour market transitions in a humane and rational way.

Nothing could be further from the truth: if UC were ever to work in the way that its designers hope, it would undermine stable employment to an even greater extent than that achieved by the previous tax credit system, while exposing a growing number of working households to the insecurities and indignities associated with conditionality. This is why it has been suggested that "the consequences of universal credit will be catastrophic, for those claiming the benefit of course, but also for the government that implements it" (Tucker 2017), although in the case of any political fallout, at least, this remains to be seen.

We have come a very long way indeed from Beveridge's vision. His "national minimum" was never unconditional: access to social insurance depended on participation in paid employment, and unemployment benefit could be withdrawn if a reasonable offer of employment, one respecting fair treatment at work and the payment of a living wage, was not taken up. The policy of seeking to maintain stability of wages and employment through collective bargaining and macroeconomic policy was not only ethically motivated, but was incentive-compatible in a way which is very far from the case with UC.

The current framework creates perverse incentives on all sides, but particularly for employers. Firms are relieved from the need to pay a living wage and actively encouraged to create insecure and low-paying jobs. They can shift the burden of providing subsistence on to the state, which is faced with the prospect of an exponential increase in this form of social security expenditure, at the same time as the tax base is being eroded. As employers have no need to invest in the training and skills development which would be needed to make it possible for them to pay higher and more stable wages, productivity is further undermined. There can hardly have been a time when the mechanisms of labour market policy were so carefully aligned to produce the opposite of a beneficial result; and the case for a return to a version of Beveridge's "national minimum" has never been stronger.

That there may be a change underway was signalled by the about-turn in government policy in 2015 which saw the adoption of a new version of the statutory minimum wage, a "national living wage" (NLW). While still below the level of the (entirely separate) living wage set by the NGO Citizens UK as a benchmark for firms, the NLW will still make a significant difference to pay determination, as the government intends it to reach a level of 60 per cent of median wages by 2020, more or less where the statutory minimum wage currently stands in France and Germany. The change was announced by the then Chancellor of the Exchequer, George Osborne, in the July 2015 Summer Budget, apparently without first consulting the Low Pay Commission, whose role was thereby significantly diminished. One of the main motivations for introducing the NLW was to reduce expenditure on tax credits. Thus the change will not necessarily lead to an improvement in household incomes. It is nevertheless a straw in the wind, a belated recognition of the powerful efficiency case (in addition to the ethical one) for a high wage floor.

Political change: new ideas in political organisation and more frequent hung Parliaments

As discussed earlier, Momentum played a significant part in Jeremy Corbyn's success; and in many ways Labour is now being driven by an integrated combination of political support and democratic upsurge – with echoes of the "new" unionism that drove the development of the original Labour Party during the nineteenth century. The way that Momentum has performed against its objectives – side-stepping the industrial media in the process – also suggests that new ideas do not have to be limited to policy packages. Whilst Corbyn has described his approach as a "new kind of politics", this could equally well be argued for the way that the left-wing agenda has been evolved and promoted. Although the trade union movement is now a shadow of its former self, Momentum has in many ways built upon the foundations it laid down – such as collectivism and mobilisation of support – and brought them up to date. The landslide election of Jeremy Corbyn as leader of the Labour Party, the ease with which he won the subsequent leadership challenge, and the unexpected 2017 general election result are testament to that. The Conservatives, on the other hand, played by the rules that had worked so well for neoliberal administrations for almost forty years – only to find that these appear to have less traction than they once did.

Nonetheless, Labour did not win the 2017 general election; and the traditionally adversarial nature of British politics seems to have crumbled recently. Since the 2008 crisis, only Cameron's Conservative administration had any sort of clear majority; and even that was very likely to have been the result of a single key issue – membership in the European Union. On this, as well as other issues, the electorate is unusually divided. Whilst this may be in part a reflection of the consequences of growing inequality in the UK, it also means that the potential influence of any democratic movement, one way or another, could have a more decisive effect than if the electorate was more united. In a contest where more parties take a share of the vote, it may be possible for a smaller party to either have a disproportionate influence – as UKIP did – or even form a government.

All of this suggests that Corbyn's Labour Party may well be able to orchestrate a shift in the insecurity cycle. But if so, would it amount to just a few adjustments within the neoliberal universe, or a complete shift in the overall conventional wisdom? The shift from liberalism towards "Keynesianism" was part of a movement, internationally, as indeed was the return to liberalism during the time of Margaret Thatcher and Ronald Reagan. The fallout from the UK's vote to leave the EU suggests that international pressures – and legal frameworks – may well have a significant impact on what any radical government is able to achieve. But perhaps the bigger question is what might happen elsewhere in the world; and how this might impact neoliberal thinking and institutions.

We have already seen that there is a strong link between Momentum in the UK and Bernie Sanders's supporters in the US. Both politicians subsequently performed significantly better than anticipated, although neither movement has yet taken power. The combination of a shift in politics on both sides of the Atlantic – perhaps with changes in parts of Europe – might be enough to spark a shift in the conventional wisdom. But it would still have to overcome the formidable neoliberal "life support system". To make this headway, the track record of the insecurity cycle so far strongly suggests that at least one very significant crisis is required – and probably more than one, if the shift is from free market liberalism towards a more socially oriented approach to capitalism.

The original shift away from liberalism was slow, grudging and driven by sustained social pressure. It was renewed by each of the recurring recessions and financial crises that characterise "free" market capitalism – and two world wars – but it took about a century and a half. By comparison, a mere decade of social pressure, mostly the result of industrial under-performance, was enough to trigger an abrupt reversal in the insecurity cycle away from social interventionism. This suggests that it would take a crisis of epic dimensions to undo the neoliberal paradigm.

However, it has to be remembered that the two alternatives tried so far — the "Keynesian consensus" and neoliberalism — are not the only approaches available. The fact that both have turned out to have serious faults suggests that perhaps the largest contributor to a cyclical shift may yet be played by new ideas. Perhaps some of these will emerge from the UK Labour Party's current consultation process with PEG. But like Keynes's ideas during the Second World War, any new ideas will have to demonstrate credible results if they are to stand any chance of enduring.

Brexit: a further twist in the cycle

Into this heady mix there now comes an event with unrivalled potential for political and economic disruption — Brexit. The Brexit vote was nothing more or less than a response to the deep insecurities which have come to afflict British society. The call of the Leave campaign for voters to "take back control" by rejecting European Union (EU) membership vividly captured the mood of the time. But Brexit promises anything but a return to conditions of economic security.

Britain in the 1960s was far from being the haven of stability and equality that the Leave campaign would have had us believe. The country was less diverse and tolerant than it is today; and gender and racial divides were far more pronounced. The 1960s were nevertheless a period of full employment and steady growth in household incomes. This was a time when the values of nationhood were not in conflict with those of solidarity and mutual support. The pro-Brexit campaign highlighted these associations, which were particularly resonant for the large number of over-60s who voted Leave.

The paradox of the Brexit vote is that the loss of this world has practically nothing to do with the European Union. It is in part the consequence of the rise of global economic forces which every industrial nation has had to come to terms with. They would have affected Britain even in the absence of EU membership. But the European Union has, if anything, mitigated the effects of globalisation, by promoting cooperation between its member states on issues of social, environmental and consumer protection. If the EU has not done more to embed its vision of the social market economy in the laws and practices of its member states, this is largely due to the influence of the UK. And as our analysis in earlier chapters has shown, it is above all British domestic policies, pursued by successive governments with a more or less neoliberal orientation, which have been responsible for the economic insecurities facing large parts of the population today.

Brexit will do nothing to end Britain's insecurity cycle. On the contrary, it is likely to exacerbate it. In the event of a "hard" Brexit, with Britain leaving the EU with no deal in place, the imposition of tariffs on agricultural goods imported into the UK from mainland Europe will lead to an increase in food prices. These will fall most heavily on the poorest and most vulnerable income groups. It is unlikely that the imposition of tariffs on goods exported from the UK into the mainland will leave British-based manufacturers unaffected, or that UK-based service firms can simply shrug off the loss of access to EU markets which is likely to follow once single market rules on non-discrimination no longer apply. The re-imposition of customs controls will impose significant processing and transaction costs and put at risk transnational supply chains and sectors dependent on just-in-time production. These effects may be offset by a continued fall in the value of sterling; but this cannot be relied upon as many other factors are in play in setting the level of the pound. Currency depreciation adds to the risk of rising food prices and higher inflation more generally, putting further pressure on living standards.

Even if UK producers could, in due course, switch trade away from Europe to rapidly growing overseas markets, this process would take time. It would not be helped by the loss of the more than fifty preferential trade deals which the UK currently has with third countries only as a result of its EU membership. The EU has no free trade agreements with a number of other countries, which include the USA, India and China; thus a hard Brexit would not put Britain at any disadvantage in trading with them. But nor would it help the UK, as following Brexit, it would be in just the same position as the EU-27 when it came to dealing with these nations. The UK's new-found freedom to strike its own trade deals would take time to bear fruit as negotiating bilateral agreements is a lengthy process which, on past experience, can go on for years. But the EU would also be cutting deals with third countries; and it is not obvious that the UK would be better-off going its own way when negotiating with larger and economically more powerful nations.

Thus, the most likely effect of a hard Brexit will be a reduction in the volume of the UK's overseas trade in both goods and services, higher prices for food and other imported goods, and some slowing of production. It is very hard to know what the size of these effects would be; but even the least pessimistic scenarios of forecasting models, such as the Cambridge Centre for Business Research's (CBR) Macro-economic Model of the UK economy (UKMOD), anticipate the need for increases in government expenditure and a loosening of monetary policy to counterbalance the effects of a slowdown in economic growth (Gudgin *et al.* 2017). There would have to be a major shift in government policy away from the current focus on austerity and fiscal "neutrality" for this to happen. A left-wing government, unfettered by commitments to maintain austerity, would be in a position to take the necessary steps to counter the negative effects of Brexit – although it could also avoid some of these effects by opting for a "softer" form of Brexit involving continued participation in the single market or its near equivalent, which in the winter of 2017-18 was the Labour opposition's publicly stated policy.

Hard Brexit could lead to a more radical alternative. This is the option of unilateral free trade associated with Economists for Brexit and the Institute of Free Trade.[11] According to this scenario, once free of the EU, the UK would simply abolish all tariffs on incoming goods. For the reasons we discussed earlier, this move would almost certainly not be reciprocated. But that wouldn't matter: according to the proponents of tariff abolition, British industry, once fully exposed to the winds of international competition, would be stimulated to raise its game, finally achieving the productivity break-through which has eluded policy makers for most of the past century.

This result cannot be ruled out. But for such a fundamental transition to be seamless would be unprecedented for any industrial nation. Such a strategy is more likely to involve huge and disruptive change for most of the working population. It would be an extreme form of the "creative destruction" which Schumpeter (1942) argued was fundamental to capitalist innovation. But in the short term, it could only intensify the conditions of uncertainty and insecurity which drove the Brexit vote in the first place.

Yet it may also fail to bring any long-term benefits. The assumption that tariff abolition will lead to one-off productivity gains is simply that – an *assumption*. It is part of a dogmatic belief that free market competition cures all ills. It would be the British equivalent of "shock therapy" of the kind inflicted on post-socialist countries in the aftermath of the fall of the Berlin Wall. In its more extreme forms, as in the countries of the former Soviet Union, this led to deindustrialisation, population decline and huge concentrations of wealth and power. Even at its most benign, as in the countries of central and eastern Europe which had the benefit of EU membership during much of their transition, it has produced rising inequality, social fragmentation and the rise of authoritarian politics.

In short, unilateral free trade is a huge gamble, which means that no British government is likely to take it unless all other options have failed. But it does at least have the merit of being a coherent response to Brexit, in the sense of taking full advantage of the opportunities it offers for a realignment of economic policy. None of the other post-Brexit options is even coherent.

As we have seen, a "hard" Brexit without tariff abolition will still lead to the loss of frictionless trade, not just with the EU but with numerous third countries; and is likely to be accompanied by a lengthy period of reduced growth as firms deal with rising costs and households deal with falling incomes. It is hard to see how a policy of diminishing trade while increasing costs can be sold as a basis for the country's economic revival, yet alone improved social cohesion.

What then of the prospects for a "soft" Brexit? If this means continuing to participate in the European Economic Area (EEA), the UK will retain single market access at the cost of ceding control over large parts of its regulatory policy to the EU-27. If the UK is part of the EEA, it might as well be in the EU, where it can at least have some influence over decision-making. For this reason, EEA participation is not a plausible long-term option. It could be one means of delivering a post-Brexit "transition period" as the economy adjusts to a new trading regime. Perhaps less plausibly, it could lead to a decision to rejoin the Union at some future point. How this might be brought about can only be a matter of speculation at this point. But it is unlikely that the UK would be able to negotiate the opt-outs, for example, on membership of the single currency, which it currently has.

If it does not go down the EEA route in the longer term, the UK will most likely end up with a trade agreement with the EU along the lines of the EU–Canada Comprehensive Free Trade Agreement (CETA). This would enable it to repatriate regulatory decision-making, at the cost of losing the benefit of the single market's rules on non-discrimination. The exact nature of this trade-off can only be guessed at for the time being. But the essential point to bear in mind is that *it will be a trade-off*: a CETA-style deal will not give British-based service firms, including, critically, those based in the City, their current level of access to mainland European markets. Moreover, it remains to be seen how long it will take for the UK to negotiate a free trade agreement with the EU, or with third countries for that matter. In the interim (which could be a decade or more), the basis for its foreign trade relations will be at best unclear – and at worst chaotic.

So there are essentially no good options with Brexit. Of course, some groups will benefit from it, including policy "entrepreneurs" from free market think tanks, media and technology firms intent on undermining the EU's antitrust policies, hedge funds expert in speculating on extreme economic events, and foreign interests hostile to the European project. Some of these appear to have been involved in funding the Leave campaign, the financing of which remains opaque (Hellier 2015; Cadwallader 2017). For Britain's political class, the benefits of Brexit are much more uncertain. For a while, Brexit was a cause which could be used – however misleadingly – to shift the blame for the multiple insecurities associated with forty years of neoliberalism. But as it becomes increasingly clear that Brexit cannot be made to work, support for it even here is starting to drain away. If this continues, Brexit will be abandoned or – an outcome which is distinctly possible but likely to please no-one – implemented in name only.

Brexit highlights the insecurities caused by neoliberal policies, but provides no solution to them. Without the 2016 referendum, social and economic policy would still have reached a turning point. Brexit accelerates that process and throws the policy choices facing the country into sharp relief. Whatever form it eventually takes, Brexit has broken the neoliberal consensus.

Conclusions

The financial sector's continued pursuit of ever more creative ways of channelling credit to those with less than perfect credit profiles suggests that the inequality gap is both limiting consumers' ability to consume and forcing them into debt. The logical policy response should therefore include an ambitious and forward-looking industrial strategy aimed at generating improvements in employment, wage and income security – and in the process, a reduced reliance on debt. But widening inequality has implications for more than the financial sector's contribution to a possible future crisis; in addition to the consequences of the low-paid, often insecure, work available to many – not infrequently accompanied by sub-standard rented accommodation – an increasing number of UK residents are also being forced into using food banks, further ratcheting up a sense of crisis.

Building an economy based on the consumption of largely foreign-made products – often paid for with foreign-sourced debt – makes little sense in itself. But with limited (if any) wage growth for the vast majority of the UK's labour force, sooner or later, there will be no more capacity to take on additional debt to fund further consumption, with obvious effects on GDP growth. The knock-on effects of this on the insecurity cycle – particularly with regard to crisis and democratic upsurge – could clearly be significant.

In light of the large numbers of people whose lives are blighted by the forces described above, is not difficult to understand the enthusiastic and growing support for both Jeremy Corbyn's vision of society and politics and the newly revived Labour Party. However, the policies that have created – and sustain – Britain's low-wage, insecure, consumption-based economy for most, are at least for the present, still in place. As a result, it would be reasonable to expect that the numbers of those affected will continue to increase, as in turn, will pressure for change.

The insecurity cycle will undoubtedly shift; the real questions are in which direction and by how much. The situation within British society and its associated economy clearly has pressures which are difficult if not impossible to address under the current economic model. But resistance to change is likely to continue. Brexit will undoubtedly be a popular scapegoat for anything and everything that goes wrong within the British economy, regardless of its actual cause. But with similar difficulties in the US and much of the rest of Europe, the problems clearly run much deeper than the UK's relationship with the European Union – and may well require a solution with a larger footprint than either.

Whilst many of the undesirable social developments discussed earlier will be entirely unacceptable to many, historically, there have also been powerful segments of society having no problem with them at all. This is especially true in cases where any change might adversely impact their own personal or financial interests. Thus, fundamental change is likely to meet resistance from those interest groups who benefit most from maintaining the status quo. Whether the next shift in the insecurity cycle will take place within the existing paradigm – or result in a decisive change of that paradigm – largely depends upon what happens next – as well as when it happens. What will be the deciding factor? In all likelihood, as Harold Macmillan may (or may not) have observed, it will be "events, dear boy – events".

However, at the time of writing, there are also signs which might suggest that things are not necessarily doomed to deteriorate still further before the insecurity cycle moves the British socio-economic system towards a more equitable position. The Labour Party's performance in the 2017 general election clearly demonstrates that there is far more political backing for Jeremy Corbyn's "new kind of politics" than many had hitherto supposed; even a number of those who had previously ruled out the idea of serving in a

Corbyn cabinet – notably the former Party leader, Ed Miliband – have since abruptly changed their minds (Merrick 2017). It is also worth noting that Winston Churchill had not considered Clement Attlee's Labour Party to be a significant threat in the run up to the 1945 general election. Churchill's subsequent defeat swiftly gave birth to the Keynesian consensus that ultimately delivered the most radical improvements in social and economic security and equality Britain has seen – so far.

It is also significant that it is not just the Labour Party feeling the need to distance itself from neoliberal policy. As with the Liberal Party during the years before the First World War, there is also evidence of a faction within the current Conservative Party which perceives these policies as being both electorally and socially risky. The Conservative Party's 2017 general election manifesto went so far as to state: "We do not believe in untrammelled free markets. We reject the cult of selfish individualism. We abhor social division, injustice, unfairness, and inequality" (Conservative Party Manifesto 2017, p. 9). The Conservatives also promised "not only to guarantee but enhance workers' rights and protections", insisted that "the government's agenda will not be allowed to drift to the right" (ibid., p. 7), and asserted the need for "a state that is strong and strategic" (ibid., p. 8).

But unfortunately, rather than producing legislation reminiscent of the spirit of the Liberal social reforms, the reputed author of these words – the prime ministerial aide, Nick Timothy – was instead sacked, apparently as a scapegoat for the loss of the Conservative's majority. The resulting minority government has so far failed to propose any concrete measures which might "enhance" workers' rights; and Theresa May has recently – in direct contradiction of her own manifesto – delivered a speech in direct support of free market capitalism. Many others within the Conservative Party remain completely comfortable with "libertarian" – that is, deregulatory – solutions to Britain's social and economic problems, seeing Brexit as a means to this end. And any opposing faction, even if it were of significant size, still lacks the support of credible statesmen, such as Lloyd George and Winston Churchill, who saw the Liberal social reforms of the early twentieth century into law, often against significant opposition from within their own party as well as elsewhere.

Nonetheless, the Liberal social reforms were still not enough to satisfy the increasingly organised and empowered interest groups that would ultimately create a new political force – the Labour Party. In the same way that many of those supporting this new movement distrusted the Lib-Lab pact and the compromises it forced upon the first Labour MPs, it seems more than likely that those passages in the Conservative manifesto intended to woo Labour voters, failed to win their trust. Instead, the surge of support for Jeremy Corbyn's revitalised Labour Party appears to be – as with the original Labour Party during the nineteenth and early twentieth centuries – rooted in a strong grass roots movement, rather than a response to a Westminster soundbite; there is, for example, no obvious Conservative Party equivalent to Momentum. Also, as in the inter-war years, the Labour Party appears to be facing divided opposition. During the earlier period, the result was the effective demise of the split Liberal Party and the sharp polarisation of politics – a situation which has some resonance with the present.

This then means that three of the four necessary preconditions for a shift in the insecurity cycle are now in place – democratic pressure, political support and different, if not (so far) new ideas. Much of this has resulted from the experience of key interest groups – notably labour and the re-emergent poor – during the past almost four decades of free market capitalism; in other words – from their point of view at least – a chronic crisis. What appears to be missing at present is either an acute crisis, capable of breaking the neoliberal consensus, or possibly a strong political conviction that the direction of policy needs to radically change.

Whilst, historically, change has usually involved an acute crisis, there is some evidence that a more voluntary policy re-think might now be possible. The current chronic crisis has produced cracks in neoliberal confidence. Although the 2017 Conservative Party manifesto clearly failed to convince the electorate, its inclusion of policy directions that at least appear to repudiate the neoliberal consensus suggests a recognition that deeper changes may indeed already be underway, with the tenets of free market economics no longer being taken entirely for granted in policy-making circles.

In Britain, this is partly the result of successive evidence-based reports by influential organisations – ranging from the International Red Cross, Oxfam, Church Action on Poverty, Joseph Rowntree Foundation, Trussell Trust, Resolution Foundation and Young Women's Trust to the Bank of England, Office of National Statistics and World Economic Forum. These not only document the extent of social and economic deprivation and the systemic factors driving it but also the adverse consequences of these developments for both social cohesion and stability and macroeconomic performance. As before, when the insecurity cycle has shifted towards greater social protectionism, there is growing recognition that poverty and unemployment are not the fault of their victims.

Internationally, even components of the neoliberal "life support" system appear to have their doubts. The International Monetary Fund (IMF), hitherto an unswerving supporter of both neoliberalism and austerity, has recently produced reports questioning their longer-term effects on both the economy and society. The IMF's acknowledgement that inequality has damaging effects on macroeconomic performance – and that GDP growth is not only stronger, but crucially, also far more sustainable, when the fruits of that growth are significantly more evenly distributed than they are at present – also support the idea that a re-evaluation of the economy and its relationship with society is long overdue.

Ways by which this re-evaluation might be accomplished could well emerge from the recently revitalised movement for economic pluralism and developments in economics education, including shifts in both formal programmes of study and the development of open-access platforms reaching-out to a wider public audience. Alongside education, another potentially influential development is the emergence of organisations like the Progressive Economic Group (PEG) as a forum for policy innovation. Like Momentum, PEG has bypassed traditional routes and processes; and as a result, it is far more difficult for evolved neoliberal structures to smother. But unlike Momentum, PEG is not aligned with any one political party, but instead offers new, problem-centred policy ideas to any who wish to develop and implement them.

Perhaps the most encouraging aspect of the workings of the insecurity cycle is that whilst smaller movements within the existing policy paradigm often seem to have been hard fought, taking significant time to achieve, both of the complete shifts that the cycle has experienced to date have, by comparison, occurred almost overnight. Free market libertarianism has once again clearly demonstrated that it consistently produces unbalanced and unsustainable socio-economic conditions; it was ultimately these conditions that gave rise to a much fairer, cohesive and, above all, more workable structure under Clement Attlee and the governments of the Keynesian consensus that followed. The next turn of the insecurity cycle still has the potential to deliver such outcomes.

Notes

1 For further elaboration and information, see https://peg.primeeconomics.org.
2 See Tribe (2008) for a further discussion.
3 See, for example, Konzelmann *et al.* (2017); and Konzelmann and Wilkinson (2016).
4 See, for example, Hicks (1937); Harrod (1937); and Meade (1937).
5 For further information, see www.core-econ.org/about/.
6 See, for example, De Nardi (2015) for a survey of work in this area.
7 See, for example Baxter (1869) and Giffen (1913) for early contributions and Atkinson and Harrison (1978) for a survey of this literature.
8 The Family Resources Survey, for example, contains questions about liquid wealth; and the British Household Panel Survey contains questions about housing wealth, with questions about liquid wealth being included in 1995, 2000 and 2005 and pension wealth in 2001 and 2005 (Crossley and O'Dea 2010; Emmerson and Wakefield 2009).
9 For further elaboration, see Chapter 6.
10 For a further discussion, see Chapters 8 and 9.
11 For further elaboration, see Chapter 10.

References

Abbas, Ali, Nazim Belhocine, Asmaa ElGanainy and Mark Horton (2010) *A Historical Public Debt Database*. IMF Working Paper wp/10/245. Washington, DC: International Monetary Fund. [Online]. Available at: www.imf.org/en/Publications/WP/Issues/2016/12/31/A-Historical-Public-Debt-Database-24332 (Accessed: 30 October 2017).

Abbas, M. and A. Croft (2011) "Cameron denies austerity drive caused UK riots". *Reuters*. 11 August. [Online]. Available at: www.reuters.com/article/2011/08/11/us-britain-riot-idUSTRE7760G820110811 (Accessed: 30 October 2017).

Abdelal, R. and J. Ruggie (2009) "The principles of embedded liberalism: social legitimacy and global capitalism", in D. Moss and J. Cisternino (eds) *New Perspectives on Regulation*. Cambridge, MA: The Tobin Project, pp. 151–62. [Online]. Available at: www.tobinproject.org/sites/tobinproject.org/files/assets/New_Perspectives_Ch7_Abdelal_Ruggie.pdf (Accessed: 30 October 2017).

Abel-Smith, Brian and Peter Townsend (1965) *The Poor and the Poorest: A New Analysis of the Ministry of Labour's Family Expenditure Surveys of 1953–4 and 1960*. Occasional Papers on Social Administration No. 17. London: G. Bell and Sons.

Adams, W.S. (1953) "Lloyd George and the labour movement". *Past and Present* 0(3): 55–64.

Adams, Zoe and Simon Deakin (2014a) *Re-regulating Zero Hours Contracts*. Liverpool: Institute of Employment Rights.

Adams, Zoe and Simon Deakin (2014b) "Institutional solutions to inequality and precariousness in labour markets". *British Journal of Industrial Relations* 53: 779–809.

Adams, Zoe and Simon Deakin (2016) "Article 4: the right to a fair remuneration", in N. Bruun, K. Lörcher, I. Schömann and S. Clauwaert (eds) *The European Social Charter and the Employment Relation*. Oxford: Hart.

Addison, Paul (1994) *The Road to 1945: British Politics and the Second World War*. London: Pimlico.

AER (1992) "A plea for pluralistic and rigorous economics". *American Economic Review* 89(2): xxv.

Ahlering, B. and S. Deakin (2007) "Labour regulation, corporate governance and legal origin: a case of institutional complementarity?" *Law & Society Review* 41: 865–908.

Allen, Katie (2014) "Accounting for drugs and prostitution to help push UK economy up by £65bn". *The Guardian*. 10 June. [Online]. Available at: www.theguardian.com/business/2014/jun/10/accounting-drugs-prostitution-uk-economy-gdp-eu-rules (Accessed: 30 October 2017).

All-Party Parliamentary Group (2014) *Feeding Britain: A Strategy for Zero Hunger in England, Wales, Scotland and Northern Ireland.* London: The Children's Society. [Online]. Available at: https://foodpovertyinquiry.files.wordpress.com/2014/12/food-poverty-feeding-britain-final.pdf (Accessed: 30 October 2017).

Alvaredo, Facundo, Anthony Atkinson and Salvatore Morelli (2016) "The challenge of measuring UK wealth inequality in the 2000s". *Fiscal Studies* 37(1): 13–33. [Online]. Available at: http://onlinelibrary.wiley.com/doi/10.1111/j.1475-5890.2016.12084/epdf (Accessed: 30 October 2017).

Archbishop of Canterbury (1985) *Faith in the City: The Archbishop of Canterbury's Commission on Urban Priority Areas.* London: Church House Publishing. [Online]. Available at: www.churchofengland.org/media/55076/faithinthecity.pdf (Accessed: 30 October 2017).

Armingeon, K. and L. Baccaro (2012) "Political economy of the sovereign debt crisis: the limits of internal devaluation". *Industrial Law Journal* 41: 254–75.

Armour, J., H. Hansmann, R. Kraakman and M. Pargendler (2017) "What is corporate law?", in R. Kraakman *et al.* (eds) *The Anatomy of Corporate Law* (3rd edn) Oxford: Oxford University Press, pp. 1–34.

Atkinson, Anthony (1991) "Keynes Lecture in Economics: what is happening to the distribution of income in the UK?" *Proceedings of the British Academy* 82: 317–51.

Atkinson, Anthony (2015) *Inequality: What Can Be Done About It?* Cambridge, MA: Harvard University Press.

Atkinson, Anthony and A.J. Harrison (1978) *Distribution of Personal Wealth in Britain.* Cambridge: Cambridge University Press.

Azoulai, L. and R. Dehousse (2012) "The European Court of Justice and legal dynamics of integration", in E. Jones, A. Menon and S. Weatherill (eds) *The Oxford Handbook of the European Union.* Oxford: Oxford University Press, pp. 350–64.

Baker, Andy (1989) *The Cairo Parliament, 1943–44.* Leigh-on-Sea, Essex: Partizan Press.

Baker, A. (2015) "Varieties of economic crisis, varieties of ideational change: how and why financial regulation and macroeconomic policy differ". *New Political Economy* 20(3): 342–66.

Bale, Tim, Monica Polletti and Paul Webb (2016) "What we know about Labour's £3 supporters – and whether they'll help Jeremy Corbyn again". *The New Statesman.* [Online]. Available at: www.newstatesman.com/politics/staggers/2016/07/what-we-know-about-labours-3-supporters-and-whether-theyll-help-jeremy (Accessed: 30 October 2017).

Barker, Derek (2013) "The Manningham Mills Strike, 1890–91: 'low wages, good water and no unions'". *Northern History* 50(1): 93–114.

Barnard, Catherine (2009) "'British jobs for British workers': the Lindsey oil refinery dispute and the future of local labour clauses in an integrated EU market" *Industrial Law Journal* 38(3): 245–77.

Barnard, C. (2012) *EU Employment Law* (4th edn). Oxford: Oxford University Press.

Barnard, C. (2013) *The Substantive Law of the EU: The Four Freedoms* (4th edn). Oxford: Oxford University Press.

Barnard, C. and S. Deakin (2012) "Social policy and labour market regulation", in E. Jones, A. Menon and S. Weatherill (eds) *The Oxford Handbook of the European Union.* Oxford: Oxford University Press, pp. 542–55.

Barnard, C., S. Deakin and R. Hobbs (2003) "Opting out of the 48-hour week: employer necessity or individual choice? An empirical study of the operation of Article 18(1)(b) of the Working Time Directive in the United Kingdom". *Industrial Law Journal* 32: 223–52.

Barnes, James Strachey (1929) *Universal Aspects of Fascism*. London: Williams & Norgate.

Bartels, L. (2016) *The UK's Status in the WTO after Brexit*. Faculty of Law, University of Cambridge, Working Paper. [Online]. Available at: https://ssrn.com/abstract=2841747 (Accessed: 30 October 2017).

Bartlett, C.J. (1972) *The Long Retreat*. London: Macmillan.

Baxter, R.D. (1869) *The Taxation of the United Kingdom*. London: Macmillan.

BBC (1999) *The Mayfair Set*, produced by Adam Curtis. Available at: www.youtube.com/playlist?list=PLFE72F513E549B5DD (Accessed: 30 October 2017).

BBC (2011) "Keynes v Hayek: two economic giants go head to head". *BBC News*. 3 August. [Online]. Available at: www.bbc.co.uk/news/business-14366054 (Accessed: 30 October 2017).

BBC (2013) "Red Cross launches food aid campaign". *BBC News*. 11 October. [Online]. Available at: www.bbc.co.uk/news/uk-24487146 (Accessed: 30 October 2017).

BBC (2015a) "Political opinion polls since May 2012". *BBC News*. 20 January. [Online]. Available at: www.bbc.co.uk/news/uk-politics-27330849 (Accessed: 30 October 2017).

BBC (2015b) "Third of UK population 'fell below the poverty line'". *BBC News*. 20 May. [Online]. Available at: www.bbc.co.uk/news/uk-32812601 (Accessed: 30 October 2017).

BBC (2016) "Economic rebellion". *The World of Business*. 31 March. [Online podcast]. Available at: https://itunes.apple.com/gb/podcast/the-world-of-business/id73330642?mt=2 (Accessed: 30 October 2017).

BBC (2017a) "Brexit: Article 50 has been triggered – what now?". *BBC News*. 29 March. [Online]. Available at: www.bbc.co.uk/news/uk-politics-39143978 (Accessed: 30 October 2017).

BBC (2017b) "Uber loses its licence to operate in London". *BBC News*. 22 September. [Online]. Available at: www.bbc.co.uk/news/uk-england-41358640?intlink_from_url=www.bbc.co.uk/news/live/uk-england-london-41135743 (Accessed: 30 October 2017).

Beaver, Patrick (1985) *The Match Makers: The Story of Bryant & May*. London: Henry Melland.

Beath, J. (2002) "UK industrial policy: old tunes on new instruments?" *Oxford Review of Economic Policy* 18(2): 221–39.

Becht, M., C. Mayer and H. Wagner (2008) "Where do firms incorporate? Deregulation and the cost of entry". *Journal of Applied Corporate Finance* 14: 241–56.

Beckett, Andy (2002) "Blueprint for Britain". *Guardian*. 4 May, p. 17.

Beckett, Andy (2003) *Pinochet in Piccadilly: Britain and Chile's Hidden History*. London: Faber and Faber.

Behling, Felix and Mark Harvey (2015) "The evolution of false self-employment in the British construction industry: a neo-Polanyian account of labour market formation". *Work, Employment and Society* 29: 969–88.

BEIS (2017) *Trade Union Membership 2016: Statistical Bulletin*. London: Department of Business, Energy and Industrial Strategy.

Béland, D. (2005) "Ideas and social policy: an institutionalist perspective". *Social Policy & Administration* 39(1): 1–18.

Bell, Torsten (2016) "Theresa May wants to help 'just managing' families? Start with the 14p stealth tax". *New Statesman*. 30 September. [Online]. Available at: www.

newstatesman.com/politics/staggers/2016/09/theresa-may-wants-help-just-managing-families-start-14p-stealth-tax (Accessed: 30 October 2017).

Bellofiore, R. and J. Halevi (2011) "A Minsky moment? The subprime crisis and the new capitalism", in C. Gnos and L. Rachon (eds) *Credit, Money and the New Capitalism*. Cheltenham: Edward Elgar, pp. 13–32.

Benhold, Katrin (2017) "London's streets, black cabs and Uber fight for a future". *New York Times*. 4 July. [Online]. Available at: www.nytimes.com/2017/07/04/world/europe/london-uk-brexit-uber-taxi.html (Accessed: 30 October 2017).

Bennett, Gill (1999) *"A Most Extraordinary and Mysterious Business": The Zinoviev Letter of 1924*. Historians, LRD History Note No. 14. London: Foreign and Commonwealth Office, February.

Berg, Andrew and Jonathan Ostry (2011) "Equality and efficiency: is there a trade-off between the two or do they go hand-in-hand?" *Finance and Development*. September, pp. 12–15. [Online]. Available at: www.imf.org/external/pubs/ft/sdn/2011/sdn1108.pdf (Accessed: 30 October 2017).

Berman, S. (1998) *The Social Democratic Movement*. Cambridge, MA: Harvard University Press.

Bernanke, Ben (2004) "The great moderation". Meetings of the Eastern Economic Association: Washington, DC, 20 February. [Online]. Available at: www.federalreserve.gov/boarddocs/speeches/2004/20040220/default.htm (Accessed: 30 October 2017).

Beveridge, William (1942) *Social Insurance and Allied Services*. Cmnd. 6404.

Beveridge, W. (1944) *Full Employment in a Free Society*. London: Liberal Publications Department.

Bingham, T. (2010) *The Rule of Law*. London: Penguin.

Black, Joseph, Leonard Conolly, Kate Flint, Isobel Grundy, Don LePan, Roy Liuzza, Jerome McGann, Anne Prescott, Barry Qualls and Claire Waters (2015) *The Broadview Anthology of British Literature*. London: Broadview Press.

Blanchard, O. (1987) "Neoclassical synthesis", in John Eatwell, Murray Milgate and Peter Newman (eds) *Palgrave Dictionary of Economics*, Volume 3. London: Palgrave MacMillan, pp. 634–6.

Blanchard, O., G. Dell Ariccia and P. Mauro (2010) *Rethinking Macroeconomic Policy*. IMF Staff Position Note SPN 10/03. 12 February. [Online]. Available at: www.imf.org/external/pubs/ft/spn/2010/spn1003.pdf (Accessed: 30 October 2017).

Bluestone, Barry and Bennett Harrison (1982) *The De-industrialization of America*. New York: Basic Books.

Blundell, John (2003) *Waging the War of Ideas*. London: Institute of Economic Affairs.

Blundell, John (2013) "Lady Thatcher and the IEA". *Centre for Policy Studies Blog*. London: Centre for Policy Studies. [Online]. Available at: www.cps.org.uk/blog/Lady-Thatcher-and the-IEA (Accessed: 30 October 2017).

Blyth, Mark (1997) "Any more bright ideas? The ideational turn of comparative political economy". *Comparative Politics* 29(2): 229–50.

Blyth, Mark (2002) *Great Transformations: Economic Ideas and Institutional Change in the Twentieth Century*. Cambridge: Cambridge University Press.

Blyth, Mark (2013) "Paradigms and paradox: the politics of economic ideas in two moments of crisis". *Governance* 26(2): 197–215.

Bogg, A. and Dukes (2017) "Article 11 ECHR and the right to collective bargaining: *Pharmacists Defence Association Union v Boots Management Services Ltd.*". *Industrial Law Journal* (forthcoming).

Booth, Charles (1893–1903) *Life and Labour of the People in London* (17 volumes). London: Macmillan. [Online]. Available at: https://openlibrary.org/works/OL5152881W/Life_and_labour_of_the_people_in_London (Accessed: 30 October 2017).

Bootle, R. (2017) *Making a Success of Brexit and Reforming the EU*. London: Brealey.

Bord, V. and J. Santos (2012) "The rise of the originate to distribute model and the role of banks in financial intermediation". *Federal Reserve Bank of New York Economic Policy Review*. July, pp. 21–34. [Online]. Available at: www.newyorkfed.org/research/epr/12v18n2/1207bord.pdf (Accessed: 30 October 2017).

Borth, Christy (1945) *Masters of Mass Production*. Indianapolis, IN: Bobbs-Merrill Company.

Bourne, Ryan (2013) "Lady Thatcher's relationship with Friedrich Hayek and Milton Friedman". *Pieria*. 10 April. [Online]. Available at: www.pieria.co.uk/articles/lady_thatchers_relationship_with_friedrich_hayek_and_milton_friedman (Accessed: 30 October 2017).

Bourne, Ryan (2017) "Brexit is the start, not the end, of the process". London: Institute for Free Trade. [Online]. Available at: http://ifreetrade.org/article/brexit_is_the_start_not_the_end_of_the_process (Accessed: 30 October 2017).

Boyer, George (1988) "What did unions do in nineteenth century Britain?" *Journal of Economic History* 48(2): 319–32.

Braun, B. (2015) "Preparedness, crisis management and policy change: the Euro area at the critical juncture of 2008–2013". *British Journal of Politics and International Relations* 17(3): 419–41.

Brewer, M., T. Clark and A. Goodman (2002) *The Government's Child Poverty Target*. Commentary 88. London: Institute for Fiscal Studies.

Briggs, Asa (1961) *Social Thought and Social Action: A Study of the Work of Seebohm Rowntree, 1871–1954*. London: Longmans.

Briggs, Asa (2014 [1959]) *The Age of Improvement, 1783–1867* (2nd edn). London: Routledge.

Briggs, Daniel (2012) *The English Riots of 2011: A Summer of Discontent*. Hook, Hampshire: Waterside Press.

Bronstein, Jamie and Andrew Harris (2012) *Empire, State and Society: Britain Since 1830*. Oxford: Wiley-Blackwell.

Brown, Gordon (1999) "The conditions for full employment". *Mais Lecture*. City University London, 9 October. [Online]. Available at: http://webarchive.national archives.gov.uk/20100407174407/www.hm-treasury.gov.uk/speech_chex_191099.htm (Accessed: 30 October 2017).

Bruun, N., K. Lörcher, I. Shömann and S. Clauwaert (eds) (2017) *The European Social Charter and the Employment Relation*. Oxford: Hart.

Buckler, S. and D. Dolowitz (2004) "Can fair be efficient? New Labour, social liberalism and British economic policy". *New Political Economy* 9(1) (March): 23–38.

Bulmer, S. and K. Armstrong (1998) *The Governance of the European Single Market*. Manchester: Manchester University Press.

Burke, Michael (2013) "Companies are hoarding cash: that's why growth is so slow". *Guardian*. 27 October. [Online]. Available at: www.theguardian.com/commentis-free/2013/oct/27/companies-hoarding-cash-slow-growth (Accessed: 30 October 2017).

Burn, G. (1999) "The state, the city and the Euromarkets". *Review of International Political Economy* 6: 225–61.

Burn, G. (2006) *The Re-Emergence of Global Finance*. Basingstoke: Palgrave Macmillan.

Burnell, Emma (2014) "Just how red is Ed Miliband?" *Guardian*. 16 December. [Online]. Available at: www.theguardian.com/commentisfree/2014/dec/16/miliband-red-ed-john-prescott-labour-leader (Accessed: 30 October 2017).

Burnett, John (1994) *Idle Hands: The Experience of Unemployment 1790–1990*. London: Routledge.

Burn-Murdoch, John, Martin Stabe and Anna Leach (2017) "UK general election 2017 poll tracker". *Financial Times*. 20 August. [Online]. Available at: https://ig.ft.com/elections/uk/2017/polls/ (Accessed: 30 October 2017).

Burns, C. and N. Carter (2012) "Environmental policy", in E. Jones, A. Menon and S. Weatherill (eds) *The Oxford Handbook of the European Union*. Oxford: Oxford University Press, pp. 511–25.

Byron, George Noel Gordon (1844) *The Life, Letters and Journals of Lord Byron*. London: John Murray.

Cadwallader, Carole (2017) "The Great British Brexit robbery: how our democracy was hijacked". *The Observer*. 7 May. [Online]. Available at: www.theguardian.com/technology/2017/may/07/the-great-british-brexit-robbery-hijacked-democracy (Accessed: 30 October 2017).

Cain, C.P. and A.G. Hopkins (1993) *British Imperialism: Crisis and Deconstruction, 1914–1990*. Harlow: Longman.

Cairncross, Alec (1985) *Years of Recovery: British Economic Policy, 1945–1951*. New York: Methuen.

Callaghan, James (1976) *Leader's Speech*. Labour Party Conference, Blackpool. [Online]. Available at: www.britishpoliticalspeech.org/speech-archive.htm?speech=174 (Accessed: 30 October 2017).

Cambridge 27, The (2001) "Opening up economics". *Post-Autistic Economics Newsletter* 7, July, Article 1. [Online]. Available at: www.paecon.net/PAEtexts/Cambridge27.htm (Accessed: 30 October 2017).

Cameron, David (2006a) *Scarman Lecture*. 24 November. [Online]. Available at: http://conservative-speeches.sayit.mysociety.org/speech/599937 (Accessed: 30 October 2017).

Cameron, David (2006b) *Leader's Speech*. Conservative Party Conference, Bournemouth, 4 October. [Online]. Available at: www.britishpoliticalspeech.org/speech-archive.htm?speech=314 (Accessed: 30 October 2017).

Cameron, David (2011) "London riots: Prime Minister's statement in full". *Telegraph*. 11 August. [Online]. Available at: www.telegraph.co.uk/news/uknews/crime/8691034/London-riots-Prime-Ministers-statement-in-full.html (Accessed: 30 October 2017).

Cameron, David (2013) *EU Speech at Bloomberg*. 23 January. [Online]. Available at: www.gov.uk/government/speeches/eu-speech-at-bloomberg (Accessed: 30 October 2017).

Cappelletti, M., M. Seccombe and J. Weiler (eds) (1986) *Integration through Law: Europe and the American Federal Experience*. Berlin: de Gruyter.

Carlin, Wendy and David Soskice (1990) *Macroeconomics and the Wage Bargain: A Modern Approach to Employment, Inflation and the Exchange Rate*. Oxford: Oxford University Press.

Carswell, Douglas and Hannan, Daniel (2008) *The Plan: Twelve Months to Renew Britain* (London: Lulu.com).

"Cato" (1940) *Guilty Men*. London: Faber & Faber.

Charlton, John (1999) *"It Just Went Like Tinder": The Mass Movement and New Unionism in Britain 1889*. London: Redwords.

Chase, Malcolm (2007) *Chartism: A New History*. Manchester: Manchester University Press.

Cheffins, B. (2008) *Corporate Ownership and Control: British Business Transformed.* Oxford: Oxford University Press.

Chen, D. and S. Deakin (2014) "On heaven's lathe: state, rule of law, and economic development". *Law and Development Review* 8: 123–45.

Chesshyre, Robert (1975) "Willie kisses rival Maggie by the sea". *Observer.* 9 February. [Online]. Available at: www.margaretthatcher.org/document/102484 (Accessed: 30 October 2017).

Chick, Martin (1998) *Industrial Policy in Britain, 1945–1951: Economic Planning, Nationalisation and the Labour Governments.* Cambridge: Cambridge University Press.

Chick, Victoria, Ann Pettifor and Geoff Tily (2016) *The Economic Consequences of Mr Osborne, Fiscal Consolidation: Lessons from a Century of UK Macroeconomic Statistics.* London: Policy Research in Macroeconomics (PRIME). [Online]. Available at: http://static1.squarespace.com/static/541ff5f5e4b02b7c37f31ed6/t/56ec 3ccaa3360 c829bb2a001/1458322639033/The+Economic+Consequences+of+Mr+Osborne +2016+final+v2.pdf (Accessed: 30 October 2017).

Chinn, Carl (1995) *Poverty amidst Prosperity: The Urban Poor in England, 1834–1914.* Manchester: Manchester University Press.

Churchill, Winston (1929) "Disposal of the surplus". *Commons Sitting of 15 April 1929,* Series 5, Vol. 227 (Hansard). [Online]. Available at: http://hansard.millbanksystems.com/commons/1929/apr/15/disposal-of-surplus (Accessed: 30 October 2017).

Clark, George (1961) *The Seventeenth Century.* Oxford: Oxford University Press.

Clark, Kevin and David Primo (2012) "Overcoming physics envy". *New York Times.* 30 March. [Online]. Available at: www.nytimes.com/2012/04/01/opinion/sunday/the-social-sciences-physics-envy.html?mcubz=0 (Accessed: 30 October 2017).

Clark, Timothy (2017) "Rethinking the 'Chicago Boys': neoliberal technocrats or revolutionary vanguard?". *Third World Quarterly* 38(6): 1350–65.

Clarke, Anna, Charlotte Hamilton, Michael Jones and Kathryn Muir (2017) *Poverty, Evictions and Forced Moves.* York: Joseph Rowntree Foundation. [Online]. Available at: www.jrf.org.uk/report/poverty-evictions-and-forced-moves?gclid=Cj0KCQjw sNfOBRCWARIsAGITapbPP_jy0i4osCvKMkNm3_b2OBfdtuO1AeGa8Q-L0YjNPEQlG7RFPjEIaAunHEALw_wcB (Accessed: 30 October 2017).

Clarke, K. (2011) "Punish the feral rioters, but address our social deficit, too". *Guardian.* 5 September. [Online]. Available at: www.guardian.co.uk/commentis-free/2011/sep/05/punishment-rioters-help (Accessed: 30 October 2017).

Clinton, Alan (1977) *The Trade Union Rank and File: Trades Councils in Britain, 1900–1940.* Manchester: Rowman and Littlefield.

Coalition, The (2010) *Our Programme for Government.* London: Cabinet Office. [Online]. Available at: www.gov.uk/government/publications/the-coalition-our-programme-for-government (Accessed: 30 October 2017).

Cockett, R. (1995) *Thinking the Unthinkable: Think Tanks and the Economic Counter-revolution, 1931–1983.* London: Fontana Press.

Cohen, E.S. (2012) "Legal pluralism, private power, and the impact of the financial crisis on the global political economy". *Oñati Socio-Legal Series* 3(4): 679–701.

Cole, Dorothy and John Utting (1962) *The Economic Circumstances of Old People.* Occasional Papers on Social Administration No. 4. Hertfordshire: The Codicote Press.

Cole, G.D.H. (1948) *A History of the Labour Party from 1914.* London: Routledge and Keegan Paul.

Collins, Doreen (1965) "The introduction of old age pensions in Britain". *Historical Journal* 8: 246–59.

Collins, H. (1992) *Justice in Dismissal*. Oxford: Oxford University Press.

Collins, Ray (2014) "Building a one nation Labour Party: the Collins Review into Labour Party reform". London: The Labour Party. February. [Online]. Available at: http://action.labour.org.uk/page/-/Collins_Report_Party_Reform.pdf (Accessed: 30 October 2017).

Comparative Constitutions Project (2017) "Characteristics of national constitutions". [Dataset]. Available at: http://comparativeconstitutionsproject.org/ (Accessed: 30 October 2017).

Conservative Party Manifesto (2017) *Forward Together: Our Plan for a Stronger Britain and a Prosperous Future. The Conservative and Unionist Party Manifesto.* London: Conservative Party. [Online]. Available at: www.conservatives.com/manifesto (Accessed: 30 October 2017).

Consterdine, E. and J. Hampshire (2013) "Immigration policy under New Labour: exploring a new juncture". *British Politics* 3: 275–96.

Cook, Chris (2005) *The Routledge Companion to Britain in the Nineteenth Century, 1815–1914.* London: Routledge.

Cooper, Niall and Sarah Dumpleton (2013) *Walking the Breadline: The Scandal of Food Poverty in 21st Century Britain.* London: Church Action on Poverty and Oxfam, May. [Online]. Available at: http://policy-practice.oxfam.org.uk/publications/walking-the-breadline-the-scandal-of-food-poverty-in-21st-century-britain-292978 (Accessed: 30 October 2017).

Copeland, Lewis, Lawrence Lamm and Stephen McKenna (eds) (1999) *The World's Great Speeches* (4th edn). Mineola, New York: Dover Publications.

Corbo, Vittorio (1989) *Public Finance, Trade and Development: The Chilean Experience.* Policy, Planning and Research Working Papers, WPS 218, July. Washington, DC: The World Bank. [Online]. Available at: http://documents.worldbank.org/curated/en/663211468769438050/pdf/multi-page.pdf (Accessed: 30 October 2017).

Cosh, A. and A. Hughes (2008) 'Takeovers after takeovers'. Centre for Business Research Working Paper No. 363. Cambridge: University of Cambridge.

Coutts, Ken and Graham Gudgin (2015) "The macroeconomic impact of liberal economic policies in the UK". Cambridge: Centre for Business Research. [Online]. Available at: http://insight.jbs.cam.ac.uk/assets/2015_cbr-report_macroeconomic-impact-of-liberal-policies-in-the-uk.pdf (Accessed: 30 October 2017).

Coutts, Ken, Roger Tarling and Frank Wilkinson (1976) "Wage bargaining and the inflation process". *Economic Policy Review* 2, March.

Crace, John (2017) "The making of the Maybot: a year of mindless slogans, U-turns and denials". *Guardian*. 10 July. [Online]. Available at: www.theguardian.com/politics/2017/jul/10/making-maybot-theresa-may-rise-and-fall (Accessed: 30 October 2017).

Crawford, Rowena, David Innes and Cormac O'Dea (2016) "Household wealth in Great Britain: distribution, composition and changes 2006–12". *Fiscal Studies* 37(1): 35–54.

Cronin, James (1987) "Strikes and power in Britain, 1870–1920". *International Review of Social History* 32: 144–67.

Crosland, C.A.R. (1956) *The Future of Socialism*. London: Jonathan Cape.

Crossley, Thomas and Cormac O'Dea (2010) *The Wealth and Savings of UK Families on the Eve of the Crisis.* Report No. R71. London: Institute for Fiscal Studies.

[Online]. Available at: www.ifs.org.uk/publications/5200 (Accessed: 30 October 2017).

Crossley, Thomas and Cormac O'Dea (2016) "Household wealth data and public policy". *Fiscal Studies* 37(1): 5–11. [Online]. Available at: http://onlinelibrary.wiley.com/doi/10.1111/j.1475-5890.2016.12090/epdf (Accessed: 30 October 2017).

Crouch, C. (2008) "What will follow the demise of privatized Keynesianism?". *The Political Quarterly* 79(4): 476–87.

Crouch, C. (2011) *The Strange Non-death of Neoliberalism*. Cambridge: Polity Press.

Curtis, Chris (2017) "How Britain voted at the 2017 general election". YouGov. [Online]. Available at: https://yougov.co.uk/news/2017/06/13/how-britain-voted-2017-general-election/ (Accessed: 30 October 2017).

Dalton, M. (1746) *The Country Justice*. London: Lintot.

Damjanovic, D. (2013) "The EU market rules as social market rules: why the EU can be a social market economy". *Common Market Law Review* 50: 1685–718.

Davidson, Adam (2017) "Why are corporations hoarding trillions?" *The New York Times Magazine*. 20 January. [Online]. Available at: www.nytimes.com/ 2016/01/ 24/magazine/why-are-corporations-hoarding-trillions.html (Accessed: 30 October 2017).

Davis, Richard (1997) "Wellington and the 'open question': the issue of Catholic emancipation, 1821–1829". *Albion* 29(1): 39–55.

Davis, Richard (1999) "The House of Lords, the Whigs and Catholic emancipation 1806–1829". *Parliamentary History* 18(1): 23–43.

Deakin, Simon (2011) "Corporate governance and financial crisis in the long run", in P. Zumbansen and C. Williams (eds) *The Embedded Firm: Corporate Governance, Labor, and Finance Capitalism*. Cambridge: Cambridge University Press, pp. 15–41.

Deakin, Simon (2012) "The corporation as commons: rethinking property rights, governance and sustainability in the business enterprise". *Queen's Law Journal* 37: 339–81.

Deakin, Simon (2013) "Droit social et travailleurs pauvres dans la Grande-Bretagne: une perspective historique", in P. Auvergnon (ed.) *Droit social et travailleurs pauvres*. Brussels: Bruylant, pp. 143–62.

Deakin, Simon (2014) "Social policy, economic governance and EMU: alternatives to austerity", in N. Bruun, I. Schömann and K. Lörcher (eds) *Economic and Financial Crisis and Collective Labour Law in Europe*. Oxford: Hart, pp. 83–106.

Deakin, Simon (2016) "Brexit, labour rights and migration: why Wisbech matters to Brussels". *German Law Journal* 17: 14–20.

Deakin, Simon (2017a) "Reversing financialisation: shareholder value and the reform of corporate governance", in C. Driver and G. Thompson (eds) *Corporate Governance in Contention*. Oxford: Oxford University Press (forthcoming).

Deakin, Simon (2017b) "Post-Brexit, post-crisis, what is the future for social rights in Europe?". *Revue des Droits de l'Homme* 13 http://journals.openedition.org/revdh/3672?file=1 (Accessed: 24 January 2018).

Deakin, Simon (2017c) "Alignment, convergence and a symbolic Brexit" *Social Europe*, 19 December 2017 https://www.socialeurope.eu/alignment-convergence-symbolic-brexit (Accessed: 2 January 2018).

Deakin, Simon, and Christopher Markou (2017) "London Uber ban: regulators are finally catching up with technology". *The Conversation*. 25 September. [Online]. Available at: https://theconversation.com/london-uber-ban-regulators-are-finally-catching-up-with-technology-84551 (Accessed: 30 October 2017).

Deakin, S. and G. Morris (2012) *Labour Law* (6th edn). Oxford: Hart.

Deakin, Simon and Hannah Reed (2000) "The contested meaning of labour market flexibility: economic theory and the discourse of European integration", in Joanne Shaw (ed.) *Social Law and Policy in an Evolving European Union*. Oxford: Hart, pp. 71–99.

Deakin, Simon and Agit Singh (2008) 'The stock market, the market for corporate control and the theory of the firm: legal and economic perspectives and implications for public policy'. Centre for Business Research Working Paper No. 365. Cambridge: University of Cambridge.

Deakin, Simon and Giles Slinger (1997) "Hostile takeovers, corporate law and the theory of the firm". *Journal of Law and Society* 24: 124–50.

Deakin, Simon and Frank Wilkinson (2005) *The Law of the Labour Market: Industrialisation, Employment, and Legal Evolution*. Oxford: Oxford University Press.

Deakin, S., S. Fraser-Butlin, C. McLaughlin and A. Polanska (2015) "Are litigation and collective bargaining complements or substitutes for achieving gender equality? A study of the British Equal Pay Act". *Cambridge Journal of Economics* 39(2): 381-403.

Deakin, S., D. Gindis, G. Hodgson, K. Huang and K. Pistor (2017) "Legal institutionalism: capitalism and the constitutive role of law". *Journal of Comparative Economics* 45(1): 188–200.

Deakin, Simon and Frank Wilkinson (1991) "Labour Law, Social Security and Economic Inequality". *Cambridge Journal of Economics* 15: 125–48.

De Nardi, Mariacristina (2015) *Quantitative Models of Wealth Inequality: A Survey*. National Bureau for Economic Research (NBER) Working Paper No. 21106.

Denham, A. and M. Garnett (1998) *British Think Tanks and the Climate of Opinion*. London: UCL Press.

Denman, James and Paulk McDonald (1996) "Unemployment statistics from 1881 to the present day [1995]". The Government Statistical Service. January. [Online]. Available at: http://terencebunch.co.uk/articles/globalisation-the-united-states-empire-the-rise-of-thatcherism-and-the-uks-descent-into-dependency/unemployment-statistics-from-1881-to-1995-the-government-statistical-service-uk.pdf (Accessed: 30 October 2017).

Department for Communities and Local Government (2017) *English Housing Survey: Headline Report 2015–16*. London: Department for Communities and Local Government. March. [Online]. Available at: www.gov.uk/government/statistics/english-housing-survey-2015-to-2016-headline-report (Accessed: 30 October 2017).

Dernauf, Steven and Lawrence Blume (2008) *The New Palgrave Dictionary of Economics* (2nd edn), Volume 1. New York: Palgrave Macmillan.

Desai, R. (1994) "Second hand dealers in ideas: think tanks and Thatcherite hegemony". *New Left Review* 203 (January/February): 27–64.

Dewey, P.E. (1984) "Military recruiting and the British labour force during the First World War". *The Historical Journal* 27: 199–233.

Diamond, Patrick (2016) "The Conservative Party and Brexit". *The UK in a Changing Europe*. [Online]. Available at: http://ukandeu.ac.uk/the-conservative-party-and-brexit/ (Accessed: 30 October 2017).

Dibben, P. (2004) "Social movement unionism", in M. Harcourt and G. Wood (eds) *Trade Unions and Democracy: Strategies and Perspectives*. Manchester: Manchester University Press, pp. 280–302.

Dicey, A.V. (1885) *An Introduction to the Study of the Law of the Constitution*. London: Macmillan.

Dickenson, Jacqueline (2006) *Renegades and Rats: Betrayal and the Remaking of Radical Organisation in Britain and Australia*. Carlton: Melbourne University Press.

Dorfman, Jeffrey (2014) "Dispelling the myth of corporate cash hoarding". *Forbes*. 21 August. [Online]. Available at: www.forbes.com/sites/jeffreydorfman/2014/08/21/dispelling-the-myth-of-corporate-cash-hoarding/#51ec2e1c5ae5 (Accessed: 30 October 2017).

Dorling, D. (2016) "Brexit: the decision of a divided country". *British Medical Journal* 354: i3697.

Dorling, Danny, Jan Rigby, Ben Wheeler, Dimitris Ballas, Bethan Thomas, Eldin Fahmy, David Gordon and Ruth Lupton (2007) *Poverty, Wealth and Place in Britain, 1968–2005*. Bristol: The Policy Press. [Online]. Available at: www.jrf.org.uk/sites/default/files/jrf/migrated/files/2019-poverty-wealth-place.pdf (accessed 20 December 2017).

Dorssemont, F., K. Lörcher and I. Schömann (eds) (2103) *The European Convention of Human Rights and the Employment Relation*. Oxford: Hart.

Dreze, Jean and Amartya Sen (2002) *Hunger and Public Action*. Oxford: Clarendon Press.

Driver, C. and Thompson, G. (2018) *Corporate Governance in Contention*. Oxford: Oxford University Press.

DWP (2013) *Tax Credit Expenditure in Great Britain*. London: Department for Work and Pensions.

Dyson, K. (2012) "Economic and monetary union", in E. Jones, A. Menon and S. Weatherill (eds) *The Oxford Handbook of the European Union*. Oxford: Oxford University Press, pp. 453–68.

Eaton, George (2015) "600,000 apply to vote in Labour leadership contest – and Corbyn will gain". *The New Statesman*. 12 August. [Online]. Available at: www.newstatesman.com/politics/2015/08/600000-apply-vote-labour-leadership-contest-and-corbyn-will-gain (Accessed: 30 October 2017).

Eayrs, James George (1971) *Diplomacy and Its Discontents*. Toronto: University of Toronto Press.

Edwards, Jim (2017) "In the long run, Uber will cut 40,000 jobs in London". *Business Insider UK*. 1 October. [Online]. Available at: http://uk.businessinsider.com/the-london-uber-ban-and-driverless-cars-2017-9?r=US&IR=T (Accessed: 30 October 2017).

Edwards, Sebastien and Daniel Lederman (1998) *The Political Economy of Unilateral Trade Liberalization: The Case of Chile*. National Bureau of Economic Research Working Paper Series. Working Paper 6510. Cambridge, MA: NBER. [Online]. Available at: https://core.ac.uk/download/pdf/6743860.pdf (Accessed: 30 October 2017).

Egan, M. (2001) *Constructing a European Market: Standards, Regulation and Governance*. Oxford: Oxford University Press.

Egan, M. (2012) "Single market", in E. Jones, A. Menon and S. Weatherill (eds). *The Oxford Handbook of the European Union*. Oxford: Oxford University Press, pp. 407–21.

"Electoral Registers through the Years". [Online]. Available at: www.electoralregisters.org.uk/timescales.htm (Accessed: 30 October 2017).

Elkins, Z., T. Ginsburg and J. Melton (2009) *The Endurance of National Constitutions*. Cambridge: Cambridge University Press.

Elliott, M. (2017) "The Supreme Court's judgment in *Miller*: in search of constitutional principle". *Cambridge Law Journal* (forthcoming).

Emmerson, C. and M. Wakefield (2009) "Amounts and accounts: reforming private pension enrolment". Institute for Fiscal Studies, Commentary No. C110. [Online]. Available at: www.ifs.org.uk/publications/4541 (Accessed: 30 October 2017).

Emsley, John (2000) *The Shocking History of Phosphorus: A Biography of the Devil's Element*. London: Macmillan.

Engels, Frederick (1845) *Condition of the Working Class in England*. Marxists Internet Archive. [Online]. Available at: www.marxists.org/archive/marx/works/down load/pdf/condition-working-class-england.pdf (Accessed: 30 October 2017).

Equality and Human Rights Commission (2017) "Being disabled in Britain: a journey less equal". London: Equality and Human Rights Commission [Online]. Available at: www.equalityhumanrights.com/sites/default/files/being-disabled-in-britain.pdf (Accessed: 30 October 2017).

Ertman, Thomas (2010) "The Great Reform Act of 1832 and British democratization". *Comparative Political Studies* 43(8–9): 1000–22.

Evans, Eric (2004) *Thatcher and Thatcherism*. London: Routledge.

Ewing, Keith and John Hendy (2010) "The dramatic implications of *Demir and Baykara*". *Industrial Law Journal* 39: 1–50.

Ewing, K., J. Hendy and C. Jones (2016) *A Manifesto for Labour Law: Towards a Comprehensive Revision of Workers' Rights*. Liverpool: Institute of Employment Rights.

Fairbrother, P. (2002) "Unions in Britain: towards a new unionism?", in P. Fairbrother and G. Greffin (eds) *Changing Prospects for Trade Unionism: Comparisons between Six Countries*. New York: Continuum, pp. 56–89.

Ffrench-Davis, Ricardo (1983) "Import liberalisation: the Chilean experience, 1973–1982", in J.S. Valenzuela and A. Valenzuela (eds) *Military Rule in Chile: Dictatorship and Oppositions*. Baltimore, MD: Johns Hopkins Press, pp. 51–84.

Financial Services Authority (2009) *The Turner Review: A Regulatory Response to the Global Banking Crisis*. London: FSA. [Online]. Available at: www.fsa.gov.uk/pubs/other/turner_review.pdf (Accessed: 30 October 2017).

Finch, David (2016) "Hanging on: the stresses and strains on Britain's 'just managing' families". *Resolution Foundation Briefing*. London: Resolution Foundation. [Online]. Available at: www.resolutionfoundation.org/app/uploads/2016/09/Hanging-On.pdf (Accessed: 30 October 2017).

Fine, Ben (2012) "Neo-liberalism in retrospect: it's financialization, stupid", in Chang Kyung-Sup, Ben Fine and Linda Weiss (eds) *Developmental Politics in Transition: The Neo-liberal Era and Beyond*. New York: Palgrave Macmillan, pp. 51–69.

Finlayson, A. (2003) *Making Sense of New Labour*. London: Lawrence & Wishart.

Finlayson, A. (2013) "From blue to green and everything in between: ideational change and left political economy after New Labour". *The British Journal of Politics and International Relations* 15(1): 70–88.

Fischer, Karin (2009) "The influence of neoliberals in Chile before, during and after Pinochet", in Philip Mirowski and Deiter Plehwe (eds) *The Road to Mont Pelerin: The Making of the Neoliberal Thought Collective*. Cambridge, MA: Harvard University Press, pp. 306–46.

Fisher, Antony (1978) *Fisher's Concise History of Economic Bungling: A Guide for Today's Statesmen*. Ottawa, IL: Caroline House Books.

Ford, Michael (2018) "Employment tribunal fees and the rule of law: R (Unison) v. Lord Chancellor in the Supreme Court". *Industrial Law Journal* 47 (forthcoming).

Foxley, Alejandro (1983) *Latin American Experiments in Neoconservative Economics*. Berkeley, CA: University of California Press.

FPC (2017) "Financial Stability Report, June". London: Bank of England Financial Policy Committee. [Online]. Available at: www.bankofengland.co.uk/publications/Pages/fsr/2017/jun.aspx (Accessed: 30 October 2017).

Fraser, W. Hamish (1999) *A History of British Trade Unionism, 1700–1998*. London: Macmillan.

Freedland, M. and J. Prassl (eds) (2015) *Viking, Laval and Beyond*. Oxford: Hart.

Friedman, Milton (1962) *Capitalism and Freedom*. Chicago, IL: University of Chicago Press.

Friedman, Milton (1977) *Unemployment and Inflation*. Institute of Economic Affairs, Occasional Paper 51.

Friedman, Milton (1988) "Using the market for social development". *Cato Policy Report* 10(6) (November/December). [Online]. Available at: www.libertarianism. org/publications/essays/using-market-social-development (Accessed: 30 October 2017).

Friedman, Milton and Rose Friedman (1984) *Tyranny of the Status Quo*. San Diego, CA: Harcourt Brace Jovanovich.

Froud, James Anthony, John Tulloch and G.W. Nickisson (1834) "Present condition of the people: class: labourers in cities and towns". *Fraser's Magazine* 9: 72–87.

Galbraith, John Kenneth (1999) *The Affluent Society*. London: Penguin Books.

Gallacher, William (1920) *The Clydeside in War Time: Snapshots of a Stormy Period*. Glasgow: Collet's Bookshop. [Online]. Available at: https://archive.org/details/ williegallachers00gall (Accessed: 30 October 2017).

Gamble, A. (2014a) *Crisis without End? The Unravelling of Western Prosperity*. Basingstoke: Palgrave Macmillan.

Gamble, A. (2014b) "A new model economy". *Juncture* 21(1): 58–63.

Gardner, R. (1980) *Sterling-Dollar Diplomacy in Current Perspective: The Origins and the Prospects of Our International Economic Order*. New York: Columbia University Press.

Garside, W.R. (1990) *British Unemployment, 1919–1939: A Study in Public Policy*. Cambridge: Cambridge University Press.

Garside, W.R. and H.F Gospel (1982) "Employers and managers: their organizational structure and changing strategies", in Ch. Wrigley (ed.) *A History of British Industrial Relations, 1875–1914*. Brighton: Harvester, pp. 99–115.

GB Historical GIS (2017) "Population statistics, total population". *A Vision of Britain through Time*. [Online]. Portsmouth: University of Portsmouth. Available at: www. visionofbritain.org.uk/unit/10061325/cube/TOT_POP (Accessed: 30 October 2017).

Ghosh, J. (2007) *Principles of the Internal Market and Direct Taxation*. Oxford: Key Haven.

Giffen, Robert (1913) *Statistics*. London: Macmillan.

Gilbert, Bentley (1966) *Evolution of National Insurance in Britain: The Origins of the Welfare State*. London: Michael Joseph.

Gilbert, Bentley (1976) "David Lloyd George: land, the budget and social reform". *The American Historical Review* 81(5): 1058–66.

Glasgow Digital Archives (2017) "The Battle of George Square (Bloody Friday) 1919". [Online]. Available at: http://gdl.cdlr.strath.ac.uk/redclyde/redclyeve14. htm (Accessed: 30 October 2017).

Goldstein, J. and R. Keohane (1993) *Ideas and Foreign Policy: An Analytical Framework*. Ithaca, NY: Cornell University Press.

Goodhart, Charles (2003) "A central bank economist", in P. Mizen (ed.) *Central Banking, Monetary Theory and Practice*, Volume 1. Cheltenham: Edward Elgar, pp. 13–61.

Goodhart, Charles (2004) "The Bank of England 1970–2000", in R. Michie and P. Williamson (eds) *The British Government and the City of London in the Twentieth Century*. Cambridge: Cambridge University Press, pp. 340–71.

Goodwin, Matthew and Oliver Heath (2016) *Brexit Vote Explained: Poverty, Low Skills and Lack of Opportunities*. York: Joseph Rowntree Foundation. [Online]. Available at: www.jrf.org.uk/report/brexit-vote-explained-poverty-low-skills-and-lack-opportunities (Accessed: 30 October 2017).

Goodwin, Matthew and Oliver Heath (2017) *The UK 2017 General Election Examined: Income, Poverty and Brexit*. York: Joseph Rowntree Foundation. [Online]. Available at: www.jrf.org.uk/report/uk-2017-general-election-vote-examined?gclid =Cj0KCQjwjdLOBRCkARIsAFj5-GAXxOexekP0ePDsc94Gt8d7wOFGcGHy8 BuRi_cTY8533pf0rMQfkkoaAvEKEALw_wcB (Accessed: 30 October 2017).

Graeber, D. (2011) *Debt: The First Five Thousand Years*. New York: Melville House.

Green Cowles, M. (2012) "The Single European Act", in E. Jones, A. Menon and S. Weatherill (eds) *The Oxford Handbook of the European Union*. Oxford: Oxford University Press, pp. 107–20.

Greener, I. (2001) "Social learning and macroeconomic policy in Britain". *Journal of Public Policy* 21: 133–52.

Greenspan, A. (1999) *Testimony of the Chairman of the Board of Governors of the US Federal Reserve System, Mr. Alan Greenspan, before the Joint Economic Committee of the US Congress on 17 June 1999*. [Online]. Available at: www.bis.org/review/ r990707a.pdf (Accessed: 30 October 2017).

Greenspan, A. (2002) "World finance and risk management". *Remarks by Federal Reserve Chairman Alan Greenspan at Lancaster House*. London, 25 September. [Online]. Available at: www.federalreserve.gov/boarddocs/speeches/2002/200209253/default.htm (Accessed: 30 October 2017).

Gregory, T.E., F.A. von Hayek, A. Plant and L. Robbins (1932) "Spending and saving: public works from rates, to the Editor of the *Times*". *The Times*. 19 October, p. 10, Issue 46268, Col. A.

Griffiths, C.V.J. (2004) "Philipps, Wogan, second Baron Milford (1902–1993)". *Oxford Dictionary of National Biography*. Oxford: Oxford University Press.

Griffiths, R. (2012) "The founding fathers", in E. Jones, A. Menon and S. Weatherill (eds) *The Oxford Handbook of the European Union*. Oxford: Oxford University Press, pp. 181–92.

Grundmann, Stefan (2011) *European Company Law: Organization, Finance and Capital Markets* (Cambridge: Intersentia).

Guardian Letter (2015) "Jeremy Corbyn's opposition to austerity is actually mainstream economics". *Guardian*. 23 August. [Online]. Available at: www.theguardian.com/ politics/2015/aug/23/jeremy-corbyns-opposition-to-austerity-is-actually-mainstream-economics (Accessed: 30 October 2017).

Guardian Letter (2017a) "Labour's proposals could be just what the economy needs". *Guardian*. 4 June. [Online]. Available at: www.primeeconomics.org/articles/guws-3cyv3ctq9g7vg754p2zyymvc2f (Accessed: 30 October 2017).

Guardian Letter (2017b) "Labour's policies drowned out by Corbyn memes". *Guardian*. 12 May. [Online]. Available at: www.theguardian.com/politics/2017/may/12/ labour-policies-drowned-out-by-corbyn-memes (Accessed: 30 October 2017).

Guardian and London School of Economics (2011) *Reading the Riots: Investigating England's Summer of Disorder*. (Phase One). [Online]. Available at: ttp://eprints.lse.ac. uk/46297/1/Reading%20the%20riots(published).pdf (Accessed: 30 October 2017).

Gudgin, Graham, Ken Coutts, Neil Gibson and Jornad Buchanan (2017) "The macroeconomic impact of Brexit: using the CBR Macroeconomic Model of the UK Economy (UKMOD)". CBR Working Paper No. 483. Cambridge: Centre for Business Research. [Online]. Available at: www.cbr.cam.ac.uk/publications/ working-papers/ (Accessed: 30 October 2017).

Hall, Peter (1986) *Governing the Economy: The Politics of State Intervention in Britain.* Oxford: Oxford University Press.

Hall, Peter (1989) *The Political Power of Economic Ideas.* Princeton, NJ: Princeton University Press.

Hall, Peter (1993) "Policy paradigms, social learning and the state: the case of economic policy-making in Britain". *Comparative Politics* 25(3): 275–96.

Hall, P. and R. Taylor (1996) "Political science and the three new institutionalisms". *Political Studies* 44(5): 936–57.

Hall, Stuart and Bill Schwartz (1985) "State and society, 1880–1930", in Mary Langen and Bill Schwartz (eds) *Crises in the British State, 1880–1930.* London: Hutchinson, pp. 7–32.

Hannan, D. (2016) *What Next?* London: Head of Zeus.

Hannan, D. (2017) "Brexit explained". London: Institute for Free Trade. [Online]. Available at: http://ifreetrade.org/article/brexit_explained (Accessed: 30 October 2017).

Hansard (1965) "House of Commons' Official Report", 17 November 1965, Vol. 720 cc1155–284. [Online]. Available at: http://hansard.millbanksystems.com/ commons/1965/nov/17/economic-affairs#S5CV0720P0_19651117_HOC_286% 7Cpublisher=hansard%7Ctitle=%7Cdate=17 (Accessed: 30 October 2017).

Hansard, T.C. (1826) *The Parliamentary Debates: Forming a Continuation of the Work Entitled the Parliamentary History of England from the Earliest Period to the Year 1803,* Vol. 13. London: T.C. Hansard.

Hansmann, H. and R. Kraakman (2001) "The end of history for corporate law". *Georgetown Law Journal* 89: 439–68.

Harari, Daniel (2017a) *Household Debt: Statistics and Impact on Economy.* House of Commons Briefing Paper No. 7584, 12 June. London: House of Commons Library. [Online]. Available at: http://researchbriefings.parliament.uk/Research-Briefing/Summary/CBP-7584#fullreport (Accessed: 30 October 2017).

Harari, Daniel (2017b) *Productivity in the UK.* House of Commons Briefing Paper No. 6492, September. London: House of Commons Library. [Online]: Available at: http://researchbriefings.files.parliament.uk/documents/SN06492/SN06492.pdf (Accessed: 30 October 2017).

Harberger, Arnold (1985) "Observations on the Chilean economy, 1973–1982". *Economic Development and Cultural Change* 33 (April): 451–62.

Harcourt, Geoff (1987) "Bastard Keynesianism", in John Eatwell, Murray Milgate and Peter Newman (eds) *Palgrave Dictionary of Economics*, Volume 1. London: Palgrave MacMillan, pp. 203–4.

Harling, Philip (2001) *The Modern British State: An Historical Introduction.* Cambridge: Polity Press.

Harmer, Harry (2014) *The Longman Companion to the Labour Party, 1900–1998.* London: Routledge.

Harris, Jose (1972) *Unemployment and Politics: A Study of English Social Policy 1886–1914.* Oxford: Oxford University Press.

Harris, R. (2000) *Industrializing English Law: Entrepreneurship and Business Organization 1720–1844.* Cambridge: Cambridge University Press.

Harrison, Royden (2000) *The Life and Times of Sidney and Beatrice Webb: The Formative Years 1858–1905.* London: Macmillan.

Harrod, R.F. (1937) "Mr. Keynes and traditional theory". *Econometrica* 5 (January): 74–86.

Harvey, David (2005) *A Brief History of Neoliberalism*. Oxford: Oxford University Press.

Hattenstone, Simon (2015) "Jeremy Corbyn: 'I don't do personal'". *Guardian*. 17 June. [Online]. Available at: www.theguardian.com/politics/2015/jun/17/jeremy-corbyn-labour-leadership-dont-do-personal (Accessed: 30 October 2017).

Hawtrey, R.G. (1925) "Public expenditure and the demand for Labour". *Economica* 13 (March): 38–48.

Hay, Colin (1999) "Crisis and the structural transformation of the state: interrogating the process of change". *The British Journal of Politics and International Relations* 1(3): 317–44.

Hay, Colin (2001) "The 'crisis' of Keynesianism and the rise of neoliberalism in Britain: an ideational institutionalist approach", in J. Campbell and O. Pederson (eds) *The Rise of Neoliberalism and Institutional Analysis*. Princeton, NJ: Princeton University Press, pp. 193–218.

Hay, Colin (2004) "Credibility, competitiveness and the business cycle in 'third way' political economy: a critical critique of economic policy in Britain since 1997". *New Political Economy* 9(1): 39–45.

Hay, Colin (2011) "Pathology without crisis? The strange demise of the Anglo-Growth Model". *Government and Opposition* 46(1): 1–31.

Hay, Colin (2013a) "Treating the symptom, not the condition: crisis definition, deficit reduction and the search for a new British growth model". *The British Journal of Politics and International Relations* 15: 23–37.

Hay, Colin (2013b) *The British Growth Crisis: A Crisis of and for Growth*. SPERI Paper No. 1. Sheffield: Sheffield Political Economy Research Institute. [Online]. Available at: http://speri.dept.shef.ac.uk/wp-content/uploads/2013/01/SPERI-Paper-No.-1-%E2%80%93-The-British-Growth-Crisis-FINAL1.pdf (Accessed: 30 October 2017).

Hay, John (1983 [1975]) *The Origins of the Liberal Welfare Reforms 1914*. London: Macmillan.

Haydu, J. (1998) "Making use of the past: time periods as cases to compare and as sequences of problem solving". *American Journal of Sociology* 104(2): 339–71.

Haydu, J. (2010) "Reversal of fortune: path dependency, problem solving and temporal analysis". *Theory and Society* 39(1): 39–48.

Hayek, Friedrich (1982) *Law, Legislation and Liberty: A New Statement of the Liberal Principles of Justice and Political Economy*. London: Routledge.

Hayek, Friedrich (2001 [1944]) *The Road to Serfdom*. London: Routledge.

Helleiner, E. (1994) *States and the Re-emergence of Global Finance*. Ithaca, NY: Cornell University Press.

Hellier, David (2015) "Why are the hedge funds supporting Brexit?". *Guardian*. 6 November. [Online]. Available at: www.theguardian.com/business/2015/nov/06/why-are-the-hedge-funds-supporting-brexit (Accessed: 30 October 2017).

Hern, Alex (2015) "Are driverless cars the future of Uber?". *Guardian*. 3 February. [Online]. Available at: www.theguardian.com/technology/2015/feb/03/are-driverless-cars-the-future-of-uber (Accessed: 30 October 2017).

Hickman, T. (2011) *Public Law after the Human Rights Act*. Oxford: Hart.

Hicks, J.R. (1937) "Mr. Keynes and the 'classics': a suggested interpretation". *Econometrica* 5 (April): 147–59.

Hill, C.P. (1985) *British Economic and Social History, 1700–1982* (5th edn). London: Edward Arnold.

Hills, John (2004) *Inequality and the State*. Oxford: Oxford University Press.

Himmelfarb, Gertrude (1991) *Poverty and Compassion: The Moral Imagination of the Late Victorians*. New York: Vintage Books.

Hinarejos, A. (2015) *The Euro Area Crisis in Constitutional Perspective*. Oxford: Oxford University Press.

Hitchens, Peter (2015) "My evening with Jeremy Corbyn". MailOnline. 7 September. [Online]. Available at: http://hitchensblog.mailonsunday.co.uk/2015/09/my-evening-with-jeremy-corbyn.html (Accessed: 30 October 2017).

HMSO (1944) *Employment Policy*. Cmd. 6527. London: HMSO, May.

HM Treasury (2000) *Tackling Poverty and Making Work Pay: Tax Credits for the 21st Century. The Modernisation of Britain's Tax and Benefit System No. 6*. London: HM Treasury. [Online]. Available at: http://dera.ioe.ac.uk/9893/1/Tackling_poverty_and_making_work_pay_-_tax_credits_for_the_21st_century.pdf (Accessed: 30 October 2017).

HM Treasury (2005) *Freedom of Information Disclosures: The Provision of Financial Assistance to Slater Walker Bank in 1975*. [Online]. Available at: http://hm-treasury.gov.uk/about/information/foi_disclosures/foi_slater_walker.cfm (Accessed: 30 October 2017).

HM Treasury (2008) *Freedom of Information Disclosures: Estimates of the Cost of Black Wednesday 1992*. [Online]. Available at: http://webarchive.nationalarchives.gov.uk/+/www.hm-treasury.gov.uk/about/information/foi_disclosures/foi_erm4_090205.cfm (Accessed: 30 October 2017).

Holehouse, Matthew (2014) "Poor going hungry because they can't cook, says Tory peer". *The Telegraph*. 8 December. [Online]. Available at: www.telegraph.co.uk/news/politics/11279839/Poor-going-hungry-because-they-cant-cook-says-Tory-peer.html (Accessed: 30 October 2017).

Holton, Robert (1976) *British Syndicalism, 1900–1914*. London: Pluto Press.

Hood, A. and P. Johnson (2016) "Are we 'all in this together'?" *Observation*. London: Institute for Fiscal Studies. [Online]. Available at: www.ifs.org.uk/publications/8210 (Accessed: 30 October 2017).

Hood, Andrew, Agnes Keiller Norris and Tom Waters (2017) "Significant cuts to two parts of the benefit system to be phased in from next week". *Observation*. London: Institute for Fiscal Studies. [Online]. Available at: www.ifs.org.uk/publications/9117 (Accessed: 30 October 2017).

House of Commons Business, Skills and Innovation Committee (2016) "Oral evidence: working practices at Sports Direct". HC 219, 7 June. [Online]. Available at: www.parliament.uk/business/committees/committees-a-z/commons-select/business-innovation-and-skills/inquiries/parliament-2015/working-practices-at-sports-direct-inquiry-16-17/ (Accessed: 30 October 2017).

Howitt, Peter (1987) "Macroeconomics: relations with microeconomics", in John Eatwell, Murray Milgate and Peter Newman (eds) *Palgrave Dictionary of Economics*, Volume 3. London: Palgrave Macmillan, pp. 273–6.

Howlett, M. and J. Rayner (2006) "Understanding the historical turn in the policy sciences: a critique of stochastic, narrative, path dependency and process-sequencing models of policy-making over time". *Policy Sciences* 39(1): 1–18.

Howson, Susan and Donald Winch (1977) *The Economic Advisory Council, 1930–1939: A Study in Economic Advice during Depression and Recovery*. Cambridge: Cambridge University Press.

Hoyle, David (1992) *The Levellers: Libertarian Radicalism and the English Civil War*. Libertarian Heritage No. 5. London: Libertarian Alliance. Available at: www.libertarian.co.uk/lapubs/libhe/libhe005.pdf (Accessed: 30 October 2017).

Hughes, K. (2016) "Written submission for the Joint Committee on Human Rights, human rights implications of Brexit". September.

Hunt, Alex (2014) "UKIP: the story of the UK Independence Party's rise". *BBC News.* 21 November. [Online]. Available at: www.bbc.co.uk/news/uk-politics-21614073 (Accessed: 30 October 2017).

Hunter, Alex (1966) *Competition and the Law.* London: George Allen & Unwin.

Inman, Philip (2017) "MPs and charities urge car leasers to publish sub-prime loan figures". *Guardian.* 2 July. [Online]. Available at: www.theguardian.com/money/2017/jul/02/car-leasers-publish-sub-prime-lending-figures-mps-charities (Accessed: 30 October 2017).

Institute for Fiscal Studies (2017) *Living Standards, Inequality and Poverty Spreadsheet.* London: Institute for Fiscal Studies. [Online]. Available at: www.ifs.org.uk/tools_and_resources/incomes_in_uk (Accessed: 30 October 2017).

Internationalist Communist Union (2001) "#55 – The 1926 General Strike – its implications for the future struggles of the working class". *Internationalist Communist Forum.* [Online]. Available at: www.union-communiste.org/en/2001-06/55-the-1926-general-strike-its-relevance-for-the-future-struggles-of-the-working-class-1469 (Accessed: 30 October 2017).

International Socialist Archives (2006) "Red Clydeside". *International Socialist.* 21 June. Available at: www.redflag.org.uk/articles/art005.html (Accessed: 30 October 2017).

Ireland, P. (1999) "Company law and the myth of shareholder ownership". *Modern Law Review* 62: 32–57.

Jackson, Michael, John Leopold and Kate Tuck (1993) *Decentralization of Collective Bargaining: An Analysis of Recent Experience in the United Kingdom.* New York: Palgrave Macmillan.

Jarley, P. (2002) "American unions at the start of the 21st century: going back to the future?", in P. Fairbrother and G. Greffin (eds) *Changing Prospects for Trade Unionism: Comparisons between Six Countries.* New York: Continuum, pp. 200–37.

Jeffries, Julie (2005) "The UK population: past present and future", in Roma Chapell (ed.) *Focus on People and Migration.* London: HMSO, pp. 1–17.

Jenkins, Simon (2006) *Thatcher & Sons: A Revolution in Three Acts.* London: Penguin Books.

Johnston, A. (2011) "Towards a sustainable European company law: a normative analysis of the objectives of EU law, with the Takeover Directive as a test case". *European Law Review* 36: 302–5.

Jones, F., D. Anan and S. Shah (2008) "The distribution of household income 1977–2006/7". *Economic and Labour Review* 2(12): 18–31.

Jones, Owen (2016) *Chavs: The Demonization of the Working Class.* London: Verso.

Jones, Peter (2013) *The 1848 Revolutions.* New York: Routledge.

Jones, Rupert (2013) "The payday lender that charged 16,734,509.4%". *Guardian.* 16 March. [Online]. Available at: www.theguardian.com/money/2013/mar/16/payday-lender (Accessed: 30 October 2017).

Jones, Rupert (2015) "Average monthly rent hits record high of £816, highlighting housing shortage". *Guardian.* 16 October. [Online]. Available at: www.theguardian.com/money/2015/oct/16/average-monthly-rent-hits-record-high-of-816-highlighting-housing-shortage (Accessed: 30 October 2017).

Jones, Russell (1987) *Wage and Employment Policy 1936–1985.* London: Allen and Unwin.

Joseph, Keith and J. Sumption (1979) *Equality.* London: John Murray.

Judd, Dennis (2012) *George VI*. London: I.B. Tauris.

Kahn, R. (1984) *The Making of Keynes's General Theory*. Cambridge: Cambridge University Press.

Kaldor, Nicholas (1976) "Inflation and recession in the world economy". *Economic Journal* 86 (December): 713–14.

Kaldor, Nicholas (1986) *The Scourge of Monetarism*. Oxford: Oxford University Press.

Kalecki, M. (1943) "Political aspects of full employment". *Political Quarterly* 14(4): 322–31.

Katelouzou, D. and M. Siems (2015) "Disappearing paradigms in shareholder protection: leximetric evidence for 30 countries, 1990–2013". *Journal of Corporate Law Studies* 15: 127–60.

Kawalerowicz, Juta and Michael Biggs (2015) "Anarchy in the U.K.: economic deprivation, social disorganization, and political grievances in the London riot of 2011". *Social Forces* 94(2): 673–98. [Online]. Available at: http://users.ox.ac.uk/~sfos0060/2011.pdf (Accessed 20 December 2017).

Keay, A. (2013) *The Enlightened Shareholder Value Principle and Corporate Governance*. London: Routledge.

Keegan, W., D. Marsh and D. Roberts (2017) *Six Days in September: Black Wednesday, Brexit and the Making of Europe*. London: OMFIF.

Keeler, J.T. (1993) "Opening the window for reform mandates, crises, and extraordinary policy-making". *Comparative Political Studies* 25(4): 433–86.

Keen, Richard and Ross Turner (2016) "Statistics on migrants and benefits". House of Commons Briefing Paper Number CBP 7445, February. [Online]. Available at: http://researchbriefings.files.parliament.uk/documents/SN06955/SN06955.pdf (Accessed: 30 October 2017).

Kennedy, Paul (1988) *The Rise and Fall of Great Powers*. London: Unwin Hyman.

Kenner, J. (2003) *EU Employment Law: From Rome to Amsterdam and Beyond*. Oxford: Hart.

Kentish, Ben (2017) "Third of private rented homes fail basic health and safety standards, new analysis finds". *The Independent*. 10 August. [Online]. Available at: www.independent.co.uk/news/uk/home-news/private-rental-homes-health-safety-standards-fail-third-landlords-lease-flats-houses-a7883016.html (Accessed: 30 October 2017).

Keynes, John Maynard (1923) *A Tract on Monetary Reform*. London: Macmillan.

Keynes, John Maynard (1924a) "Alfred Marshall, 1842–1924". *The Economic Journal* 34(135): 311–72.

Keynes, John Maynard (1924b) "Does unemployment need a drastic remedy?". *Nation and Athenaeum*.

Keynes, John Maynard (1925) *The Economic Consequences of Mr. Churchill*. London: L. and V. Woolf.

Keynes, John Maynard (1926) *The End of Laissez Faire*. London: Hogarth Press.

Keynes, John Maynard (1928) "How to organize a wave of prosperity". *The Evening Standard*. 31 July. Available at: https://webspace.utexas.edu/hcleaver/www/368/368keynesprosperity.html (Accessed: 30 October 2017).

Keynes, John Maynard (1933) *The Means to Prosperity*, London: Macmillan. Available at: http://gutenberg.ca/ebooks/keynes-means/keynes-means-00-h.html (Accessed: 30 October 2017).

Keynes, John Maynard (1937a) "How to avoid a slump: looking ahead, 1. The problem of the steady level". *The Times*. 12 January, p. 13, Issue 47580, Col. G.

Keynes, John Maynard (1937b) "How to avoid a slump: "dear" money, II. The right time for austerity". *The Times*. 13 January, p. 13, Issue 47581, Col. G.

Keynes, John Maynard (1937c) "How to avoid a slump: a board of public investment? III. Opportunities of policy". *The Times*. 14 January, p. 13, Issue 47582, Col. G.

Keynes, John Maynard (1940) *How to Pay for the War: A Radical Plan for the Chancellor of the Exchequer*. London: Macmillan.

Keynes, John Maynard (1997 [1936]) *The General Theory of Employment, Interest and Money*. New York: Prometheus Books.

Keynes, John Maynard (2010 [1919]) "The economic consequences of the peace", in J.M. Keynes, *Essays in Persuasion*. London: Palgrave Macmillan.

Keynes, John Maynard (2011 [1930]) *A Treatise on Money: The Pure Theory of Money and the Applied Theory of Money*. Eastford, CT: Martino Fine Books.

Keynes, John Maynard and Hubert Henderson (2010) "Can Lloyd George do it?", in J.M. Keynes, *Essays in Persuasion*. New York: Palgrave Macmillan, pp. 86–125.

Khomami, Nadia (2017) "The US Bernie Sanders campaigners lending Jeremy Corbyn a hand". *Guardian*. 30 May. [Online]. Available at: www.theguardian.com/politics/2017/may/30/the-us-sanders-campaigners-lending-corybn-hand-bernie-momentum (Accessed: 30 October 2017).

Kingon, Suzanne (2004) "Ulster opposition to Catholic emancipation, 1828–9". *Irish Historical Studies* 34(134): 137–55.

Klugmann, James (1968) *History of the Communist Party of Great Britain*, Volume 1: *Formation and Early Years, 1919–1924*. London: Lawrence & Wishart.

Konzelmann, S. and F. Wilkinson (2016) *Co-Operation in Production, the Organization of Industry and Productive Systems: A Critical Survey of the 'District' Form of Industrial Organization and Development"*. Centre for Business Research, University of Cambridge. Working Paper No. 481, September.

Konzelmann, S., M. Fovargue-Davies and F. Wilkinson (2017) "Britain's industrial evolution: the structuring role of economic theory". *Journal of Economic Issues* (forthcoming).

Kuhn, T. (1962) *The Structure of Scientific Revolutions*. Chicago, IL: Chicago University Press.

Kynaston, D. (1994) *The City of London, Volume 1: A World of Its Own, 1815–1890*. London: Chatto and Windus.

Labour Party Manifesto (1945) *Let Us Face the Future: A Declaration of Labour Policy for the Consideration of the Nation*. [Online]. Available at: http://labourmanifesto.com/1945/1945-labour-manifesto.shtml (Accessed: 30 October 2017).

Labour Party Manifesto (1966) *Time for Decision*. [Online]. Available at: www.labour-party.org.uk/manifestos/1966/1966-labour-manifesto.shtml (Accessed: 30 October 2017).

Labour Party Manifesto (1997) *New Labour Because Britain Deserves Better*. [Online]. Available at: http://labourmanifesto.com/1997/1997-labour-manifesto.shtml (accessed 20 December 2017).

Labour Party Manifesto (2017) *For the Many, Not the Few*. [Online]. Available at: www.labour.org.uk/index.php/manifesto2017 (Accessed: 30 October 2017).

Lagarde, C. (2011) "Don't let fiscal brakes stall global recovery". *Financial Times*. 15 August. [Online]. Available at: www.ft.com/cms/s/0/315ed340-c72b-11e 0-a9ef-00144feabdc0.html#axzz2WqN55Zpq (Accessed: 30 October 2017).

Laidler, D. (1999) *Fabricating the Keynesian Revolution: Studies of the Inter-War Literature on Money, the Cycle and Unemployment*. Cambridge: Cambridge University Press.

Lansley, Stewart and Joanna Mack (2015) *Breadline Britain: The Rise of Mass Poverty*. London: Oneworld Publications.

Laursen, F. (2012) "The Treaty of Maastricht", in E. Jones, A. Menon and S. Weatherill (eds) *The Oxford Handbook of the European Union*. Oxford: Oxford University Press, pp. 121–34.

Lawrence, F. (2016) "The gangsters on England's doorstep". *Guardian*. 11 May. [Online]. Available at: www.theguardian.com/uk-news/2016/may/11/gangsters-on-our-doorstep (Accessed: 30 October 2017).

Lazonick, William and Mary O'Sullivan (2000) "Maximizing shareholder value: a new ideology for corporate governance". *Economy and Society* 29(1): 13–35.

League of Nations (1945) *Industrialization and World Trade*.

Lee, Geoffrey (2008) *The People's Budget: An Edwardian Tragedy*. London: Shepheard-Walwyn.

Le Monde (2000) "Open letter from economics students to professors and others responsible for the teaching of this discipline". *Le Monde*. 17 June. [Online]. Available at: www.autisme-economie.org/article142.html (Accessed: 30 October 2017).

Linker, R.W. (1976) "The English Roman Catholics and emancipation: the politics of persuasion". *Journal of Ecclesiastical History* 27(2): 151–80.

Lo, Andrew and Mark Mueller (2010) "Warning: physics envy may be hazardous to your wealth!". [Online]. Available at: https://arxiv.org/pdf/1003.2688.pdf (Accessed: 30 October 2017).

Loopstra, Rachel and Doireann Lalor (2017) *Financial Insecurity, Food Insecurity and Disability: The Profile of People Receiving Emergency Food Assistance from the Trussell Trust Foodbank Network in Britain*. Salisbury: The Trussell Trust. [Online]. Available at: www.trusselltrust.org/wp-content/uploads/sites/2/2017/07/OU_Report_final_01_08_online2.pdf (Accessed: 30 October 2017).

Lovell, John (1969) *Stevedores and Dockers: A Study of Trade Unionism in the Port of London, 1870–1914*. London: Palgrave Macmillan.

Lucas, R. (2003) "Macroeconomic priorities". *American Economic Review* March: 1–14.

Lucas, R. and T. Sargent (1979) "After Keynesian macroeconomics". *Federal Reserve of Minneapolis Quarterly Review* 3(2), Spring: 1–16. [Online]. Available at: www.minneapolisfed.org/research/qr/qr321.pdf (Accessed: 30 October 2017).

MacCarthy, Fiona (1994) *William Morris: A Life for Our Time*. London: Faber & Faber.

Maccoby, S. (2002) *English Radicalism: 1853–1886*. New York: Routledge.

Macgregor, D.H., A.C. Pigou, J.M. Keynes, W. Layton, A. Salter and J.C. Stamp (1932a) "Private spending: money for productive investment, a comment by economists". *The Times*. 17 October, p. 13, Issue 46266, Col. E.

Macgregor, D.H., A.C. Pigou, J.M. Keynes, W. Layton, A. Salter and J.C. Stamp (1932b) "Spending and saving: what are natural resources, the economists' reply". *The Times*. 21 October, p. 15, Issue 46270, Col. E.

Machin, G.I.T. (1979) "Resistance to Repeal of the Test and Corporation Acts, 1828". *Historical Journal* 22(1): 115–39.

Mackail, J.W. (1899) *The Life of William Morris, Volume 2*. London: Longmans, Green & Co. [Online]. Available at: https://archive.org/details/lifeofwilliammor02mack-uoft (Accessed: 30 October 2017).

Magdoff, H. and P. Sweezy (1987) *Economic History As It Happened, Volume 4: Stagnation and the Financial Explosion*. New York: Monthly Review Press.

Maher, Imelda (1995) "The new Sunday: re-regulating Sunday trading". *Modern Law Review* 58: 72–86.

Mahoney, J. (2000) "Path dependence in historical sociology". *Theory and Society* 29(4): 507–48.

Mahoney, J. and K. Thelen (2010) *Explaining Institutional Change: Ambiguity, Agency and Power*. Cambridge: Cambridge University Press.

Maidment, Jack (2017) "Ed Miliband 'could return to Labour frontbench under Jeremy Corbyn'". *The Telegraph*. 12 June. [Online]. Available at: www.telegraph.co.uk/news/2017/06/12/ed-miliband-could-return-labour-frontbench-jeremy-corbyn/ (Accessed: 30 October 2017).

Malthus, Thomas (1798) *An Essay of the Principle of Population, as It Affects the Future Improvement of Society, with Remarks on the Speculation of Mr. Godwin, Mr. Condorcet and Other Writers*. London. [Online]. Available at: www.esp.org/books/malthus/population/malthus.pdf (Accessed: 30 October 2017).

Mann, Michael (1988) *States, War and Capitalism*. Oxford: Blackwell.

Mansfield, Katie (2016) "Now FOUR polls put LEAVE camp ahead as Project Fear sees British voters desert Cameron". *The Express*. 6 June. [Online]. Available at: www.express.co.uk/news/politics/677155/Brexit-IN-THE-LEAD-as-Project-Fear-sees-voters-desert-Cameron-EU-referendum (Accessed: 30 October 2017).

Mansfield, Malcolm (1994) "Naissance d'une définition institutionelle du chômage en Grande-Bretagne (1860–1914)", in Malcolm Mansfield, Robert Salais and Noel Whiteside (eds) *Aux sources du chômage 1880–1914*. Paris: Belin, pp. 295–323.

Marr, Andrew (2007) *A History of Modern Britain*. London: Macmillan.

Marriott, John (1948) *Modern England: 1885–1945, A History of My Own Times* (4th edn). London: Methuen & Company. [Online]. Available at: https://archive.org/details/in.ernet.dli.2015.54679 (Accessed: 30 October 2017).

Martin, Ben (2015) "Jeremy Corbyn's economic policies could be 'highly damaging', economists warn". *The Telegraph*. 3 September. [Online]. Available at: www.telegraph.co.uk/finance/economics/11840928/Jeremy-Corbyns-economic-policies-could-be-highly-damaging-economists-warn.html (Accessed: 30 October 2017).

Martin, Ross (1980) *TUC: The Growth of a Pressure Group, 1868–1976*. Oxford: Clarendon Press.

Martynova, M. and L. Renneboog (2008) "A century of corporate takeovers: what have we learned and where do we stand?". *Journal of Banking & Finance* 32: 2148–77.

Marx, Karl (2015 [1887] [1867]) *Capital: A Critique of Political Economy*, Volume 1. London: Lawrence and Wishart. Marx/Engels Internet Archive. [Online]. Available at: www.marxists.org/archive/marx/works/download/pdf/Capital-Volume-I.pdf (Accessed: 30 October 2017).

Marx, Karl (1904 [1859]) *A Contribution to the Critique of Political Economy*. Chicago, IL: Charles Kerr & Company. [Online]. Available at: https://gruppegrundrisse.files.wordpress.com/2012/06/a-contribution-to-the-critique-of-political-economy-marx.pdf (Accessed: 30 October 2017).

Marx, Karl (1951 [1863]) *Theories of Surplus Value*. London: Lawrence & Wishart. [Online]. Available at: www.bard.edu/library/arendt/pdfs/Marx-Surplus.pdf (Accessed: 30 October 2017).

Marx, Karl and Frederick Engels (1948) *The Manifesto of the Communist Party*. Marxists Internet Archive [Online]. Available at: www.marxists.org/archive/marx/works/download/pdf/Manifesto.pdf (Accessed: 30 October 2017).

Marxist Internet Archive (2007) *The Reds and the General Strike: The Lessons of the First General Strike of the British Working Class*. London: The Dorritt Press. [Online].

Available at: www.marxists.org/history/international/comintern/sections/britain/pamphlets/1926/reds.htm (Accessed: 30 October 2017).

Matthijs, Matthias (2011) *Ideas and Economic Crises in Britain: From Attlee to Blair (1945–2005)*. New York: Routledge.

May, Theresa (2016) *Statement from the New Prime Minister, Theresa May*. London, 13 July. [Online]. Available at: www.gov.uk/government/speeches/statement-from-the-new-prime-minister-theresa-may (Accessed: 30 October 2017).

Mayhew, Henry (1861 [1851]) *London Labour and the London Poor; Cyclaepedia of the Condition and Earnings of Those that Will Work, Those that Cannot Work and Those that Will Not Work*, Volume 1. London: Griffin, Bohn and Company.

McBriar, Alan (1987) *An Edwardian Mixed Doubles: The Bosanquets versus the Webbs. A Study in British Social Policy 1890–1929*. Oxford: Clarendon Press.

McCready, H.W. (1955) "British Labour and the Royal Commission on Trade Unions, 1867–9". *University of Toronto Quarterly* 24(4): 390–409.

McDonald-Gibson, Charlotte (2013) "Exclusive: Red Cross launches emergency food aid plan for UK's hungry". *Independent*. 10 October. [Online]. Available at: www.independent.co.uk/news/uk/home-news/exclusive-red-cross-launches-emergency-food-aid-plan-for-uk-s-hungry-8872496.html (Accessed: 30 October 2017).

McHugh, Declan (2015) "Why did Labour use this system to elect its leader?" *The New Statesman*. 8 September. [Online]. Available at: www.newstatesman.com/politics/elections/2015/09/why-did-labour-use-system-elect-its-leader (Accessed: 30 October 2017).

McIvor, Arthur (2000) *A History of Work in Britain, 1880–1950*. London: Palgrave Macmillan.

McKibben, Ross (1974) *The Evolution of the Labour Party, 1910–1924*. Oxford: Oxford University Press.

McNeil, Kate, and Chris Pond (eds) (1988) *Britain Can't Afford Low Pay: A Programme for a National Minimum Wage*. London: Low Pay Unit.

Meade, James (1937) "A simplified model of Mr. Keynes' system". *Review of Economic Studies* 4: 98–107.

Meade, James (1982) *Wage Fixing*. London: Allen and Unwin.

Mearns, Andrew (1883) *The Bitter Cry of Outcast London: An Inquiry into the Condition of the Abject Poor*. London: James Clarke & Company. [Online]. Available at: www.attackingthedevil.co.uk/pdfs/bittercry.pdf (Accessed: 30 October 2017).

Merrick, Rob (2017) "Ed Miliband says he is keen to return to frontline politics alongside Jeremy Corbyn". *Independent*. 14 October. [Online]. Available at: www.independent.co.uk/news/uk/politics/ed-miliband-jeremy-corbyn-return-job-frontbench-2015-election-defeat-a8000246.html (Accessed: 30 October 2017).

Metcalf, David (2008) "Why has the British national minimum wage had little or no impact on employment?". *Journal of Industrial Relations* 50(3): 489–511.

Middlemas, Keith (1986) *Power, Competition and the State, Volume 1: Britain in Search of Balance, 1940–61*. Stanford, CA: Hoover Institution Press.

Middlemas, Keith (1990) *Power, Competition and the State, Volume 2: Threats to the Post-war Settlement, 1914–1974*. London: Macmillan.

Middlemas, K. and J. Barnes (1969) *Baldwin: A Biography*. London: Macmillan.

Middleton, R. (1982) "The Treasury in the 1930s: political and administrative constraints to acceptance of the 'new' economics". *Oxford Economic Papers* 34: 48–77.

Minford, P. (2017) "From project fear to project prosperity". London: Economists for Trade. [Online]. Available at: www.economistsforfreetrade.com/wp-content/

uploads/2017/08/From-Project-Fear-to-Project-Prosperity-An-Introduction-15-Aug-17-2.pdf (Accessed: 30 October 2017).

Minsky, H. (2008 [1986]) *Stabilizing an Unstable Economy*. London: McGraw-Hill.

Mirowski, Philip (1992) "Do economists suffer from physics envy?". *Finnish Economic Papers* 5(1): 61–8. [Online]. Available at: http://taloustieteellinenyhdistys.fi/images/stories/fep/f1992_1f.pdf (Accessed: 30 October 2017).

Mirowski, Philip (1999) *More Heat Than Light: Economics as Social Physics, Physics as Nature's Economics*. Cambridge: Cambridge University Press.

Mirowski, Philip (2013) *Never Let a Serious Crisis Go to Waste: How Neoliberalism Survived the Financial Meltdown*. London: Verso.

Mishra, Pankaj (2017) "The rise of Jeremy Corbyn and the death throes of neoliberalism". *The New York Times Magazine*. 20 June. [Online]. Available at: www.nytimes.com/2017/06/20/magazine/the-rise-of-jeremy-corbyn-and-the-death-throes-of-neoliberalism.html?mcubz=0 (Accessed: 30 October 2017).

Mishra, Ramesh (1984) *The Welfare State in Crisis: Social Thought and Social Change*. New York: Saint Martin's.

Mitchell, James, Kostas Mouratidis and Martin Weale (2005) *The Long-term Relationship between Poverty and Debt*. York: Joseph Rowntree Foundation. 17 November. [Online]. Available at: www.jrf.org.uk/report/long-term-relationship-between-poverty-and-debt (Accessed: 30 October 2017).

Moggridge, D. (1992) *Maynard Keynes: An Economist's Biography*. London: Routledge.

Moore, Jane and John Strachan (2010) *Key Concepts in Romantic Literature*. New York: Palgrave Macmillan.

Moore, Roger (1982) "Free market economics, trade union law and the labour market". *Cambridge Journal of Economics* 6(3): 297–315.

Moravcsik, A. (1998) *The Choice for Europe: Social Purpose and State Power from Messina to Maastricht*. Ithaca, NY: Cornell University Press.

Morgan, Kenneth (1985) *Labour in Power, 1945–1951*. Oxford: Oxford University Press.

Morgan, Kenneth (1990) *The People's Peace: British History 1945–1990*. Oxford: Oxford University Press.

Morgan, Kenneth (2001) *Britain since 1945: The People's Peace*. Oxford: Oxford University Press.

Morgan, Kenneth (2017 [2011]) "The new Liberal Party from dawn to downfall, 1906–1924". *Les Cahiers du MIMMOC*. [Online]. Available at: http://mimmoc.revies.org/671; DOI: 10.4000/mimmoc.671. (Accessed: 30 October 2017).

Morris, William (1884) "Work in a factory as it might be". *Justice*. 28 June. Marxists Internet Archive. [Online]. Available at: www.marxists.org/archive/morris/works/1884/justice/13fact3.htm (Accessed: 30 October 2017).

Murray, Bruce (2009) "The people's budget: a century on". *Journal of Liberal History* 64: 4–13.

Mynors, H.C.B. (1941) "Bank of England". *London Gazette*. 19 September, Issue 35279, p. 5489. [Online]. Available at: www.thegazette.co.uk/London/issue/35279/page/5489 (Accessed: 30 October 2017).

Mynors, H.C.B. (1942) "Bank of England". *London Gazette*. 3 April, Issue 35511, p. 1540. [Online]. Available at: www.thegazette.co.uk/London/issue/35511/page/1540 (Accessed: 30 October 2017).

New Statesman (2017) "Theresa May on calling an early election: full statement". *New Statesman*. 18 April. [Online]. Available at: www.newstatesman.com/politics/

elections/2017/04/theresa-may-calling-early-election-full-statement (Accessed: 30 October 2017).

Nickell, Stephen (1985) "The governments' policy for jobs: an analysis". *Oxford Review of Economic Policy* 1(2): 98–115.

Nissel, Muriel (1987) *People Count: A History of the General Register Office*. London: HMSO.

Nörr, K.W. (1998) "A symbiosis with reserve: social market economy and legal order in Germany", in P. Koslowski (ed.) *The Social Market Economy: Theory and Ethics of the Economic Order*. Frankfurt: Springer, pp. 220–47.

Novitz, T. (2017) "Collective bargaining, equality and migration: the journey to and from Brexit". *Industrial Law Journal* 46: 109–33.

Obendorfer, L. (2014) "A new economic governance through secondary legislation? Analysis and constitutional assessment: from new constitutionalism, via authoritarian constitutionalism to progressive constitutionalism", in N. Bruun, K. Lörcher and I. Schömann (eds) *The Economic and Financial Crisis and Collective Labour Law in Europe*. Oxford: Hart, pp. 25–54.

Ogden, C. and F. Melville (1987) "Thatcher: we are building a property democracy". *Time Magazine*. 26 June. [Online]. Available at: www.time.com/time/magazine/article/0,9171,964699,00.html (Accessed: 30 October 2017).

O'Gorman, Frank (1989) *Voters, Patrons, and Parties: The Unreformed Electoral System of Hanoverian England, 1734–1832*. Oxford: Clarendon Press.

Ogus, Anthony (1982) "Great Britain", in Peter Köhler and Hans Zacher (eds) *The Evolution of Social Insurance 1881–1981: Studies of Germany, France, Great Britain, Austria, and Switzerland*. London: Pinter, pp. 150–264.

O'Hagan, Ellie Mae (2015) "Jeremy Corbyn and the fight for the soul of Britain's Labour Party: can a socialist from North London wrestle back Labour from the big banks and Blairites?". *Foreign Policy*. 11 August. [Online]. Available at: http://foreignpolicy.com/2015/08/11/britains-bernie-sanders-is-about-to-win-big-jeremy-corbyn-labour/ (Accessed: 30 October 2017).

Ohlin Report (1956) "Social aspects of European economic cooperation". *International Labour Review* 74: 99–123.

Oliver, M. and H. Pemberton (2004) "Learning and change in 20th century British economic policy". *Governance: An International Journal of Policy, Administration and Institutions* 17(3): 515–41.

ONS (Office for National Statistics) (2010) *Households – Savings Ratios*. [Online]. Available at: www.statistics.gov.uk/CCI/nscl.asp?ID=5927 (Accessed: 30 October 2017).

ONS (Office for National Statistics) (2015) *Wealth in Great Britain Wave 4: 2012–2014*. London: Office for National Statistics. [Online]. Available at: www.ons.gov.uk/peoplepopulationandcommunity/personalandhouseholdfinances/incomeandwealth/compendium/wealthingreatbritainwave4/2012to2014 (Accessed: 30 October 2017).

ONS (Office for National Statistics) (2017) "Migration Statistics Quarterly Report February 2017". London: Office of National Statistics. [Online]. Available at: www.ons.gov.uk/peoplepopulationandcommunity/populationandmigration/internationalmigration/bulletins/migrationstatisticsquarterlyreport/feb2017 (Accessed: 30 October 2017).

Osborne, George (2012) "George Osborne's speech to the Conservative conference: full text". *New Statesman*. 8 October. [Online]. Available at: www.newstatesman.

com/blogs/politics/2012/10/george-osbornes-speech-conservative-conference-full-text (Accessed: 30 October 2017).

Osborne, Peter (2013) "David Cameron may have finished off the Tories – but he had no choice". *The Telegraph*. 23 January. [Online]. Available at: www.telegraph. co.uk/news/newstopics/eureferendum/9821289/David-Cameron-may-have-finished-off-the-Tories-but-he-had-no-choice.html (Accessed: 30 October 2017).

Ostry, J., P. Loungani and D. Furceri (2016) "Neoliberalism: oversold?". *Finance and Development* June: 38–41.

Oxfam (2013) *The Cost of Inequality: How Wealth and Income Extremes Hurt Us All*. Oxfam Media Briefing. Ref: 02/2013. 18 January. [Online]. Available at: www. oxfam.org/sites/www.oxfam.org/files/cost-of-inequality-oxfam-mb180113.pdf (Accessed: 30 October 2017).

Palley, T. (2013) "Europe's crisis without end: the consequences of neoliberalism". *Contributions to Political Economy* 32: 29–50.

Parkinson, Justin (2016) "Who are the JAMS (the 'just about managing')?". *BBC News*. 21 November. [Online]. Available at: www.bbc.co.uk/news/uk-politics-38049245 (Accessed: 30 October 2017).

Pautz, H. (2011) "New Labour in government: think tanks and social policy reform, 1997–2001". *British Politics* 6: 187–209.

Peck, Jamie (2010) *Constructions of Neoliberal Reason*. Oxford: Oxford University Press.

Peden, G.C. (1984) "The Treasury view on public works and employment in the interwar period". *The Economic History Review* 37(2) (May): 167–81.

Pelkmans, J., D. Hanf and J. Chang (eds) (2008) *The EU Internal Market in Comparative Perspective: Economic, Political and Legal Analyses*. Brussels: Peter Lang.

Pelling, Henry (1968) *Popular Politics and Society in Victorian Britain*. London: Macmillan.

Pelling, Henry (1984) *The Labour Governments, 1945–51*. London: Macmillan.

Perry, Matt (2005) *The Jarrow Crusade: Protest and Legend*. Sunderland: University of Sunderland Press.

Phillips, A.W. (1958) "The relation between unemployment and the rate of change of money wage rates in the United Kingdom, 1861–1957". *Economica* 26(100): 283–99.

Phillips, John A. and Charles Wetherell (1995) "The Great Reform Act of 1832 and the political modernization of England". *American Historical Review* 100: 411–36.

Picchio del Mercado, Antonella (1992) *Social Reproduction: The Political Economy of the Labour Market*. Cambridge: Cambridge University Press.

Pierson, P. (2004) *Politics in Time: History, Institutions and Social Analysis*. Princeton, NJ: Princeton University Press.

Piketty, Thomas (2014) *Capital in the 21st Century*. Cambridge, MA: Harvard University Press.

Polanyi, K. (2001 [1944]) *The Great Transformation: The Political and Economic Origins of Our Time*. Boston, MA: Beacon Press.

Pollack, Mark (2012) "The Council of Ministers and European Council", in E. Jones, A. Menon and S. Weatherill (eds). *The Oxford Handbook of the European Union*. Oxford: Oxford University Press, pp. 321–35.

Pollard, Sidney (1982) *The Wasting of the British Economy, British Economic Policy 1945–Present*. London: Croom Helm.

Pollard, Sidney (1983) *The Development of the British Economy* (3rd edn): *1914–1980*. London: Edward Arnold.

Pollard, Sidney (1992) *The Development of the British Economy* (4th edn): *1914–1990*. London: Edward Arnold.

PRA (2017) *PRA Statement on Consumer Credit*. London: Bank of England Prudential Regulatory Authority. 4 July. [Online]. Available at: www.bankofengland.co.uk/pra/Documents/publications/reports/prastatement0717.pdf (Accessed: 30 October 2017).

Prassl, Jeremias (2013) "Freedom of contract as a general principle of EU law? Transfers of undertakings and the protection of employer rights in EU labour law". *Industrial Law Journal* 42: 434–46.

Prassl, Jeremias (2018) *Humans as a Service: The Promises and Pitfalls of Work in the Gig Economy*. Oxford: Oxford University Press.

Ptak, R. (2009) "Neoliberalism in Germany", in P. Mirowski and D. Plehwe (eds) *The Road from Mont Pèlerin*. Cambridge, MA, and London: Harvard University Press, pp. 98–138.

Pugh, Martin (2012) *State and Society: A Social and Political History of Britain since 1870* (4th edn). London: Bloomsbury.

Puttick, Keith (2018) "From mini to maxi jobs? Low pay, 'progression', and the duty to work (harder)". *Industrial Law Journal* (forthcoming).

Radcliffe Committee (1959) *Radcliffe Committee Report*, chapter VI. [Online]. Available at: www.federalreserve.gov/pubs/rfd/1959/334/rfd334.pdf (Accessed: 30 October 2017).

Raunio, T. (2012) "The European Parliament", in E. Jones, A. Menon and S. Weatherill (eds) *The Oxford Handbook of the European Union*. Oxford: Oxford University Press, pp. 365–79.

Raw, Louise (2009) *Striking a Light: The Bryant & May Matchwomen and Their Place in Labor History*. London: Continuum UK.

Reid, M. (1982) *The Secondary Banking Crisis 1973–5: The Inside Story of Britain's Biggest Banking Upheaval*. London: Macmillan.

Report of the Interdepartmental Committee on Physical Deterioration (1904) Cd 2175. [Online]. Available at: https://babel.hathitrust.org/cgi/pt?id=umn.31951002383925x;view=1up;seq=3 (Accessed: 30 October 2017).

Resolution Foundation (2016) "Britain's 'just managing' families have experienced a 13 year income squeeze". Press Release. 29 September. [Online]. Available at: www.resolutionfoundation.org/media/press-releases/britains-just-managing-families-have-experienced-a-13-year-income-squeeze/ (Accessed: 30 October 2017).

Riddell, P. (1991) *The Thatcher Era and Its Legacy*. Cambridge, MA: Blackwell.

Rider, B., D. Chaikin and C. Abrams (1987) *Guide to the Financial Services Act 1986*. Bicester, UK: CCH Editions.

Roberts, Dan (ed.) (2011) *Reading the Riots: Investigating England's Summer of Disorder*. London: Guardian Books.

Robertson, D.H., P. Sraffa and G.F. Shove (1930) "Increasing returns and the representative firm: a symposium". *The Economic Journal* 40(157): 79–116.

Robinson, Joan (1962) "Review of H.G. Johnson *Money, Trade and Economic Growth*". *Economic Journal* 72: 690–2.

Robinson, Joan (1965) *Collected Economic Papers*, Volume 3. Oxford: Blackwell.

Robinson, Joan (1969 [1933]) *The Economics of Imperfect Competition* (2nd edn). New York: St. Martin's Press.

Robinson, Joan (1973) *After Keynes*. Oxford: Basil Blackwell.

Robinson, Joan (1978) *Contributions to Modern Economics.* New York: Academic Press.

Robinson, Joan (1979) *The Generalization of the General Theory.* London: Macmillan.

Robinson, Joan and Frank Wilkinson (1977) "What has become of employment policy?". *Cambridge Journal of Economics* 1(1): 5–14.

Rogers, Daniel (2012) *Age of Fracture.* Cambridge, MA: Harvard University Press.

Rogers, Jon (2017) "The return of Blair? Labour supporters of ex-PM could split party as they plot new group". *The Express.* 2 July. [Online]. Available at: www. express.co.uk/news/politics/823781/Labour-Tony-Blair-Jeremy-Corbyn-Blairites-breakaway-party-Liz-Kendall (Accessed: 30 October 2017).

Rothbard, M. (1978) *For a New Liberty: The Libertarian Manifesto* (2nd edn). New York: Collier-Macmillan.

Rowley, A. (1974) *The Barons of European Industry.* London: Croom Helm.

Rowntree, Seebohm (1901) *Poverty; A Study of Town Life.* London: Macmillan. [Online]. Available at: https://archive.org/details/povertyastudyto00rowngoog (Accessed: 30 October 2017).

Rubinstein, William (2003) *Twentieth-Century Britain: A Political History.* New York: Palgrave Macmillan.

Ruggie, J. (1982) "International regimes, transactions and change: embedded liberalism in the postwar economic order". *International Organization* 36(2): 379–415.

Ruskin, John (1921 [1860]) *Unto This Last.* New York: E.P. Dutton and Company. [Online]. Available at: https://archive.org/details/untothislast00rusk (Accessed: 30 October 2017).

Russell, Dean (2015) "Labour's identity crisis lost it the election". *The Commentator.* 19 May. [Online]. Available at: www.thecommentator.com/article/5860/labour_s_identity_crisis_lost_it_the_election (Accessed: 30 October 2017).

Saez, Emmanuel and Gabriel Zucman (2014) *Wealth Inequality in the United States since 1913: Evidence from Capitalized Income Tax Data.* National Bureau of Economic Research (NBER) Working Paper No. 20625. [Online]. Available at: www.nber. org/papers/w20625 (Accessed: 30 October 2017).

Salter, W.E.G. and W.B. Reddaway (1966) *Productivity and Technical Change.* Cambridge: Cambridge University Press.

Samuelson, Paul (1955) *Economics* (3rd edn). New York: McGraw-Hill (and other editions).

Sánchez, Juan and Emircan Yurdagul (2013) "Why are corporations holding so much cash?". *Federal Reserve Bank of Saint Louis: The Regional Economist.* January, pp. 4–8. [Online]. Available at: www.stlouisfed.org/Publications/Regional-Economist/January-2013/Why-Are-Corporations-Holding-So-Much-Cash (Accessed: 30 October 2017).

Sanderson, P., D. Seidl and J. Roberts (2017) "Taking soft regulation seriously? Managers' perceptions of the legitimacy of corporate governance codes and 'comply-or-explain' in the UK and Germany". *Regulation and Governance* (forthcoming).

Saner, Ermine (2017) "Will the end of Uber in London make women more or less safe?". *Guardian.* 25 September. [Online]. Available at: www.theguardian.com/life-andstyle/2017/sep/25/will-the-end-of-uber-in-london-make-women-more-or-less-safe (Accessed: 30 October 2017).

Saunders, Robert (2008) "Chartism from above: British elites and the interpretation of Chartism". *Historical Research* 81(213): 463–84.

Saville, John (1987) *1848: The British State and the Chartist Movement.* Cambridge: Cambridge University Press.

Saville, John (1957–58) "The welfare state: an historical approach". *New Reasoner* 3: 1–24.

Scally, Robert (1975) *The Origins of the Lloyd George Coalition: The Politics of Social Imperialism, 1900–1918*. Princeton, NJ: Princeton University Press.

Schabas, Margaret (1993) "What's so wrong with physics envy?", in Neil Di Marchi (ed.) *Non-natural Social Science: Reflecting on the Enterprise of More Heat Than Light*. Annual Supplement to Volume 25, *History of Political Economy*. Durham, NC: Duke University Press, pp. 45–53.

Schenk, C. (2004) "The new City and the state in the 1960s", in R. Michie and P. Williamson (eds) *The British Government and the City of London in the Twentieth Century*. Cambridge: Cambridge University Press, pp. 322–39.

Schmidt, S. and A. Wonka (2012) "European Commission", in E. Jones, A. Menon and S. Weatherill (eds) *The Oxford Handbook of the European Union*. Oxford: Oxford University Press, pp. 336–49.

Schmidt, V. (2008) "Discursive institutionalism: the explanatory power of ideas and discourse". *Annual Review of Political Science* 11: 303–26.

Schmidt, V. (2009) "Putting the political back into political economy by bringing the state back in yet again". *World Politics* 61(3): 516–46.

Schmidt, V. (2010) "Taking ideas and discourse seriously: explaining change through discursive institutionalism as the fourth 'new institutionalism'". *European Political Science Review* 2(1): 1–25.

Schmidt, V. (2011) "Reconciling ideas and institutions through discursive institutionalism", in D. Beland, R. Cox (eds) *Ideas and Politics in Social Science Research*. Oxford: Oxford University Press, pp. 47–64.

Schnyder, G. and M. Siems (2013) "The ordoliberal variety of neoliberalism", in S. Konzelmann and M. Fovargue-Davies (eds) *Banking Systems in the Crisis: The Faces of Liberal Capitalism*. London: Routledge, pp. 250–68.

Schumpeter, Joseph (1942) *Capitalism, Socialism and Democracy*. New York: Norton.

Shleifer, Andre and Robert Vishny (1997) "A survey of corporate governance". *Journal of Finance* 52(2): 737–83.

Silverwood, J. (2013) "Creative consolidation or punctuated equilibrium? The orthodox paradigm in the UK economy". [Online]. Available at: www.psa.ac.uk/sites/default/files/762_330_0.pdf (Accessed: 30 October 2017).

Simor, J. (2017) "Why it's not too late to step back from the Brexit brink". *The Guardian*. 7 October. [Online]. Available at: www.theguardian.com/commentisfree/2017/oct/07/why-its-not-too-late-to-step-back-from-brexit (Accessed: 30 October 2017).

Simpson, B. (1999) "A milestone in the legal regulation of pay: the National Minimum Wage Act 1999". *Industrial Law Journal* 28: 1–32.

Sims, George (1889) *How the Poor Live and Terrible London*. London: Chatto & Windus, Piccadilly. [Online]. Available at: https://archive.org/details/howpoorliveandho00sims (Accessed: 30 October 2017).

Singh, Agit (1975) "Takeovers, economic natural selection and the theory of the firm: evidence from post-war United Kingdom experience". *Economic Journal* 85(339): 497–515.

Singh, Arj (2017) "Labour pledges crackdown on bad landlords to ensure rented homes are 'fit for human habitation'". *Independent*. 30 April. [Online]. Available at: www.independent.co.uk/news/uk/politics/labour-rented-homes-housing-bad-landlords-unfit-fridge-freezer-tenants-tax-a7711076.html (Accessed: 30 October 2017).

Skidelsky, Robert (1994) *Politicians and the Slump: The Labour Government of 1929–33*. London: Papermac.

Skousen, Mark (1997) "The perseverance of Paul Samuelson's *Economics*". *Journal of Economic Perspectives* 11(2): 137–52.

Slater, J. (1977) *Jim Slater: Return to Go*. London: Futura Publications.

Smith, Adam (1999 [1776]) *The Wealth of Nations*. London: Penguin Books.

Smith, Anthony (2002) *The Strike for the People's Charter in 1842*. PhD Thesis. London School of Economics, London, United Kingdom. [Online]. Available at: http://etheses.lse.ac.uk/1687/1/U173775.pdf (Accessed: 30 October 2017).

Smith, Harold (1998) "The British Women's Suffrage Campaign, 1866–1928". *Seminar Studies in History*. London: Longman.

Snell, Keith (1985) *Annals of the Labouring Poor*. Cambridge: Cambridge University Press.

Social Justice Policy Group (2006) *The State of the Nation Report: Economic Dependency*. London: Social Policy Justice Group. [Online]. Available at: www.centreforsocial-justice.org.uk/library/breakdown-britain-economic-dependency (Accessed: 30 October 2017).

Solar, P. (1995) "Poor relief and English economic development before the Industrial Revolution". *Economic History Review (NS)* 42: 1–22.

Spaak Report (1956) "Rapport des chefs de délégation aux ministres des affaires étrangères". Brussels, 21 April.

Spielvogel, Jackson (2018) *Western Civilization since 1300* (10th edn). Boston, MA: Cengage.

Sraffa, P. (1926) "The laws of returns under competitive conditions". *The Economic Journal* 36(144): 535–50.

Stanley, L. (2014) "We're reaping what we sowed: everyday crisis narratives and acquiescence to the age of austerity". *New Political Economy* (ahead-of-print): 1–23.

Stead, W.T. (1883) "Outcast London: where to begin?". *The Pall Mall Gazette*. 23 October. [Online]. Available at: www.attackingthedevil.co.uk/pmg/where.php (Accessed: 30 October 2017).

Stedman Jones, Gareth (1971) *Outcast London*. New York: Pantheon.

Stephens, M. (2007) "Market deregulation and its consequences". *Housing Studies* 22(2): 201–20.

Stewart, Heather, Anushka Asthana and Rowena Mason (2016) "EU referendum: Boris Johnson calls Cameron's Project Fact 'baloney'". *Guardian*. 1 March. [Online]. Available at: www.theguardian.com/politics/2016/feb/29/eu-referendum-boris-johnson-calls-camerons-argument-baloney (Accessed: 30 October 2017).

Stiglitz, J. (2016) *The Euro and Its Threat to the Future of Europe*. London: Allen Lane.

Stock, J. and M. Watson (2002) "Has the business cycle changed and why?". *NBER Macroeconomics Annual*, Volume 17. Cambridge, MA: The MIT Press. [Online]. Available at: www.nber.org/chapters/c11075.pdf (Accessed: 30 October 2017).

Strange, Susan (1971) *Sterling and British Policy: A Political Study of an International Currency in Decline*. Oxford: Oxford University Press.

Streeck, Wolfgang (2016) *How Will Capitalism End? Essays on a Failing System*. London: Verso.

Streeck, W. and K. Thelen (2005) *Beyond Continuity: Institutional Change in Advanced Political Economies*. Oxford: Oxford University Press.

Supiot, A. (2015) *La gouvernance par les nombres*. Paris: Fayard.

Talbot, L. (2012) *Progressive Corporate Governance for the Twenty-First Century*. London: Routledge.

Tanner, Duncan (1990) *Political Change and the Labour Party, 1900–1918*. Cambridge: Cambridge University Press.

Tarrant, A. and A. Biondi (2017) "EU law is no barrier to Labour's economic programme". *Renewal: A Journal of Social Democracy*. [Online]. Available at: http://renewal.org.uk/ (Accessed: 30 October 2017).

Taylor, Miles (1996) "Rethinking the chartists: searching for synthesis in the historiography of Chartism". *Historical Journal* 39(2): 479–95.

Taylor, N. (2009) "Tensions and contradictions left and right: the predictable disappointments of planning under New Labour in historical perspective". *Planning, Practice and Research* 24(1) (February): 57–70.

Taylor, Robert (1996) "Industrial relations", in David Marquand and Anthony Seldon (eds) *The Ideas That Shaped Post-war Britain*. London: Harper Collins, pp. 88–121.

Taylor, Robert (2004) "The rise and fall of the social contract", in Anthony Seldon and Kevin Hickson (eds) *New Labour, Old Labour: The Blair, Wilson and Callahan Governments*. London: Routledge, pp. 70–104.

Tebbit, Norman (2005) "An electoral curse yet to be lifted". *Guardian*. 10 February. [Online]. Available at: www.guardian.co.uk/politics/2005/feb/10/freedomof information.economy (Accessed: 30 October 2017).

Thane, Pat (1982) *Foundations of the Welfare State*. London: Longman.

Thane, Pat (1984) "The working class and state 'welfare' in Britain, 1880–1914". *Historical Journal* 27: 877–900.

Thatcher, Margaret (1993) *The Downing Street Years*. New York: Harper Collins.

Thelen, K. (2004) *How Institutions Evolve: The Political Economy of Skills in Germany, Britain, the United States and Japan*. Cambridge: Cambridge University Press.

Thompson, E.P. (1955) *William Morris: Romantic to Revolutionary*. London: Lawrence & Wishart.

Timmins, N. (1996) *The Five Giants*. London: Fontana Press.

Titmuss, Richard (1950) *Problems of Social Policy*. London: Longmans, Green.

Torr, Dona (1956) *Tom Mann and His Times, Volume 1: 1856–1890*. London: Lawrence & Wishart.

Torrance, David (2010) *Noel Skelton and the Property Owning Democracy*. London: Biteback Publishers.

Toussaint, Eric (2009) "The Keynesian revolution and the neoliberal counter-revolution". *Global Research*. 15 July.

Townsend, Peter (1955) "The family life of old people: an investigation in East London". *The Sociological Review* 3(4): 179–95.

Treanor, Jill (2015) "Royal Bank of Scotland: from bailout to sell-off". *Guardian*. 3 August. [Online]. Available at: www.theguardian.com/business/2015/aug/03/royal-bank-of-scotland-from-bailout-to-sell-off-rbs (Accessed 20 December 2017).

Tribe, Keith (2008) "Britain, economics (20th century)", in Stephen Durlaugh and Lawrence Blume (eds) *The Palgrave Dictionary of Economics*. Basingstoke: Palgrave Macmillan, pp. 552–62.

Tribe, Keith (2009) "Liberalism and neoliberalism in Britain: 1930–1980", in Philip Mirowski and Deiter Plehwe (eds) *The Road to Mont Pelerin: The Making of the Neoliberal Thought Collective*. Cambridge, MA: Harvard University Press, pp. 306–46.

Truman, Harry (1950) "Statement by the President Upon Signing the Order Concerning the Point 4 Program". *Public Papers, Harry S. Truman, 1945–1953*. [Online]. Available at: www.trumanlibrary.org/publicpapers/index.php?pid=869&st=&st1= (Accessed: 30 October 2017).

Trussell Trust (2017a) *Early Warnings: Universal Credit and Food Banks*. Salisbury: The Trussell Trust. [Online]. Available at: www.trusselltrust.org/wp-content/uploads/sites/2/2017/04/Early-Warnings-Universal-Credit-and-Foodbanks.pdf (Accessed: 30 October 2017).

Trussell Trust (2017b) End of Year Stats. [Online]. Available at: www.trusselltrust.org/news-and-blog/latest-stats/end-year-stats/#fy-2011-2012 (Accessed: 30 October 2017).

Tucker, Pilgrim (2017) "Universal credit has poleaxed the jobless: now for low income workers". *The Guardian*. 24 October. [Online]. Available at: www.the-guardian.com/commentisfree/2017/oct/24/jobless-poleaxed-universal-credit-workers-low-income-financial-penalties (Accessed: 30 October 2017).

Tyler, Imogen (2015) "'Being poor is not entertainment': class struggles against poverty porn". *Social Action and Research Foundation*. 2 September. [Online]. Available at: www.the-sarf.org.uk/being-poor-is-not-entertainment-class-struggles-against-poverty-porn-by-imogen-tyler/ (Accessed: 30 October 2017).

UMKC (2001) *Economics Needs Fundamental Reform – and Now is the Time for Change*. Kansas City, MO: Association for Evolutionary Economics Summer School, June. [Online]. Available at: www.autisme-economie.org/article132.html (Accessed: 30 October 2017).

Varian, Hal (1987) "Microeconomics", in John Eatwell, Murray Milgate and Peter Newman (eds) *Palgrave Dictionary of Economics*, Volume 3. London: Palgrave Macmillan, pp. 461–3.

Varoufakis, Yanis (2015) *And the Weak Suffer What They Must? Europe, Austerity and the Threat to Global Stability*. London: Bodley Head.

Varoufakis, Yanis (2017) *Adults in the Room: My Battle with Europe's Deep Establishment*. London: Bodley Head.

Vatican Pontifical Council for Justice and Peace (2011) *Towards Reforming the International Financial and Monetary Systems in the Context of Global Public Authority*. [Online]. Available at: www.zenit.org/article-33718?l=english (Accessed: 30 October 2017).

Visser, J., S. Hayter and R. Gammerano (2015) *Trends in Collective Bargaining Coverage: Stability, Erosion or Decline?* Geneva: International Labour Organization.

Waddington, David (1992) *Contemporary Issues in Public Disorder: A Comparative and Historical Approach*. New York: Routledge.

Wadsworth, Jonathan, Swati Dhingra, Gianmarco Ottavanio and John Van Reenan (2016) *Brexit the Impact of Immigration on the UK*. CEP Brexit Brief No. 5. London: London School of Economics. [Online]. Available at: http://cep.lse.ac.uk/pubs/download/brexit05.pdf (Accessed: 30 October 2017).

Walker, Robert (2014) *The Shame of Poverty*. Oxford: Oxford University Press.

Walsh, J. (2000) "When do ideas matter? Explaining the successes and failures of Thatcherite ideas". *Comparative Political Studies* 33(4): 483–516.

Warham, Dror (1995) *Imagining the Middle Class: The Political Representation of Class in Britain, c. 1780–1840*. Cambridge: Cambridge University Press.

Watson, Steven (1953) "The budget and the Lords: the crisis of 1909–11". *History Today* 3(4): 240–8.

Watt, D.C. (1984) *Succeeding John Bull: America in Britain's Place, 1900–1975*. Cambridge: Cambridge University Press.

Watts, B., S. Fitzpatrick, G. Bramley and D. Watkins (2014) *Welfare Sanctions and Conditionality in the UK*. York: Joseph Rowntree Foundation. [Online]. Available at: www.jrf.org.uk/sites/default/files/jrf/migrated/files/Welfare-conditionality-UK-Summary.pdf (Accessed: 30 October 2017).

Weatherill, S. (1995) *Law and Integration in the European Union*. Oxford: Oxford University Press.

Webb, Sidney (1887) *Facts for Socialists: From the Political Economists and Statisticians*.

Webb, Sidney (1889) "The basis of socialism", in G. Bernard Shaw (ed.) *Fabian Essays in Socialism*. New York: Humbolt Publishing Company, pp. 1–43. [Online]. Available at: http://files.libertyfund.org/files/298/0066_Bk.pdf (Accessed: 30 October 2017).

Webb, Sidney and Beatrice Webb (1920) *The History of Trade Unionism*. London: Longmans.

Webb, Sidney and Beatrice Webb (1909) *The Public Organisation of the Labour Market: Being Part Two of the Minority Report of the Poor Law Commission*. London: Longmans, Green & Co.

Wheeler, Brian (2015) "Lords v Commons: tax credit battle gets constitutional". *BBC News*. 27 October. [Online]. Available at: www.bbc.co.uk/news/uk-politics-3461 4716 (Accessed: 30 October 2017).

Whitehead, Phillip (1985) *The Writing on the Wall: Britain in the Seventies*. London: Michael Joseph.

Wilensky, Harold (1975) *The Welfare State and Equality*. Berkeley, CA: University of California Press.

Wilkinson, Frank (1974) "The outlook for wages". *Prospects for Economic Management 1973–77*. University of Cambridge, Department of Applied Economics.

Wilkinson, Frank (2001) "The theory and practice of wage subsidisation: some historical reflections", in Fran Bennet and Donald Hirsch (eds) *Tax Credit and Issues for the Future of In-Work Support*. York: Joseph Rowntree Foundation, pp. 94–125. [Online]. Available at: www.jrf.org.uk/report/employment-tax-credit-and-issues-future-work-support (Accessed: 30 October 2017).

Wilkinson, Frank (2007) "Neoliberalism and New Labour policy: economic performance, historical comparisons and future prospects". *Cambridge Journal of Economics* 31(6): 817–43.

Wilkinson, Frank (2012) "Real wage, the customary standard of life and economic progress". *Cambridge Journal of Economics* 36(6): 1497–534.

Wilks-Heeg, S. (2009) "New Labour and the reform of English local government, 1997–2007: privatizing parts that Conservatives couldn't reach?". *Planning, Practice and Research* 24(1) (February): 23–39.

Williams, Karel (1981) *From Pauperism to Poverty*. London: Routledge and Kegan Paul.

Williams, Rowan (2011) "Time for us to challenge the idols of high finance". *Financial Times*. 1 November. [Online]. Available at: www.ft.com/content/a561a4f6-0485-11e1-ac2a-00144feabdc0 (Accessed 20 December 2017).

Wills, J. (2001) "Community unionism and trade union renewal in the UK: moving beyond the fragments at last?" *Transactions of the Institute of British Geographers* 26: 465–83.

Wilson, Jeremy (2016) "MOMENTUM: the inside story of how Jeremy Corbyn took control of the Labour party". *Business Insider UK*. 3 March. [Online]. Available at: http://uk.businessinsider.com/momentum-the-inside-story-of-how-jeremy-corbyn-took-control-of-the-labour-party-2016-2 (Accessed: 30 October 2017).

Winter, J.M. (1986) *The Great War and the British People*. New York: Macmillan.

Wohl, Anthony (1977) *The Eternal Slum Housing and Social Policy in Victorian London*. London: Edward Arnold.

Woodroofe, Kathleen (1977) "The Royal Commission on the Poor Laws 1905–09". *International Review of Social History* 22: 137–64.

Woodward, Llewellen (1967) *Great Britain and the War of 1914–1918*. London: Methuen.

World Economic Forum (2012) *The Global Risks Report 2012*. [Online]. Available at: www.ledevoir.com/documents/pdf/davos2012.pdf (Accessed: 30 October 2017).

World Economic Forum (2017) *The Global Risks Report 2017*. [Online]. Available at: www.weforum.org/reports/the-global-risks-report-2017 (Accessed: 30 October 2017).

Wrigley, Ch. (1982) "The government and industrial relations", in Ch. Wrigley (ed.) *A History of British Industrial Relations, 1875–1914*. Brighton: Harvester, pp. 135–58.

Wrigley, E.A. (1988) *Continuity, Chance and Change: The Character of the Industrial Revolution in England*. Cambridge: Cambridge University Press.

Yergin, Daniel and Joseph Stanislaw (2002) *The Commanding Heights: The Battle for the World Economy*. New York: Touchstone.

YouGov (2017a) *Headline Voting Intention*. 18–19 April. [Online]. Available at: https://d25d2506sfb94s.cloudfront.net/cumulus_uploads/document/04xxn42p3e/TimesResults_170419_VI_Trackers_GE_W.pdf (Accessed: 30 October 2017).

YouGov (2017b) *Voting Intention and Seat Estimates*. 7 June. [Online]. Available at: https://yougov.co.uk/uk-general-election-2017/ (Accessed: 30 October 2017).

YouGov (2017c) *Why People Voted Labour or Conservative at the 2017 General Election*. 12–13 June. [Online]. Available at: https://yougov.co.uk/news/2017/07/11/why-people-voted-labour-or-conservative-2017-gener/ and https://d25d2506sfb94s.cloudfront.net/cumulus_uploads/document/01h35vzc5b/InternalResults_170613_Coding_WhyConLab_W.pdf (Accessed: 30 October 2017).

Young, Hugo (2013) *One of Us: A Biography of Margaret Thatcher*. London: Pan Books.

Young Women's Trust (2017) *Worrying Times: Young Women's Trust Annual Survey 2017*. London: Young Women's Trust. [Online]. Available at: www.youngwomenstrust.org/assets/0000/7887/YWT_Worrying_Times_A4_8pp_06_AW_LOW.pdf (Accessed: 30 October 2017).

Youngson, A.J. (1967) *Britain's Economic Growth 1920–1966*. New York: Routledge.

Index

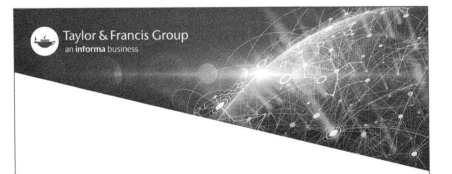

Printed and bound by CPI Group (UK) Ltd, Croydon, CR0 4YY

01/05/2025

01858432-0006